A Text Book Of

BUILDING DESIGN AND DRAWING

For
SEMESTER - IV

SECOND YEAR DEGREE COURSE IN CIVIL ENGINEERING

As Per New Revised Syllabus of Shivaji University, Kolhapur
(Effective From 2015)

Vivekanand G. Shetti
M. E. (Struct. Engg.), M.I.E.
Assistant Professor,
D.Y. Patil College of Engg. and Technology
Kasba Bavada, KOLHAPUR

A. D. Pawar
M. E. (Civil) Construction & Management
Assistant Professor, NICMAR, PUNE CAMPUS
S.T.E.S's, Formerly, SKN - Sinhgad Institute of Technology & Science
Kusgaon (Bk), LONAVALA

Mrs. V. S. Limaye
M. Tech. (Civil), M.P.M.
Associate Professor of Civil Deptt.
Sinhgad College of Engineering
Vadgoan (Bk.) PUNE

N3375

BUILDING DESIGN AND DRAWING (S.E. CIVIL SEM. IV - SU) ISBN 978-93-5164-466-8

First Edition : February, 2015

© : **Authors**

The text of this publication, or any part thereof, should not be reproduced or transmitted in any form or stored in any computer storage system or device for distribution including photocopy, recording, taping or information retrieval system or reproduced on any disc, tape, perforated media or other information storage device etc., without the written permission of Authors with whom the rights are reserved. Breach of this condition is liable for legal action.

Every effort has been made to avoid errors or omissions in this publication. In spite of this, errors may have crept in. Any mistake, error or discrepancy so noted and shall be brought to our notice shall be taken care of in the next edition. It is notified that neither the publisher nor the authors or seller shall be responsible for any damage or loss of action to any one, of any kind, in any manner, therefrom.

Published By :
NIRALI PRAKASHAN
Abhyudaya Pragati, 1312, Shivaji Nagar,
Off J.M. Road, PUNE – 411005
Tel - (020) 25512336/37/39, Fax - (020) 25511379
Email : niralipune@pragationline.com

Printed By :
REPRO INDIA LTD.
50/2 T.T.C. MIDC,
Industrial Area, Mahape, Navi Mumbai
Tel - (022) 2778 2011

DISTRIBUTION CENTRES

PUNE

Nirali Prakashan
119, Budhwar Peth, Jogeshwari Mandir Lane
Pune 411002, Maharashtra
Tel : (020) 2445 2044, 66022708, Fax : (020) 2445 1538
Email : bookorder@pragationline.com

Nirali Prakashan
S. No. 28/27, Dhyari,
Near Pari Company, Pune 411041
Tel : (020) 24690204 Fax : (020) 24690316
Email : dhyari@pragationline.com
bookorder@pragationline.com

MUMBAI
Nirali Prakashan
385, S.V.P. Road, Rasdhara Co-op. Hsg. Society Ltd.,
Girgaum, Mumbai 400004, Maharashtra
Tel : (022) 2385 6339 / 2386 9976, Fax : (022) 2386 9976
Email : niralimumbai@pragationline.com

DISTRIBUTION BRANCHES

NAGPUR
Pratibha Book Distributors
Above Maratha Mandir, Shop No. 3, First Floor,
Rani Jhanshi Square, Sitabuldi, Nagpur 440012,
Maharashtra, Tel : (0712) 254 7129

BENGALURU
Pragati Book House
House No. 1, Sanjeevappa Lane, Avenue Road Cross,
Opp. Rice Church, Bengaluru – 560002.
Tel : (080) 64513344, 64513355,
Mob : 9880582331, 9845021552
Email:bharatsavla@yahoo.com

JALGAON
Nirali Prakashan
34, V. V. Golani Market, Navi Peth, Jalgaon 425001,
Maharashtra, Tel : (0257) 222 0395
Mob : 94234 91860

KOLHAPUR
Nirali Prakashan
New Mahadvar Road,
Kedar Plaza, 1st Floor Opp. IDBI Bank
Kolhapur 416 012, Maharashtra. Mob : 9850046155

CHENNAI
Pragati Books
9/1, Montieth Road, Behind Taas Mahal, Egmore,
Chennai 600008 Tamil Nadu, Tel : (044) 6518 3535,
Mob : 94440 01782 / 98450 21552 / 98805 82331, Email : bharatsavla@yahoo.com

RETAIL OUTLETS

PUNE

Pragati Book Centre
157, Budhwar Peth, Opp. Ratan Talkies,
Pune 411002, Maharashtra
Tel : (020) 2445 8887 / 6602 2707, Fax : (020) 2445 8887
Pragati Book Centre
Amber Chamber, 28/A, Budhwar Peth,
Appa Balwant Chowk, Pune : 411002, Maharashtra,
Tel : (020) 20240335 / 66281669
Email : pbcpune@pragationline.com

Pragati Book Centre
676/B, Budhwar Peth, Opp. Jogeshwari Mandir,
Pune 411002, Maharashtra
Tel : (020) 6601 7784 / 6602 0855
PBC Book Sellers & Stationers
152, Budhwar Peth, Pune 411002, Maharashtra
Tel : (020) 2445 2254 / 6609 2463

MUMBAI
Pragati Book Corner
Indira Niwas, 111 - A, Bhavani Shankar Road, Dadar (W), Mumbai 400028, Maharashtra
Tel : (022) 2422 3526 / 6662 5254, Email : pbcmumbai@pragationline.com

www.pragationline.com info@pragationline.com

Dedicated To ...
      Our Beloved Parents

... **Authors**

PREFACE

It gives us immense pleasure to present this book on **"Building Design and Drawing"**.

This book is written mainly for the Second Year Students of Civil Engineering of Shivaji University, Kolhapur.

The text book has been thoroughly prepared according to Six Units as per revised curriculum of 2014. An attempt is made to give due justice to the use of plans in building design and drawing activities. The authors with their professional and academic experience have taken all efforts to present the text in lucid manner. The theoretical matter has been explained with number of diagrams and illustrations supported by solved examples and Appendices of Several Plans.

Nirali Prakashan put the book, what we thought into reality. Our sincere thanks to Shri. Dineshbhai Furia, Shri. Jignesh Furia and Shri. M.P. Munde. The book could be completed in time, due to sincere and hard work of Nirali Prakashan's staff namely Mr. Akbar Shaikh, Ms. Deepali Lachake (Co-ordinator), Mr. Kiran Velankar, Mrs. Roshan Khan and Miss Chaitali Takale. We thanks them them all.

Our special thanks to our family members, student and all those who directly or directly or indirectly supported us in this project.

We are also thankful to Mr. Virdhaval Shinde, Branch Manager, Kolhapur Office and Mr. Ashok Nanaware, Branch Manager, Sangli District for their valuable help and efforts for promotion of our book.

Valuable suggestions from our esteemed readers to improve the text will be most welcome and highly appreciated.

Ganesh Jayanti,
23rd January, 2015

Authors

SYLLABUS

SECTION I

Unit 1: (05 Hours)
Site Selection Criteria
Principles of Building Planning, Significance, Sun path diagram, Wind Diagram, Orientation, Factors affecting, Criteria under Indian condition.

Unit 2: (10 Hours)
Building Planning Byelaws and Regulations as per SP-7, 1983 National Building code of India group 1 to 5.
Planning of Residential Building (Bungalows, Row Bungalows, Apartments and Twin Bungalows), Procedure of Building Permission, Significance of Commencement, Plinth Completion or Occupancy Certificate.

Unit 3: (05 Hours)
Low Cost Housing: Materials and Methods (Conceptual introduction only), Maintenance, Repairs, Rehabilitation of Structures (Conceptual introduction only), Concept of Green Building and Rating.

SECTION II

Unit 4: (08 Hours)
Plumbing System, Various Materials for systems like A-PVC, C-PVC, GI and HDPE.
Various Types of Traps, Fittings, Chambers, Need of Septic Tank, Concept of Plumbing and Drainage Plan, Introduction to Rainwater Harvesting, Concept of Rain Water Gutters. Rainwater Outlet and Down Take Systems.
Electrification: Concealed and Open Wiring, Requirements and Location of various points, Concept of Earthing.
Fire Resistance in Building: Fire protection precautions, Confining of fire, Fire Hazards, Characteristics of fire resisting materials, Building materials and their resistance to fire.

Unit 5: (08 Hours)
Ventilation: Definition and necessity of Ventilation, Functional requirement, Various systems and selection criteria.
Air-conditioning: Purpose, Classification, Principles, Systems and Various Components of the same.
Thermal Insulation: General concept, Materials, Methods.
Introduction to Acoustics: Absorption of sound, Various materials, Conditions for good acoustics.
Sound Insulation and Methods of Noise Control.

Unit 6: (08 Hours)
Paints: Different types and application methods.
Plastering, Pointing and various techniques.
Wall cladding, Skirting, Dado work with various materials.
Miscellaneous finishes such as POP, Gypsum plaster.

CONTENTS

Section - I

CHAPTER 1 : SITE SELECTION CRITERIA — 1.1 – 1.16

CHAPTER 2 : BUILDING PLANNING AND BYE LAWS — 2.1 – 2.104

CHAPTER 3 : LOW COST HOUSING — 3.1 – 3.34

Section - II

CHAPTER 4 : PLUMBING SYSTEMS AND ELECTRIFICATION — 4.1 – 4.66

CHAPTER 5 : HEAT, VENTILATION AND AIR-CONDITIONING SYSTEMS IN BUILDING — 5.1 – 5.82

CHAPTER 6 : PAINTS AND PLASTERS — 6.1 – 6.24

Unit 1
SITE SELECTION CRITERIA

1.1 FACTORS FOR SITE SELECTION OF RESIDENTIAL BUILDINGS

There are many factors which must be taken into account while selecting a site for commercial and residential buildings. Some of these factors are as given below.

1. Shape of the plot
2. Location of the plot
3. Availability of amenities
4. Water table
5. Sewerage system.

1. **Shape of the Plot:** Geometry of the plot for any kind of construction is very important which can largely effect the appearance of your structure. Shape of the plot should be such that the construction can be easily made with cost low as possible. And also in the future you can further expand it. A plot with more routes will be considered a good one.

2. **Location of the Plot:** The surrounding area of the residential plot is very important. It affects the price and the beauty of the plot. Plot should be taken in the area provided with a lot of services. And in a suitable environment free from all kind of pollutions. Efforts should be make to buy it near to main road. Because such plots are more valuable as compared to the plots situated away from the main road.

3. **Availability of Amenities:** Plot for a residential building should be taken in the area provided with much number of amenities such as Electricity, Telephone, Fax, Internet, Gas, School, Colleges, University etc. and the most important is the good and fast transport system, so that communication become more fast and quick.

4. **Water Table:** The water table at the site of residential building should not be very high. Otherwise it will effect the quality of water which are used for drinking and domestic purposes. A plot with normal water table will be more preferred as compared with other plots having high water table.

5. **Sewerage System:** There should be proper sewerage system at the site of residential plots so that the extra water of houses can be easily drawn out especially in rains and floods. If in case there is no sewerage system the dirty water affect the building and as well as the occupants.

Factors for Site Selection of Commercial Building

The following are the few factors which must be taken into account while selecting a site for commercial building.
1. Location.
2. Climate of region.
3. Availability of raw materials.
4. Cost and time frame.
5. Population of the region.

1. **Location:** The value of a commercial building depends upon its location, whether it is located in the center of the region or at the borders or on the main road or away from the main road. For a good commercial building it should be on the main road and in the center of the region.
2. **Climate of Region:** The strength and stability of building mainly depends upon the climate of the region in which it is going to be constructed. As commercial buildings are very important and expensive from economic point, so it must be constructed according to the terms and conditions of region, so that it can remain safe from floods, rains, snowfalls etc.
3. **Availability of Raw materials:** Usually commercial buildings require more construction materials as compared to a normal residential house. So before construction of the commercial building it must be sure that raw materials are available nearby. Otherwise it will become uneconomical.
4. **Cost and Time Frame:** Before the construction of commercial building a thorough investigation should be made for the cost and time frame for the commercial building. Cost and time frame mainly depends upon the location and the availability of raw materials.
5. **Populations of the Region:** Commercial buildings are constructed to meet the need of the local population. So for this purpose it must be constructed in the region having sufficient population in which the commercial building can restore its cost.

1.2 PRINCIPLES OF PLANNING

Before planning a structure, the planner collects all relevant information such as climatic conditions, site location, thorough understanding of present and future requirement of owner and user, existing bye-laws, etc. and tries to adopt following principles of planning with due consideration to various constraints:

1. Aspect
2. Prospect
3. Roominess
4. Grouping
5. Privacy
6. Circulation
7. Elegance
8. Sanitation
9. Orientation
10. Economy.

1.2.1 Aspect

Occupant of building should be in a position to get maximum benefit of natural gift of sunlight, fresh air, scenery etc. to suit various activities at different hours of the day.

To achieve this

(i) Doors and windows are placed in external walls to derive benefits of sunlight, wind etc.

(ii) Different rooms are placed in accordance with the activity in room.

Aspect is an important consideration not only from view point of environment but also from view point of hygiene and proper aspect for units can be achieved by proper orientation of the structure which is discussed at length later. Aspect is related with placing of doors and windows in the external walls of the structure.

Aspect depends upon the direction of sun, breeze and rain. Sun diagram for South West India is shown in Fig. 1.1.

In whole day, Sun rises at East and sets at West; slightly tilting towards South and wind blows in West or South-West and North-West direction.

A room is said to have aspect to particular direction, if it receives light or air from that direction. From the Sun diagram shown in Fig. 1.1, it is clear that

(i) Bedrooms should have West, South West or North West aspect to get good breeze during summer.

(ii) From view point of sunlight, living room should have South or South East aspect.

(iii) Early in the morning, sun rays are welcomed by the lady working in kitchen, from view point of hygiene, warmth and light. Hence, kitchen should have Eastern aspect preferably or North East aspect.

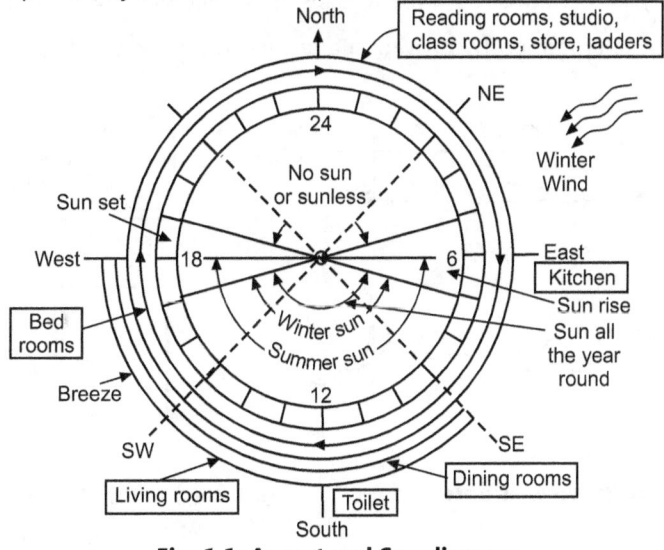

Fig. 1.1: Aspect and Sun diagram

(iv) North aspect is very good for library, study room, drawing halls, photo studios, workshops, stores, stairs, classrooms, because there will not be direct sunlight from North and only diffused light will be available.

(v) Toilets should not be placed in East-West direction, but should be placed on South side so that South West wind takes away all foul gases.

Further, according to building bye laws, the minimum opening area of habitable rooms and kitchen (excluding doors) should not be less than $\frac{1}{10}^{th}$ of floor area of the room for dry climate and $\frac{1}{6}^{th}$ floor area for wet climate. It is preferable to have windows on two sides of a room instead of providing on one side only. This helps in having continuous flow of fresh air.

1.2.2 Prospect

Prospect means positioning of doors, windows in external walls of structure so as to reveal certain desired views at the same time concealing undesired views from inside. Through desired arrangements of doors and windows particular space is camouflaged into its surroundings.

Windows enable to enjoy views of gardens, fountains, hill top, Sunrise or Sunset which can be further enhanced by providing vista. A vista is an enframed segment of a view. Fig. 1.2 (a) and (b) show view of a hill top and inspire as actually observed. In Fig. 1.2 (c) and (d), the same view is enframed by providing a large window or opening in the living room wall.

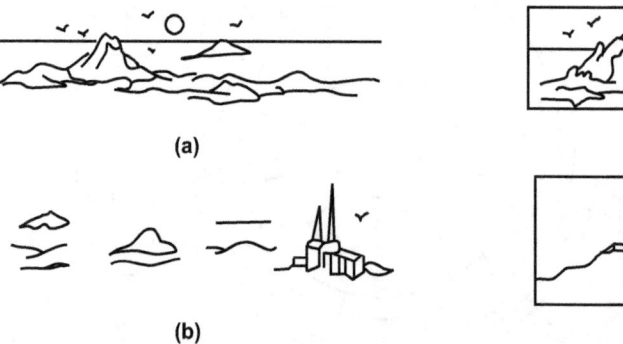

(a)   (c)

(b)   (d)

Fig. 1.2: (a) & (b) View as observed   **Fig. 1.2: (c) & (d) The view enframed by vista i.e. large window**

Prospect can also be achieved by providing projecting windows since, such windows not only provide pleasing appearance, but also help in concealing as shown in Fig. 1.2 (e), (f) and (g), prospect is necessary for enlightenment of the user.

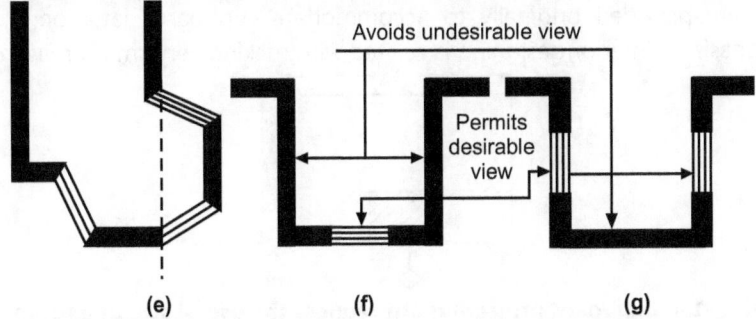

Fig. 1.2: (e), (f) & (g) Projected windows increase pleasing appearance and conceal undesired views such as cementry, slum areas, garbage dumps, etc.

1.2.3 Roominess

Roominess is the "feel" obtained of the room when one enters it and can be achieved as follows:

(a) Roominess can be effected by carefully adjusting the length, breadth and height of the building: Consider the dimensions of a living room shown in Fig. 1.3 (a) and (b).

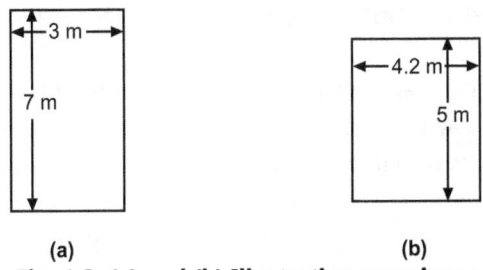

(a) (b)
Fig. 1.3: (a) and (b) Illustrating roominess

In Fig. 1.3 (a), L : B ratio is more than 2. A person in this room will feel like moving through a long tunnel.

In Fig. 1.3 (b), L : B ratio is less than 1.5. Here more comfort is experienced; illustrating roominess. It is advisable to keep L : B ratio between 1.2 to 1.5.

In public buildings such as clubs, the minimum height specified by bye-laws may be provided to create awareness of closeness whereas in badminton halls, foyers, churches, museum, etc., an increased height gives a monumental effect.

(b) Colours: From aesthetic point of view, light colours illuminate room thus enhancing its appearance, whereas dark colour conveys a gloomy feeling. Also use of varying colours to walls depending on light direction, reflection and proportion of room is required to be made.

(c) Interior arrangement: Planning and positioning of interior cupboards, table-sets etc. play a very important role in effective roominess. A cupboard projecting out reduces the useful size of the room. Therefore, it is good planning if offsets in the wall are provided originally to accommodate cupboards later on. Recently, the emphasis on interior designing is related with making very small areas 'roomy'.

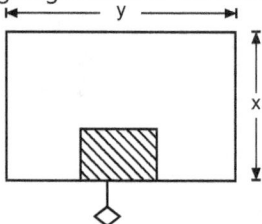

Fig. 1.4: Cupboard projecting out reduces the useful size of a room

Principle of roominess is especially very important since it is absolutely essential to have *maximum feeling of space* with *minimum dimensions* to achieve economy.

1.2.4 Grouping

Grouping means arranging various rooms in such a way that, functions of the rooms and movement of its users can be co-ordinated. It helps in easily performing various functions in sequence and with least interference. A few examples are given below to illustrate this:

(i) Administrative department of hospitals, factories, office buildings should be centrally located, preferably on ground floor, so that various departments will have an easy access to it.

(ii) Kitchen should be near dining room and main entrance, at the same time, it should be preferably away from the living room. This helps the lady in kitchen to perform multiple functions with lesser strain.

(iii) In case of factory manufacturing say steel furniture, various processes like receipt of material, processing the same, cutting, bending, welding, grinding, assembling, spray painting, packing, despatching etc. are required to be arranged in a sequence.

Incorrect grouping drastically affects circulation, privacy, sanitation.

1.2.5 Privacy

It is one of the important principles in planning of a building and more so, in respect of residential buildings. Privacy requires consideration in two ways:

(a) Privacy of a part or all parts of building from another building: For example: Swimming tank or an indoor gymnastic hall will require privacy from adjoining buildings. This can be achieved by properly planning entrances, raising compound walls, planting closely spaced tall trees, providing louvers, jallies, creepers on trollis, etc.

(b) Privacy of one room from another: Privacy is of supreme importance in bedroom, bathroom, water closets, urinals, strong room, safe deposit vaults in banks, cabins of top executives etc. This can be achieved by:
- Proper grouping of rooms.
- Positioning doors suitably. It will be noticed that in Fig. 1.5 (a) if door is placed at the centre of shorter side, more privacy is lost than if the door is kept at one side [Fig. 1.5 (b)]. If door is placed at one side of longer wall, more privacy is achieved. [Fig. 1.5 (c)].
- Privacy can also be achieved by providing screens, hanging shutters, vertical Sun breakers, etc.
- When entrance from one room to another room is direct, privacy is lost. However, if it is through common passage, privacy is not affected. *Access from bedrooms to bath room and W.C. should always be independent.*
- Providing a curtain wall in front of doors of public toilet avoids direct view of closing and opening of door from outside.
- For better privacy, staggered openings are preferred.

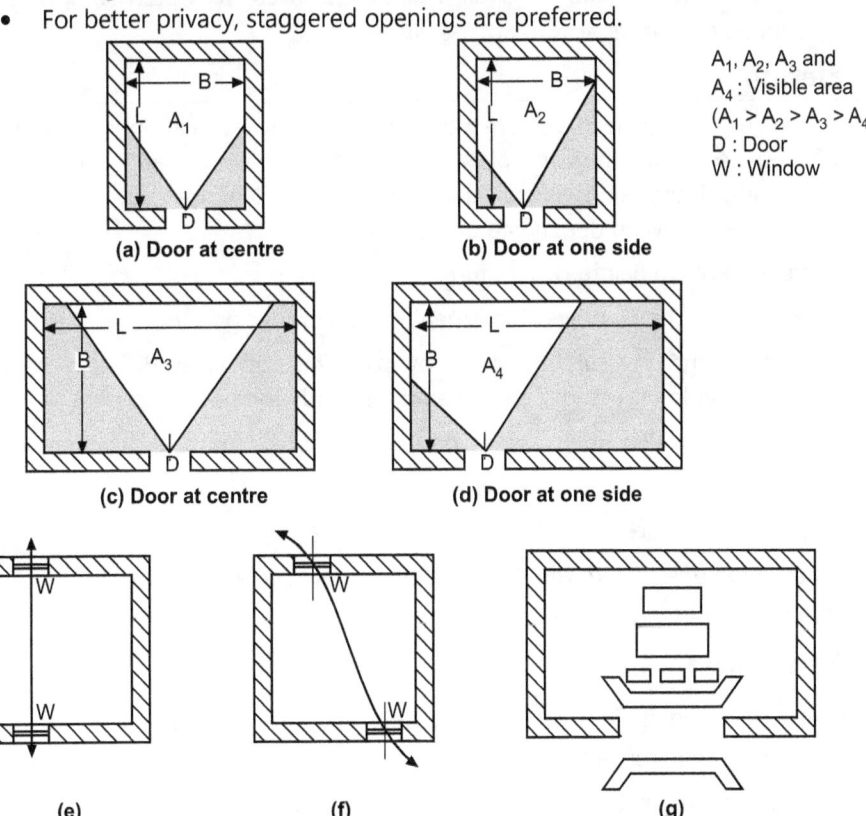

A_1, A_2, A_3 and A_4 : Visible area
$(A_1 > A_2 > A_3 > A_4)$
D : Door
W : Window

Fig. 1.5: Effect of positioning of door on privacy

1.2.6 Circulation

Circulation indicates movement inside the building in the horizontal plane or in vertical plane.

- **(a) Horizontal Circulation:** It depends upon the functional inter-relation of the rooms i.e. living, dining, kitchen should be interconnected by passages, corridors. The passage should be short and wide, otherwise they will increase travel distance and obstruct movement. To have free movement in corridor, doors should not open into corridor. For better circulation, staircases should be centrally placed as far as possible. Also use of foyer is made in public building. Bifurcated stairs facilitate easy circulation.

- **(b) Vertical Circulation:** It is the movement in vertical direction from one floor to another floor and can be achieved by use of stair cases, ramps, lifts, escalator.

Passages, staircases should be well illuminated, well ventilated and must satisfy minimum requirements as regards tread, rise, landings etc.

1.2.7 Elegance

A functionally well planned structure may not necessarily invite attention of the user due to lack of elegance. Thus, the principle of elegance deals with beautifying the structure outwardly thereby integrating it with the surrounding. Elegance may be improved by combination of the following depending on economy:

(a) Increasing plinth height of structure.

(b) Use of arches for windows, door openings, decorative grills etc.

(c) Disturbing the vertical monotony by planning rooms at different heights. For example: duplex structures, combination of plinth and rendering stilt.

(d) Use of decorative building stones, providing different forms of ornamental plaster.

(e) Combination of flat and sloping roofs.

(f) Making various designs in R.C.C.

(g) Integration of structure with surroundings by proper landscaping.

(h) Skillful combination of external colours.

1.2.8 Sanitation

It consists of providing light ventilation, cleanliness, water supply and sanitary amenities as per the different requirements.

- **(i) Light:** Arrangements of windows, ventilators should be made so as to illuminate the maximum portion of the room uniformly. Vertical windows of the same dimensions as horizontal windows provide more natural light. Minimum window area should be provided as per the local governing rules but generally more than 10% of the floor area. Door openings are not to be considered for light and ventilation requirements.

(ii) **Ventilation:** This is a prime requirement to maintain the hygiene of any occupant as lack of fresh air produces headache, sleepiness, suffocation, etc. Natural ventilation may be sought through windows and ventilators. As far as possible, cross ventilation should be achieved. Artificial ventilation may be sought by way of air-conditioning, use of fans, exhaust fans etc.

(iii) **Cleanliness / water supply / sanitary amenities:** Ample water-supply facilities by way of underground sumps, overhead tanks with pumping facility, as well as sanitary amenities like bathrooms, water closets, lavatories, urinals etc. with adequate flushing cisterns are primary requirements of any building.

Cleanliness may be achieved by non-absorbent flooring materials with proper slope, provision of rain water pipes for terrace, adequate slopes and dados in baths, water closets etc.

1.2.9 Orientation

It consists of fixing direction of major axis of building so as to derive maximum benefit from the elements of nature such as sun, wind, rain, in achieving functional comfort inside the building. If length of building is in East-West direction, then its orientation is North South. Orientation is very important principle of planning since only after proper orientation, desired aspect can be achieved.

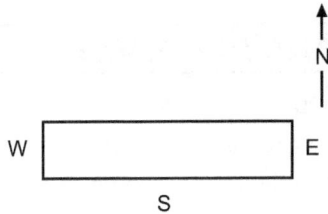

Fig. 1.6: North-South orientation

Poor orientation increases operation, and maintenance cost.

For optimum orientation,

(i) A building should receive maximum solar radiation in winter and minimum in summer.

(ii) In hot climates, verandahs or chajjas or sun breakers may be provided. Hospital, school, drawing offices, library should be located on North side. i.e. long sides of these should face North whereas South and West side should be protected by verandahs.

Verandahs should NOT be provided on North facing.

(iii) To reduce intensity of sun rays.
- (a) Tall trees may be planted on sunny side.
- (b) Walls of minimum area may be provided on East and West side.
- (c) Rooms which are occupied throughout the day are placed on North, whereas bedrooms may be located on West or in the direction of prevailing wind.

(iv) From ventilation point of view, height of a house should not be more than twice the width of the street.

No part of the building is allowed to project beyond the set back distance as shown in Fig. 1.6.

1.2.10 Economy and Practical Considerations

Economy: Last but not the least, any planning would fail if the cost incurred is not considered. However, a structure requiring less investment initially may prove to be costlier in the long run due to high maintenance cost. Although one constructs house during his life time, a costly structure may not be practically feasible. Hence an optimum policy should be framed wherein the functional utility, comfort, as well as cost of the structure.

Practical considerations like scope for future extension without dismantling or damaging strength and stability of the structure, feasibility of converting a room for overlapping purposes etc. should also be considered.

1.3 SUN PATH AND WIND DIAGRAMS

Sun path diagrams map the path of the sun across the sky. They show the position of the sun relative to the site, both by time of day and time of year. A plan of the objects that will shade the site (currently and in the future) can be drawn onto the sun path diagram.

This diagram can then be used to assess the shading effect on the site and help you make decisions about the position of the house on the site, and in particular the position of the north facing windows (the primary solar collectors). If compromise is necessary, as a minimum, you should aim for unrestricted sun on solar collecting windows between 9 am and 3 pm in winter.

A sun path diagram is a three dimensional map of the path of the sun across the sky. You can draw onto this map objects such as trees, buildings and hills that will shade the site. This information will allow you to plan the position of your building and the solar collecting windows of that building to capitalize on the heat from the sun in winter.

Objects that are close to the site, such as adjacent buildings, will shade different parts of the site differently so several sun chart diagrams may be required to plot different parts of the site. Distant objects will shade the whole site in essentially the same way. By moving around the compass bearings on the sun path diagram taking altitude angles for objects that may shade the site you can map these objects onto the sun path diagram.

The links below take you straight the relevant sun path diagrams of your area, you can download the Adobe Acrobat PDF file to print and use. If your region does not have a sun path diagram you can use that of a nearby region, the differences will be insignificant.

Sun path diagrams can tell you a lot about how the sun will impact your site and building throughout the year. Stereographic sun path diagrams can be used to read the solar azimuth and altitude for a given location.

Stereographic Sun Path Diagrams:

Stereographic sun path diagrams are used to read the solar azimuth and altitude throughout the day and year for a given position on the earth. They can be likened to a photograph of the sky, taken looking straight up towards the zenith, with a 180° fish-eye lens. The paths of the sun at different times of the year can then be projected onto this flattened hemisphere for any location on Earth.

Note that these stereographic diagrams are not exactly like a fish-eye photo: such an image would be flipped left-to-right. These diagrams are from the point of view of the sky looking down at the ground, you can superimpose it on a map or a plan of the building without being confused. (You can see this by following the hour lines from east to west on the diagram.)

- **Azimuth Lines:** Azimuth angles run around the edge of the diagram.
- **Altitude Lines:** Altitude angles are represented as concentric circular dotted lines that run from the center of the diagram out.
- **Date Lines:** Date lines start on the eastern side of the graph and run to the western side and represent the path of the sun on one particular day of the year. In Ecotect, the first day of January to June are shown as solid lines, while July to December are shown as dotted lines.
- **Hour Lines/Analemma:** Hour lines are shown as figure-eight-type lines that intersect the date lines and represent the position of the sun at a specific hour of the day. The intersection points between date and hour lines give the position of the sun.

Reading the Sun Position (Step-by-Step).

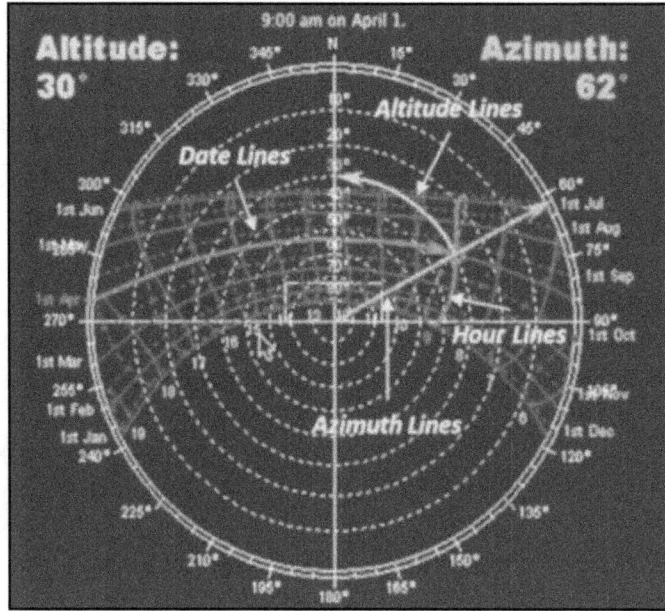

Fig. 1.7

1. Locate the required hour line on the diagram.
2. Locate the required date line, remembering that solid lines are used for January-June and dotted lines for July-December.
3. Find the intersection point of the hour and date lines. Remember to intersect solid with solid and dotted with dotted lines.
4. Draw a line from the very center of the diagram, through the intersection point, out to the perimeter of the diagram.
5. Read the azimuth as an angle taken clockwise from north. In this case, the value is about 62°.
6. Trace a concentric circle around from the intersection point to the vertical north axis, on which is displayed the altitude angles.
7. Interpolate between the concentric circle lines to find the altitude. In this case the intersection point sits exactly on the 30° line.
8. This gives the position of the sun, fully defined as an azimuth and altitude.

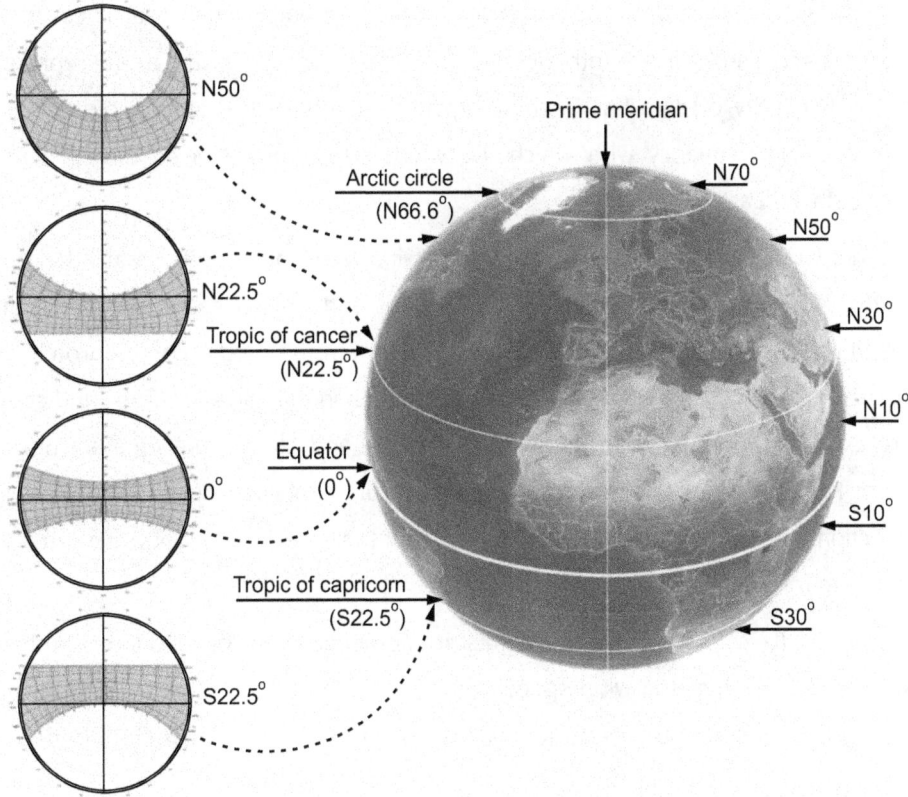

Fig. 1.8: Sun charts illustrating the variation in the sun's movement in relation to latitude

1.4 WIND ROSE

A wind rose gives a very succinct but information-laden view of how wind speed and direction are typically distributed at a particular location. Presented in a circular format, the wind rose shows the frequency of winds blowing from particular directions. The length of each "spoke" around the circle is related to the frequency of time that the wind blows from a particular direction. Each concentric circle represents a different frequency, emanating from zero at the center to increasing frequencies at the outer circles. The wind roses shown here contain additional information, in that each spoke is broken down into discrete frequency categories that show the percentage of time that winds blow from a particular direction and at certain speed ranges. All wind roses shown here use 16 cardinal directions, such as north (N), NNE, NE, etc.

The wind rose is a method of graphically representing the occurrence of winds at a location, showing their strength, direction and frequency. It is a very useful representation as a large quantity of data has been summarised in a simple graphical plot. The wind rose indicates the frequency with which the wind blows from a given direction (N - North, S - South, E - East, W - West).

The wind rose in Fig. 1.9 (a) shows the wind direction conditions at a height of 10 m, in this case distributed over 16 wind directions and 9 wind speed classes including calm (0-0.4 m/s). The wind direction indicates the direction the wind is coming from. The number of wind directions and wind speed classes can change as required. The wind speed classes are explained in Fig. 1.9 (a). Rings for 3, 6, 9, 12 and 15% of the time are also indicated. From Fig. 1.9 (a), we can see that the most common wind direction is West. From this direction, the wind comes approximately 12% of the time. From Fig. 1.9, we can also see that it is calm for 7.02% of the time.

Fig. 1.9 (b) shows the wind speed distribution irrespective of wind direction for the same station. We see that the wind speeds between 2.5 and 4.5 m/s are the most common, at 27.7% of the time. Wind speeds greater than 16.5 m/s occur less than 0.1% of the time.

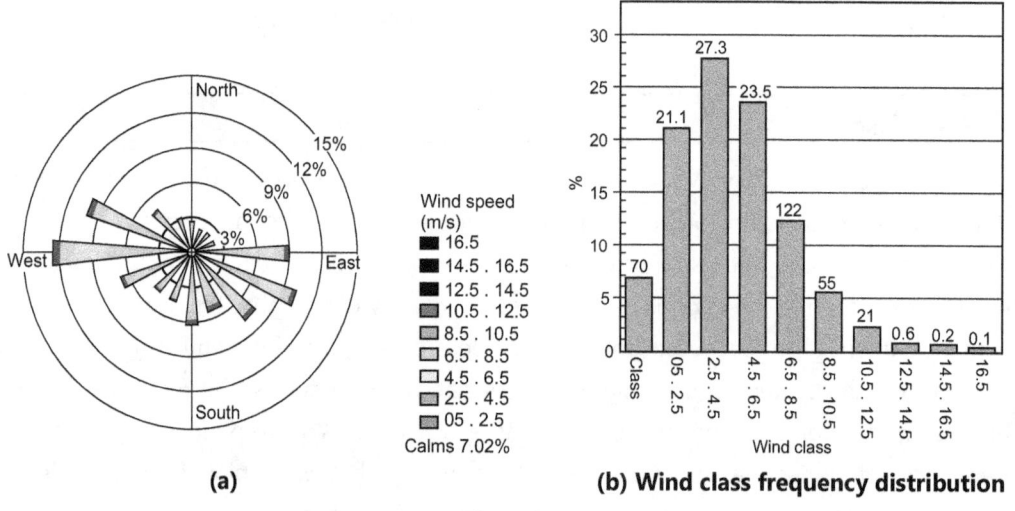

Fig. 1.9

1.5 ORIENTATION

Orientation is the positioning of a building in relation to seasonal variations in the sun's path as well as prevailing wind patterns. Principles of good orientation Good orientation, combined with other energy efficiency features, can reduce or even eliminate the need for auxiliary heating and cooling, resulting in lower energy bills, reduced greenhouse gas emissions and improved comfort. It takes account of summer and winter variations in the sun's path as well as the direction and type of winds, such as cooling breezes.

Good orientation can help reduce or even eliminate the need for auxiliary heating and cooling, resulting in lower energy bills, reduced greenhouse gas emissions and improved comfort.

Ideally, choose a site or home with good orientation for your climatic and regional conditions and build or renovate to maximize the site's potential for passive heating and passive cooling, adjusting the focus on each to suit the climate. For those sites that are not ideally oriented, there are strategies for overcoming some of the challenges.

In hot humid climates and hot dry climates with no winter heating requirements, aim to exclude direct sun by using trees and adjoining buildings to shade every façade year.

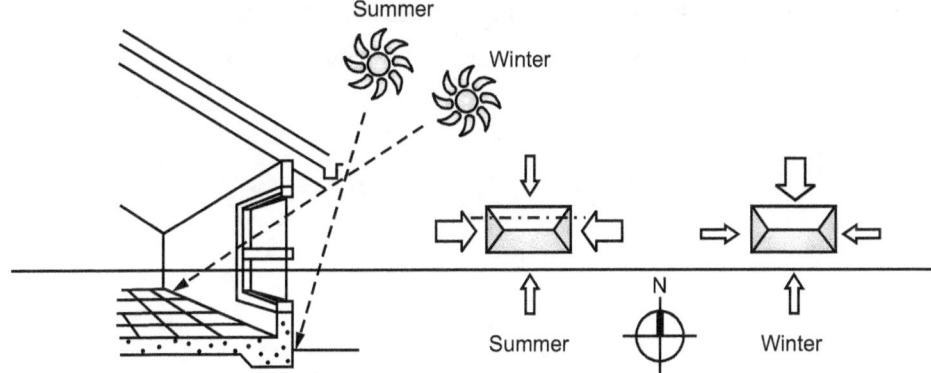

Fig. 1.10: Average daily solar radiation on vertical surfaces

In all other climates a combination of passive solar heating and passive cooling is desirable. The optimum balance between capturing sunlight (solar access) and capturing cooling breezes is determined by heating and cooling needs.

North orientation is generally desirable in climates requiring winter heating, because the position of the sun in the sky allows you to easily shade northern façades and the ground near them in summer time with simple horizontal devices such as eaves, while allowing full sun penetration in winter.

North-facing walls and windows receive more solar radiation in winter than in summer. As shown in the diagram, the opposite is true for other directions and why, in mixed or heating climates, it is beneficial to have the longer walls of a house facing north to minimize exposure to the sun in summer and maximize it in winter.

QUESTIONS

1. What is the necessity of planning a building?
2. (i) Explain "Aspect" as a principle of planning a building.
   (ii) State how "Prospect" is different from "Orientation". Explain with sketches.
   (iii) State the aspect you will provide for kitchen, bedroom, factory building.
   (iv) Explain factors affecting the orientation of a building.
3. What is roominess? State general norms for the ratio between length and width. State effect of shape of a room on roominess.
4. Write short note on "Circulation" as a principle of planning.
5. Describe how the factor 'Economy' dominates the principles of planning.
6. Write a short note on orientation.
7. Explain the requirements of "sanitation" in building as regards:
   (i) Light and ventilation, (ii) Cleanliness, (iii) Sanitary apartment.

■■■

Unit 2

BUILDING PLANNING AND BYE LAWS

2.1 BUILDING BYE-LAWS

Dwellings and buildings have always set out to provide protection from environmental elements for their occupants. Historically, designers of buildings followed traditionally established precedents and relief for decisions on their own experience of traditional solutions. The acceleration of technical development, which is now in progress in the field of building, presents ever increasing functional problems. Experience of previous practice is of only limited value in tackling the new situations which arise. Fortunately, technical progress has also given rise to research which helps to make clear the fundamental principles underlying many environmental phenomena, to provide standards to guide designers and methods of analysis and means for the prediction of conditions to be expected in the new buildings.

Depending upon weather conditions, availability of land, population to be accommodated, local government authorities prepare certain rules and regulations to control the development of various parts of the locality. These rules and regulations covering the requirements of building, ensuring safety of public through open spaces, minimum size of rooms and height and area limitations are known as building bye-laws. It is mandatory, under Maharashtra Regional Town Planning Act 1966, for local authorities to prepare development plans for area under their control. The development plan for any locality is prepared in consultation with experts in various subjects such as town planning, law, health, civil engineering, traffic, general administration etc. Rules are framed to control the growth in various parts of local areas. While planning any developmental project, the architect should follow these regulations. He should submit his proposal with the help of different drawings to the local authority and get it approved before the execution of project.

2.2 NECESSITY OF BYE-LAWS

A well planned and architecturally designed layout may have to be abandoned because the design does not benefit the statutory requirements in one or other respects. With all liberties in planning and designing, an architect has to shape and trim his layout if need be so as to make the resulting plan to the mark of the rules and regulations enforced by the concerned authorities. There are building regulations and bye-laws laid down by the Municipal authorities in their jurisdiction. In other areas similar statutes are made applicable by the Town Planning authorities. In Rural areas the Revenue authorities are concerned with this.

These regulations dictate upon:
1. Lines of building frontages,
2. Built-up area of buildings,
3. Open spaces around buildings and their heights,
4. Provision as to size, height and ventilation of rooms and apartments,
5. Water supply and sanitary provisions,
6. Structural design or sizes and sections.

The knowledge of the regulations and bye-laws, which influence the building design, needs to be considered as a sound basis for the professional architects and the students as well. While giving the details of structural elements, according to the rules and regulations, certain additional details are given here. This will help students in providing suitable sizes and sections without going in for detailed calculations. However, it is advised that students should calculate and design various members as far as possible.

If bye-laws are not followed, development will take place without proper amenities and healthy environment and all construction activities will aim at only making profit. Therefore, building bye-laws are necessary for the following objects:
1. Building bye-laws help the architects or the engineers in planning developmental projects.
2. Bye-laws help in carrying out systematic growth of various parts of locality and avoid haphazard development.
3. Building bye-laws ensure safety against fire, pollution, health hazards and building failure.

2.2.1 Basic Definitions

1. **Act:** It shall mean:
   (i) The Bombay Provincial Municipal Corporation Act - 1949.
   (ii) The Maharashtra Regional and Town Planning Act - 1966.
   (iii) Urban land (C and R) Act - 1976.
2. **Balcony:** A horizontal projection including a handrail or balustrade to serve as a passage or sitting out place.
3. **Basement or Cellar:** Storey of a building below or partly below ground level.
4. **Building:** The word building shall have the same meaning assigned thereto as under the B.P.M.C. Act 1949.
5. **Built-up Area:** Area covered immediately above the plinth level by the building or external area of any upper floor whichever is more excepting the areas permitted in the open spaces.
6. **Building Height:** The vertical distance measured in the case of flat roofs, from the average level of the ground around and contiguous to the building to the highest

point of the building and in the case of pitched roofs, upto the mid-point between the eaves level and the ridge. Architectural features serving no other function except that of decoration shall be excluded for the purpose of ascertaining height.

7. **Carpet Area:** The net floor area of all habitable rooms within an apartment excluding the area of walls.
8. **Chajja:** A sloping or horizontal structural overhang usually provided over openings on external walls to provide protection from sun and rain.
9. **Courtyard or Chowk:** A space permanently open to the sky, enclosed fully or partially by building and may be at ground level or any other level within or adjacent to a building.
10. **Detached Building:** A building whose walls and roofs are independent of any other building with open space on all sides as specified.
11. **Development:** 'Development' with its grammatical variations means the carrying out of buildings, engineering, mining or other operations in or over or under land or water, or the making of any material change, in any building or land, or in the use of any building or land and includes redevelopment and layout and sub-division of any land, reclamation; 'to develop' shall be constructed accordingly.
12. **Drainage:** The removal of any liquid by a system constructed for the purpose.
13. **Enclosed Staircase:** A staircase separated by the fire resistant walls and door(s) from the rest of the building.
14. **Existing Building or Use:** A building structure or its use existing authorisedly before the commencement of these rules.
15. **Floor Area:** It shall mean covered area of a building at any floor level.
16. **Front:** The space between the boundary line of plot abutting the means of access / roads / street and the building. The plot shall be deemed to front on all such means of access.
17. **Habitable Room:** It means a room constructed or intended for human habitation.
18. **Occupancy:** Principal occupancy for which a building or a part of building is used or intended to be used.
    (a) **Residential buildings:** These shall include any building in which sleeping accommodation is provided for normal residential purposes with or without cooking or dining or both facilities.
    (b) **Educational buildings:** These shall include any building used for school, college or day care purposes for more than 8 hours per week involving assembly for instructions, education or recreation incidental to education.
    (c) **Institutional buildings:** These shall include any building or a part thereof which is used for purposes such as medical or other treatment or case of persons, informity care of infants etc.

(d) Assembly buildings: These shall include any building or a part of a building where groups of people congregate or gather for amusement, recreation, social, religious, patriotic, civil, travel and similar purposes.

(e) Business buildings: These shall include any building or a part of a building which is used for transaction of business for keeping of account for similar purposes.

(f) Office buildings: The premises where sole or principal use is to be used as an office or for office purpose; which includes, administration, clerical work, handling money, telephone and telegraph operating and operating computers.

(g) Industrial building: These shall include any building or part of a building or structure in which products or materials of all kinds and properties are fabricated, assembled or processed.

(h) Public building: Except where otherwise defined means a building owned and used by Government or Semi-Government or public registered trusts for public purposes.

19. **Parking Space:** An area enclosed or unenclosed, covered or open, sufficient in size to park vehicles, together with a drive way connecting the parking space with a street or alley and permitting ingress or egress of vehicles.

20. **Plinth:** The position of a structure between the surface of the surrounding ground and surface of the floor, immediately above the ground.

21. **Plinth Area:** The maximum built up covered area measured externally at the floor level or the basement or of any storey whichever is higher.

22. **Room Height:** The vertical distance measured from the finished ceiling/slab surface. In case of pitched roofs, the room height shall be the vertical distance measured from the finished floor surface upto the mid-point of the sloping roof.

23. **Row Housing:** A row house with only front rear and interior open space.

24. **Semi-detached Building:** A building detached on three sides with open spaces as specified. Provided, however, that semi-detached construction will be permitted only when the intention is to save construction cost by having one common wall and when the two buildings in the two adjoining plots are designed jointly.

25. **Site or Plot:** A parcel / piece of land enclosed by definite boundaries.

26. **Storey:** The portion of a building included between the surface or any floor and the surface of the floor next above it, or if there be no floor above it, then the space between any floor and the ceiling next above it.

27. **Tenement:** An independent dwelling unit with a kitchen.

28. **Volume Plot Ratio (V.P.R.):** The ratio of volume of building measured in cubic metres to the area of plot measured in square metres and expressed in metres.

29. **Width of Road:** The whole extent of space within the boundaries of road when applied to a new road, as laid down in the city survey map or development plan or prescribed road lines by any act or law and measured at right angles to the course or intended course of direction of such road.

2.3 DEVELOPMENT CONTROL RULES FOR PLAN PREPARATION

2.3.1 Plot Size

As per the development plan, a site or plot is a parcel, or piece of land enclosed by definite boundaries.

Following are the rules for various types of zones.

Residential and Commercial Zone:

(Excluding weaker section housing schemes undertaken by public authorities).

The minimum size of plots in residential layouts shall be of 50 sq. m subject to the following further provisions:

(a) Plots having area upto 125 sq. m shall be permitted only for row housing schemes and the width of such plots shall be between 4.5 to 8 m.

(b) Plots having area between 125 sq. m to 250 sq. m shall be permitted only for row housing or semi-detached housing and the width of such plots shall be between 8 to 12 m.

(c) Plots above 250 sq. m shall be permitted for row housing, semi-detached or detached housing and the width of plots in this category shall be above 12 m and no dimension of plot shall be less than 12 m.

The above rules will also apply to sub-division schemes, layouts and building construction pattern in commercial zones.

For special housing schemes, for Low Income Group and Economically Weaker section of society and slum clearance schemes, the minimum plot size shall be 20 sq. m with a minimum width of 3.6 m or the size as prescribed by Government from time to time.

Industrial Zones: The width of plot shall not be less than 15 m and the size of plot shall not be less than 300 sq. m.

Cinema Theatres / Assembly Halls: The minimum size of plot for cinema theatre / assembly buildings used for public entertainment with fixed seats shall be on the basis of seating capacity of the building at the rate of 3 sq. m per seat or as prescribed by Government from time to time.

Mangal Karyalaya: The minimum size of plot shall be 1000 sq. m.

Petrol Filling Stations:

The minimum size of plot shall be

(a) 30.5 m × 15.75 m – for petrol filling stations without service bay.

(b) 36.5 m × 30.5 m – for petrol pump with service bay.

2.3.2 Means of Access

Every building existing or proposed shall have public or internal means of access. Any building shall not in any way encroach upon or diminish the area set apart as means of access. The means of access shall be clear of marginal open space of at least 3 m from the existing building line. The plot shall abut on a public means of access like street / road. If it is not, then the width of road shall be as per the following Table 2.1.

Table 2.1

Length of means of access in m	Width of means of access in m	
	When development is only on one side of means of access	When development is on both sides of means of access
Upto 75	5.0	6.0
150	6.5	7.5
300	8.0	9.0
Above 300	11.0	12.0

For all industrial buildings, theatres, cinema houses, assembly halls, stadia, educational buildings, markets which attract large crowd, width of road shall be as per the following Table 2.2.

Table 2.2

Length of means of access in m	Width of means of access (minimum) in m
Upto 200	12
Above 200	15

The length of means of access shall be determined by the distance from the farthest plot (building) to the public street. The length of the subsidiary access way shall be measured from the point of its origins to the next wider road on which it meets. In case of U-loop, the length shall be considered as half the length of the loop.

Intersection of Roads: At junctions of roads meeting at right angles or at less than $60°$, the rounding off shall be done as shown in Figs. 2.1 and 2.2.

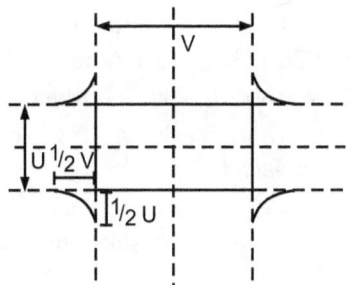
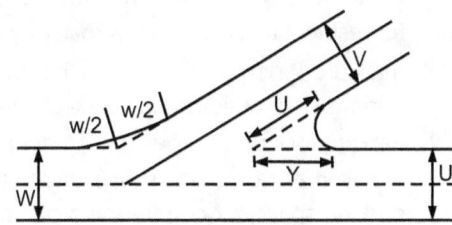

Fig. 2.1: Rounding off intersections at junctions

Fig. 2.2: Rounding off intersections at junctions

2.3.3 Open Spaces

In any layout or sub-division of land admeasuring 4000 sq. metres or more, 10% of the entire plot area shall be reserved as recreation of space which shall as far as possible be provided in one place. In case of very large layout, distribution of total open space in the various sectors may be allowed, provided that no such space at any place admeasures less than 200 sq. m. The shape and location of such open space shall be such that it can be properly utilized as play ground. The minimum dimensions of such recreational space shall not be less than 7.5 m and if the average width of such recreational space is less than 24 m, the length shall not exceed 2.5 times the average width.

For the open spaces having area 570 sq. m or above, a two storeyed structure having built up area equal to 15% of open space shall be permitted out of which 10% built up area shall be allowed on ground floor and 5% on first floor for the purpose of pavilion or Gymnasia or other activities which are related to open spaces.

If the open space is not directly approachable from all the buildings in the layout, an independent means of access having minimum width of 5 m shall be provided.

2.3.4 Floor Area Ratio (F.A.R.)

To maintain designed population in different parts of the city and to avoid haphazard growth of the city, local authority lays down certain controls on F.A.R., height of the building, total covered area, tenement density, Volume Plot Ratio (V.P.R.) etc.

Floor area means covered area of a building at any floor level. The quotient obtained by dividing the total floor area on all floors excluding exempted area by the area of plot is called floor area ratio or Floor Space Index (F.S.I.).

$$\text{F.A.R. or F.S.I} = \frac{\text{Total covered area on all floors}}{\text{Plot area}}$$

2.3.4.1 For Calculation of Covered Area or F.A.R. Following Areas are Excluded

(i) Projections for cornice, chajja, roof or weather shade having width less than 0.75 m.

(ii) An unenclosed canopy not exceeding 5 m in length, 2.5 m in width in the form of a cantilever and having a minimum clear height of 2.1 m below the canopy.

(iii) In residential buildings, a balcony at roof level above floor of a width 1.2 m measured perpendicular to the building line having maximum $1/3^{rd}$ length of perimeter of building and 10% of the floor area of each floor.

(iv) Parking lock up garages having height upto 2.4 m.

(v) A basement or cellar space under a building constructed on stilts and used as a parking space, air conditioning plant rooms.

(vi) Electric cabin or substation, watchman's cabin of maximum size 1.6 sq. m, pump house, garage shaft, fire hydrants, electric fittings, water tanks.

(vii) Stair case room, lift rooms above the topmost floor, architectural features, chimneys.

(viii) Well, plant, nursery, water pool, uncovered swimming pool, platform round a tree, fountain, bench, ramps, compound wall, gate, overhead water tank on top of the building.

Different rules are framed for congested area relating to the existing congested areas specified in the development plan and existing Gaothans of villages included in the municipal limits. The permissible F.A.R. shall be 1.5 for purely residential building and 2.00 for building with mixed residential and commercial use. The permissible tenement density shall be 250 T/Ha.

In case of buildings, having residential and commercial use, the commercial use will be permitted only on ground floor. The F.A.R. permissible for residential use is 1.5 and commercial use is 0.5. In case of educational, public health and charitable buildings in congested area. F.A.R. shall be 1.5. But under special circumstances, F.A.R. equal to 2.25 is permitted.

Permissible F.A.R. for buildings in areas other than congested area is given in Table 2.3.

2.3.4.2 Area Measurement of a Building

Following definitions explain various forms of building coverage:

Covered Area:

It is the ground covered above plinth. Area occupied by compound wall, uncovered porches, is not included in the covered area.

Plinth Area:

It is the built up covered area measured at the floor level of a building.

Following areas shall be included:

(i) Areas of walls at floor level excluding plinth offsets, projections beyond claddings when building consists of columns.

(ii) Internal shafts of sanitary installations less than 2 m² in area, air conditioning ducts, lifts.

(iii) Porches and other cantilevers provided.

(iv) Area of Barsati at terrace.

Following areas shall not be included:
(i) Lofts.
(ii) Internal shafts of sanitary installations greater than 2 m² in area.
(iii) Unclosed balconies.
(iv) Towers, turrets and domes unless they form a storey.
(v) Architectural bans, cornices.
(vi) Vertical sun breakers.

Floor Area:

It is the usable covered area of the building at any floor level.

Thus, Floor area = Plinth area − Walls

Following areas shall be included:
(i) Doors and other openings.
(ii) Internal pillars and supports.
(iii) Plasters along the walls exceeding 300 m².

Following areas shall not be included:
(i) Plasters along the walls less than 300 m².
(ii) Fire places projecting beyond face of wall.

Built-up Area:

It is the area covered by all floors of a building. It includes everything covered under roof. Area occupied by balcony, staircase is excluded from the built up area.

Carpet Area:

It is defined as actual area of usable room at any floor level (Literally means the area where carpet can be laid). It does not include sanitary accommodations, verandahs, corridors and passages, stores in domestic buildings, staircases, and shafts for lifts, garages, air condition ducts and plant room.

2.3.5 Marginal Distances

As per the building regulations, spaces open to sky should be left around the buildings. This open space is useful from the following aspects: (a) to meet light and ventilation requirements, (b) to facilitate fire fighting operation, (c) to serve the purpose of future expansion of streets, (d) to reduce noise level and entry of pollutants in the building by planting trees, (e) to reduce loss due to fire in case the adjoining building catches fire.

The open space left between the street and building is called as front margin, open space on back sides is called as rear margin and on sides is called as side margin.

In congested areas front margin, for residential buildings facing roads 4.5 m or more in width shall be 1.5 m. For shops and commercial buildings, minimum front margin shall be 2.25 m. For educational, public health and charitable buildings, a clear open space of 3 m all around the building shall be provided. Provisions for open spaces applicable for areas other than congested areas for residential buildings, residential cum office or shop buildings permissible on plots are given in Table 2.3.

Table 2.3

Far. front/Rear/Side Margins/Tenement Densities/Heights to different categories in Non-congested residential zones

Sr. No.	Description of Road	Minimum plot size in m^2	Minimum frontage in m	Minimum setback from road front in m	Minimum side and rear open space in m	Maximum permissible Ground coverage in m^2	Maximum height permissible in m	Far	Tenement Density/ Maximum No. of storeys permissible	Remarks
1	2	3	4	5	6	7	8	9	10	11
1.	National/State Highway, or road as specified by the Municipal Commissioner	750	18	6 m from the D. P. road line.	Half the height of the building minus three subject to minimum of 3 m (side and rear)	1/2 or 1/3	18 m	1	250 Tenements per Ha/G + 7 or G + 6	
2.	M.D.R.O.D.R. and other roads 24 m wide and above	600	18	4.5 for purely residential tenements and 6 m for other uses on groundfloor.	Half the height of the building minus three subject to minimum of 3 m (side and rear)	1/2 or 1/3	18 m	1	250 Tenements per Ha/G + 7 or G + 6	
3.	Roads of width below 24 m wide and above 15 m.	500	15	4.5 for purely residential tenements and 6 m for other uses on groundfloor.	Half the height of the building minus three subject to minimum of 3 m (side and rear)	1/2 or 1/3	18 m	1	250 Tenements per Ha/G + 7 or G + 6	
4.	Road of width below 15 m and above 9 m.	250	12	4.5 for purely residential tenements and 6 m for other uses on groundfloor.	Half the height of the building minus three subject to minimum of 3 m (side and rear)	1/2 or 1/3	12 m	1	250 Tenement per Ha/G + 3 or G + 2	
5.	Road of width below 9 m and above 6 m.	250	12	4.5 for purely residential tenements and 6 m for other uses on groundfloor.	Half the height of the building minus three subject to minimum of 3 m (side and rear)	1/2 or 1/3	12 m	1	250 Tenement per Ha/G + 3 or G + 2	

Sr. No.	Description of Road	Minimum plot size in m²	Minimum frontage in m	Minimum setback from road front in m	Minimum side and rear open space in m	Maximum permissible Ground coverage in m²	Maximum height permissible in m	Far	Tenement Density/ Maximum No. of storeys permissible	Remarks
1	2	3	4	5	6	7	8	9	10	11
6.	Road of width 12 m and below.	125 250	8 to 12	3.00	side margin 2.25 m of 2.25 m only on one side in case of semidetached rear margin 3.00	1/2 or 1/3	10 m	1	250 Tenement per Ha/G + 3 or G + 2 (i) G + 1 (ii) G + 2 with side and rear margin of 3 m.	In case of categories 6, 7 and 8 marginal distance of any building shall be minimum 3.00 m from peripheral boundary of the layout.
7.	Row Housing on Roads of width of 12 m and below.	50 125	4 to 8	3.00	side margin 2.25 rear margin 1.50	1/2 or 1/3	10 m	1	250 Tenement per Ha/G + 3 or G + 2 G − 1	
8.	Row Housing for Economically weaker reaction/ Low income group.	20 50	4	1.0 m from pathway / 2.25 m from road boundary.	side margin 2.25 rear margin 1.50	One full plot area after leaving areas under set backs	10 A	1	400 Tenements per Ha. size of the tenements should be between 20 and 30 sq. m.	

The provisions regarding built up area, permissible F.A.R. and open spaces for buildings other than residential buildings are given in Table 2.4.

Table 2.4

Type of building	Maximum permissible F.A.R.	Built-up area (maximum permissible)	Minimum open space
1. Educational buildings	1.0	1/3rd of plot area	6 m on all sides from boundaries of plot.
2. Institutional buildings (Hospitals, health centres)	1.0	1/3rd of plot area	6 m on all sides from boundaries of plot.
3. Cinema theatres, assembly halls	1.0	–	Front set back 12 m side and rear open space 6 m.
4. Public entertainment halls, Mangal karyalaya	1.0	1/3rd of plot area	Front open space 12 m side and rear open space 6 m.
5. Buildings in commercial zones	1.5	Half of plot size	4.5 m along peripheri.

When a building abuts two or more streets, the setbacks from the streets shall be such as if the building was fronting each such street.

2.3.6 Height of Building

The height of building is decided by two factors; either by the width of the street on which it fronts, or the minimum width or rear space. The height of the building is measured upto the tie beam in case of pitched roof and upto the surface of roof in case of flat roof. In case of pitched roof, the pitch is not expected to exceed 45 degrees or the height of parapet by three feet in case of flat roof. No plinth or any part of a building or out-houses shall be less than 30 (60 cm according to some authorities) above the determined level of the central part of the abutting street or foot-path, or the highest part of a service lane or any portion of the ground within 3 m distance of such a building. Table 2.5 below gives a typical example of building heights with reference to street widths.

Table 2.5

Sr. No.	Width of street	Height of the building
1.	Upto 8 m	Not more than $1\frac{1}{2}$ times the width of the street.
2.	8 m to 12 m	Not more than 12 m.
3.	Above 12 m	Not more than width of the street, and not more than 21 m.

The height of the building with respect to the rear space is fixed by two imaginary lines – the horizontal line and the diagonal line. The horizontal line is drawn at right angles to the road, through the centre of the front line. The location of this horizontal line is taken at the higher point along the line. See Fig. 2.3. The diagonal line is drawn in the direction of the building at $63\frac{1}{2}$ degrees from where the horizontal lines meet the rear boundary. No part of the building is allowed to project beyond the diagonal line except that for minor part such as smoke chimneys, turrets etc.

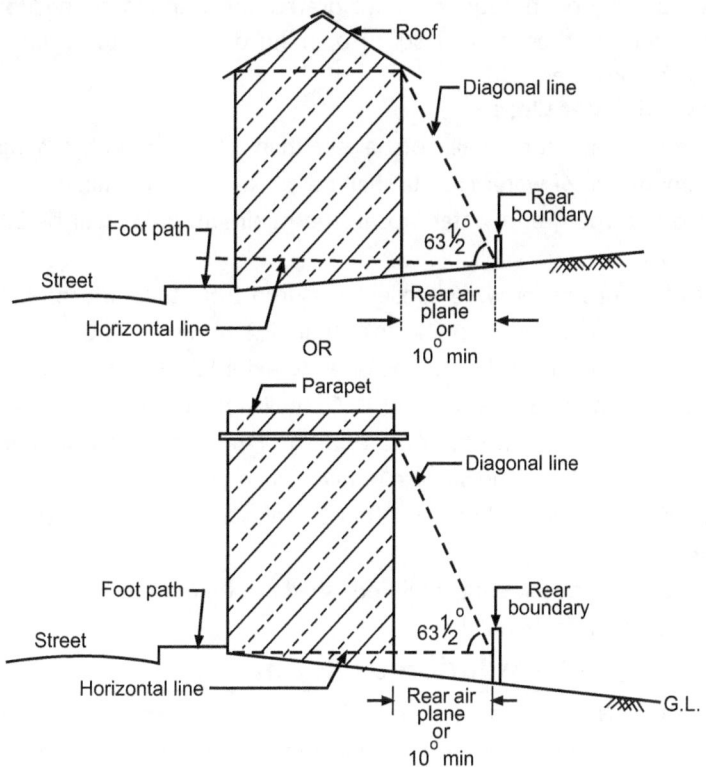

Fig. 2.3: Height of buildings with reference to rear space

2.3.7 Provisions Regarding Room Sizes

(a) Habitable Rooms:

Size: No habitable room shall have a floor area of less than 9.5 sq. m except those in the hostels attached to recognised educational institutions where minimum size of a room shall be 7.5 sq. m. The minimum width of a habitable room shall be 2.4 m. One full side of a habitable room in which windows for minimum light and ventilation are provided shall abut on the required open space.

Height: The height of any room for human habitation including that of kitchen shall not be less than 2.75 m measured from the surface of the floor to the lowest point of ceiling. For centrally air conditioned rooms, the height shall not be less than 2.4 m.

(b) Kitchen:

Size: The area of the kitchen shall not be less than 5.5 sq. m with a minimum width of 1.8 m. If the kitchen is also intended for use as a dining room, the minimum floor area shall be 9.5 m with minimum width of 2.4 m.

Every room to be used as a kitchen shall have means for washing of kitchen utensils which shall lead directly or through a sink to grated and trapped connection to the waste pipe. Window of area not less than 1 sq. m opening directly on to an interior or exterior open space shall be provided.

(c) Bathrooms and Water Closets:

Size: The size of bathroom shall not be less than 1.8 sq. m with a minimum width of 1.2 m. The minimum size of water closets shall be 1.1 sq. m with a minimum width of 0.9 m. If it is combined bathroom and water closet, the minimum area shall be 2.8 sq. m with a minimum size of 1.2 m.

The height of bathroom or water closet measured from the surface of the floor to the lowest point in the ceiling shall not be less than 2.2 m. Every bath or W.C. shall be so situated that atleast one of its walls shall be open to external air with the size of opening not less than 0.3 sq. m in area. Bathroom and W.C. shall not be constructed directly over any room other than water closet, washing place, bath or terrace. Bathroom and W.C. shall be enclosed by walls or partitions and surface of every such wall shall be finished with a smooth impervious material to a height of not less than 1 m above the floor of such room.

(d) Store Rooms:

Size of a store room in residential buildings shall not be more than 3 sq. m. The height of store room shall not be less than 2.2 m.

2.3.8 Lighting and Ventilation of Room

All habitable rooms including kitchen shall have, for the admission of light and air, one or more openings, such as windows, fan, lights, opening directly to the external air or into an open verandah not more than 2.4 m in width.

Where lighting and ventilation requirements are not met through day lighting and natural ventilation, the same shall be ensured through artificial lighting and mechanical ventilation.

The minimum aggregate area of openings of habitable rooms and kitchens, excluding doors shall not be less than $1/8^{th}$ floor area.

For ventilating the spaces for W.C. and bathrooms if not opening on the front side, rear and interior open spaces, shall open onto the ventilation shaft. The minimum size of such ventilation shaft are given in Table 2.6.

Table 2.6

Height of building in m	Minimum area of ventilation shaft in sq. m	Minimum side of shaft in m
Upto 12	3	1.5
18	4.5	1.8
20	6	1.8

2.3.9 Drainage and Sanitation

There are some regulations for minimum requirements for water supply and sanitary conveniences for different types of buildings:

(a) **Residential Buildings:** There shall be one bathroom with a tap, one water closet and one sink per dwellings. The minimum requirement of water shall be 135 litres per day per head.

(b) **For shops and Commercial Offices:** There shall be one water closet for every 25 persons, drinking water fountain for every 100 persons and wash basin, one for every 25 persons.

(c) **Hotels:** There shall be one water closet per 100 persons for males and 2 for 100 persons for females. There shall be urinals one for 50 male persons.

(d) **Educational Buildings:** There shall be one water closet per 30 pupils in nursery schools. For other educational institutions, 1 W.C. per 80 boys and 1 W.C. per 50 girls shall be provided. There shall be 1 urinal per 20 boys. Separate W.C. and urinals shall be provided for male and female teaching staff. The requirement of water shall be 45 lit. per head per day for day schools and for boarding schools 135 lit. per head per day.

(e) **Hospitals:** There shall be one water closet for every 8 beds, 2 wash basins per 30 beds and 1 bathroom for every 8 beds. In addition, there shall be separate water closets and urinals for male and female administrative staff. For hospitals, requirement of water shall be 340 litres per head per day.

(f) **Government and Public Buildings:** There shall be one water closet for every 25 male persons, one for every 15 female persons. There shall be one urinal for 7 – 20 male persons and additional one urinal for every 20 male persons. The requirement of water shall be calculated at the rate of 45 litres per head per day.

(g) **Cinema Threatres and Auditoria:** There shall be 1 W.C. per 100 persons for males upto 400 persons and additional W.C. 1 per 250 persons above 400 persons. For females, there shall be 3 water closets per 100 persons upto 200 persons and 2 additional W.C. per 100 persons if the number is more than 200. There shall be one urinal for 25 male persons.

Separate wash basins for male and female persons at rate of 1 for every 200 persons shall be provided. Separate urinals for male and water closets for male and female staff shall be provided. The requirement of water shall be 15 litres per seat of accommodation.

(h) Industries: There shall be one water closet per 15 male persons and additional one for every 20 persons. There shall be one water closet per 12 female persons and additional one for next 13 female persons. There shall be urinals one per 20 persons and additional 1 for every 20 persons. Drinking water requirement is 30 litres per head per day.

2.3.10 Parking

Parking spaces for cars scooters and cycles shall be provided to each building depending upon the type of building and number of users. The space requirement for motor vehicles shall be 2.5 m × 5 m, for scooters - 3 sq. m, for cycles - 1.4 sq. m.

Table 2.7 shows provision for off street parking space for vehicles.

Table 2.7: Off street parking space

Sr. No.	Occupancy	One Parking space for every	Congested Area			Non-congested Area		
			Car Nos.	Scooter Nos.	Cycle Nos.	Car Nos.	Scooter Nos.	Cycle Nos.
1.	Residential (i) Multi-family residential	(a) 1 tenement having carpet area more than 80 sq. m.	1	2	2	1	2	2
		(b) 2 tenements having carpet area between 40 sq. m. to 80 sq. m.	–	2	4	1	4	4
		(c) 4 tenements having carpet area upto 40 sq. m.	–	4	8	1	4	4
	(ii) Lodging establishments, tourist homes, hotels with lodging accommodation.	(d) Every five guest rooms.	2	2	4	3	4	4

contd. ...

	(iii) Restaurants	(e) For Grade I hotel, eating houses, 18 sq. m. of area of restaurant including kitchen, pantry hall, dining rooms etc.	2	2	2	2	4	4
		(f) For Grade II and III hotels, eating houses etc. for an area of 80 sq. m. or part thereof.	–	4	8	1	4	4
2.	Institutional (Hospital Medical Institutions)	Every 20 beds.	3	2	4	3	4	4
3.	Assembly (theatres) cinema houses, concert halls, Assembly halls including those on colleges and Hostels and Auditorium for Educational buildings.	40 seats	3	5	10	3	10	10
4.	Educational	100 sq. m. or fraction thereof the administrative area and public service area.	2	2	4	2	4	4
5.	Government or semipublic or private business buildings and Auditoriums for Educational buildings.	100 sq. m. carpet area fraction thereof.	2	2	4	2	4	4

contd. ...

6.	(a) Mercantiles (markets, departmental stores, shops and other commercial users).	100 sq. m. carpet area fraction thereof.	2	2	4	2	4	4
	(b) Wholesale	100 sq. m. carpet area fraction thereof.	2	2	4	2	4	2
	(c) Hazardous building	100 sq. m. carpet area fraction thereof.	1	2	4	1	4	4
7.	Industrial	Every 300 sq. m. or fraction thereof.	1	2	4	1	4	8
	Storage Type		1	2	4	1	4	8
	Plots less than 200 sq. m. (any use)		–	2	4	–	2	4
	Plots less than 100 sq. m.		–	2	4	–	2	4

2.4 BUILDING LINE AND CONTROL LINE

The line upto which the plinth of a building adjoining the street or an extension of a street or future street may lawfully extend is called as **building line**. It includes the lines prescribed, if any scheme or development plan or under any other law, in force. The line refers to the line of building frontage which is known as set back or front building line.

Control Line: In case of buildings such as cinema theatres, factories, commercial concerns which attract large number of vehicles should be setback a further distance apart from the building line. The line upto which such buildings can be constructed is known as **control line**. The distance of control line from centre of adjoining street or road may be about one and half times that of building line. The distances of the lines of building frontages is decided by the category of the city zone in which the site of proposed building is located. In the development plan, the present width and future likely widening of each street and road is marked. The minimum distance from the centre line of road is prescribed for the line building frontages. The space in front of the building helps in future widening of the road, reducing noise, dust from abutting buildings and preventing creation of blind corners at the intersection of the streets. This space also helps in maintaining open spaces for air, sun etc.

Table 2.8: Distances of building and control lines

Type of Road	In open and agricultural country		Ribbon development along approaches		Actual limits in urban areas	
	Building line m	Control line m	Building line m	Control line m	Building line m	Control line m
1. National and state highway	30	56	18	30	30	45
2. Major district roads	24	45	9	15	15	24
3. Other district roads	15	24	6	9	9	25
4. Village roads	12	18	6	9	9	25

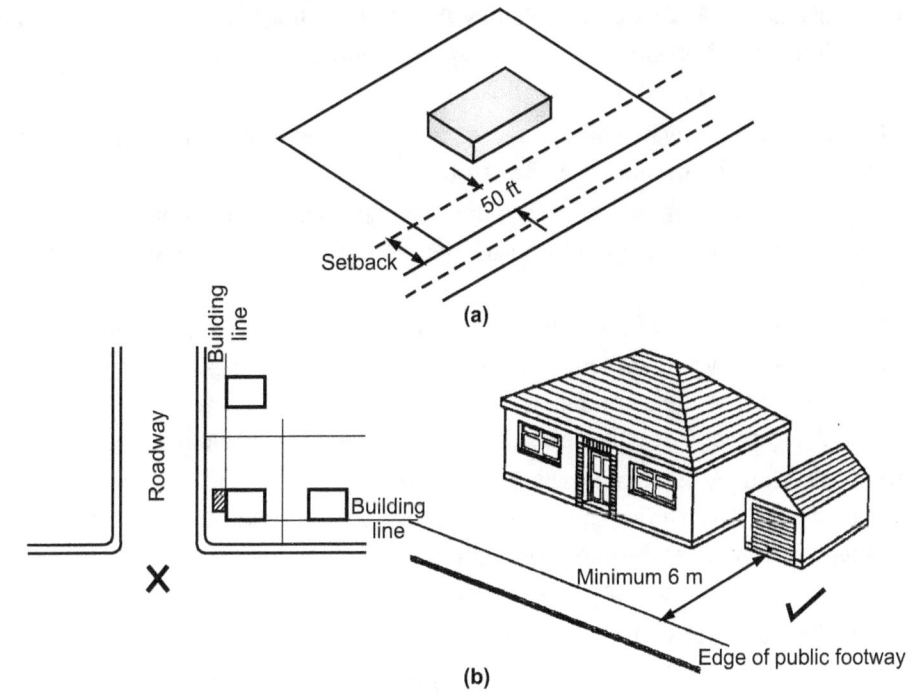

Fig. 2.4

2.5 PLANNING OF RESIDENTIAL BUILDINGS

As per National Building Code of India (SP : 7-1970) Residential Buildings (Group A) are those buildings in which sleeping accommodation is provided for normal residential purposes, with or without cooking or dining or both facilities. It is a building, where one dwells or resides permanently or for a considerable time can be called as a residential building; it may be a bunglow, a block of flats, a hill side cottage or a hotel. Every type of residential building serves the purpose of dwelling in one way or the other, only there is difference of type. Buildings of group A are further sub-divided as follows:

(i) **Sub-division A-1: Lodging or Rooming Houses:** These include any building or group of buildings under the same management, in which separate sleeping accommodation for a total of not more than 15 persons, on either transient or permanent basis with or without dining facilities, but without cooking facilities for individuals, is provided.

A lodging or rooming house is classified as a dwelling in sub-division A-2 if no room in any of its private dwelling units is rented to more than three persons.

(ii) **Sub-division A-2: One or two Family Private Dwellings:** These include any private dwelling which is occupied by members of a single family and has a total sleeping accommodation for not more than 20 persons.

If rooms in a private dwelling are rented to outsiders, these should be for accommodating not more than 3 persons.

If sleeping accommodation for more than 20 persons is provided in any one residential building, it should be classified as a building sub-division A-3 or A-4 as the case may be.

(iii) **Sub-division A-3: Dormitories:** These include any building in which group sleeping accommodation is provided, with or without dining facilities, for persons who are not members of the same family, in any one room or a management, for example, school and college dormitories, students and other hostels and military barracks.

(iv) **Sub-division A-4: Apartment Houses (Flats):** These include any building or structure in which living quarters are provided for three or more families living independently of each other and with independent cooking facilities, for example, apartment houses, mansions and chawls.

(v) **Sub-division A-5: Hotels:** These include any building or group of buildings under single management in which sleeping accommodation, with or without dining facilities, is provided for hire to more than 15 persons who are primarily transient, for example, hotels, inns, clubs and motels.

2.6 SITE SELECTION

In case of buildings, particularly residential, selection of a site and designs of a building before its construction, are two important aspects. Every individual has a desire to live in an ecofriendly atmosphere with a good aspect for all the natural benefits like light, air etc.

Therefore, before starting planning of any residential building, following main points should be considered by planner.

(a) Climate of site and its effects.

(b) Living habits of the owner and his requirements.

(c) Budget of owner.

(d) Bye-laws and regulations for sanctioning.

(e) Materials of construction and method of construction.

2.7 TYPES OF STRUCTURE

1. Load bearing structure.
2. Framed structure.
3. Composite structure.

1. Load Bearing Structure:

In this method, the entire load of the structure is transmitted through the brick or stone masonry walls of a structure. The walls are supported on continuous foundations, which are resting on firm soil at shallow depth. Load bearing structure can be constructed maximum upto four storeys, but usually two storeys are constructed. In this type of structure, beam and trusses etc. rest on a load bearing walls.

2. Framed Structures:

Framed structures consist of frames. These frames are formed by columns, slabs, footings and beams. The columns are created usually on independent foundations and braced together by beams at floor levels and roof levels. In some cases, instead of providing independent foundations, combined or raft foundations are provided depending on the underlying soil and load conditions.

3. Composite Structure:

This is a combination of load bearing and framed structure. The outer walls can be of load bearing type, whereas column and structure can be provided internally. Thus, floors and roof are supported by walls as well as by frame. This type of construction is generally adopted for industrial buildings or ware houses where span are very large.

2.7.1 Comparison Between Different Types of Structures

The three types of structures described above can be compared with respect to the following aspects: (Refer Table 2.9)

Table 2.9

Aspect	Load bearing	Frame structure	Composite structure
Soil/Foundation strata	Soil of good S.B.C. available at shallow depth.	Can be suitable for any type of soil at any depth.	Soil of good S.B.C. available at shallow depth.
Floor space	Thick walls cause reduction in floor space.	More floor area due to thinner walls.	Intermediate floor space available.
Height (No. of storeys)	Allowed upto 4 storeys.	Multistoreyed construction possible.	Allowed upto 2 to 3 storeys.
Time of construction	Slow and time consuming construction.	Fast and speedy construction.	Intermediate time required.
Economy	Economical upto 2 storeys.	Economical for multistoreyed buildings.	Less cost than framed structure upto 2 to 3 floors.
Flexibility in planning.	Less flexible due to load bearing walls.	Flexible due to walls serving as partition only.	Internal arrangement can be modified.
Resistance to vibration	Susceptible to vibration due to machines and earthquake.	Withstand machine vibration and earthquake forces if provision is made in design.	Better than load bearing.

2.8 ARRANGEMENT OF ROOMS FOR RESIDENTIAL BUILDINGS

1. Drawing Room or Living Room:

It is the main room and living area where friends are entertained and family members relax. It can also be used as a combined drawing and dining room. It should be situated on the front entrance of a building and should not provide direct access to the bedrooms and toilet block. It should be spacious to accommodate furniture for sitting, well lighted, ventilated and adjacent to dining room.

An important factor in arranging the living room is due consideration to seating accommodation of different groups. The size and shape of the furniture depends upon the living standard of the family and allied purposes it is going to serve. The living room may be used as bed room, it may be combined kitchen-cum-living room or it may accommodate the dining space or have attached dining recess. There would be many variety of the shape and size of the living rooms to suit all types of activities which may be accommodated in them. (Refer Table 2.10). Rooms are generally more satisfactory if rectangular than square, but irregular shapes with long and narrow rooms should be avoided.

Doors and windows should be planned in view of the 'aspect', 'prospect' light and ventilation, as well as to leave good wall-spaces against which furniture can be placed. Doors should be as few as possible and not less than 0.9 m in width 1.1 m is preferable.

Table 2.10: Approximate sizes of various furniture pieces

Name	Size
(1) Large couch or settee	0.9 m × 2.1 m or 0.75 m × 2.05 m
(2) Reclining or club chair	0.75 m × 0.9 m or 0.65 m × 0.75 m
(3) Twin chair or sofa	0.75 m × 1.35 m
(4) Office chair or small chair	0.45 m × 0.45 m
(5) Chair without arms for dining	0.45 m × 0.45 m
(6) Writing table	1.35 m × 0.75 m
(7) Small desk	1.20 m × 0.60 m
(8) Bridge or card table	0.90 m × 0.90 m
(9) Coffee or card table	1.0 m diameter
(10) End table or end piece	0.60 m × 0.30 m or 0.60 m diameter

2. **Dining Room:**

   Dining room should be adjacent or attached to kitchen. For attached dining room, the activities of kitchen should be screened by a screen wall or partition. Location of drawing, dining and kitchen should be side by side. A wash basin should be provided attached or inside the dining room. It is preferred, that the dining and drawing room remain connected through connecting door. Also according to the recent trends, these two rooms are combined into one big size room.

   The floor area of the separate dining room depends on the type of furniture and the minimum number of persons to be served at a time. The dining room may also serve alternative purposes such as children's study room, occasional sitting room for ladies etc. It should be well lighted and ventilated. There should be as few doors as possible, one joining either to living room or connecting passage and another for providing access to kitchen. Provision of one or two cupboards for keeping plates, crockery, glasses etc. and a wash-basin is essential for convenience.

3. **Kitchen:**

   In every house kitchen is one of the important rooms. The primary function in the kitchen is food preparation and service and may accommodate in addition to these dining, cleaning space etc.

   Kitchen should be located in a corner of the house such that smoke of the kitchen does not spread in all the rooms of the house. There should be no connection with toilet block provision of cooking shelves, cupboards, storage shelves and washing utensils should be made in the kitchen. The sequence of operations needs to be taken into account while planning the kitchen. The operation in connection with meals start with collection of goods, grains, flour, vegetables, dairy and poultry products, and storing them. The food is to be prepared and cooked. The next step is to keep food in readiness to be served and then service or distribution of food. Rest of the food to be stored and preserved. The used plates and dishes need to be washed and put away.

   It is essential to have good lighting in kitchens both by day and night. Windows should be planned preferably with north and east aspect to give even and adequate lighting for all working areas. A flooring of non-absorbent and smooth nature should be provided. The equipment of the working kitchen comprises of sink of size (60 cm × 45 cm × 25 cm) and at least 0.75 cm to 0.9 m height from floor level. Cooking range (chulla), working table, water storage, storage cabinets, larder and refrigerator.

4. Bed Room:

This room should be located on one side of the building. It is should have at least one of its walls as an external wall so as to maintain good natural ventilation and light in the room. This room should be directly in front of the prevailing direction of wind. Attached bath and W.C. is preferable for modern planning. There should be no connection with the kitchen. The bed room should be located so as to maintain privacy. The probable bed room furniture comprises of the following pieces.

1. Double bed – size 1.35 to 1.45 m × 2 to 2.10 m.
2. Single bed – size 0.9 × 2.0 m.
3. Single cot – size 0.75 × 1.80 m.
4. Small chair – size 0.45 m × 0.45 m.
5. Small arm chair – size 0.65 m × 0.45 m.
6. Divan, port or settee – size 0.75 × 1.65 m.
7. Dressing stool – size 0.45 × 0.38 m.
8. Chest of drawers (small) – size 0.45 × 0.90 m.
9. Chest of drawers (large) – size 0.60 × 0.30 m.
10. Bed side table – size 0.60 × 0.30 m.
11. Small dressing table – size 0.45 × 0.90 m.

Above sizes are indicative of plan dimensions.

5. Store Room:

For storing food grains and other articles it is preferable to place them in a store room. Ventilation and natural lightning is less important for this room. The left out space after fulfilling the requirements for all other rooms may be used as a store room.

6. Pantry:

This is a small room which is attached to a dining room cooked food is kept in this room. This room should have cupboards and shelves.

7. Guest Room:

This room should be located on one side of the front verandah. It may not have connection with other rooms except with the dining room. Separate toilets should be provided to the guest room to maintain privacy.

8. Dressing Room:

This room should remain attached with bed room and bath and W.C. This room should have provisions of a dressing table, cupboard etc.

9. **Bath and W.C.:**

   Bath and W.C. may be separate or they combined in one room. If bath and W.C. are to be attached with a bed room, then they are generally combined. Both W.C. and bath should be well ventilated. There should be at least one separate bath and W.C. in the house, other than combined with the bed rooms. All the W.C. and bath rooms should have at least one of their wall as external walls so as to facilitate proper ventilation. Dado or glazed tiles should be provided or otherwise walls should be finished with smooth water-proof cement coat. They should also be provided with the necessary fixtures. Size and type of W.C. pans, wash basins, electrical installations for hot water, plumbing fixtures, washing machine etc. control the size of bathrooms and WC.

10. **Verandah:**

    For economic use of space the provision of verandah is becoming minimum in modern planning. But a certain amount of free space area for corridor and verandah (covered) is required to provide independent access to different rooms, seating space and for drying cloths etc. A minimum width of 1.2 m and having a length equal to that of a front room may be provided.

11. **Puja or Prayer Room:**

    A small room or space at least 1.2 m × 2.5 m should be provided for prayer by the side of bed room. This room should be lighted and ventilated.

12. **Stair:**

    Provision of a stair even for a single storyed building is necessary for the purpose of inspection, cleaning of the roof and also as outdoor sleeping area during peak summer nights. For storied building the location of a staircase should be such that each floor or flat is separated from general movement of stair. For family use it should be located centrally and most of the rooms should have easy approach for the stair provided that their privacy of any room does not suffer.

13. **Lobby:**

    It is a hall at the entrance of which remains connected to the other parts of the building through corridors.

14. **Porches:**

    It is constructed in the front of the building. This adds to the elevation of the building. Car can be parked in it temporarily.

15. **Garage and Servant's Room:**

    These rooms are connected in the back open space of the plot. They are always made in separate blocks.

16. **Corridor:**

    It is a covered common passage in the building for independent entrance to various rooms.

2.9 SIZE OF ROOMS FOR RESIDENTIAL BUILDINGS

This depends upon the standard of living and income of the individual family. Big size rooms are generally preferred. A bed room should not be over-congested by placing too-many furnitures. For luxurious planning, the size of a drawing or living room can be made as big as possible. But considering all the points as indicated above some average dimensions for High Income Group (H.I.G.), Middle Income Group (M.I.G.); Low Income Group (L.I.G.) and maximum size as per code of practice for building bye-laws are given below for general guidance. (Refer Plate No. 1 to 16 for).

Table 2.11

Name of the room	H.I.G. All dimensions	M.I.G.	L.I.G.	Minimum (as per I.S.)
		Length × Breadth are in metres		
Drawing room	5.0 × 4.2 to 7.2 × 5.5	4.2 × 3.6 to 4.5 × 4.0	3.5 × 3.0	9.5 sq.m.
Dining room	4.0 × 3.5 to 5.0 × 4.0	3.5 × 3.1 to 7.0 × 3.1 (drawing + dining)	3.0 × 2.8	7.5 sq.m.
Bed room	4.8 × 4.2	4.6 × 3.6	3.5 × 3.0	9.5 sq.m.
Office room	4.0 × 3.6	3.5 × 3.0	–	–
Guest room	4.0 × 3.6	3.5 × 3.0	–	–
Store	3.0 × 3.0	3.0 × 2.8	2.25 × 1.5	3.0 sq.m.
Kitchen	3.5 × 3	2.0 × 2.5	2.5 × 2.2 (Breadth min.)	4.5 sq.m. (Kitchen and dinning combined 5.0 sq.m.)
Pantry	3.0 × 2.5	–	–	–
Dressing	3.5 × 3.0	3.0 × 2.5	–	–
Bath and W.C. (combined)	3.5 × 2.5	3.0 × 1.6	2.10 × 1.5	1.0 × 1.8
Bath (separate)	3.0 × 2.0	2.0 × 1.5	1.50 × 1.20	1.0 × 1.2
W.C. (separate)	2.5 × 2.0	1.8 × 1.2	1.1 × 1.0	0.9 × 1.0
Box room	1.8 × 1.8	–	–	–
Servant's room	3.0 × 3.0	3.0 × 2.5	–	–
Garage (min. height 2.4 m)	5.8 × 5.5	5.0 × 2.80	–	5.0 × 2.5
Porch	6.0 × 3.0 to 4.8 × 3.0	–	–	–

BUILDING DESIGN AND DRAWING (SU)　　　　　　　　　BUILDING PLANNING AND BYE LAWS

2.10 PLANNING OF A RESIDENTIAL COMPLEX

To describe various types of drawings, which are required to be drawn by the architecture, a set of different drawings is furnished here. **(For additional set of drawings refer end pages of this chapter)**

1. Plate No. 1 – Shows layout of a residential complex which includes arrangement of different buildings, internal roads, garden etc.
2. Plate No. 2 – Shows typical floor plans for first, third and fifth floors.
3. Plate No. 3 – Shows typical floor plans for second, fourth and sixth floors.
4. Plate No. 4 – Shows parking floor plan.
5. Plate No. 5 – Shows front elevation.
6. Plate No. 6 – Shows terrace floor plan.
7. Plate No. 7 – Shows floor plan for lift, machine room, and R.C.C. water storage tank.
8. Plate No. 8 – Shows section and side elevation.
9. Plate No. 9 – Shows perspective of a building.
10. Plate No. 10 – Shows perspective view of the complex.
11. Plate No. 11, 12, 13, 14 – Show typical floor plans of other buildings in the same residential complex.
12. Plate No. 15 – Shows centre line plan of a building.
13. Plate No. 16 – Shows structural drawing showing R.C.C. design details, schedule of R.C.C. footing and columns.

SOLVED EXAMPLES

Planning of Typical R.C.C. Stairs:

Example 2.1: *Plan a dog legged stair for a building with the following data:*

(i) Vertical distance between the floors = 3.6 m.

(ii) Size of stair hall 2.5 m × 5 m.

(iii) Thickness of the floor slab = 140 mm.

(iv) Thickness of the waist slab and landing slab = 100 mm.

Solution: Assume, Rise = 150 mm
and Tread = 250 mm

$$\text{Width of the flight} = \frac{2.5}{2}$$
$$= 1.25 \text{ m}$$

∴ $$\text{Height of each flight} = \frac{3.6}{2}$$
$$= 1.8 \text{ m}$$

∴ $$\text{Number of risers required} = \frac{1.8 \times 1000}{150}$$
$$= 12 \text{ in each flight}$$

Number of treads in each flight = 12 – 11
= 11

∴ Space required for treads = 11 × 250 = 2750 mm
∴ Space left for passage = 5 – 1.25 – 2.75 = 1.00 m

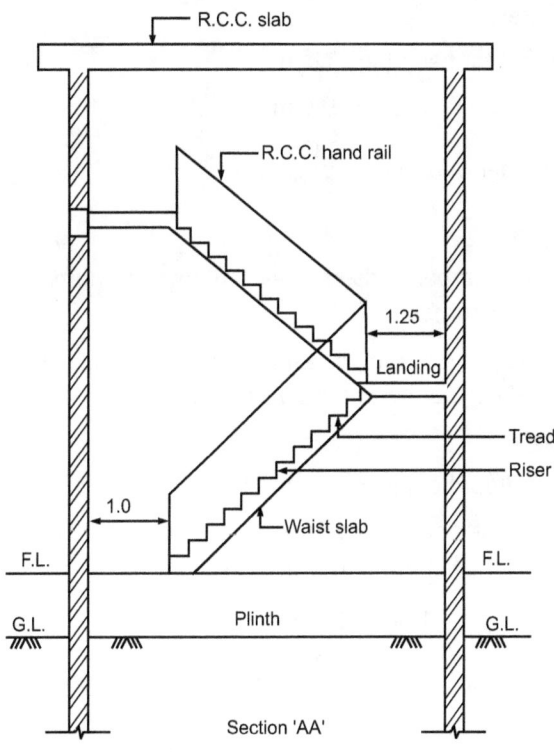

Fig. 2.5

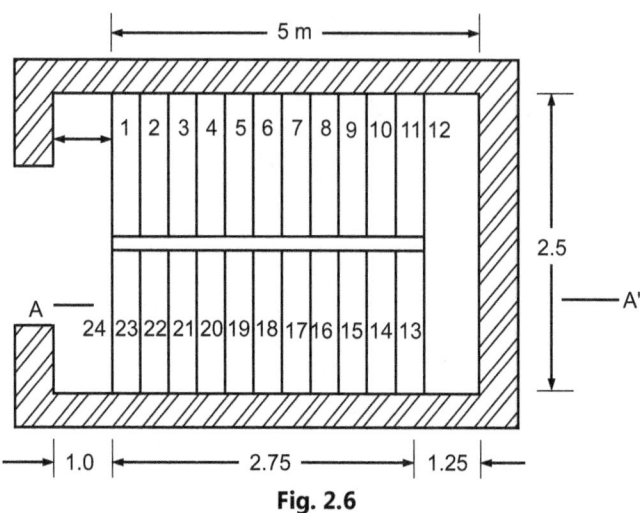

Fig. 2.6

Example 2.2: *Calculate number of risers and treads in each flight for dog legged stair, floor to floor height is 3.3 m and riser is 150 mm.*

Solution: Given data:

$$\text{Floor to floor height} = 3.3 \text{ m}$$
$$\text{Riser} = 150 \text{ mm}$$
$$\therefore \text{Total number of risers} = \frac{3300}{150}$$
$$= 22$$

Assuming two flights, number of risers in each flight = 11 number and number of treads in each flight = 11 – 1 = 10 number.

Example 2.3: *Plan a staircase for a residential building in which the vertical distance between each floor is 3.36 m. The size of the stair hall is limited to 4.5 × 3 m.*

Solution: Given data:

(i) Floor to floor height = 3.36 m

Let, Width of landing = 1.5 m
 = Width of stairs

Assume, Rise = 16 cm

$$\therefore \text{Total number of risers} = \frac{3.36 \times 100}{16}$$

= 21 risers ⇒ 11 in first flight
10 in second height

Provide 11 risers in each flight

∴ Number of treads in first flight = 11 – 1 = 0

in second flight = 10 – 9 = 9

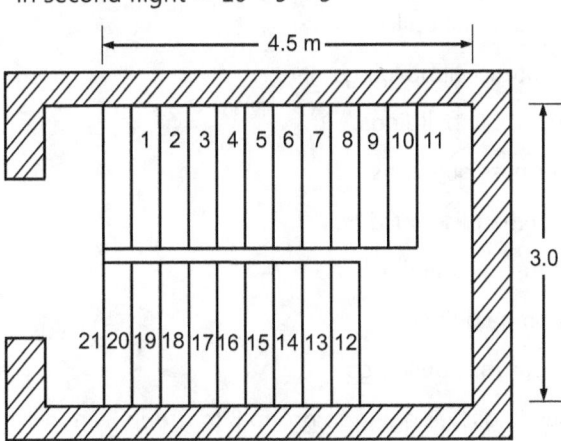

Fig. 2.7

2.11 PLANNING OF PUBLIC BUILDINGS

The design of public building depends upon the nature of the building. Every building has a special character of it's own. The function of the building is to be ascertained initially. Then the different components or blocks or units are to be planned. The units are then joined together to form the whole building. The site of various units depend on the number of person that will be occupied in that room, furniture requirements, space required for circulation etc. There are no hard and fast rules to ascertain the dimension of each block or unit in these building. Minimum dimensions are needed to be fixed on the basis of space needs, thermal comfort, lightning, ventilation requirement etc. of that specified building unit.

2.12 TYPES OF BUILDINGS

National Building Code of India (Sp: 7-1970) defines the building as "any structure for what so ever purpose and of what's ever materials constructed and every part there of whether used as human habitation or not and includes foundations, plinth, walls, floors, roofs, chimneys, plumbing and building services, fixed platforms, balcony cornice or platform projection, part of a building or any thing fixed there to or any wall enclosing or intended to enclose any land or space and signs and outdoor display structures."

According to National Building Code of India (1970), buildings are classified based on occupancies, as follows.

- Group A : Residential buildings.
- Group B : Educational buildings.
- Group C : Institutional buildings.
- Group D : Assembly buildings.
- Group E : Business buildings.
- Group F : Merchandise buildings.
- Group G : Industrial buildings.
- Group H : Storage buildings.
- Group I : Hazardous buildings.

In this chapter, buildings belonging to group B to group F are discussed.

2.13 TOWNSHIP AND ROLE OF PLAN SANCTIONING AUTHORITY

A new concept in the field of planning, which is responsible for the development of an area around an urban centre. Maharashtra Government has passed the resolution in the year 2004 for the said purpose.

Concept paper on this aspect was widely accepted in International Infrastructure summit in 2002, which was organized by Government of Maharashtra in collaboration with Maharashtra Economic Development Council.

There is a dire need to promote private investment in housing sector to facilitate housing at reasonable price and also to create hassleless environment for the residents. This need aroses from the fact that 50% (or even more) of population of India is forecasted to be living in urban areas by 2041. Hence, a step towards fulfillment of this demand is essentially to promote integrated townships.

Policy decision for promotion of townships:

(i) Physical and social infrastructure to be borne by private developers.

(ii) 100% direct foreign investment for development.

In November 2005, S.T. Policy was announced for Pune District and in 2006-07, township policies for whole states are in place including corporation and councils.

- **(iii) Applicability:** Gist of policy – general Applicable in Local bodies and area under it and in R.P. area in Residential as well as in agricultural zone.
- **(iv) Area Requirement:** The minimum land required shall not be less than 100 acres (i.e. 40 ha) which is unbroken, uninterrupted with access road of width 18 m.
- **(v) Declaration:** The area declaration is through MRTP Act, 1966. If it is under R.P, then section 18(3) is to be followed whereas if area development is under DP then section 44(2) is followed.

For Infrastructure Facilities:

All the infrastructure facilities are to be provided and maintained by the developer of the area. e.g. 140 lit/cap/day of water supply, inside road planning development and maintenance.

Drainage and Garbage Disposal:

The least possible D and G is to be pass on to municipal corporation for which reuse, recycle eco-friendly techniques are to be implemented.

Power: Developer himself shall ensure about continuous and quality power supply. Back up generators for supply may also be employed for the said purpose.

Environment: Without major changes for topographical features and hampering ecological systems environment is to be protected. All the land is to be put for different land uses namely:

General Norms:

1. **Residential use of land:** Total use is of 60%, 10% of which are of 40 sq.m. tenements.
2. **Commercial:** Proper distribution within the area is essential as it caters for the adjoining urban areas.
3. **Educational area:** Within the area, considering pattern of projected primary to secondary education facilities are to be provided (preferable at walkable distances).
4. **Public utilities:** Utilities play an important role in common man's life and these are to be located suitably to serve the residents considering aspirations and need. e.g. Electric power substations, bus stations, fire brigade, sewarage and garbage disposal etc.

   Transport and Communication: The main access to area shall be minimum 18 m wide and the road work within the area should satisfy prevailing bye-laws with minimum width of 9 m.

Service Industries: Suitable locations offers other than residential area without environmental pollution impact.

Amenity Space: 5% of total area, which is to be evenly distributed and within which markets, essential shopping, townhall, libraries etc. are to be suitably placed.

Health facilities: Main objective is to provide P.H.C. within the area, but one way go for hospital location if projected population is more.

Parks, Gardens and Playgrounds: Minimum 20%, exclusive of open space layouts.

Development Control Regulations:

(A) If Township is developed within:
- Residential Zone:

FSI of 1.0 of gross is provided in RP and corporation areas.

- Agriculture – No development Zone:

RP – 0.5 with 50% open area.

Additional 0.5 may be allowed with premium of ₹ 500/sq. ft. or by referring ready reckoner of the area, whichever is more.

- Corporation - FSI – 0.2, additional 0.80 .... (same as above)

(B) Planting the trees:
- Residential zone - 150 trees/hectare to be planted and maintained.
- No development zone – 400 trees/hectare.

(c) D.C. Rules:

For the areas, regional plan rules and local body regulations are applicable.

2.13.1 Procedure for Township Project Approval by Plan Sanctioning Authority

1. Locational Clearance by the Government.
2. Letter of intent from collector.
3. Final approval by the collector in consultation with Deputy Director Town planning.

1. Locational Clearance:

To be submitted to Government with copy to be submitted to Director, Town Planning. Following document are to be submitted:

(a) Ownership and development rights.

(b) Village map indicating the boundaries of the said township.

(c) Part plan of R.P. / D.P.

Scrutiny: Checking of the above said documents and on site is to be worked out within stipulated time of 90 days and within this survey the following points are to be detailed in:

(i) Character of the land (continuous, broken, unbroken etc.).

(ii) Command area of irrigation.

(iii) Water bodies and forest areas.
(iv) Historical monuments/Archeological sites.
(v) Land ownership (To clarify about disputes if any).
(vi) NOC of irrigation and other departments.

The Locational Clearance is granted by issuing notification in Gazette by the Government. If the entire ownership is with the developer then township shall be declared under sections 18(3)/ 44(2) of MRTP Act, but in case of partial ownership (of minimum 50%), procedure under the sections 20, 37 is to be followed.

Validity of locational clearance is for one year and if can be renewed after submitting the application to the Government.

2. Letter of Latent:

The developer shall submit the application in prescribed format to Collector/ Municipal Commissioner with the following documents attached the rein:

(i) Ownership and development rights with 50% ownership of land, tribal land if any.
(ii) Environmental clearance.

The scrutiny procedure for the above said submissions is worked out within 45 days within which and letter of intent is to be given the validity of which is for six months and which can be renewed.

3. Final Approval: To Collector / Municipal Commissioner:

For getting the Final Approval the following steps are to be carried out by the developer:

(a) Submission of layout plans of entire Township area, sector wise detailed building plans and details of phasing.
(b) Agreement with bank guarantee of 15% of its development cost.

The approval is granted by the collector, in consultation with Deputy Director, Town planning.

While approving all the documents, are thoroughly scrutinized for the following aspects:

(i) Amalgamation of land.
(ii) Layout (Road hierarchy, Ventilation areas, Open spaces etc.).
(iii) Building plans.
(iv) Land utilization.
(v) FSI statement.

Appeal: An appeal can be filed within 40 days in case of any aggrievence by the order of collector / municipal commissioner, to

(i) Director Town planning – (R.P. Area).
(ii) The Government - (Municipal Corporation).

Implementation and Completion:
1. Basic infrastructure to be completed to the satisfaction of the collector / municipal commissioner as per the relevant phase.
2. Total span for completion is of ten years.
3. Occupation certificates for individual buildings are allotted by the collector / municipal commissioner in consultation with Town Planning.
4. Final completion certificate for the scheme is granted in consultation with Town Planning Department and after producing NOC from MPCB, Forest Department and Chief Fire officer.

Interpretation:

Any dispute arose, is to be referred to the State Government, where decision is final and finding.

Special concessions for Township Projects are as under:
- (i) **N.A. Permission:** The procedure is automatic, no separate permission is required.
- (ii) **Stamp Duty:** 50% of prevailing rates of Mumbai Stamp Act.
- (iii) **Grant of Government land:** Land to be leased at market rate to the developer.
- (iv) **Relaxation:** From Mumbai Tenancy and Agriculture Land Act (condition of being agriculturist is removed).
- (v) Exemption for Ceiling of Agriculture Land.
- (vi) Exemption for Ceiling under ULC Act, 1976.
- (vii) Partial exemption for Scrutiny Fee.
- (viii) **Floating FSI:** Within the township, Floating FSI is permitted. Unused FSI of one plot can be used anywhere in the whole township.
- (ix) Development charges: 50% of the normal are charged.
- (x) For star category Hotels, Hospitals and Multiplexes concession to property tax is offered.

Latest Status of Township Projects:

The Government has given Locational clearance for 14 projects. Out of these four has got final approval and the schemes are running phasewise.

In Pune, ongoing townships are:
- (i) Blue Ridge: Hinjewadi, IT-park.
- (ii) Amonara: Hadapsar.
- (iii) Nanded City: Sinhgad road.
- (iv) I–Vel City: Jambe.
- (v) Magarpatta City.

Characteristic features of Magarpatta City:
Following sustainable systems are provided within the area:
- Solar water heaters
- Extensive Greening of City
- Rain water harvesting
- Vermiculture pits
- Use of Eco-friendly materials (recycled) – like Flyash, City farming.

Other Civic Amenities:
- Magarpatta City School
- Gymkhana
- Shopping Area
- Gardens
- Cafeteria.

Socio-Economic Status:
- The model has established a different model for urban settlements of workspace and residential in same premises.
- Migration or displacement of the original land residents has stopped.
- Lifestyle is upgraded.

2.14 FORMATION OF CO-OPERATIVE SOCIETY

The Maharastra Co-operative Societies Act, 1960 provide two definitions namely:
1. Housing society means a society the object of which is to provide its members with:
   (i) Open plots for housing,
   (ii) Dwelling houses,
   (iii) Flats.
2. Housing society, the object of which is to provide, in case of open plots, houses or flats already acquired by its members, common amenities and services.

Life within a housing co-operative is based on common management and sharing. Such management is intricate and different. The relationship thus established creates a bond between members, which inspires them to undertake further activities and social life on a shared basis.

The essence of the co-operative movement is that the people concerned should themselves look after the management of their affairs including economic betterment and social welfare.

"Co-operative Society" under Section 4 of the Maharastra Co-operative Societies Act, 1960 means a voluntary organization formed with the object of promoting mutual aid, economic interest or general welfare of its members in accordance with co-operative principles.

As laid down in this Act or these Rules, the Registrar may refuse to register that society if it is likely to be economically unsound or which may have adverse effect of development of the Co-operative movement.

Procedure of Formation of a Co-operative Society:

To form a Co-operative Society, **Section 6 of the Maharastra Co-operative Societies Act, 1961** lays down the conditions for registering a society which is among others, that a minimum of ten members would be required to own the various units in the building. These persons should be from different families.

Also, these persons should be competent to enter into a contract under the Indian Contracts Act 1872.

Every developer has to form a Co-operative Housing Society at one point of time or another. With the limited amount of options available with regard to management of the affairs of the building i.e. (a) Condominium (b) Private Limited Company and (c) Co-operative Society, (excluding the unrealistic rental housing), it will not be an exaggeration to state that in atleast 90% cases particularly in Mumbai the Promoters and/or the Builders have formed a Co-operative Housing Society. The flat purchasers normally do not know the basic requirement for Registration of Co-operative Housing Society. It is here that apart from the statutory obligations cast upon the builder, the builder as a friend, philosopher and guide of promoters helps in forming a Co-operative Housing Society.

Earlier, unless the registration proposal was signed by 90% of the flat purchasers, the society could not be formed. Now, even if 60% of the total number of flat purchasers is willing to form a Society, then the Co-operative Society can be formed.

The Society has to be registered with the Registrar of Co-operative Societies. The application for registration has to be made in **Form-A. Under section 8 of the Act,** 1960 states that for the purposes of registration, an application shall be made to the Registrar in the prescribed form and shall be accompanied by four copies of the proposed bye-laws of the society and such registration fee as may be prescribed in this behalf. The application should be signed by at least 10 persons (such persons being a member of a different families) and who are qualified under the said Act.

The procedure for Registration of a society begins with electing a Chief Promoter in a meeting of the Promoter who has the authority to sign the necessary documents on behalf of the promoter members and open a bank account in the name of the proposed Society after obtaining the necessary permission from the Registrar.

The Chief Promoter will apply to the registrar for reservation of name of the Society of the proposed society and permission to collect share-capital. The name once reserved is valid for 3 months. He will then deposit the collected share money in the bank account of the proposed Society. This has to be done only after receiving the name reservation from the registrar and after collection of the necessary share capital.

The application for registration should be accompanied with the scheme showing economic feasibility of the proposed Society, bank balance certificate, and list of persons who have contributed to the share-capital and the entrance fee of the proposed Society.

The registrar will enter the particulars in register of application maintained in **Form "B"** and give serial number and issue receipt in acknowledgement of the same.

Afterwards, if the registrar is satisfied that a proposed society has complied with the provisions of the said Act and the rules and its proposed bye-laws are not contrary to this Act or to the rules, he shall within 2 months from the date of receipt of the application register the society and its bye-laws.

The other documents necessary for Housing Societies are as follows:

The person who has legally acquired or intends to acquire a plot or flat in the proposed Society can join in application for registration of a Society. The following procedures have to be fulfilled:

- The documents pertaining to the purchase of land/building.
- Title clearance certificate.
- Sanctioned/Proposed plan and layouts for construction of building / houses.
- Proof of payment of stamp-duty and registration of documents.
- Certificate from the architect showing the scheme of construction.
- In case of Builder promoted Societies, **Form-Z** and for others **Form-X** is to be submitted.
- 60% of the total members should join in the Registration Proposal.

(i) Registration is optional in the case of a flat owner to another person in a registered Co-operative Society. This is because under section 41 of the Maharashtra Co-operative Societies Act, 1960, any instrument relating to a transfer of shares in a society is exempted from compulsory registration.

(ii) A flat owner to another person in an unregistered society, registration is advisable. This is because registration of a document safeguards the interest of a purchaser.

In the Rules framed under the Act known as Maharashtra Co-operative Societies Rules, 1961, the Registrar classifies the societies under section 12 and Rule 10 where housing societies is classified into three categories:

(a) Tenant Ownership Housing Society: Where land on which the houses are built and constructed is obtained either on lease-hold or free-hold basis by the society for the joint activities of the members.

(b) Tenant Co-partnership Housing Society: It is a housing society, which holds both land and building either on lease-hold or free-hold basis and allots the flats or other premises in the building to its members.

(c) Other Housing Societies: It consists of (a) House Mortgage Society (b) House Construction Societies.

Every society must make by-laws regarding the object of the society, privileges, rights, duties and liabilities of members. And such society cannot legally incur any obligations not directly connected with the furtherance of these objects. The objects for which a society is formed should be clearly, definitely and exhaustively set forth in the by-laws as provided under Rule 8 and section 10 of the Act. Any act which is beyond the objects specified in the by-laws is ultra vires and void and if thereby any loss is incurred the official responsible will be personally liable.

The validity of Membership in Co-operative Society:

In order to become a member of the society, a person has to comply with the provisions of by-laws of a society besides complying with the provisions of Section 22 and Rule 19. For instance, a housing society may require any declaration as to the holding of any other premises in the area of operation of the society. Whether a particular person is validly admitted as member of the society or not is to be seen by the Registrar and not by the Co-operative Court under section 91 of the Act.

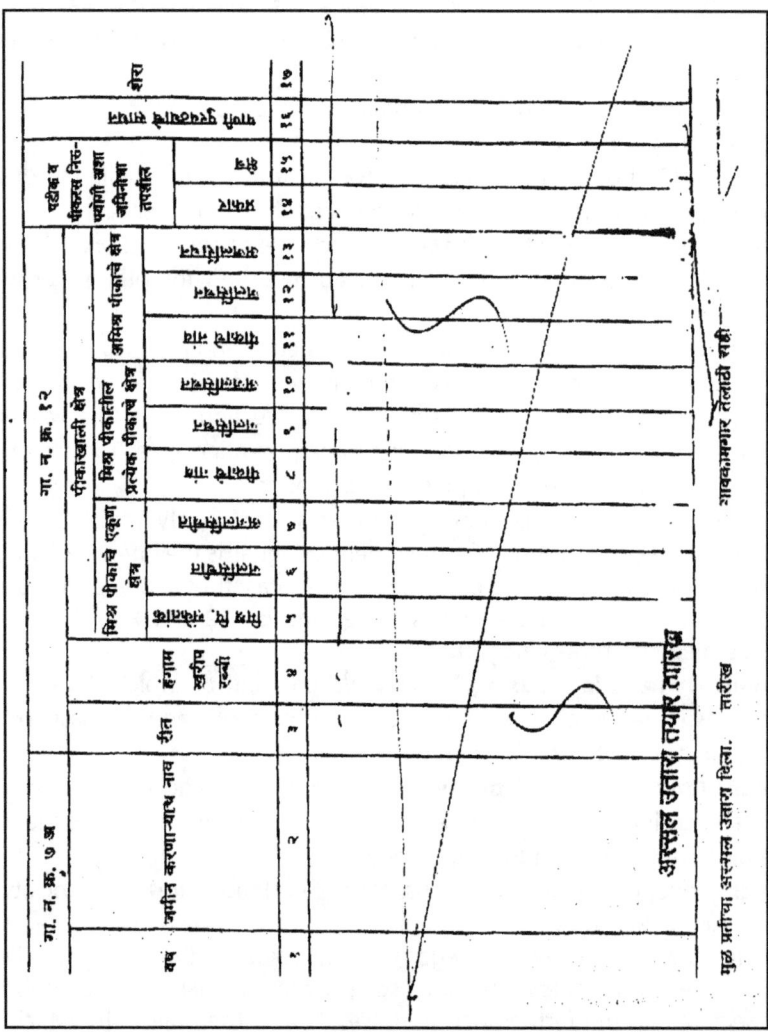

Fig. 2.8

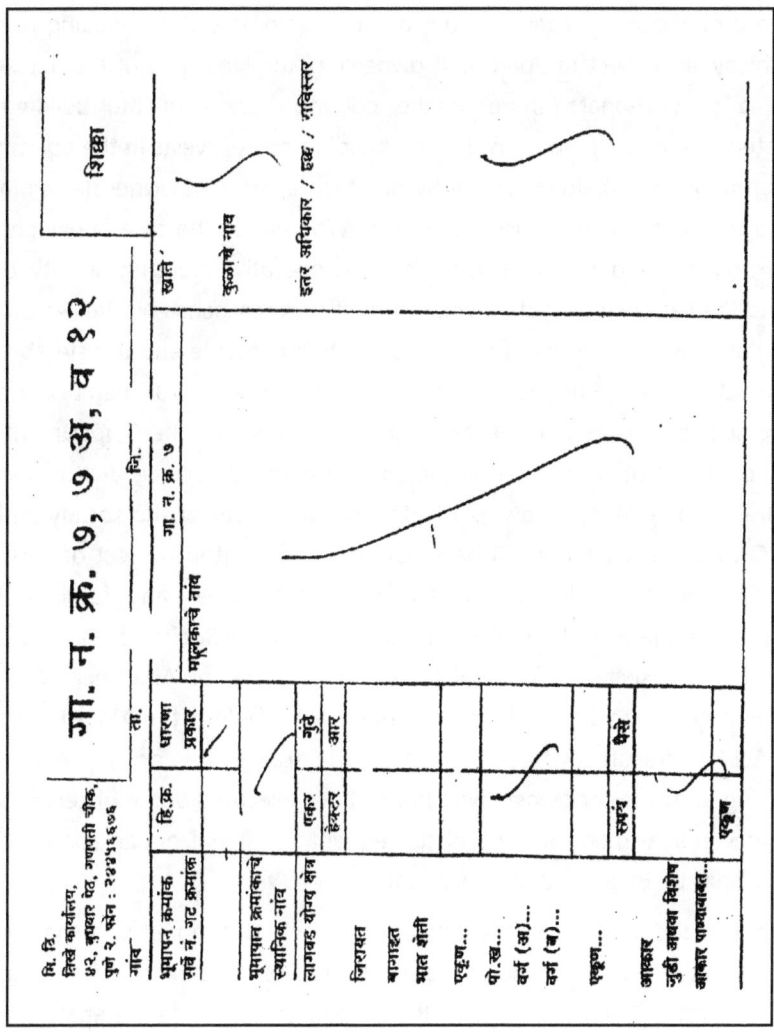

Fig. 2.9

2.15 FORMATION OF APARTMENT OF OWNERSHIP

The Maharashtra Apartment Ownership Act, 1970 provides for the ownership of an individual apartment in a building and to make such apartment heritable and transferable property. **An Apartment** means an part of property intended for any type of independent use, including one or more rooms or enclosed spaces located on one or more floors in a building intended to be used for residence, office, practice of any profession or for carrying on any occupation, trade, or business or for any other type of independent use and with a direct exit to a public street, road or highway or to a common area leading to such street, road or highway. In respect of apartment ownership, the legal title of the flat as an object, along with a proportionate share in the common areas of the building and also proportionate share in the land on which the building stands, vests in the apartment owner. That means, the building belongs to jointly but each apartment owner has an independent right to his apartment to the exclusion of others. Whereas, in the case of ownership flat, the title to the building and the land vests in a co-operative housing society or a limited company and the flat owner is not a owner of the flat in real sense but he has only a right to occupy the flat. This is a species of property, which is heritable and transferable. In case of Maharashtra Ownership Flat Act there should be atleast 10 members for forming co-operative society and in apartment ownership there should be 5 apartments in one or more building. In case of Ownership Flat Act or Co-operative Societies Act the assessment of the flats will be in the name of owner of the land or builder or the society and in case of Apartment Ownership Act there will be separate assessment in respect of each apartment and its percentage of undivided interest in common areas and facilities. In case of Ownership Flat Act, there will be registration of Co-operative Society or Pvt. Ltd Company as contemplated under section 10 of MOF Act and in case of Apartment Ownership Act declaration is required to be made in prescribed form before the Magistrate as required under the Act. All transfers of apartments by the sole owner or all the owners of the property (being an owner or owners who has or have executed and registered a declaration in form "A") to an apartment owner and subsequent transfers from an apartment owner to his transferee shall be by a Deed of Apartment.

In the case of the first Deed of Apartment the party of the first part shall be either the sole owner or all the owners of the property who has or have executed and registered the Declaration in form "A" and the party of the second part shall be the apartment owner. In the case of subsequent Deeds of Apartment, the party of the first part shall be the apartment owner and the party of the second part shall be his transferee.

2.16 7/12 ABSTRACT

The Village Form VII-XII is a combine form incorporating village forms VII and XII. kept together. Village Form VII is an index of all the rights by survey numbers and survey numbers whereas village form XII gives details of crops, fallows, survey and boundary marks. It is a combined form. The upper part is form no. VII and the lower part of V.F. No. XII. The village Form VII-XII is as shown below:

VILLAGE FORM VII
Record of Rights
(Adhikar Abhilekh Patrak)

[Rules 3, 5, 6 and 7 of the Maharashtra Land Revenue Record of Rights and Registers (Preparation and Maintenance) Rules, 1971]

Village: Hamadabad   Taluka: Satara

Survey No.	Sub-division of Survey number	Tenure	Name of the occupant	Khata No.
191		Occupant Class I	Shantabai *alias* Kanta Bhandu Kadam (1) (107) [(1) Hirabai Ramchandra Shinde 0-8=0.	127 Name of the tenant Rent ₹ P ....
	Local name of the field Cultivable area	H.A. 1 29	(2) Kalavati Dharmaji Shinde 0-8-0] (127) Ganesh Parbati Dhane	Other rights: Dattatraya Pandurang Dhekne recovers the maximum rent of ₹ 20 Area of 0.28
	Total Pot Kharab (uncultivable) Class (a) ..... Class (b) ..... Total Assessment Judi or special assessment	1 29 ──── ──── ₹ P 8.69	(156), (157)	assessed of ₹ 1.81 is shown in the name of Government. The transaction of 156 and 157 is against Consolidation of Holdings and Fragmentation Act(1). Boundary and Survey marks

VILLAGE FORM XII
Register of Crops
[Rules 29 of the Maharashtra Land Revenue Record of Rights and Registers (Preparation and Maintenance Rules, 1971)]

Year	Season	Code No. of mixture	Details of cropped area								Land not available for cultivation			Remarks
			Mixed crops area		Pure crops area									
					Constituent crops with area under each									
			Irrigated	Un-irrigated	Name of Crop	Irrigated	Un-irrigated	Name of Crop	Irrigated	Un-irrigated	Nature	Area	Source of Irrigation	
1	2	3	4	5	6	7	8	9	10	11	12	13	14	15
			H.A.	H.A.		H.A.	H.A.		H.A.	H.A.		H.A.		
1968-69	Kharif	...	...	0.60	Groundnut	...	0.45	Chillis	...	0.02				
					Coriander	...	0.02							
	Rabbi	...	...	0.61	Rabbi	...								
					Jowar	...	0.40							
					Kardi	...	0.03							
					Wheat	...	0.03							

A Combined Form:

This is a combined form of Record of Rights and Register of Crops. It consists of two parts (i) the upper part which in effect is an index of Village Form VI and (ii) the lower part which provides statistics of cultivation including crops and fallows. But for few exceptions listed hereafter, no change can be made in the upper part unless and until an entry is made and certified in the Register of Mutations i.e. Village Form VI. As soon as a mutation is effected in Village Form VI, the Talathi should make pencil entry in the concerned village Form VII. As soon as the said mutation entry is cancelled or modified, the pencil entry should be rubbed out and modified entry made in pencil. Immediately, after the entry in the Register of Mutation is certified, the Talathi shall record it in ink in Village Form-VII. The pencil entry facilitates checking during crop or other inspections on site and protects public against cheating by suppression of all accomplished transactions.

Authorities for Effecting Changes:

Changes in survey number, Hissa number, area including Pot-Kharab and agricultural assessment are supported by the Akarband, Kami-Jasti Patrak and Akar Phod Patrak or Hissa Form No. XII issued by the District Inspector of Land Records. Changes in tenure are made under orders of Government, Collector or other competent authority; changes in Khata number are made by the Talathi once in ten years and changes in the name of the owner and tenant and other rights are brought about by certified entries in the Village Form VI. Seldom does the local name of the field changes.

General Instructions to be Followed:

The following general instructions are to be followed in maintaining Village Form VII:

(a) No words, figures and names in Village Form VII shall ever be erased.

(b) The names, words or figures which are no longer to be retained shall be struck out by a single line drawn through them, so that the original is still quite legible.

(c) The new names, words or figures shall be written underneath that which has been struck out or if space is not enough then at the side in such a way that it is quite legible for what the new matter is substituted.

(d) The entry number in Village Form VI upon which change is based shall be written against new name, word or figure entered or omitted.

(e) If a new name or figure thus inserted is again altered by a further mutation, the same process is repeated.

(f) If the mutation simply removes a name not putting anything in its place, then it is struck out as in (b) and (d) above, nothing is to be added.

(g) Use only one page of form for each parcel of land viz. Survey number of Sub-Division of a Survey number including a Hissa.

(h) Use stiff covers, for these books or volumes and the pages or forms by strong laces, so that the pages can be turned over.

(i) Divide the village map into suitable blocks of about 100 to 150 holdings or so, number them, write up the Village Form VII in respect of them and bind them in one volume as instructed above.

VILLAGE FORM XII

Register of Crops:

The Village Form XII is also known as Register of crops. The crops grown in each agricultural season every year are required to be shown in this form. Every year when the crops are grown and standing in the fields, the Talathi is to visit the village for the purpose of crop inspection and making entries in the crop register. For this purpose the Talathi is to fix a date at least seven days in advance and arrange to inform the villagers of the fixed date. He will publicise his visit by beat of drum or other suitable method, requiring villagers to be present in their fields and evidence the entries being made in the Register of crops. The Talathi is also to give intimation of his visit to the Village Panchayat Sarpanch 'if any' and through him request the members of the Village Panchayat to accompany him (Talathi.) On the date so fixed, the Talathi shall visit every field in the presence of the villagers, the Sarpanch and the Village Panchayat members who may be present there and make entries in the said register. The Talathi is to allow the persons interested to see the entries so made.

After the enquiries made by the Talathi the Circle Inspector or any other superior officer is to visit the village for verification of the entries. Such visiting officer is to give prior intimation about his visit and after making due enquiry has to correct entries found to be incorrect.

Instructions for Maintaining Village Form XII:

- Care should be taken properly to distinguish between fallow and Pot Kharab and grass and fallow, crops in Pot Kharab should not be shown.
- But if considerable cultivation is noticed in Pot Kharab of Class (b), say 0.506 hectares i.e. five gunthas or more, then Talathi may make note of the fact and add this to the other cultivation in unassessed land and other lands not intended for cultivation shown in Village Form XI.
- While writing up the crops statistics, the Talathi should first attend to the Pot Kharab and fallow areas; and then the grass or grass and babul, if any. But the areas of these should not be finally entered at the first inspection if there is any likelihood of the area thereunder ploughed up and cropped in the Rabi season. The area under improved seeds should be distinguished by putting the indicative letter I.S. against it.
- Next to this, attention should be given to mixed crop. To save clerical labour, the Talathi should record at the beginning of each volume of Village Forms VII-XII the standard composition (Code No.) and the name of the mixture being used in writing the crops statistics.
- After completing these entries, the Talathi should count and note in the 'Remarks' column any fruit trees old enough to bear fruit of the following kinds which are scattered over the field: Mango, Tamarind, Jack, Coconut, Tad and Date Palms. He will also count and note the following kinds of fuel trees, if any, scattered over the field:
    Babul, Neem, Khair, Dhavdar and Anjan.
- He will also note the trees, the cutting of which is prohibited under the Maharashtra State Felling of Trees Act, 1966, and rules thereunder viz. Tamarind, Mahuva, Jack fruit, Khair and Teak trees and under the Maharashtra Land Revenue (Prohibition of Cutting of Trees) Rules, 1968.
- If at any time, it is directed to count any other trees, it should also be done. But when the whole or a distinct portion of the field is entirely set apart for growing pala or fruit trees or fuel trees, then the area under those trees will be given and not the number.
- Authorised crops in unoccupied land or land not included in survey number or in unassessed land leased for reclamation etc., as well as crops in Government land encroached upon should be brought to account.
- Similarly when alluvion or diluvian is noticed the Talathi should note them in the 'Remark' column for taking action when statutory limit is exceeded.
- Diluvian is fallow but crops in alluvion, before it becomes assessed area, are disregarded. Crops sown but failed, but not sown again will be accounted as crops.
- But when sown again, the first crop is disregarded and crops sown again are shown after keeping a note to the effect that "crop of ...failed".
- They will however, never be treated as two crops. All crop reaped more than once should be accounted for as second or third crop, if they are all sown and reaped in the same area.

- Another important point to remember is about the lands under the command of the Pat but have not grown irrigated crops. For the correct accounting of crops in these lands, all officers concerned should pay special attention to the proper maintenance of this record.
- In order to know the total area under green manure and the cropwise area benefited by the green manure, the area of the crop grown in the green manured field should be marked by the letters G.M. in bracket against that crop.
- It is not necessary to total the form, as the total of the cropped area is taken below Village Form XI.

Entering Area of Fallow Land:

In columns 12 and 13 of Village Form XII area in respect of fallow land is to be shown. There are eight kinds of fallow lands which are to be shown separately. Which are as follows:

Uncultivable Follows:
1. Forest-Lands under Government forest as well as private forest in a village should be taken into account for mentioning area thereof.
2. Hill and rocky tracts, desert area, rivers.
3. Non-agricultural lands, viz. area under buildings, roads, railways, burial grounds, military camping grounds, water sources etc.
4. Lands kept fallow for certain period i.e. (five years or more).
5. Grass lands and used for grazing cattle.
6. Lands other than forest consisting of useful trees.
7. Other fallow lands i.e. lands kept as fallow for a period from one year to five years.
8. Current fallow i.e. lands, kept fallow only for one season (Kharif or Rabi) in a year.

Different sources from which water is taken:

In column 14 of the Village Form XII the different sources from which water is taken for the purpose of irrigation should be noted. These sources are viz.

(a) canals, (b) tube wells, (c) wells, (d) tanks, (e) bandharas, (f) rivers and nallas.

In respect of sources viz. canals, tube wells and wells, Talathi should ascertain after enquiry on the spot whether the particular source belongs to Government or private person. Where water is lifted through electric pumps or oil engines such information should also be entered in this column whenever any crops is grown with the aid of any irrigation, the kind of irrigation should be written against it.

The classes of recognised irrigation are:

Tanks, wells, pumps (steam or oil engines working on river banks or wells), Government canals, private canals or Pats, lifts (Dhekudi).

It would suffice, if only initial letter, instead of the whole word is written over the irrigated crop e.g. T, W, S, P etc., when more than one method is used then the irrigation should be classed chiefly according to the source of water i.e. from tank or from a well; but if from a public river, then according to the method of appropriating it. Wells often supplement Pats; the crops should be classed as under Pats but (W) added to indicate Motasthal aid.

2.17 6-D FORM

Village Form VI is a diary of mutations. A record of changes in the record of rights in respect of all the particulars are shown in this form. These particulars are expected to be written in detail as required under Section 148 of the Maharashtra Land Revenue Code and the rules thereunder.

VILLAGE FORM VI
Register of Mutations
PHERPHAR PATRAK
[Rule 10 of the Maharashtra Land Revenue Record of Rights and Registers (Preparation and Maintenance) Rules, 1971]

Village: Hamadabad   Taluka: Satara   District: Satara

Serial No. of entry	Nature of right acquired	Survey and Sub-Division numbers affected	Initials or remarks by Testing officers
1	2	3	4
157	Date of mutation 11-7-69 Date of receipt of information 4-7-69	Gat. No. 191 (one only)	Consolidation Transaction is in Contravention of Consolidation Act and should be reported
	Sale (1) Khatedar Shantabai Khandu Kadam (2) Tarabai Ramchandra Shinde (3) Leelabai Dharmaji Shinde have sold undivided share of three annas and nine pies in a rupee to Baliram Parbati Dhone for ₹ 1,200 on 2-5-1969		Notices have been served Certified (Sd.) Circle Inspector 7-9-69
	Registration No. 3782 Date of intimation of mutation on the interested parties 11-7-1969 Date of intimation of certification	Date of publication of mutation on notice board 11-7-1969 (Sd.) Talathi	

Who is occupant?

The person who actually holds possession under a claim of title shall be recorded as an occupant or a Government lessee as the case may be. If there is a doubt as to actual possession the person with the strongest title should be recorded.

How to file mutation papers:

Every vardi, order, or authority upon which an entry in the register of mutations is made should be kept in a file; where they can be easily found. Akarbands and Kami-Jasti Patraks should be kept with Village Form I. Registration extracts in continuous file in the sequence of months and written reports, mutations, orders and other correspondence about mutations filed in sequence of the entries in Village Form VI.

VILLAGE FORM VI-A

Register of Disputed Cases

[Rules 5(2), 16 and 25 of the Maharashtra Land Revenue Record of Rights and Registers (Preparation and Maintenance) Rules, 1971]

Serial No.	Serial No. in Mutation Register (Village Form VI) or rough copy of Record of Rights	Survey No. and Sub-Division No.	Date of Receipt of objection	Particular of dispute with names of disputing parties	Decision of officer
1	2	3	4	5	6

VILLAGE FORM VI-B

Register of Fines under section 152 of the Maharashtra Land Revenue Code, 1966

Entry in village Form VI	Name of acquire of right or holder of document	Order of Tahsildar as to fine to be levied	Number and date of receipt
1	2	3	4
157	Shri. Sahebrao Anna Dhone		....

VILLAGE FORM VI-C

Register of Heirship Cases

Village: Hamadabad   Taluka: Satara   District: Satara

Sr. No.	Name of deceased occupant or other right holder	Date or approximate date of death	Old Khata No. in Village Form VIII-A	Names of legal heirs	Names of the heirs out of column 5 in actual possession	Order of Tahsildar as to who should be entered as occupant and/or in the other rights column	Entry in Village Form VI embodying decisions the other
1	2	3	4	5	6	7	8
3	Shri. Bapu Govindrao Dhone	7-4-1969	18	Sons: 1. Shankar 2. Ganesh 3. Dinesh 4. Dinkar Daughters: 1. Indubai Shrirang Yadao 2. Sakubai Kisan Kadam 3. Kashibai Bhiku Kadam 4. Yashoda 5. Radha (Widow)	Age 34 25 17 10 30 23 21 12 55	Shri. Shankar Bapu Dhone (as manager of joint family)	No. 167
				Out of these, Shri Shankar is the manager of Hindu undivided family.			

VILLAGE FORM VI-D

Register of New Sub-Divisions (Hissas)

Village: Hamadabad   Taluka: Satara   District: Satara

Mutation entry in Village Form VI	Survey No. or sub-division No.	Nature of change required in map	By whom done and date
1	2	3	4
161	23	123	Hissas measured on 25-12-1971 by Shri. P.H. Deshpande, P.H.S. Measurer (Sd)
		H. No. 1 .. Shri. Vasant Ram Sharma H. No. 3 .. Shri Laxman Ram Sharma H. No. 2 .. Smt. Shantabai Wife of Ram Sharma	(P.H. Deshpande) Dated 25-12-1971
168	18/2	A. 18.2	Hissas measured on 20-11-1972 by Shri. M.G. Choudhari, C.S.Z. (Sd.)
		B.	(M. G.Choudhari) Dated 20-11-1972.
191	101	H. No. 18/2A .. Shri Sitaram Rajaram Shinde H. No. 18/2B .. Shri Tukaram Rajaram Shinde 1 2 101 H. No. 1 .. Shri Sitaram Rajaram Shinde H. No. 2 .. Shri Balku Dhondu Pawar	

(**Note:** The above entries are illustrative)

Subsidiary Registers:

The four subsidiary registers, viz. (i) Village Form VI-A-Register of Disputed Cases, (ii) Village Form VI-B-Register of Fines-under-section 152 of the Maharashtra Land-Revenue Code, (iii) Village Form VI-C-Register of Heirship Cases, and (iv) Village Form VI-D-Register of New Sub-division (Hissas); are simple, self-explanatory and easy to maintain. They facilitate correct entries in Village Form-VI, appraise public of their obligations to assist Government in maintaining an accurate and up-to-date Record of Rights and ensure that the survey records on which the Record of Rights is based are also maintained up-to-date.

2.18 LIST OF DOCUMENTS

Alongwith the plan, the following documents are required to be submitted:
1. Notice to execute the proposed work in the standard form.
2. Undertaking from the architect in the standard form.
3. Extract from property register stating the details regarding the owner and land.
4. Plan from the city survey office showing boundaries of the plot and adjoining survey numbers.
5. Certificate regarding area of the plot given by a corporation or town planning department.

Resubmission: If the plans comply with the requirements of the rules and bye-laws of the sanctioning authority and the code of town planning scheme, they may be sanctioned in due course, otherwise they may have to be resubmitted as per instructions of the Authorities after complying with the same.

General requirements regarding plans, notice, certificates, undertakings, qualifications, and so on by different plan sanctioning authorities such as corporations, municipalities and others are indicated below.
1. Documents and plans
2. Number of copies
3. Owner's notice to execute the work
4. Undertaking from the supervisor
5. Building completion certificate
6. Qualifications and the experience for licensed surveyors, architects, engineers, clerks of works, structural designers, and plumbers.
7. Extracts from the property register card.

1. Documents and Plans:

The following is an extract from building rules and bye-laws of municipal corporation. The person intending to carry out the work shall send, along with the notice to be given, the following documents and plans:

(a) Correct plans and sections of every floor of the building intended to be erected which shall be drawn to a scale of not less than (10 mm = 1 m) and shall show the position, form, dimensions and means of ventilation of and access to the several parts of such a building and its appurtenances and the particular part or parts thereof, which are and those which are not intended to be used for human habitation and in the case of a building intended to be used as a dwelling house for two or more families or for carrying on any trade or business in which a number of people not exceeding twenty maximum be employed or as a place of public resort, the means of ingress and egress. Such plans and sections shall also show the depth and nature of the foundation and the proposed dimensions of all the walls, posts, columns, beams, joints, all girders; and scantling to be used in the walls, staircases, floors, and roof.

(b) A specification of each description of work proposed to be executed and of the materials to be used. Such specification shall include a description of the proposed method of drainage of the building intended to be erected and of the sanitary fittings to be used and also of the means of water supply and shall, if necessary, by the commissioner, be supplemented, by detailed calculations showing the sufficiency of the strength of any part of such a building.

(c) A block plan of such a building which shall be drawn to the scale of the largest revenue survey map at the time being in existence for the locality in which the building is, or is to be situated and shall show the positions and appurtenances of the properties, if any, immediately adjoining the width and level of the street, if any, in front and side of the street, if any, at the rear of such buildings, the levels of the foundations, and the lowest floor of such buildings, and of any yard or ground belonging there to and the means of access to such buildings.

(d) A plan showing the intended line of drainage of such a building and the intended size, depth and inclination of each drain, and the details of the arrangement proposed for the ventilation of the drains.

(e) Undertaking from the person who is appointed to supervise the execution of the work.

Plans and sections to be submitted to the corporation under the provisions of the act and the building bye-laws and rules should be drawn and signed by the surveyor, engineer, architect or structural designer licensed by the municipal commissioner.

The description of the works set out in the plans must comply with the requirements of the building bye-laws.

The structural drawings and the structural calculations which are to accompany the plans shall be prepared and signed by the structural designer licensed.

2. Number of Copies:
1. Three copies of plans for buildings in "gaothan" areas.
2. Four copies of plans for buildings in agricultural lands.
3. Five copies of plans for buildings in town planning scheme areas.

One of the above plans shall be signed by the Municipal Commissioner when signifying his approval or otherwise of the plan and shall be returned to the person by whom the same was furnished.

(a) If found necessary by the commissioner, it shall be incumbent on every person whose plans have been approved or otherwise, to submit amended plans for any deviations he proposes to make during the construction of his building work and the procedure laid down for plans therefore shall apply to all such amended plans.

(b) Every plan or amended plan mentioned above shall be coloured with fixed colours as follows:

Block Plan: The proposed work is in red; the existing work is in black grey or neutral tint and the open spaces are uncoloured. Work to be removed is to be clearly shown on the plan.

Plans and Sections: Proposed work in white lines if shown on blue ferro prints and in red lines if on white coloured prints.

Deviations: In red, if shown on blue prints and in black, if on white prints. Brick work, Wood work, RCC work, or steel work shall each be differently specified.

(c) All the drainage work and drainage lines shall be shown on original and amended plans in distinguishing colours together with the location of the sewer trap chamber and the depth of street connections.

3. **Owner's Notice to Execute the Work:**

Typical Notice
XXX Municipal Corporation

Notice under Section _____ of the XXX Provincial Municipal Corporation Act, 1949.

No.
Date

To The Municipal Commissioner,
XXX Municipal Corporation,
XXX

Sir,
Pursuant to the provisions of _____ of the XXX Municipal Corporation Act, _____, I hereby give you notice that I intend within the meaning of that section to execute the following work:

1. Description of the proposed work.
2. The purpose for which the work is intended.
3. Dimensions of the work.
4. The name and address of the person intended to be employed to supervise the work.
5. Name and address of the contractor, if any.
6. The description of walls, whether stone or brick masonry, the nature of mortar to be used.
7. The depth of the foundation and whether it is to be taken upto murum or hard rock strata.
8. Information about the projection of the balcony, whether it is on the municipal land.
9. How is the disposal of sewage water provided for?
10. Whether the land on which the proposed work is to be erected is owned by the person giving the notice.

I hereby acknowledge to have persuade the building regulations contained in Chapter XV and schedule Chapter XII of the XXX provincial Municipal Corporation Act, _____, and the bye-laws made under the said Act.

Yours faithfully,

Signature and address of the owner of the proposed work
XXX (Name of the town)

4. Undertaking from the Supervisor:

The following undertaking from the person who is appointed to supervise the execution of the work should be submitted to the Municipal Commissioner along with the notice.

To The City Engineer.   Date

XXX Municipal Corporation, XXX.

Sir,

With reference to the notice under Section ____ of the XXX Provincial Municipal Corporation Act, ____ , Submitted to you by Shri. _____ for the execution of the work _____, I wish to inform you that I have agreed to supervise the execution of the work mentioned therein.

Yours faithfully,

Licensed Surveyor	L.S. No.	_____
Licensed Engineer	L.S. No.	_____
Licensed Architect	L.S. No.	_____
Licensed Structural Designer	L.S. No.	_____

5. Building Completion Certificate:

(a) Certificate from the architect to the Corporation/Municipality:

XXX Municipal Corporation

Building Completion Certificate

I do hereby certify that the following work _____ has been (insert full particulars of the work) supervised by me and has been completed to my satisfaction, that the workmanship and the whole of the material used are good; and that no provision of the Act or the bye-laws and no requisition made, condition prescribed or order issued thereunder has been transgressed in execution of the work.

The drainage works in relation to the construction work mentioned above have been completed in accordance with your drainage rules and bye-laws and a certificate prescribed under rule_____ of schedule from Shri. XXX, a licensed plumber is sent herewith.

Signature

(Date)

License No. _____

(b) Certificate from the Corporation to the Owner:

XXX Corporation,
_____

No. _____

_____
Dated

Occupancy Certificate
(According to XXX Municipal Corporation Act of 1949)

From
The Assistant Engineer,
_____ Corporation,

_____

To
Shri. _____
Address _____

With reference to your application, dated _____ for permission to construct a building _____ at plot No. _____ the Commencement Certificate No. _____ dated _____ _____ was issued to you.

With reference to the completion certificate, dated _____ issued by your architect and submitted to this office, permission required to occupy the same building is hereby granted as per _____ Provincial Municipal Act.

XXX Sd/
Assistant Engineer

_____ Corporation

6. Qualifications and Experience:

Definitions:

1. Words and phrases which are used but not defined-herein shall have the same meanings as are assigned to them in the XXX Municipal Corporation Act, _____ referred to in these bye-laws as the "Act".

Qualifications of a Licensed Surveyor:

1. No surveyor shall be granted a license by the Commissioner as required by Section _____ unless the said person possesses the qualifications and experience as prescribed:

    (a) A degree in civil engineering of any University or a diploma or a degree in architecture of any University or Institution recognised by the Commissioner.

OR

(b) Associate membership or membership of any institution which is considered by the Commissioner to be equivalent to a University Degree in civil engineering or architecture.

OR

(c) A diploma in civil engineering of any University or institution which is recognised by the Commissioner with practical experience of at least one year of work connected with the survey and building construction.

2. Any surveyor who has been granted continuously for a period of five years immediately preceding the date on which these bye-laws come into force, a surveyor's license by the Municipal Corporation of the city of XXX or who has at least five years practical experience of work connected with the survey and building construction work, may be granted a surveyor license by the Commissioner, provided he passes the practical examination held by the City Engineer for testing the merit.

3. No architect or engineer shall be granted a license by the Commissioner as required by section ___ unless the said person possesses the qualifications as prescribed:

(a) A degree in civil engineering or a diploma in architecture of any University or institution recognised by the Commissioner in this behalf.

OR

(b) Associate membership or membership of any institution which is considered by the Commissioner to be equivalent to a University Degree in civil engineering or architecture.

(c) A diploma holder in civil engineering or equivalent, holding surveyor's license for at least 10 years before these bye-laws came into force, if he is able to produce sufficient evidence of his having done structural engineering work for the ten years.

4. No person will be granted a license by the Commissioner to work as a structural designer for carrying out the works of design and execution of RCC.
A diploma holder in civil engineering or equivalent who is already holding surveyor's license continuously for the last seven years previous to the passing of these bye-laws.

Qualifications of a clerk of works:

5. Any person who intends to work as a clerk of works may obtain a license from the Commissioner under section _____ if he produces a certificate from a licensed surveyor of having worked under him for a period of five years to the satisfaction of the licensed surveyor.

Qualifications of a Licensed Plumber:

6. (i) No plumber shall be granted a license by the Commissioner as required by _____ unless the said person holds a Degree or a Diploma in Civil Engineering or Sanitary Engineering of any University or Institution recognised by the Commissioner.

(ii) Not withstanding anything contained in clause (i), any person who does not possess the qualifications prescribed in clause (ii) may be given a plumber's license by the Commissioner, if:

(a) He was granted a plumber's License by the Municipal Corporation of the City of XXX continuously for a period of five years immediately preceding the date on which these bye-laws come into force.

OR

(b) He has extensive practical experience of not less than five years.

Provided that the Commissioner may, before granting a license to such a person, require him to pass a theoretical and practical examination.

The Architects Act, 1972 (No. 20 of 1972):

An act to provide for the registration of architects and for matters connected therewith was passed by the Parliament in 1972. The objects and reasons stated were, "Since independence and more particularly, with the implementation of the five year plans, building construction activity in our country has expanded almost on a phenomenal scale. A large variety of buildings, many of an extremely complex nature and magnitude, like multistoreyed office buildings, factory buildings and residential houses, are being constructed each year. With this increase in building activity, many unqualified persons calling themselves as architects are undertaking the construction of buildings which are uneconomical and quite frequently, unsafe, thus bringing into disrepute the profession of architects. Various organisations, including the Indian Institute of Architects, have repeatedly emphasised the need for statutory regulation to protect the general public from unqualified persons working as architects. With the passing of this legislation, it will be unlawful for any person to designate himself as an "architect" unless he has the requisite qualifications and experience and is registered under the Act."

Other professionals like engineers will be free to engage themselves in their normal vocation in respect of building construction work provided that they do not style themselves as architects.

Application for Registration:

According to this act, "Every architect who desires to have his name entered in the register shall submit an application in form No. XI, together with documentary evidence about his eligibility for registration accompanied by a draft of ₹ 50/- (Present situation) in favour of the Secretary, Council of Architecture, New Delhi, for issue of a certificate of registration and the certificate of registration shall be issued in Form XII.

Form No. XI
Application for Registration of Architects

The Secretary
Council of Architecture
New Delhi

1. Name in full (in block letters)
2. Father's name
3. Nationality
4. Date of Birth
5. Residential address
6. Professional address
7. Particulars of qualification (supported by attested copies)
8. Date of commencement of profession/service.
9. Whether practising independently/as a partner/or employed
10. Period of residence in India
11. Present address on which communication will be made
12. Any other particulars.

I hereby undertake that if admitted as a registered architect, I will be bound by the provision of the Architect's Act, 1972 and the rules and regulations framed thereunder or that may hereafter from time to time be made pursuant to the said Act.

I also enclose a draft of ₹ 50/- as registration fee for the year _____

Yours faithfully,
Encl. List of particulars endorsed.

Form No. XII

Council of Architecture of India

Certificate of Registration under sub-section (7) of Section 24 and sub-section (4) of Section 26 of the Architects Act, 1972.

Certificate of Registration

This is to certify that the name of Shri./Shrimati _____ has been entered in the register and his/her Registration No. is _____. This certificate is valid from the _____ day of _____ 20 ___ to the _____ day of 20 _____ inclusive.

Renewals

Signature of the Registrar

List of Additional qualifications.

Given under the common seal of the Council of Architecture. This _____ day of 20 _____

President
Secretary (Seal)

Extracts from the Property Register Card

City Survey: Poona, Taluka: Poona, District: Poona			
Survey No. (Shivajinagar) 560	Area (ha) (0.34)	Tenure (final plot) 26	Particulars of assessment or rent paid to the Govt. and when due for revision
Basements:			
Holder in 19 origin of the title (so far as traced)			
Lessee			
	City Survey Office SEAL		
Other encumbrances Other Remarks			
Date	Transaction	Vol. No.	New Holder (H), Lessee (L) or Encumbrances (E)	Attestation
12.4.44	As per partition deed	120	H Kiran Joshi	Sd/- Tahsildar
5.11.68	As per sale deed amount ₹ 4,32,450/- From: Kiran Joshi	S(2) 4350 – 9.4.67	Vidya Co-operative Housing Society	Sd/- Tahsildar

2.19 TDR

The main occupation in ancient time was agriculture and people used to live in villages. After mechanization was introduced, town and cities were developing and becoming more populated. Cities became more populated because people migrated to cities in search of education and jobs. As development was increasing rapidly, more and more multistoried buildings were built. To control haphazard growth of city, local bodies (corporations) introduced certain bye-laws and Development Control Rules (DCR). Due to development in the area, employment is increased and thus enhancing per capita income, hence living standards of people is increased. On the other hand due to urbanization, the pollution in air, water and land is increased to a very large extent.

2.19.1 What is TDR?

In Development Plan reservations are shown against a number of public utilities. In view of limited financial resource available with the utilities and consequently the paucity of funds for such huge compensation, the State Government have introduced the concept of Transferable Development Right. Before introducing this concept the municipalities used to compensate the land owners in terms of money as per Government value of the land. The utilities may now be upgrade / expand their services and provide better amenities to the citizens.

With this concept if any land owner hands over the possession of the reserved land to the Municipal Corporation free of cost without any encumbrance, a Development Right Certificate (DRC) will be granted to the owner to construct a built up area equivalent to permissible FSI of the land handed over by him/ her on one or more plots in the zones specified. The Municipal Corporation has a mandate to regulate the activities pertaining to Transferable Development Right.

2.19.2 Why Reservation of Land is Necessary?

The main purpose of reservation is to provide facilities to public. These facilities include basic facilities such as school, hospitals etc., recreational facilities such as play grounds, gardens etc., essential services such as fire brigade, vegetable market, water treatment plants, waste water treatment plants, etc.

2.19.3 Who is Eligible?

The owner of the plot which is reserved for a public purpose or road construction or road widening, in the DP and for additional amenities deemed to be provided in accordance with modified DCR excepting in case of an existing or retention user or to any required, compulsory or recreational open space, shall be eligible for the award of TDR. Such award will entitle the owner of land to FSI in the form of DRC which he / she may use for himself / herself or transfer to any person.

Development Rights will be granted to owner or a lessee only for reserved lands which are retainable / non-retainable under Urban Land Ceiling Act, 1976 and in respect of all other reserved lands to which the provision of the aforesaid act do not apply and on production of a certificate to this effect from the Competent Authority under the Act before Development Right shall be to such extent and subject to such conditions as Government may specify. Development Rights are available only in cases where development of a reservation has not been implemented.

Land development: TDR granting and DRC handling is worked out only after the reserved land is surrendered to Municipal Corporation free of cost and free of encumbrances after leveling of land, constructing a compound wall of 1.5 m height, providing street light, access road by the owner is completed and Municipal Commissioner is satisfied.

Issue of DRC: A DRC shall be issued by the Municipal Commissioner himself as a certificate printed on bond paper in an appropriate form. Such certificate will be a transferable and negotiable instrument after due authentication by him of all transactions etc. relating to grant of DRC. Other important aspect is transfer of name in land records.

Documents to be submitted for availing TDR:
- 7/ 12 Extract
- Fher Far (change of Ownership + other)
- Power of Attorney
- ULC Order (NOC)
- Search and Title Report
- N.A. Order
- Original Site Plan
- Zoning Demarcation
- Zone Certificate
- Demarcation
- Architect Area Certificate
- Tax NOC
- Six files to be submitted: To TDR department, Road department, Legal department, Bhoomi and Zindagi department, Bhoomi praman, D.P. Department.

Creation of TDR: Plot area minimum: 500 sq.m / 5000 sq. ft.

Zones: A, B, C (PUNE CASE)

(A) Congested zone (FSI – 1.5 to 2.0) in core of the city. TDR is generated here but it is not applicable or cannot be loaded on the plan within this area. Hence, it can be used in lower zones.

(B) Semi-congested zone which is peripheral to A zone. Development is proper and area is accessible from outside and within.

(C) Non-congested and on the outskirts of city limit peripheral to B zone.

Utilization of TDR:

Development rights shall not be used in A zone and some other congested area. Development rights shall not be used on plots for housing schemes of slum dwellers for which additional FSI is permissible and the areas where permissible FSI is less than 1.0.

Development Rights shall not be used on the plots fronting on arterial road with 30 m width in zone B. It can be subjected on rest of the area to other regulations.

Transfer of area: A to B OR C, B to B OR C, C to C only.

Development Right Certificate may be used on one or more plots of land whether vacant or already developed or by erection of additional storeys or in any other manner consistent with these regulations, but not so as to exceed in any plot a total built up FSI higher than prescribed.

(a) The FSI on receiving plots shall be allowed to be exceeded not more than 0.4 in respect of TDR available for the reserved plots.

(b) The FSI on receiving plot shall be allowed to be exceeded by further 0.4 in respect of TDR available on account of land surrendered for road widening or construction of new road from the very said plot. For utilization of TDR minimum width of road is 6 m.

Priority List for Generation of TDR:

Phased annual programme is open to public for utilization of TDR in the form of DRC (as per DP references) and used after receiving plots and in case of emergency utility may be completed initially and then DRC etc. is finalized. Following are few examples:

(a) DP Roads reservation already committed by authority during past years.

(b) DP Roads reservation responsible for improving circulation pattern.

(c) Reservation for essential municipal service such as fire brigade / water / sewage plants / vegetable market / burial / crematories etc.

(d) Parking reservations that can be developed by Municipal Corporation for multistoried parking lots.

(e) Reservation for transport.

(f) Shopping center which will yield high asset to Municipal Corporation etc.

Priority List for Utilization of TDR:

This shall be made available to the public in the office of Deputy City Engineer (DP).

(i) Grant of TDR in case where lands are under acquisition (request for the same is to be made to special LA OFFICER – for the cases after 30 September 1993-TDR introduction and acceptance).

(ii) Possession of the land has been delivered without having received part or full compensation under MRTP, BPMC Acts.

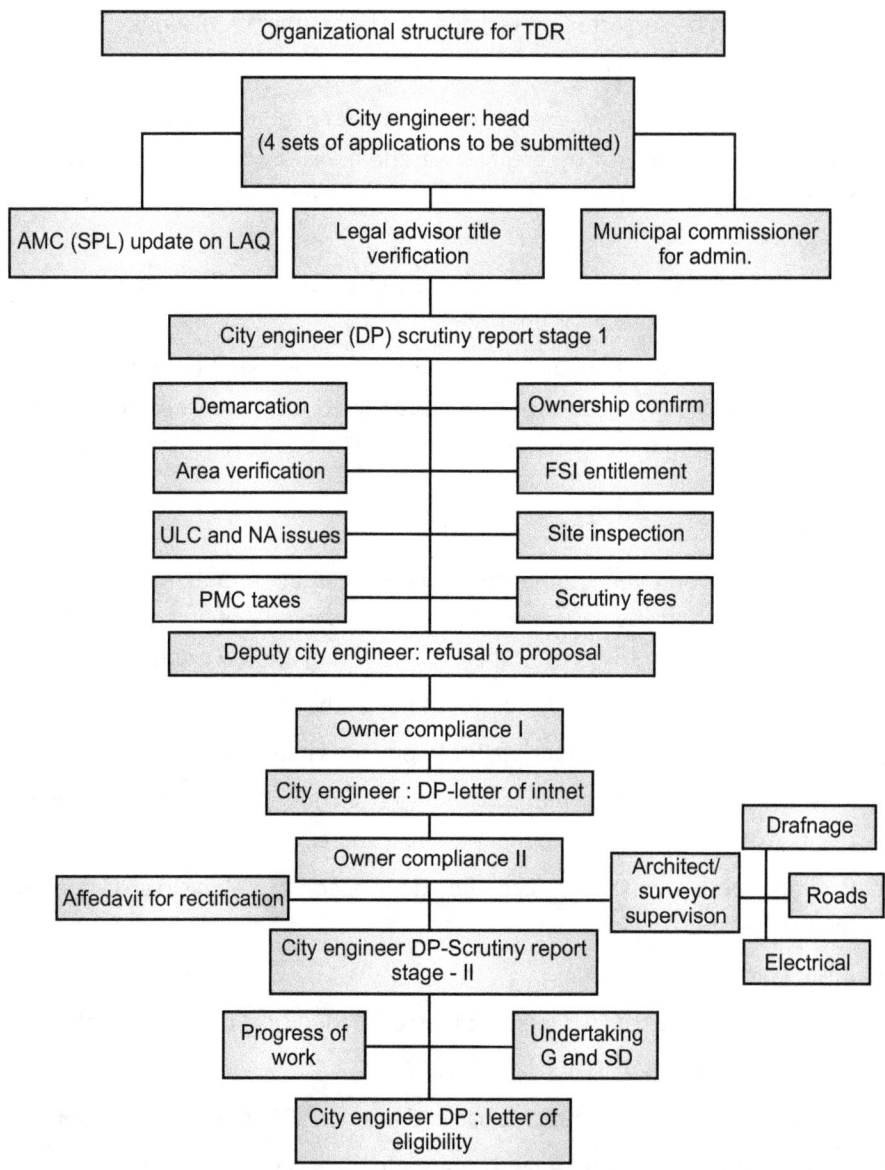

Fig. 2.10

2.20 COMMENCEMENT CERTIFICATE

1. **Format I:**

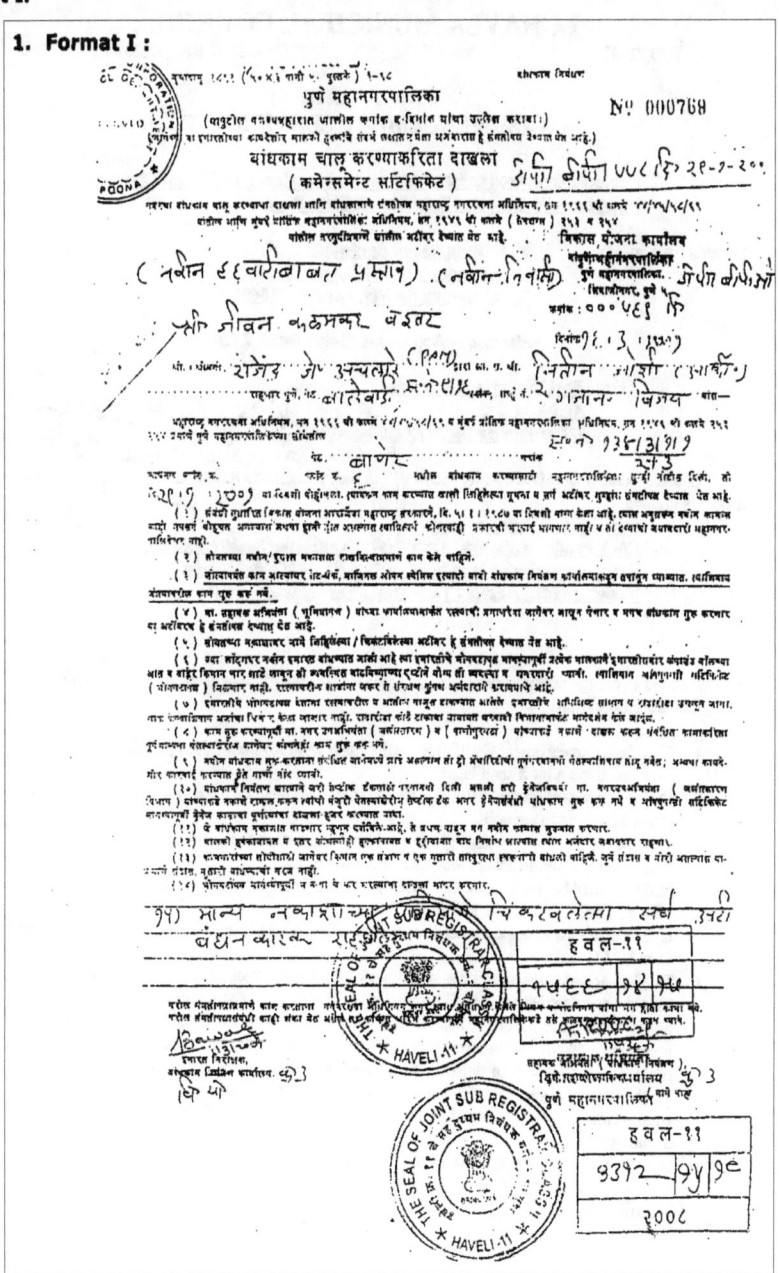

2. Format II:

2. Format II:

LONAVLA MUNICIPAL COUNCIL

Date :- 6/08/2007   No. ENG/BP/ 25/2007-2008 /527

Form No. 2 (Rule No. 5)
COMMENCEMENT CERTIFICATE

Subject :- Proposed construction on land bearing, CTS No. 186/ F & 187/6 'A' Bhangarwadi, Lonavla , Tal:- Maval, Dist:- Pune

Lonavla for Shri/Smt,   Mrs. Geeta Ashok Agrawal
C/o Virendra K. Parakh, Architect
7, Vardhaman Society, Lonavla 410401

Reference :- Application / Letter dated 7.5.2007

From Shri.Virendra K. Parakh
Architect
7, Vardhaman Society, Lonavla 410401

Commencement Certificate under section 45 of the Maharashtra Regional Town Planning Act 1966 is hereby granted to :
Mrs. Geeta Ashok Agrawal
C/o Virendra K.Parakh, Architect 7, Vardhaman Society, Lonavla 410401
For construction on land bearing CTS No. 186/ F & 187/6 'A'
Bhangarwadi, Lonavla , Tal:- Maval, Dist:- Pune

Lonavla as per the accompanying plan as amended by this office in green on the plan & on the following Conditions :

1. That the commencement Certificate shall remain valid for period first year from the date of issue and there after it shall lapse.
2. That the applicant owner shall intimate the commencement of the construction work to this office in writing in advance.
3. That the applicant owner shall give the advance intimation to the collector of Pune Revenue Branch before commencing Non-Agriculture use of land.
4. Plot/land shall be demarcated on site before commencement of the work from city survey officer , Lonavla / T.I.L.R. Vadgaon.
5. If the existing trees comes under Proposed building prior approval for tree cutting to be obtained from L.M.C.
6. This Municipal Council will not supply water for construction or drinking purpose.
7. That the construction work shall be carried out strictly as per sanctioned plan and as amended by this office in green on the plan. If during the construction any departure from sanctioned plan is intended or way of internal or external changes , prior sanction of the L.M.C. shall be necessary. A revised plan showing deviations shall be submitted and the procedure laid down for the original plans heretofore shall apply to all such amended plans. Any works done in contravention of the sanctioned plans , without prior approval of L.M.C. shall be deemed as unauthorized.
8. The owner through his licensed Architect shall give notice to L.M.C. on completion of work upto plinth level , No progress above the plinth shall be carried out unless plinth is checked and approved by L.M.C.

Contd ...2...

9. All Building material shall be SUB or exclusively within a building plot. The stocking of materials and details on public roads highways shall be prohibited except with special permission of L.M.C.
10. No temporary construction shall be permitted without prior approval of L.M.C.
11. If the electrical H.T. line is passing through or near the plot necessary N.O.C. of the concern Authority shall be submitted L.M.C. before actual commencement of the work on site.
12. If the plot is abutting on the Mumbai – Pune National Highway or and Railway line, necessary N.O.C. regarding set back distance from the concern. Authority shall be submitted to L.M.C. before Commencement of the work.
13. The structural design of building shall carried out in accordance with structural design chapter of national building code of India.
14. All material and workmanship shall be good quality confirming to Indian standard Specifications.
15. Plumbing, sanitary and electrical work shall be carried out as per the requirement of Indian standard specifications under the supervision of authorized Licensed Holder.
16. Adequate fire fighting equipments shall be installed.
17. Copy sanctioned plan shall be made available on site whenever requirement by L.M.C. and Police Authorities.
18. The owner shall be pay necessary octroi for buildings material time and is liable to show / s submit all necessary accounts as and when required by L.M.C.
19. The owner through his licensed Architect shall give notices to L.M.C. regarding completion of work in prescribed form and shall be accompanied by three sets Record plan. The built up structure shall not brought into use without occupancy certificate of L.M.C.
20. All portions of the building shall be used for the specific purpose as shown on the sanctioned Record Plan.
21. That the L.M.C. is not responsible for any Government, Technical, Privet Ownership, Area & Boundary disputes.
22. If it is noted that the information plan and other details supplied by the applicant is false or wrong the commencement of occupancy certificate shall stand cancelled & applicant will be liable for action under such consequences as maintained in relevant provisions of chapter IV of the Maharastra Regional Toning Act 1966 and the sign reserve the right to revoke or modify the permission granted.
23. Display board showing all details of development viz permission No. and date, plot No. C.T.S. No./R.S.No., Plot Area, Built up area sanctioned Nos. of tenements, Name of the developers Architects etc. shall be erected at prominent Place on site.
24. At least   trees to be planted in the plot.
25. Provision of rain water harvesting (i.e. conservation, augmentation & recycling of water) shall be done on site.

No. ENG/BP/ 25/ 2006-07
Date : 16/ 05 /2007

Chief Officer
Lonavla Municipal Council

To,
Mrs. Geeta Ashok Agrawal
C/o Virendra K.Parakh, Architect
7, Vardhaman Society, Lonavla 410401

C.F.W.C. to :
1. The Collector Of Pune (R.B.)
2. City Survey Officer, Lonavla / T.I.L.R. Vadgaon (Maval)
3. Building Inspector, L.M.C.

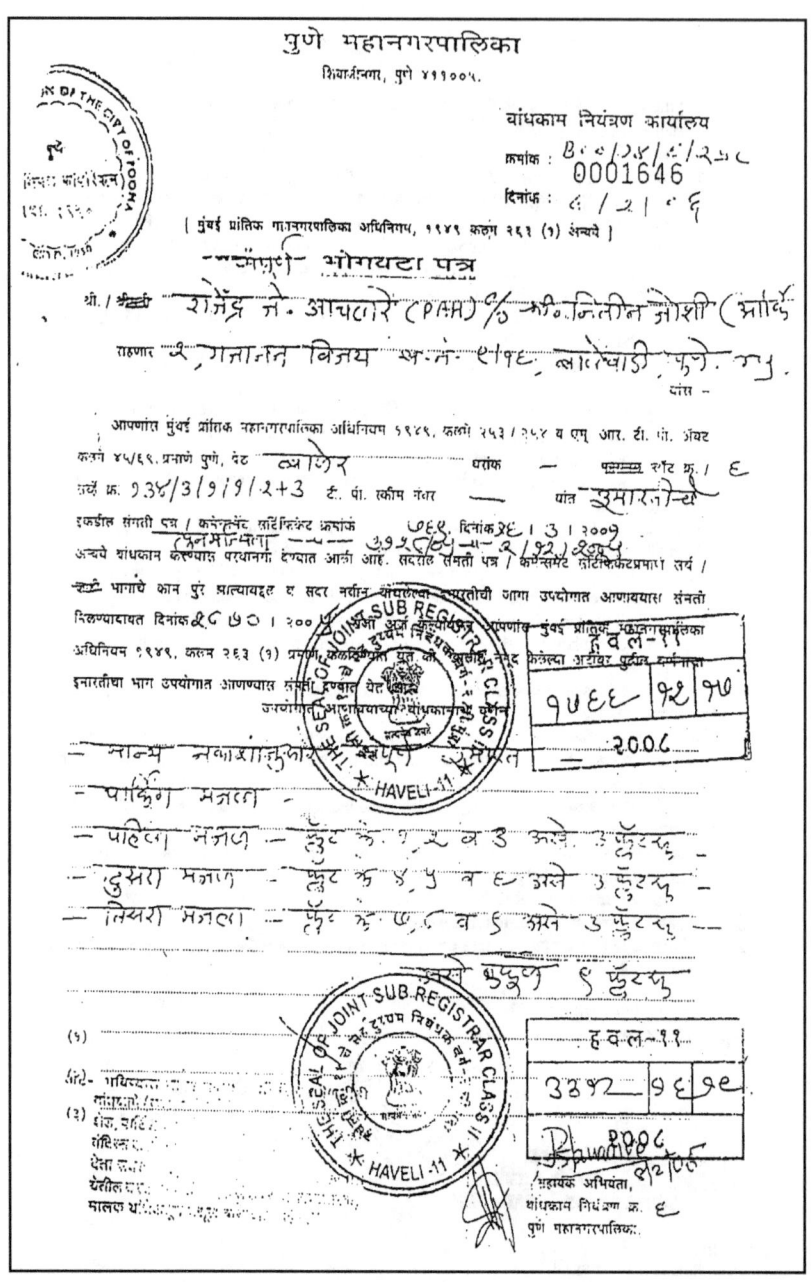

2.21 MSEB

FORM - X
प्रपत्र - एक्स

१) पूर्ण नांव : आचळरे असोसिएट,

मावळत्या ग्राहकाचा पेशा / व्यवसाय :
आणि पूर्ण पत्ता :

२) नवीन ग्राहकाचा पेशा / व्यवसाय आणि पूर्ण पत्ता : श्री. प्रशांत सुभाषराव पाटील
व्यवसाय :- व्याख्याता (Lecture)
फ्लॅट नं. ५, गौरवी अपार्टमेंट, वाळेकराची फाटा

३) विद्युत शक्ती जोडून दिलेल्या स्थळांचा पूर्ण पत्ता : पाबळकर मळा S.N. 134/3/1/1/2/3
धायरे, पुणे-४५

४) स्थापित यंत्रसामुग्रीचा संक्षिप्त तपशील भार ग्राहक क्र. व मोटर क्रमांक
: 3.00 KW
ग्राहक क्र. 160220174589
मिटर क्र. 900064859

५) कारखाना किंवा उत्पादन इत्यादीचे स्वरूप : - घरगुती

६) व्यवसायाचे हस्तांतरण नोंदणीकृत विलेखाव्दारे झाले की कराराव्दारे असे नसेल तर त्याची अंमलबावणी कशा प्रकारे झाली ? :

७) विद्यमान मालकाची (म्हणजे मावळत्या ग्राहकाची) : स्वाक्षरी व तारीख :

८) नवीन ग्राहकाची स्वाक्षरी व तारीख : 10/06/२०१८

९) विद्युत पुरवठा परवाना धारक किंवा अभियंता : दिनांक किंवा प्रभारी अभियंता यांचे अभिप्राय

१०) सुरक्षा प्रतिभूर्ति ठेव म्हणून भरलेली रक्कम
रूपये _____ पावती क्रमांक _____
दिनांक _____ प्राक्कलन क्रमांक _____

११) (असल्यास) _____

2.22 NOC FOR ROADS, NATIONAL AND STATE HIGHWAYS

Commercial centres, residential complexes, factories etc. are increasing day by day along the road side under the jurisdiction of Public Works department. The proposals for approach road are received from public. On Scrutiny of the proposals, if found suitable the permission is granted by the Chief Engineer. After obtaining permission it is necessary to make agreement in the prescribed form. The required documents, conditions and general procedures are as follows:

1. **How and Where to Apply?**

If it is adjacent to National Highway then - concerned Executive Engineer of National Highway Division. If it is adjacent to the State Highway /Major District Road/Other District Road/Village Road then - Executive Engineer Public Works Division/Zilla Parishad (Works) Division.

2. **Which Documents are Required with Application?**

(A) Documents:
- Application from Owner.
- NOC for non-agriculture of land (Copy of NA permission from Revenue Department).
- Plot ownership document.

(B) Plans:
- Index/Key plan.
- Part of village map showing survey numbers in which private property is located.
- Layout plan/site plan showing details of construction, proposed approach road, C.D. works etc.
- Access plan showing the position proposed approach roads, exact chainage of proposed approach road, position of existing approaches on both sides of proposed approach road, land width, building line, control line, centre line of road, carriageway / formation width, C.D. works etc.
- Cross-Section of approach road.
- L/Section of arterial road for 300 metres on either side of proposed access.
- Detailed plan of C.D. works and trap drain with cross section.
- Existing access plan.
- Plan showing drainage arrangement at approach road.

3. **Who Takes Decision on the Application?**
- National Highway/State Highway/Major District Road
  The Chief Engineer,
  Public Works Region Ministry of transport
  New Delhi.

- Other District road/Village road
  The Superintending Engineer
  Public Works Circle.

4. **Expected Period to Take Decision:**
   Three months approximately.

TO BE FILLED BY THE APPLICANT

To,

THE EXECUTIVE ENGINEER,

_____

_____

_____

Subject: Access Permission for approach to Private Property Abuting on National Highway / State Highway / Major District Road.

Sir,

Kindly find enclosed herewith the proposal in prescribed formats for permission to take approach road from N. H. / S. H. / M. D. R. In km. No._____ of _____ road section of N. H. / S. H. / M. D. R. No. _____ for access to private property belonging to _____ in survey no. _____ / gat no. _____ of _____ village, Taluka. _____, District _____, in triplicate.

It is requested to please accord permission for the said access.

Thanking you

Yours faithfully

(Name and Address of the applicant)

D. A.: Checklist and drawing in triplicate and other documents in single.

PROPOSAL RECEIVED ON

Details to be furnished for obtaining access permission for approach road to private property.

Name of Applicant with Address

_____

_____

_____

Sr. No.	Item	Information to be furnished by applicant	Comments SDE/DE/SDO
1.	Location of the proposed road (km. ___ & Chainage ___).		
2.	Whether within municipal limit or outside municipal limit and place?		
3.	Traffic intensity on road in MT/Day, PCU and CVD (At the nearest count post).	Do not reply	
4.	Width of road and land width available.	Do not reply	
5.	Whether there is a divided carriageway or otherwise?	Do not reply	
6.	The distance from center line of the road to the plot boundary of the private property in metres (Front and Back).		
7.	The proposed construction will be used for residential purpose or non-residential purpose.		
8.	If non-residential, mention the purpose of activity (attach the development plan sanctioned by competent authority duly attested).		
9.	The distance between tangent point of the curve of the said road and that of proposed approach road in a direction parallel to the center line of the road (For arterial road it should not be less than 500 m in Urban area and 750 m in Rural area.)		

contd. ...

10.	The width of proposed approach road. (This shall be adequate to enable safe operation of the vehicles). It should be 7.50 m to 9.00 m according to category of main road).		
11.	The radius of the access for entrance and exit road with the highway (The ruling radius of curves being 30 m and the absolute minimum 13 m).	Do not reply	
12.	Whether the private property is in plain and rolling country or in hilly terrain.	Do not reply	
13.	If on plain and rolling terrain whether it is on level ground? If on hilly terrain whether slope is less than 5%?	Do not reply	
14.	Whether vehicles entering or leaving the private property would be fully visible to the traffic using the main road?	Do not reply	
15.	Distances of building line, control line & private property boundary from the centre line of the road (Attach plan).		
16.	The type of cross drainage work proposed to be provided to allow road side drainage (pipe culvert / slab culvert) (Attach plan).		
17.	If pipe culvert is provided, give the diameter of pipe (It shall be 750 m diameter (minimum). The diameter of the pipe shall be suitably made higher to cater the road side water flow efficiently).		
18.	Is the catch water drain (as per the sketch attached) provided and its details are shown in layout plan submitted with the proposal? (If not, the proposal will not be considered).		
19.	Whether the private property is affected by land acquisition proceedings or alternative improved alignment?	Do not reply	

contd. ...

20.	Whether tree cutting is required due to proposed approach road? If yes, give details and permission for cutting/rehabilitation (Show such trees on the location/site plan).		
21.	Whether the NOC for non-agriculture of land is obtained from the Revenue Deptt.? If yes, mention No. and Date.		
22.	Whether the following document and plans are attached with the proposal? (if any one from the list is missing the application will be rejected).		
(A)	Documents: (i) Application from owner. (ii) NOC for non-agriculture of land (copy of N.A. permission from Revenue Department.) (iii) Plot ownership document.		
(B)	Plans: (i) Index / key plan. (ii) Part of village map showing survey No. in which private property is located. (iii) Layout plan / site plan showing details of construction, proposed approach road, C.D. works etc. (iv) Access plan showing the position of proposed approach roads, exact chainage of proposed approach road, position of existing approaches upto 500 m along highway on both sides of proposed approach road land width, building line, control line, center line of road, carriage way/formation width C.D. works etc. shall be shown in different colours and distances on the plan. (v) Cross – section of approach road. (vi) L/Section of arterial road for 300 m on either side of proposed access. (vii) Detailed plan of C.D. works and trap drain with cross section.		

Notes:

1. All plans should be signed by the owner.
2. The plan will be signed by the Deputy Engineer and Executive Engineer while submitting the proposal.
3. For the reference of the applicant the following plans are attached with the check list.
   (i) Existing access plan.
   (ii) Plan showing drainage arrangement at approach road.
4. The owner / owners (Licensee /Licensees) will have to enter license deed as per Annexure – I enclosed.

LICENCE FOR THE USE FOR NATIONAL HIGHWAY LAND

* Here enter details of premises i.e. land revenue no. etc.	1. Agreement to construct an approach road with necessary provision for drainage to *_____ _____ _____
* Here enter name of National Highway	_____ abutting on the _____ boundary of * _____ in kilometer _____ in Survey No. _____
* Here enter full details of the party in whose favour Licence is issued	of the village _____in the Taluka of _____ of the _____ District. An agreement made this _____ day of _____ between the President of India (hereinafter called the Government which expression shall, unless excluded by or repugnant to the context, including exclude his successors in office and assigns) of the one part and *_____
* Here enter the name of National Highway	hereinafter called " the Licensee" (Which repugnant shall, unless excluded by or repugnant to the context, include the said Licensee's successors, heirs, executors, administrators and assigns) of the other part.

contd. ...

	2. Whereas the Licensee's has applied to the Government for permission to construct on the Government land an approach road with necessary provision for drainage to his property abutting on the boundary of *_____ in kilometer _____ in the _____ Taluka of the _____ District, more particularly described in the Schedule annexed hereto and shown in the drawing attached hereto (hereinafter referred to as "the said premises").
	3. And whereas the Government have agreed to, grant such Permission on the terms and conditions hereinafter mentioned.
	4. Now, this agreement witnessed that, in consideration of the terms and conditions hereinafter continued and on the part of the licence to be observed and performed, the Government hereby grants to the licensee permission to construct an approach road with necessary drainage works to the said premises as per approved drawings attached subject to the following terms and conditions.

SCHEDULE

(here type the schedule referred to in clause 2)

In witness whereof this agreement is executed in duplicate by the parties hereto on the dates mentioned below their respective signatures.

Signed by shri.

(Name in full)	For & on the behalf of
The Licensee	The President of India
The constituted attorney	Under secretary to the
The licensees	Govt. of India
In the presence of	Ministry of Surface
1. Name in full (Signature) with designation	Transport (Roads wing)
2. Name in full (Signature) with designation	1. Name in full (Signature) with designation
	2. Name in full (Signature) with designation

N.B.: Wherever alternatived such as "at " his From their Licensee Divisional has etc. are given only Licensees Executive have applicable portion should be typed in the fair licence deed.

For Office use only

To,

_____
_____
_____

Subject: Access permission for approach road to private property abuting on national highways / state highways / major district road.
Ref.: Your Letter No. _____ Dated __/__/__.
Dear Sir,
The application submitted by you is found to be incomplete, hence it is returned herewith. The following remarks may be complied and the application may be resubmitted

_____
_____
_____

Yours sincerely
D. A: Proposal in original Executive Engineer

_____
_____
_____

For Office use only
No. 1
Proposal for permission to approach road from N. H. / S. H. / M. D. R. For the private property of _____ on N. H. / S. H. / M .D. R. in km. _____ of _____ section.

CERTIFICATE

1. The nearest existing approach road connecting on_____ (N.H./S.H./M.D.R.) is beyond _____ m. from proposed approach.
2. The nearest C.D. Work on N.H./SH/MDR is beyond _____ m from proposed approach crossing N. H. Way.
3. Portion upto 200 m length on either sides of proposed approach is straight and the road banking is not more than 0.6 m.
4. The proposal fulfils the requirements of IRC- 62, 1976.
5. There is no obstacle like other approaches or accesses, C.D. Works, Big road, side trees etc. road in curve, road in high bank or road in cutting in construction to this proposed approach, hence the permission may be granted.

Sub-divisional Engineer / Officer
Sub. Dn. ___ .

For office use only
No. 2

CERTIFICATE

Certified that the standards adopted in the case of proposed construction of approach road for the access to private property of _____ km. No._____ of _____ Section of N.H./S.H./ M.D.R._____ Location near _____ village in District _____ are as per IRC. Specification No. 62/1976.
"Guidelines for control of access on Highways."

Executive Engineer,
_____

For office use only
Letter of permission

Government of Maharashtra
Public Works Department
Public Works Region

Chief Engineer's Office,

Ph. No.
No. D-2 (HDM) /Approach Road / Dated ___/___/___

To,
The Superintending Engineer;
_____
_____

Subject: Access Permission from N. H. / S. H. /M.D.R. No. _____

In Mouza _____ S. NO. _____ in km _____
To M/s _____ grant of
Reference: _____
_____

    With reference to the letter cited above, access permission from N.H /S. H./ M.D.R. NO. ---------------- in Mouza ------------------------ Survey No. ---------------------- in km No. ------------------ for the private property of Messer's _____ is hereby granted subject to the conditions as laid down in Government of India, Ministry of Surface Transport, New Delhi's letter No. N.H./III/P17/75, dated 30/10/80.

The approach road and the cross drainage structure shall be constructed as per the rules. The road top level of the approach road shall be as shown in the approved drawing. The agency shall give guarantee to maintain the level of the approach road top as per the approved drawing. The permission for the approach road is granted subject to the following conditions:

1. For Urban area, any construction within the private land of Licensee /Licensees shall not be done within 6 m from the road boundary.
2. For rural area the proposed residential construction should not be done _____ m from the centre line of N.H./S.H./M.D.R.
3. For rural area the proposed Non-residential construction should not be done _____ m from the centre line of N.H./S.H./M.D.R.
4. Adequate drainage arrangement in the proposed construction shall be made so that the surface water should not flow over the highway / road.

D. A.: Set of
Proposal 2 Nos.
Chief Engineer
Copy to Executive Engineer, _____
_____, for information.

QUESTIONS

1. State the bye-laws regarding road width and height of building.
2. What is Floor Area Ratio (F.A.R.)? State which areas of construction are excluded while calculating floor area ratio.
3. Write a detailed note on building line and control line. Mention its distances for all types of roads.
4. Discuss the importance of built-up area, plinth area and carpet area.
5. A line plan for a Residential Building is shown in Fig. 2.11.

    Data: (a) All walls are 230 mm thick. (b) Walls indicated by ⊗ are 100 mm thick. (c) RCC framed structure. (d) Beam sizes 0.23 m × 0.38 m. (e) Column sizes 0.23 m × 0.30 m. (f) Floor to floor height 3.30 m. (g) Plinth height 0.60 m.

    Based on the data and Fig. 2.11:

    (i) Draw to a scale 1 : 50 detailed plan.
    (ii) Draw to a scale 1 : 50 detailed section A-A.
    (iii) Prepare schedule of openings and also show design for staircase.
    (iv) Assuming cost of construction ₹ 4000/- per sq.m., find cost of construction.

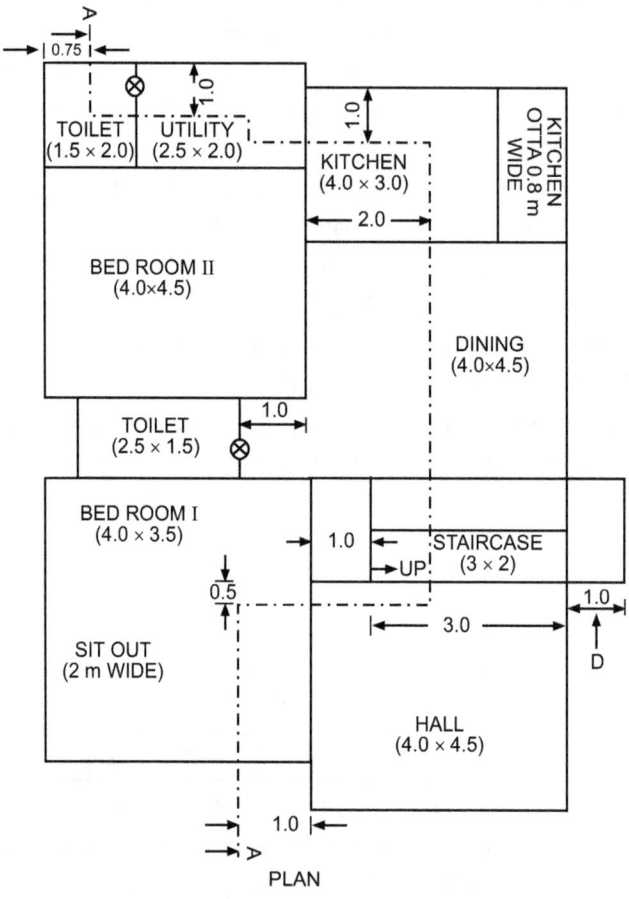

Fig. 2.11

6. A line plan for a residential building is given in Fig. 2.12. Draw to a scale of 1 : 50 or suitable:

   (a) Detailed plan for RCC framed structure.

   – All external walls and those marked ⊗ are 230 mm thick.

   – All internal walls are 115 mm thick.

   (b) Detailed section A-A assuming depth of foundation 1200 mm below G.L. Floor to floor height is 3150 mm. Riser – 175 mm, Tread – 250 mm.

   (c) Calculate X and Y dimensions.

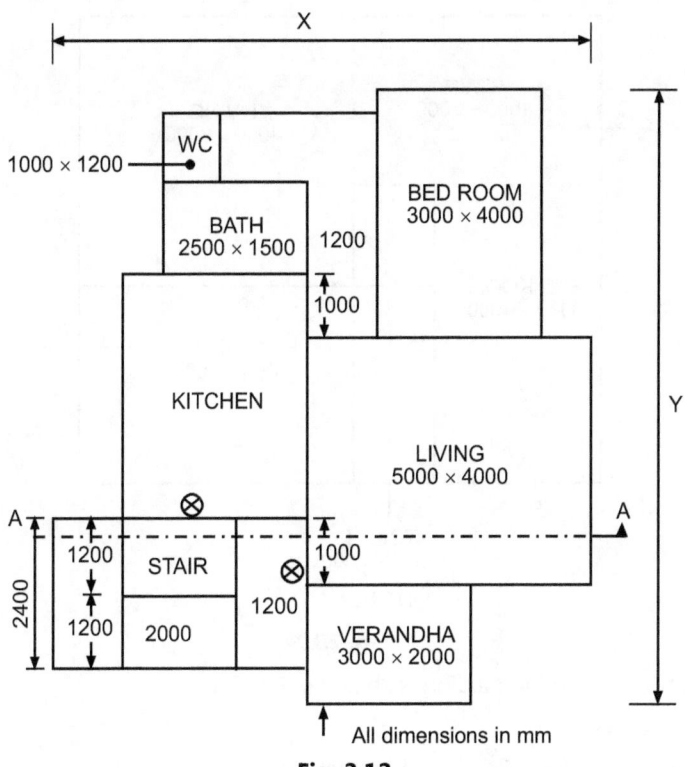

Fig. 2.12

7. Develop the line plan shown in Fig. 2.13. Scale 1 : 50.

   (i) Draw detailed plan.

   Wall thickness: external 230 thick.

   internal 150 thick.

   Doors standard size as per IS code.

   Window opening 15% of room area.

   Proof pitched to 30 degrees, hipped end, RCC.

   Assume other relevant details.

   (ii) Draw detailed section showing

   (a) Stair details

   (b) W.C. details

   (c) Foundation details.

   (iii) Prepare budget. Assume cost ₹ 5,000/- per sq.m. Calculate cost of building.

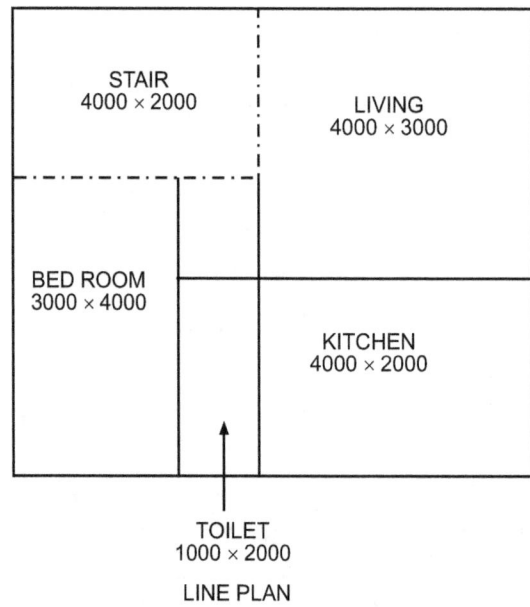

LINE PLAN

Fig. 2.13

8. A plan for a residential building is shown in Fig. 2.14.

   Draw to scale of 1 : 50

   (1) Detailed plan for R.C.C. framed structure.

   Take: External walls 230 thick

   Internal walls 115 thick

   Column size 230 × 450

   (2) Detailed section S.S.

   The different levels are:

   - Foundation level   − 1200
   - Ground level   − 450
   - Plinth level   ± 000
   - Sill level   − 900
   - Lintel level   − 2100
   - Slab level   − 3000
   - Slab above stair   − 3900

   (3) Write schedule for doors and windows.

   (4) Show North direction.

   (5) Calculate X and Y dimensions.

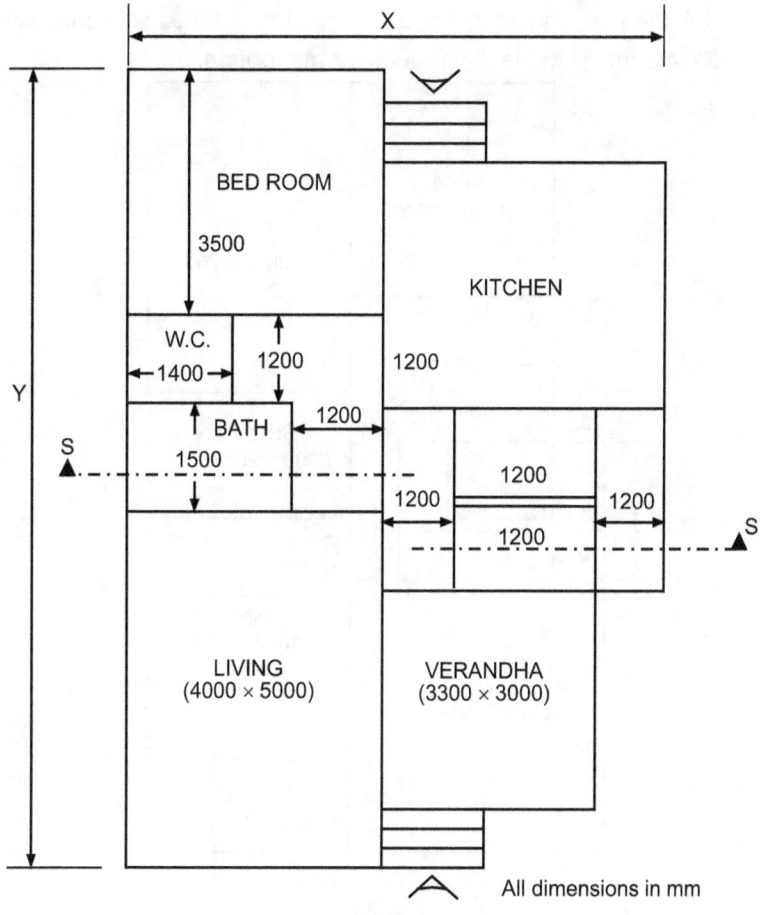

Fig. 2.14

9. (a) Draw a detailed floor plan to a scale 1 : 50 or suitable of a residential building for a given line plan as shown in Fig. 2.15.

   Data:
   1. The structure is load bearing
   2. All dimensions are in mm
   3. Thicknesses of all walls are 230 mm and those marked by encircled X are 115 mm thick.
   4. The building is single storey.
   5. Assume proper sizes of doors and windows.
   6. Consider plinth height as 900 mm (0.9 m)
   7. Give the detailed dimensions.

(b) For the line plan shown in Fig. 2.15 draw the detailed sectional elevation along line XY, assume suitable dimensions for the footing:

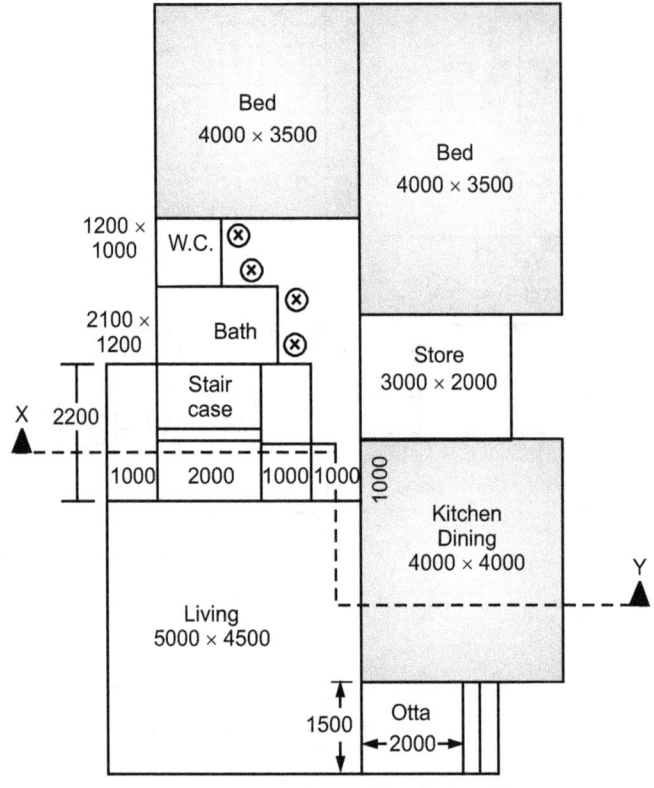

All dimensions in mm
Fig. 2.15

10. (a) Draw detailed plan to a scale a 1 : 50 of a residential building for the line plan shown in Fig. 2.16.

    Fig. 2.16 is not to scale.

    Refer the following guidelines:
    (1) The structure is load bearing.
    (2) All the walls are 230 mm thick.
    (3) The building has got ground floor only.
    (4) Access to the terrace is provided through staircase.
    (5) All dimensions are in mm.
    (6) Assume suitable sizes of doors and windows.
    (7) Locate doors and windows at suitable positions.
    (8) Provide sufficient number of doors and windows.
    (9) Take plinth height = 600 mm.
    (10) R.C.C. slab is provided on all rooms.

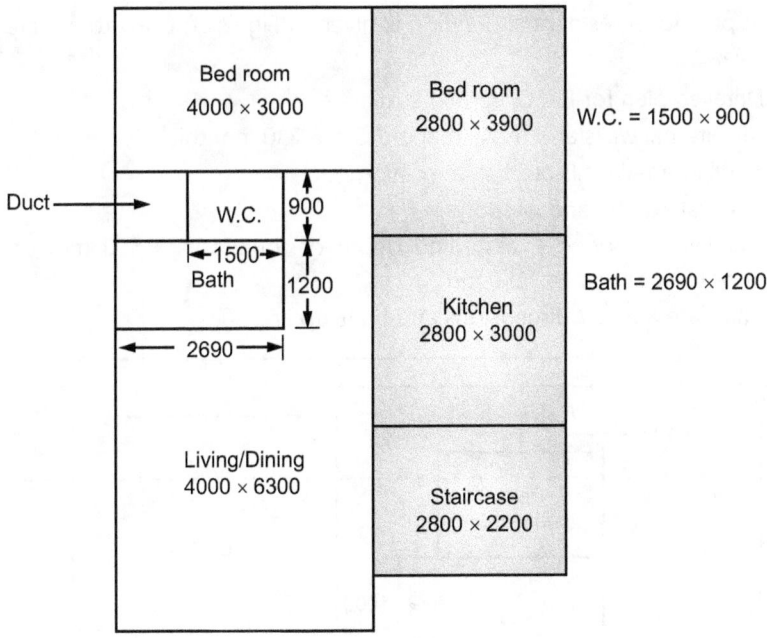

Fig. 2.16

(b) Write detailed schedule for doors and windows as per the format given:

Sr. No.	Type of door/window	No. of doors/windows	Size of opening in mm

11. Plan a residential building having G + 1 framed structure with the following requirements:

Sr. No.	Type of unit	No. of Units	Internal Area of Unit in sq. m.
1.	Living room	01	18
2.	Bed room	02	12
3.	Additional bed room with attached toilet	01	16
4.	Kitchen	01	12
5.	W.C.	01	1.5
6.	Bath	01	2.8
7.	Staircase	01	Use suitable dimensions

12. A line plan for a residential building is given in Fig. 2.17. Draw to a scale of 1 : 50 or suitable: ....
    (a) Detailed plan for R.C.C. framed structure:
        All external walls and those marked ⊗ are 230 mm thick:
        1. All internal walls are 115 mm thick;
        2. Locate doors and windows.
    (b) Detailed section A-A assuming depth of foundation 1500 mm below GL and floor to floor height 3150 mm.
    (c) Calculate X and Y dimensions and built-up area.

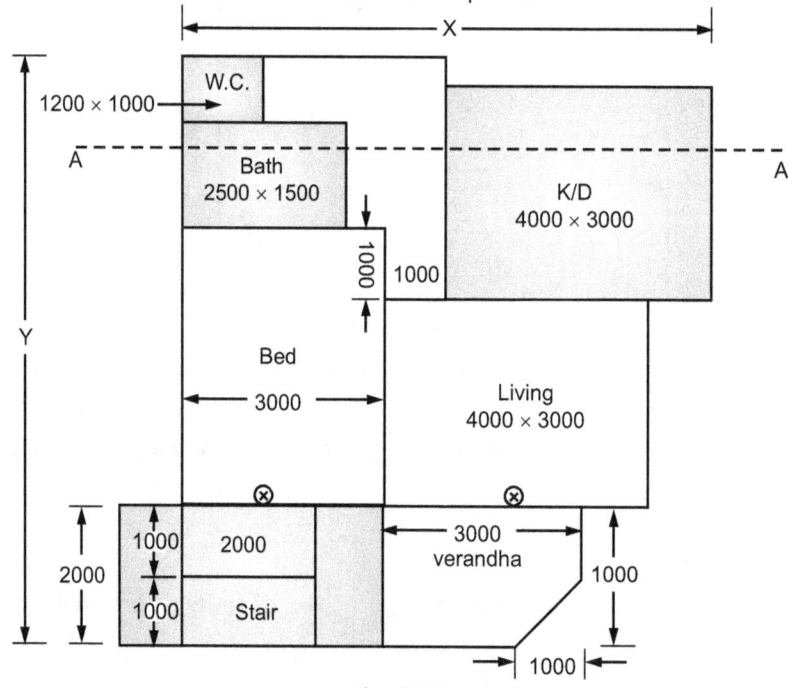

Fig. 2.17

All dimensions in mm
All external walls and those marked ⊗ are 230 thick
All internal walls are 115 thick.

13. A line plan for a residential building is given in Fig. 2.18. Draw to a scale of 1 : 50 or suitable: ....
    (a) Detailed sectional plan for R.C.C. framed structure.
        • All external walls and those of the staircase room are 230 mm thick.
        • All internal walls are 115 m thick. Locate doors and windows.
    (b) Locate columns of size 230 mm × 400 mm.
    (c) Show northline to orient the building.

(d) Detailed Section A-A, assuming depth of foundation 1000 mm below ground level. Floor to floor height is 3150 mm.

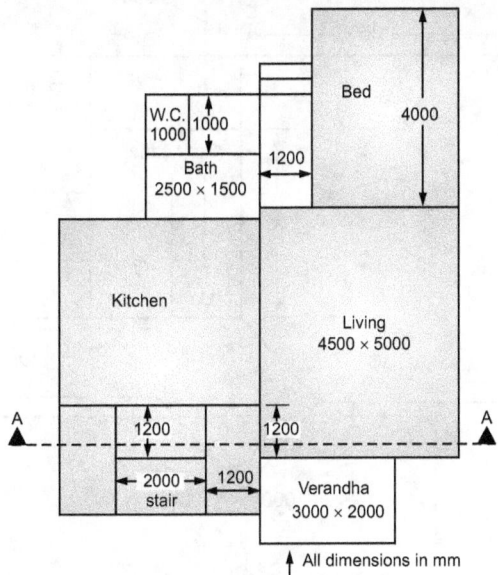

Fig. 2.18

14. Develop the line plan shown in Fig. 2.19.

    Data: Wall external BBM 230 tk.
    - Wall internal BBM 150 tk.
    - Door – As per IS code.
    - Windows – Opening 10% of floor area.
    - RCC framed structure.
    - Assume other details and state them clearly.

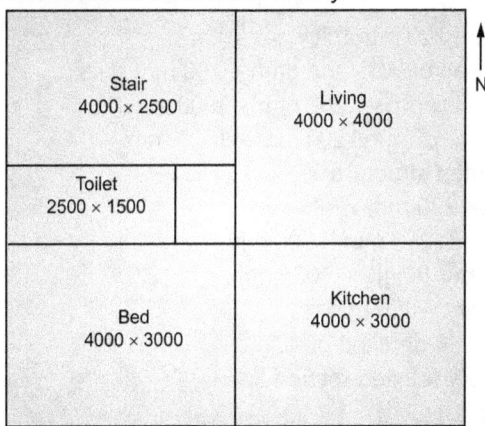

All dimensions in mm

Fig. 2.19

15. A line for a Residential Building is shown in Fig. 2.20.

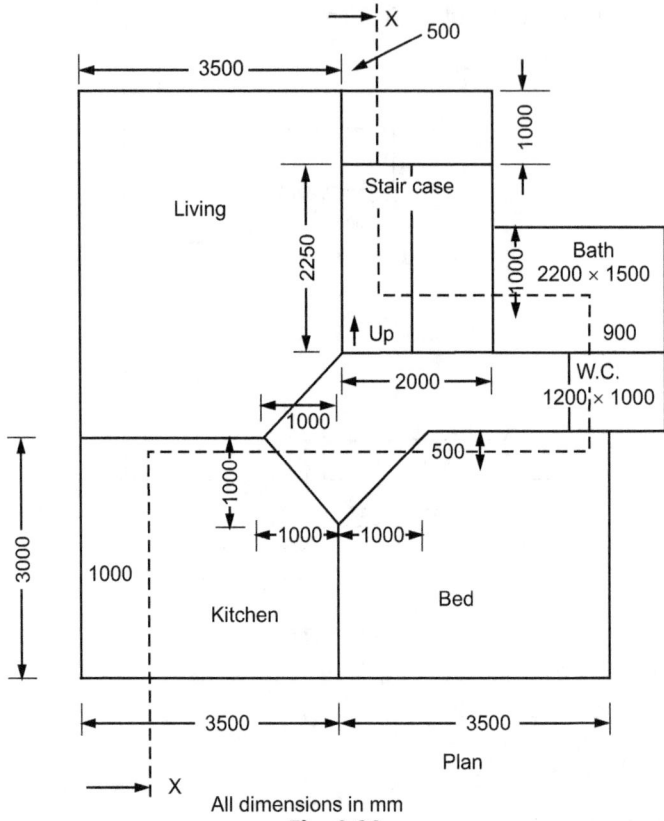

All dimensions in mm
Fig. 2.20

Data:
    (a) All walls are 230 mm thick.
    (b) Partition wall of W.C. and Bath – 100 mm thick.
    (c) Size of W.C. room – 1200 mm × 1000 mm.
    (d) Size of Bath room – 2200 mm × 1500 mm.
    (e) R.C.C. framed structure.
    (f) Beam sizes 230 mm × 380 mm.
    (g) Column sizes 230 mm × 300 mm.
    (h) Floor to floor height – 3000 mm.
    (i) Plinth height – 450 mm.

(i) Draw to a scale 1 : 50 detailed plan.
(ii) Draw to scale 1 : 50 detailed section XX.
(iii) Calculate Built-up area.
(iv) Show design calculations for a staircase.
(v) Show entrance steps at proper location in plan.

16. A line plan for a residential building is given in Fig. 2.21. Draw to scale of 1 : 50 or suitable:

   (a) Detailed plan for R.C.C. framed structure:
   - All external walls and those marked are 230 mm thick.
   - All internal walls are 115 mm thick
   - Locate doors, windows and columns of size 230 mm × 400 mm.

   (b) Detailed section AA assuming depth of foundation 1500 mm below ground level. Floor to floor height 3150 mm. Floor to ceiling height 3000 mm. Rise 175 mm, tread – 250 mm for R.C.C. stair.

   (c) Write schedule for doors and windows.

   (d) Calculate X and Y.

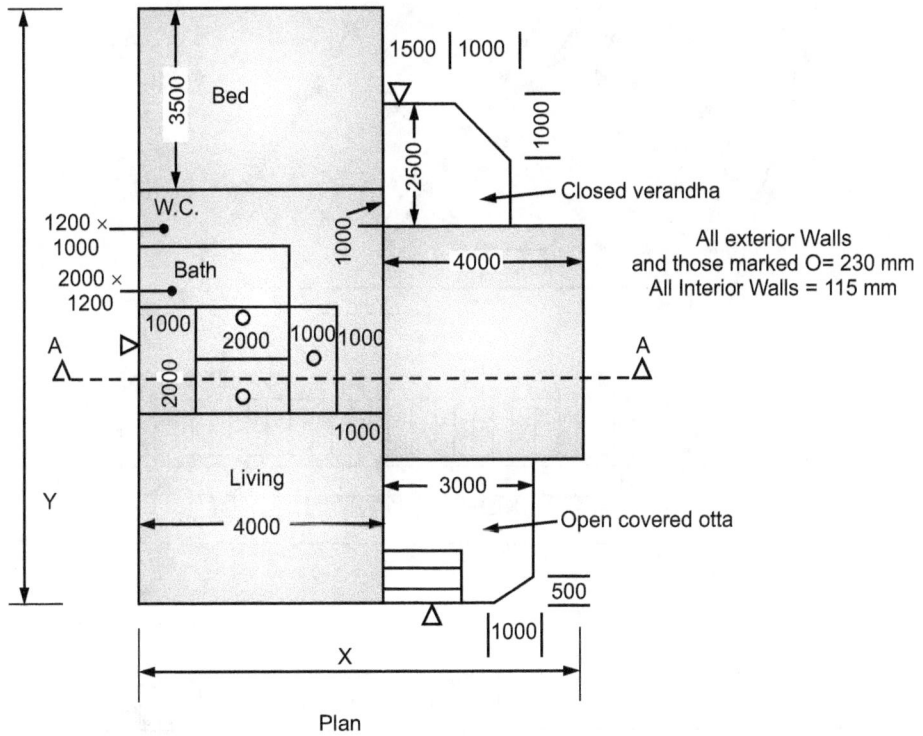

Plan

Fig. 2.21

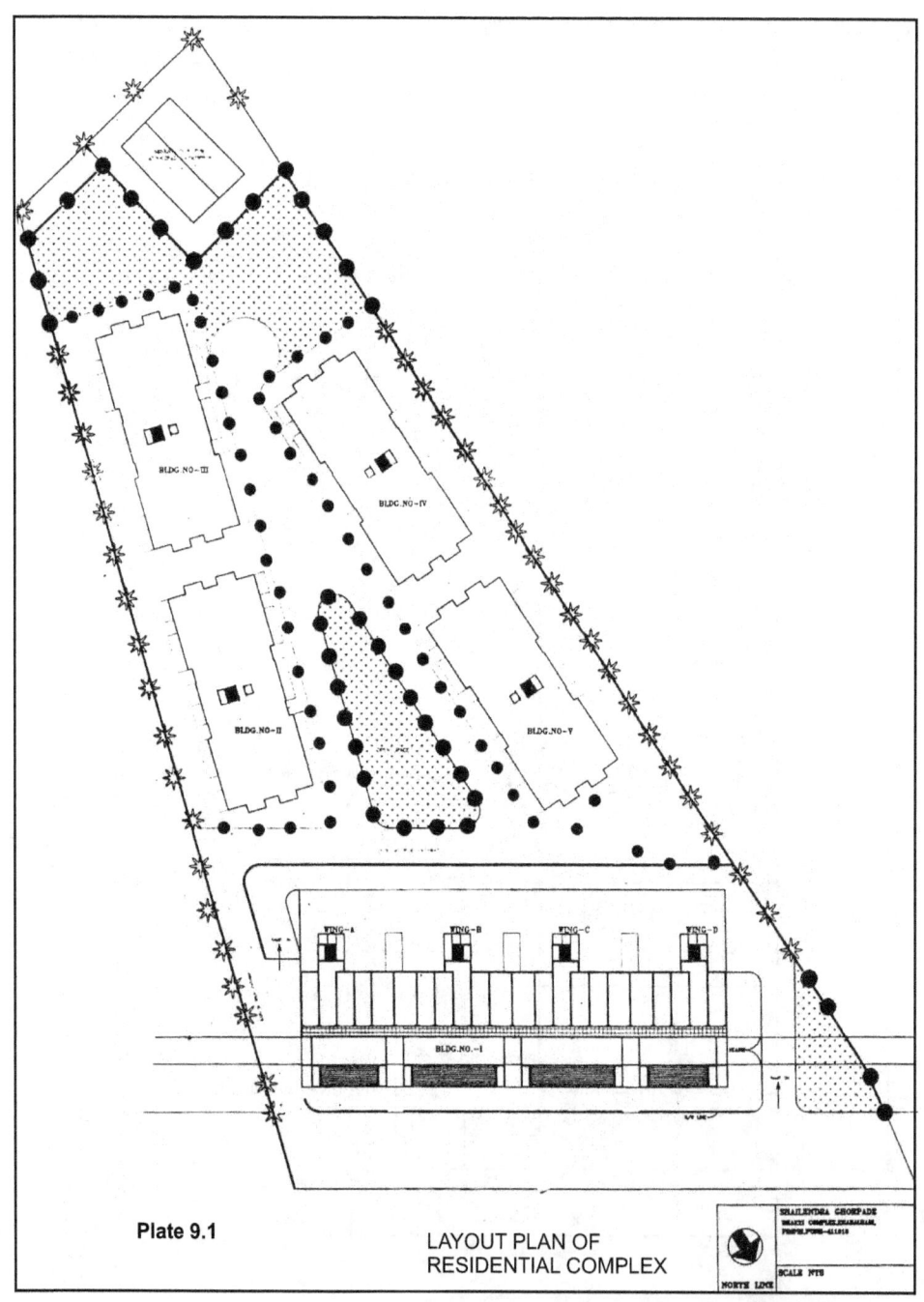

Plate 9.1 LAYOUT PLAN OF RESIDENTIAL COMPLEX

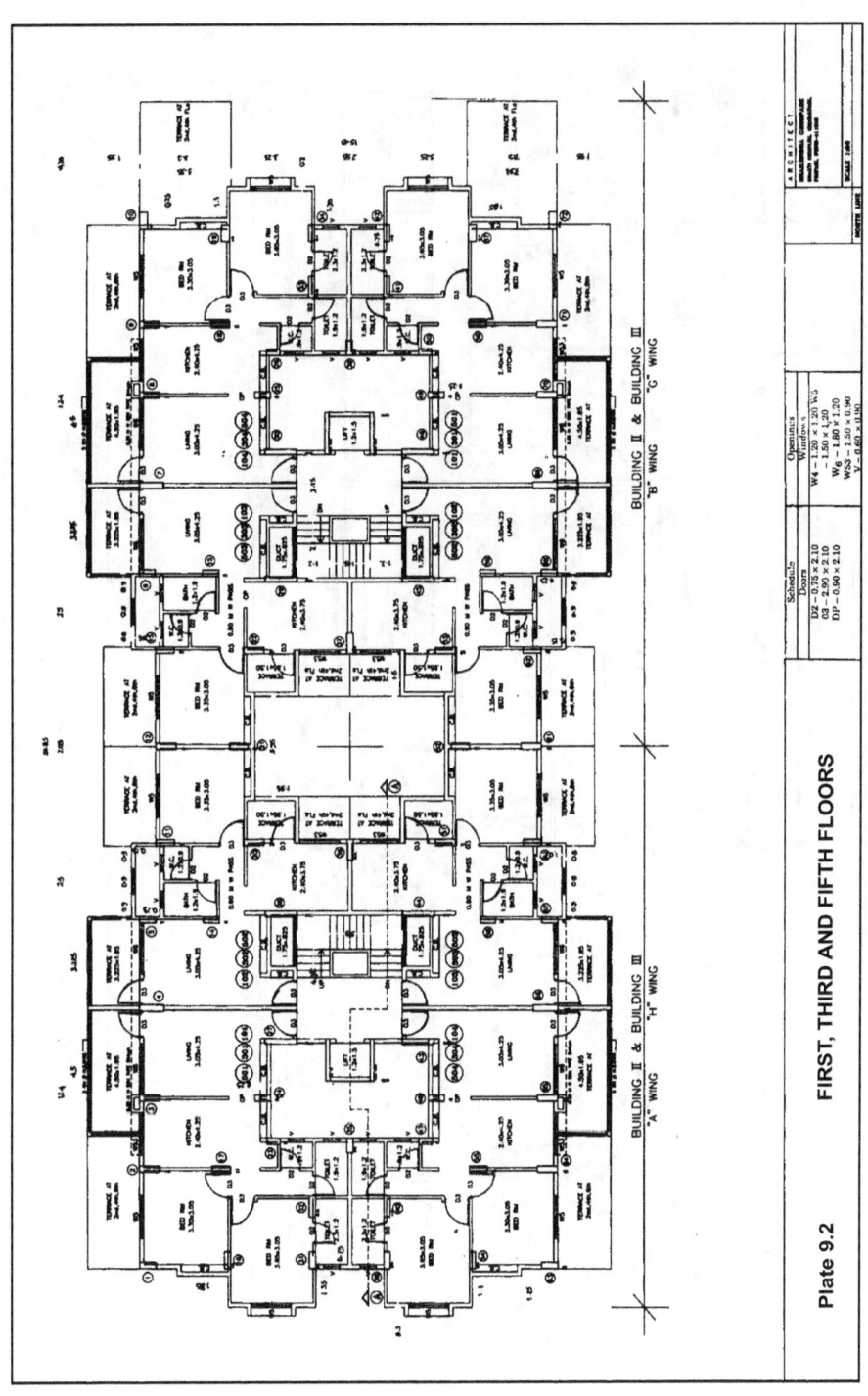

Plate 9.2 FIRST, THIRD AND FIFTH FLOORS

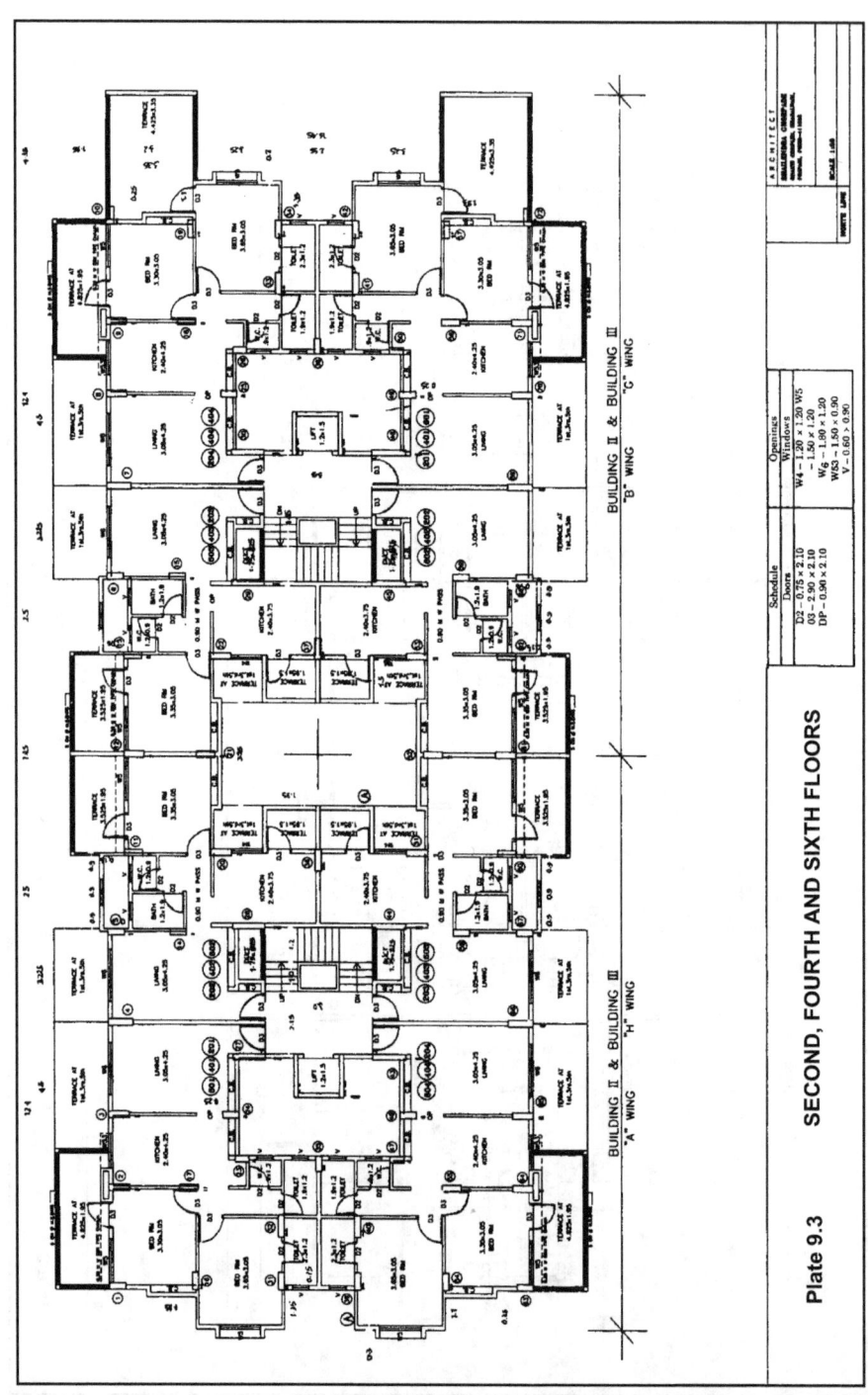

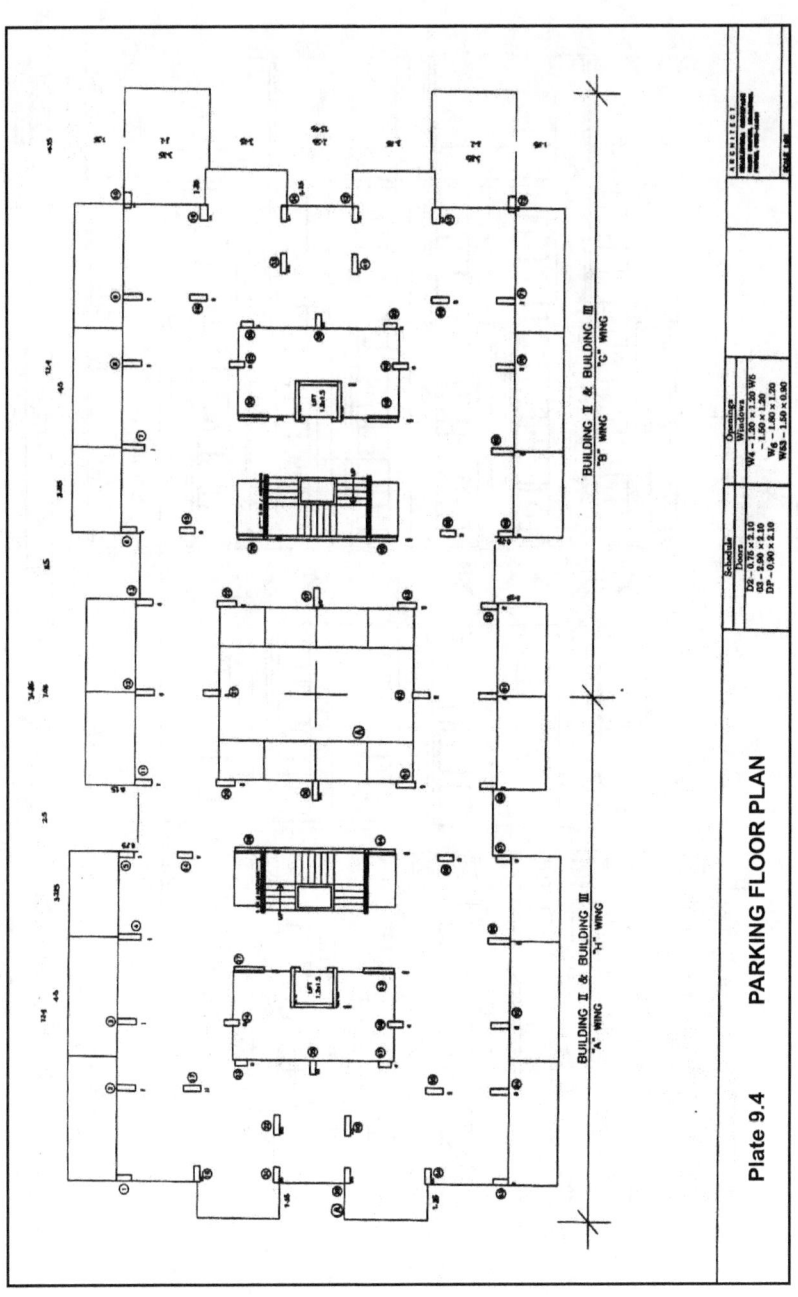

Plate 9.4 PARKING FLOOR PLAN

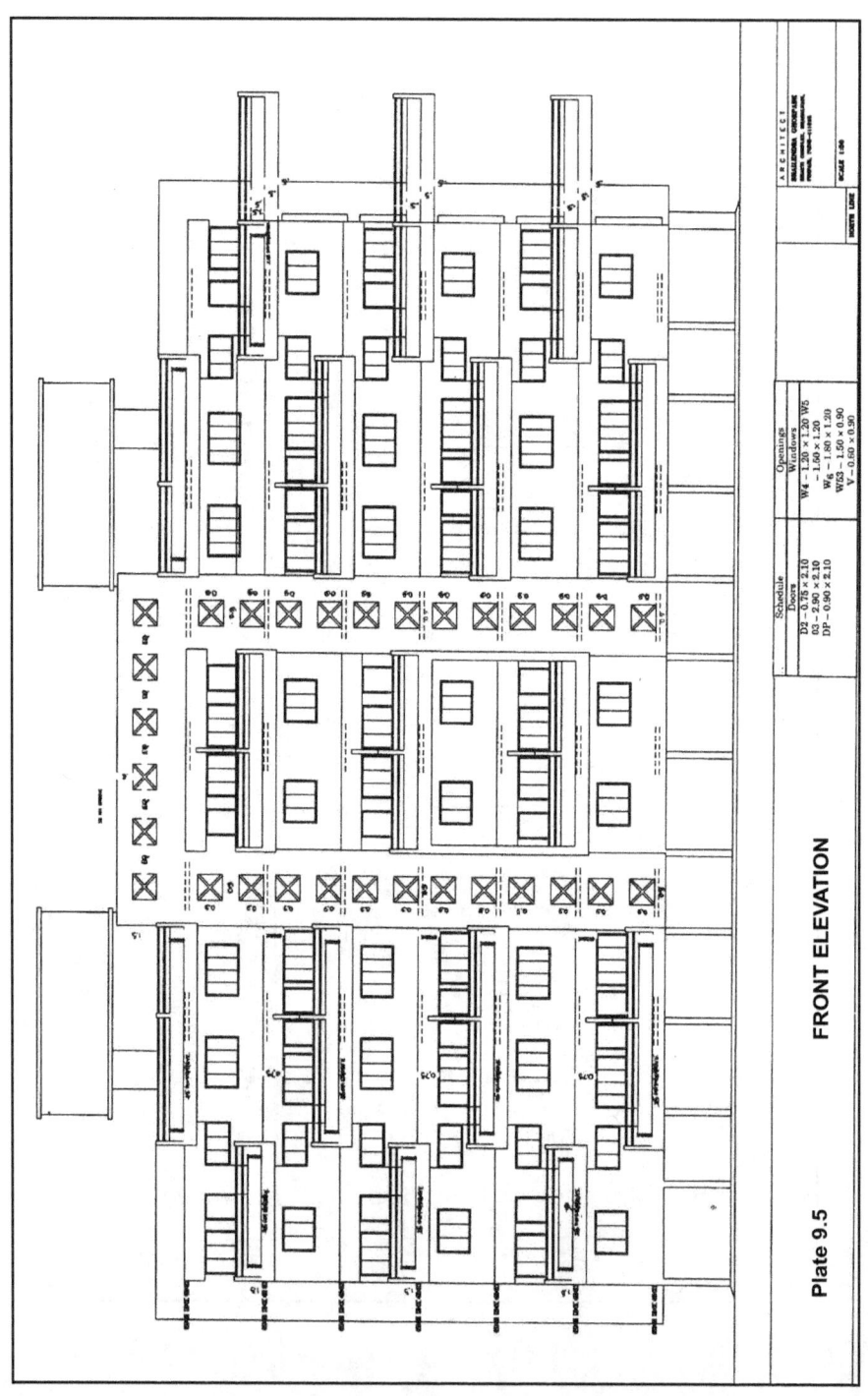

Plate 9.5 FRONT ELEVATION

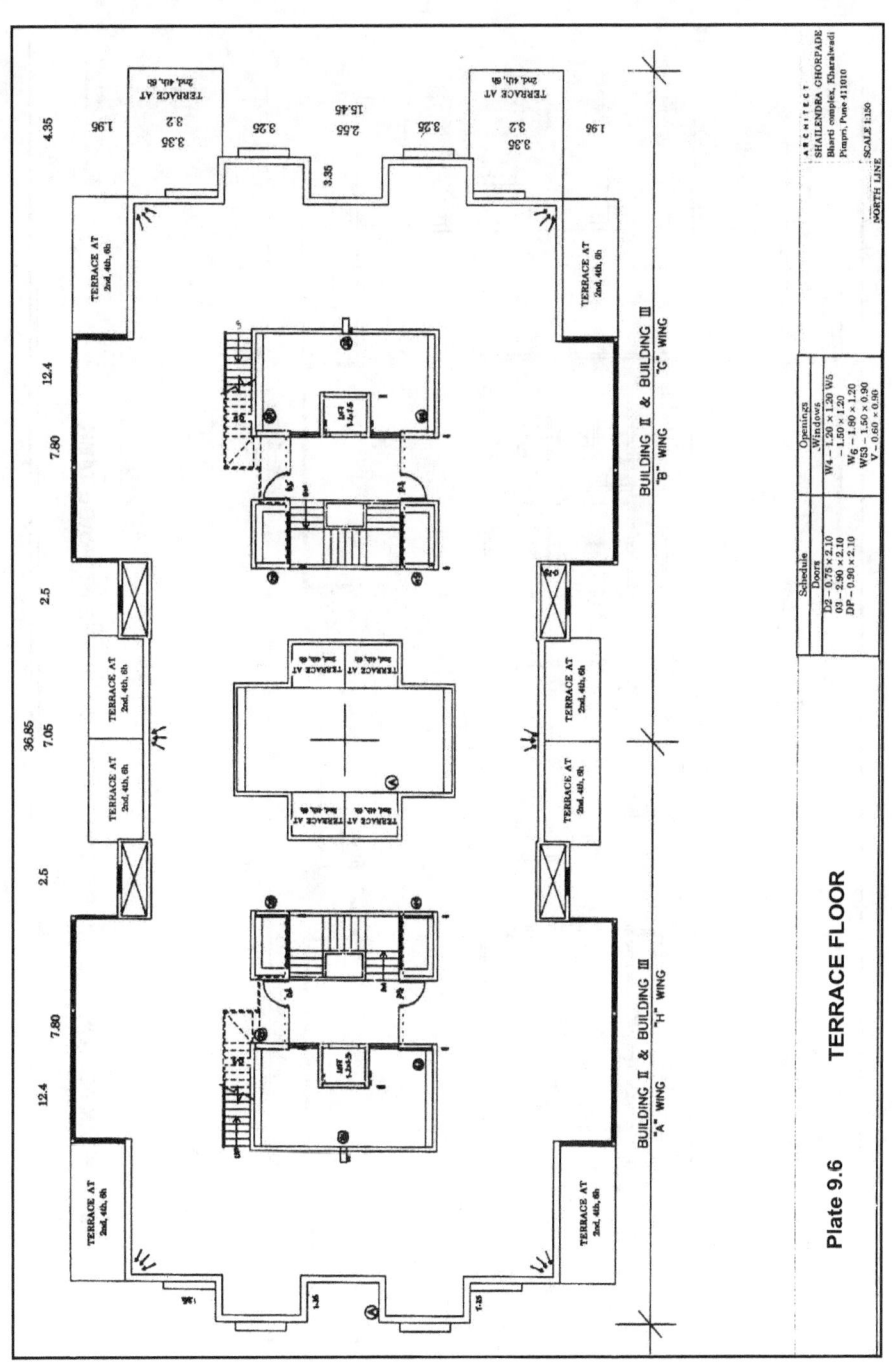

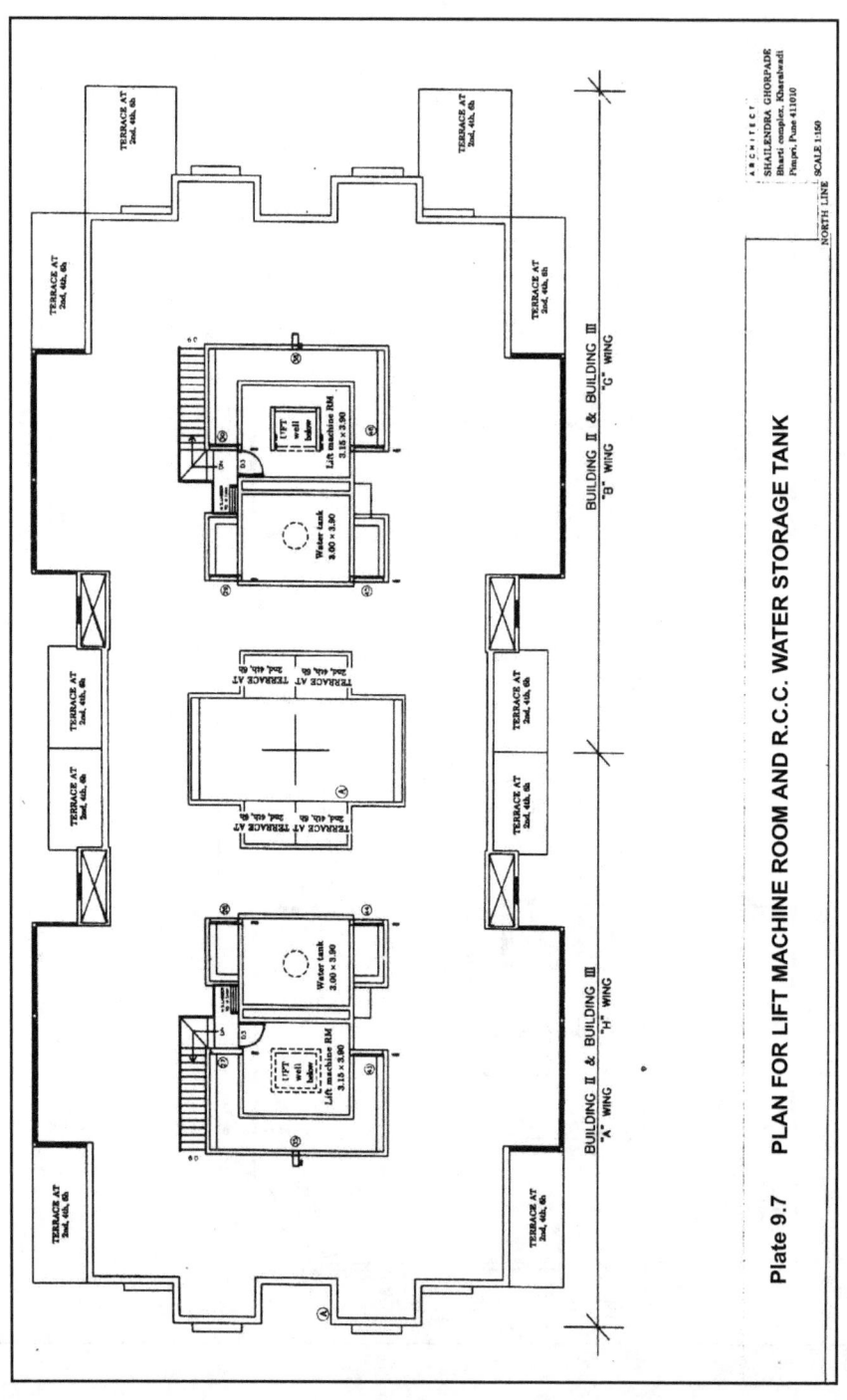

Plate 9.7 PLAN FOR LIFT MACHINE ROOM AND R.C.C. WATER STORAGE TANK

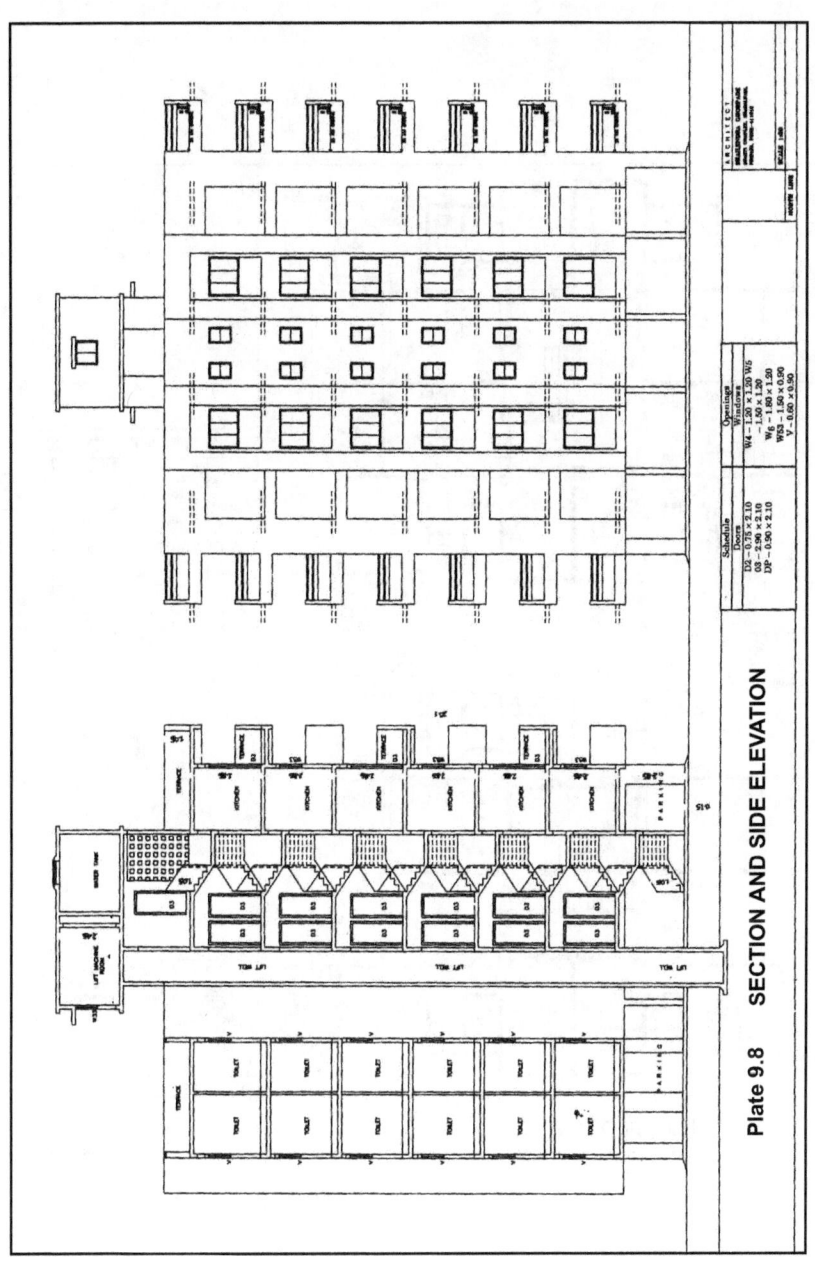

Plate 9.8 SECTION AND SIDE ELEVATION

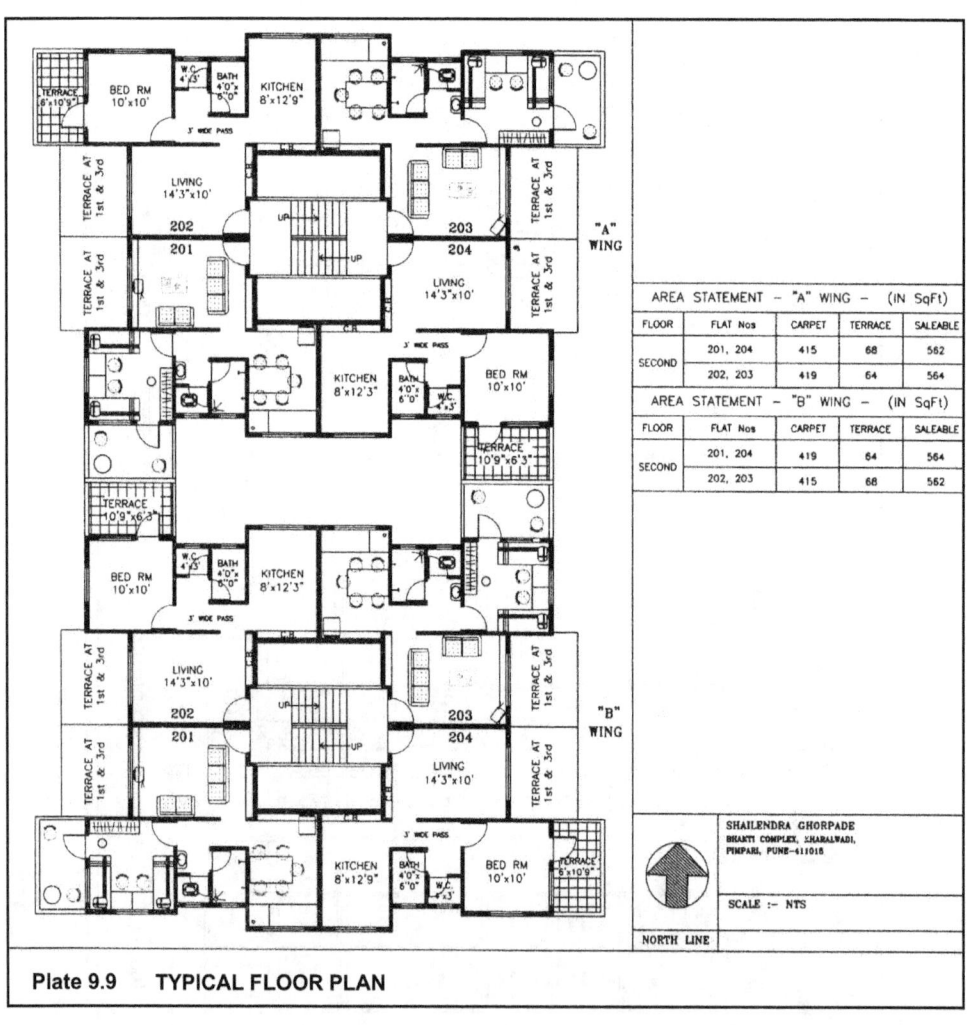

Plate 9.9 TYPICAL FLOOR PLAN

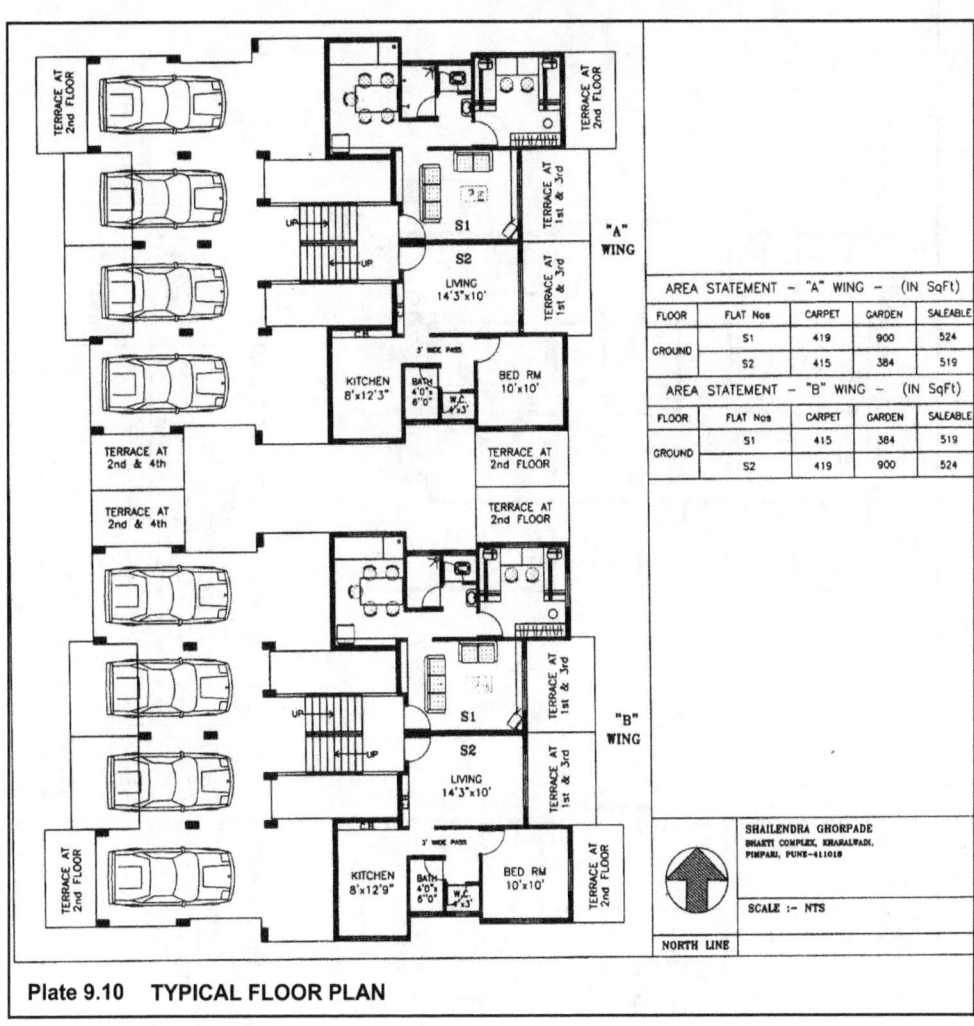

Plate 9.10 TYPICAL FLOOR PLAN

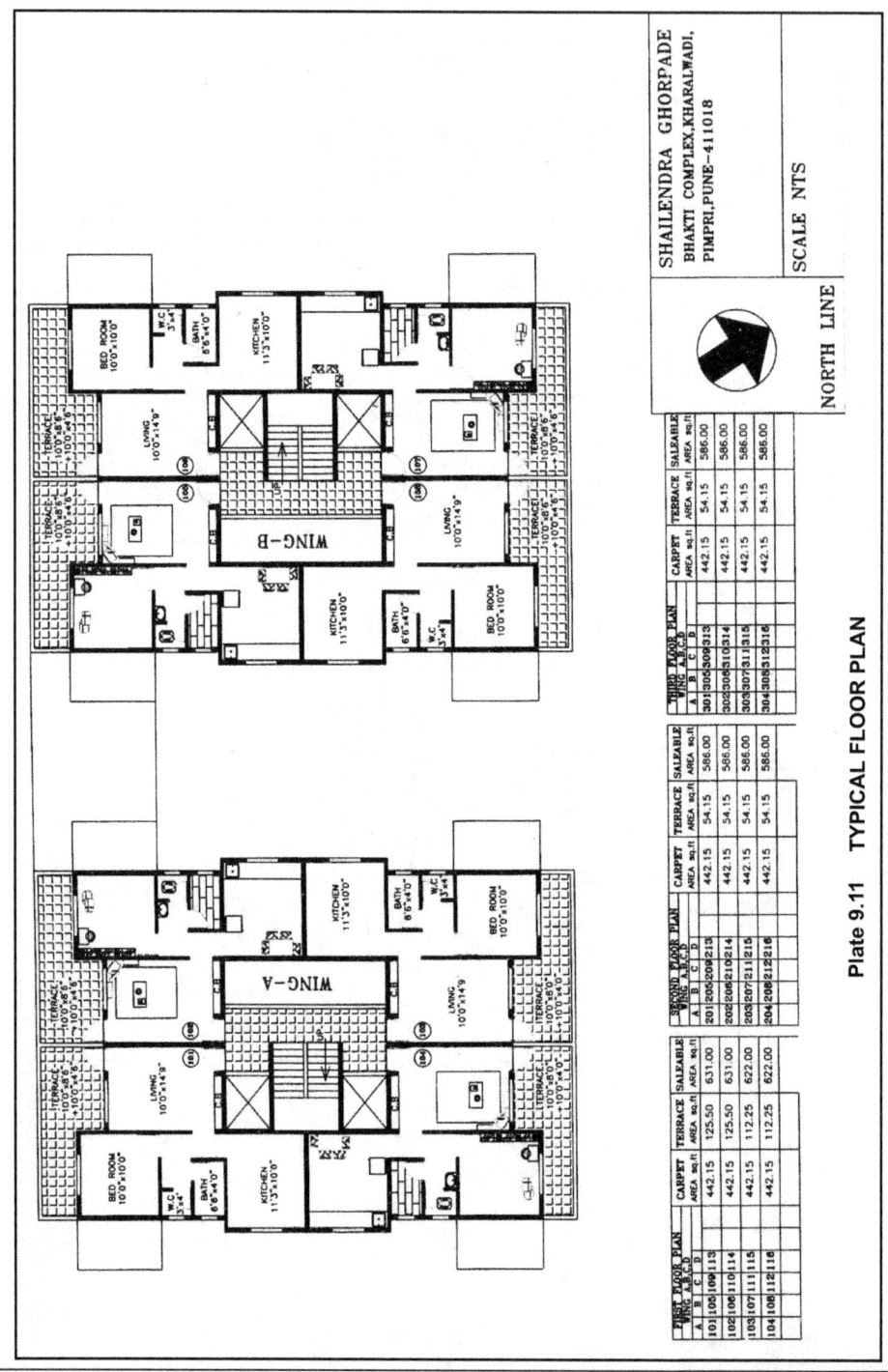

Plate 9.11 TYPICAL FLOOR PLAN

Plate 9.12 TYPICAL FIRST AND THIRD FLOOR PLAN

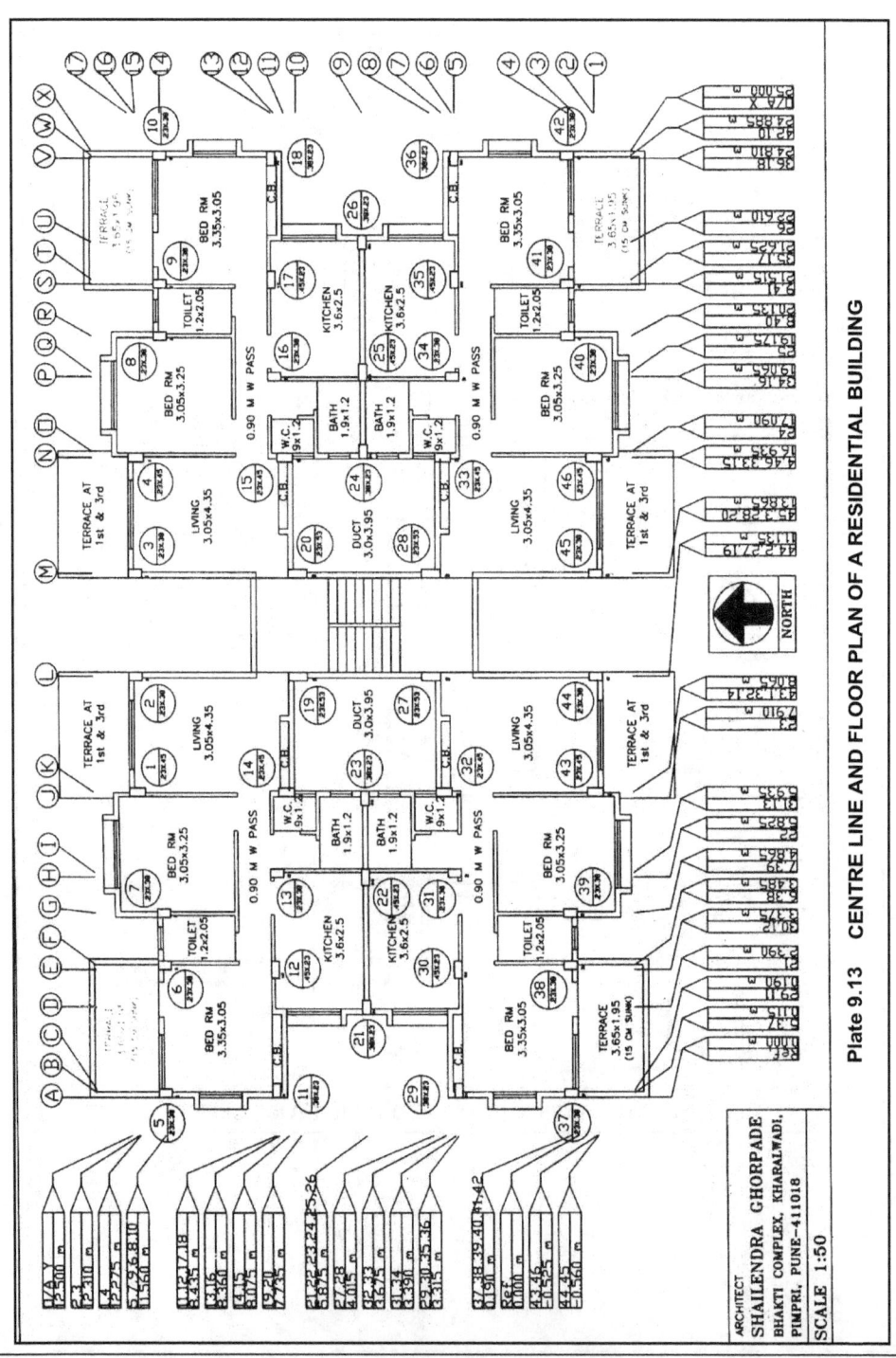

Plate 9.13 CENTRE LINE AND FLOOR PLAN OF A RESIDENTIAL BUILDING

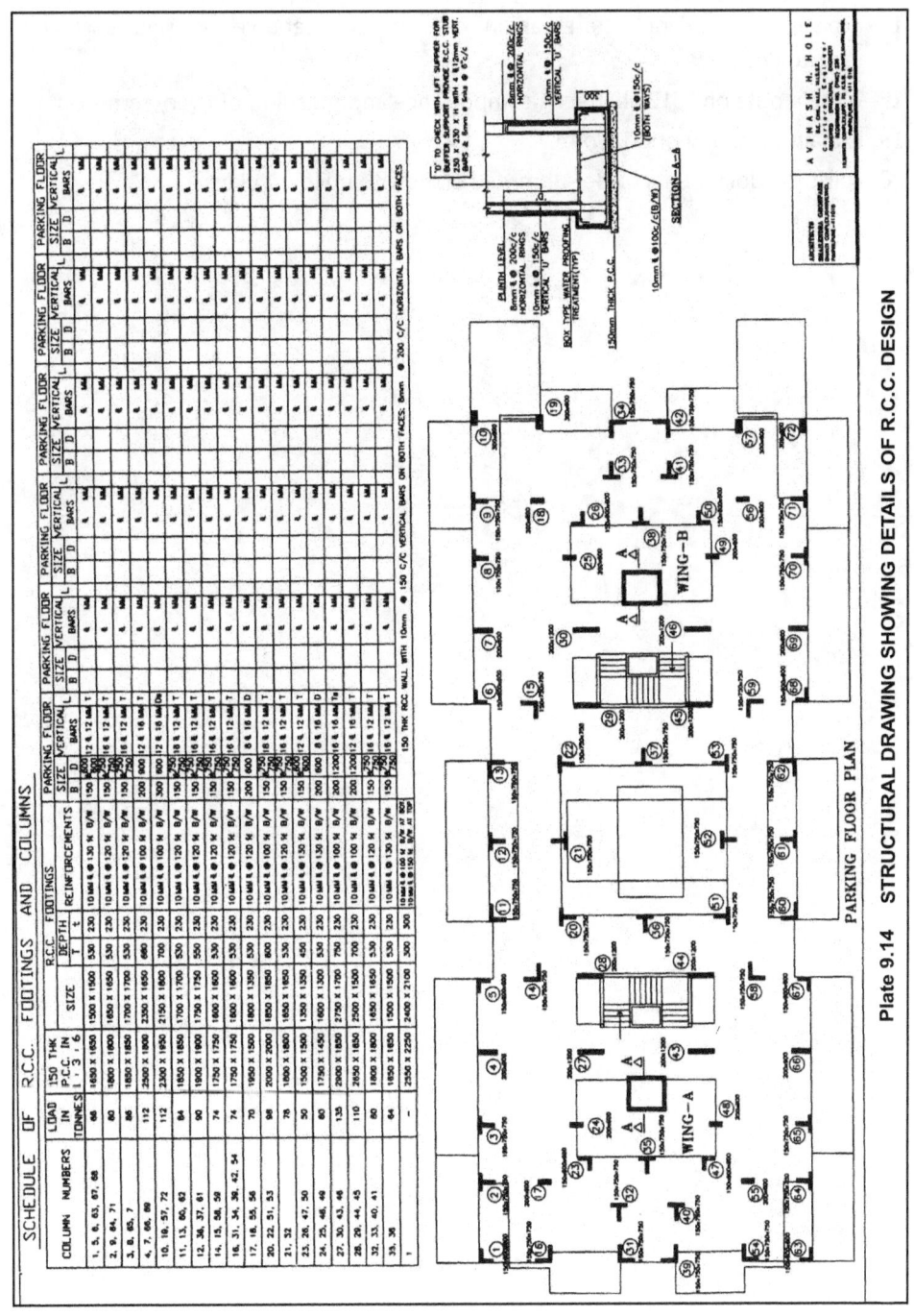

Plate 9.14 STRUCTURAL DRAWING SHOWING DETAILS OF R.C.C. DESIGN

17. Explain the working strategies in case of co-operative housing societies and apartments.
18. Write a note on 7/12 abstract, its importance and meaning of every terms on it.
19. Explain the utility of 6-D form.
20. Enlist the documents to be submitted alongwith building plans.

■■■

Unit 3
LOW COST HOUSING

3.1 LOW COST

Low Cost Housing is a new concept which deals with effective budgeting and following of techniques which help in reducing the cost construction through the use of locally available materials along with improved skills and technology without sacrificing the strength, performance and life of the structure. There is huge misconception that low cost housing is suitable for only sub-standard works and they are constructed by utilizing cheap building materials of low quality. The fact is that low cost housing is done by proper management of resources. Economy is also achieved by postponing finishing works or implementing them in phases.

3.1.1 Building Cost

The building construction cost can be divided into two parts namely:

Building material cost: 65 to 70%

Labour cost: 65 to 70%

Now in low cost housing, building material cost is less because we make use of the locally available materials and also the labour cost can be reduced by properly making the time schedule of our work. Cost of reduction is achieved by selection of more efficient material or by an improved design.

Areas from where cost can be reduced are:

- Reduce plinth area by using thinner wall concept. For example: 15 cm thick solid concrete block wall.
- Use locally available material in an innovative form like soil cement blocks in place of burnt brick.
- Use energy efficiency materials which consume less energy like concrete block in place of burnt brick.
- Use environmentally friendly materials which are substitute for conventional building components like use R.C.C. door and window frames in place of wooden frames.
- Preplan every component of a house and rationalize the design procedure for reducing the size of the component in the building.

- By planning each and every component of a house the wastage of materials due to demolition of the unplanned component of the house can be avoided.
- Each component of the house shall be checked whether if it is necessary, if it is not necessary, then that component should not be used.

3.1.2 Cost Reduction Methods

Foundation:

Normally, the foundation cost comes to about 10 to 15% of the total building and usually foundation depth of 3 to 4 ft is adopted for single or double store building and also the concrete bed of 6"(15 cm) is used for the foundation which could be avoided.

It is recommended to adopt a foundation depth of 2 ft (0.6 m) for normal soil like gravely soil, red soils etc., and use the uncoursed rubble masonry with the bond stones and good packing. Similarly the foundation width is rationalized to 2 ft (0.6 m). To avoid cracks formation in foundation the masonry shall be thoroughly packed with cement mortar of 1 : 8 boulders and bond stones at regular intervals.

It is further suggested adopt arch foundation in ordinary soil for effecting reduction in construction cost up to 40%. This kind of foundation will help in bridging the loose pockets of soil which occurs along the foundation.

In the case black cotton and other soft soils it is recommend to use under ream pile foundation which saves about 20 to 25% in cost over the conventional method of construction.

Plinth:

It is suggested to adopt 1 ft height above ground level for the plinth and may be constructed with a cement mortar of 1 : 6. The plinth slab of 4 to 6" which is normally adopted can be avoided and in its place brick on edge can be used for reducing the cost. By adopting this procedure the cost of plinth foundation can be reduced by about 35 to 50%. It is necessary to take precaution of providing impervious blanket like concrete slabs or stone slabs all round the building for enabling to reduce erosion of soil and thereby avoiding exposure of foundation surface and crack formation.

Walling:

Wall thickness of 6 to 9" is recommended for adoption in the construction of walls all-round the building and 41/2" for inside walls. It is suggested to use burnt bricks which are immersed in water for 24 hours and then shall be used for the walls.

RAT - Trap Bond Wall:

It is a cavity wall construction with added advantage of thermal comfort and reduction in the quantity of bricks required for masonry work. By adopting this method of bonding of brick masonry compared to traditional English or Flemish bond masonry, it is possible to reduce in the material cost of bricks by 25% and about 10 to 15% in the masonry cost. By adopting rat-trap bond method one can create aesthetically pleasing wall surface and plastering can be avoided.

Concrete Block Walling

In view of high energy consumption by burnt brick it is suggested to use concrete block (block hollow and solid) which consumes about only 1/3 of the energy of the burnt bricks in its production. By using concrete block masonry the wall thickness can be reduced from 20 cm to 15 cm. Concrete block masonry saves mortar consumption, speedy construction of wall resulting in higher output of labour, plastering can be avoided thereby an overall saving of 10 to 25% can be achieved.

Soil Cement Block Technology:

It is an alternative method of construction of walls using soil cement blocks in place of burnt bricks masonry. It is an energy efficient method of construction where soil mixed with 5% and above cement and pressed in hand operated machine and cured well and then used in the masonry. This masonry does not require plastering on both sides of the wall. The overall economy that could be achieved with the soil cement technology is about 15 to 20% compared to conventional method of construction.

Doors and Windows:

It is suggested not to use wood for doors and windows and in its place concrete or steel section frames shall be used for achieving saving in cost upto 30 to 40%. Similarly for shutters commercially available black boards, fibre or wooden practical boards etc., shall be used for reducing the cost by about 25%. By adopting brick jelly work and precast components, effective ventilation could be provided to the building and also the construction cost could be saved upto 50% over the window components.

Lintels and Chajjas:

The traditional RCC lintels which are costly can be replaced by brick arches for small spans and save construction cost upto 30 to 40% over the traditional method of construction. By adopting arches of different shapes, a good architectural pleasing appearance can be given to the external wall surfaces of the brick masonry.

Roofing

Normally 5"(12.5 cm) thick RCC slabs are used for roofing of residential buildings. By adopting rationally designed insitu construction practices like filler slab and precast elements the construction cost of roofing can be reduced by about 20 to 25%.

Filler Slabs

They are normal RCC slabs where bottom half (tension) concrete portions are replaced by filler materials such as bricks, tiles, cellular concrete blocks, etc. These filler materials are so placed as not to compromise structural strength, result in replacing unwanted and non-functional tension concrete, thus resulting in economy. These are safe, sound and provide aesthetically pleasing pattern ceilings and also need no plaster.

For more on filler materials check Filler Materials Used in Concrete.

Jack Arch Roof/Floor:

They are easy to construct, save on cement and steel, are more appropriate in hot climates. These can be constructed using compressed earth blocks also as alternative to bricks for further economy.

Ferrocement Channel/shell Unit:

Provide an economic solution to RCC slab by providing 30 to 40% cost reduction on floor/roof unit over RCC slabs without compromising the strength. These being precast, construction is speedy, economical due to avoidance of shuttering and facilitate quality control.

Finishing Work:

The cost of finishing items like sanitary, electricity, painting etc., varies depending upon the type and quality of products used in the building and its cost reduction is left to the individual choice and liking.

Conclusion:

The above list of suggestion for reducing construction cost is of general nature and it varies depending upon the nature of the building to be constructed, budget of the owner, geographical location where the house is to be constructed, availability of the building material, good construction management practices etc. However it is necessary that good planning and design methods shall be adopted by utilizing the services of an experienced engineer or an architect for supervising the work, thereby achieving overall cost effectiveness to the extent of 25% in actual practice.

3.2 REPAIRS AND REHABILITATION OF BUILDINGS

The existing buildings nearing its serviceability life and showing sign of breakdown does calls for technical intervention for enhancing their life and to avoid any accidental failure due to seismic event or other structural reason. The deterioration of the structures takes place due to Weathering action, Fire, Natural calamities like earthquake, Flood, Tsunami, Cyclones, soil and structure interaction (settlement of soil or soil failure), defects in construction and many more. Post the technical evaluation of such structures, the decision to repair or replace a structure or its component has to be taken. This has to be in compliance with economy, construction, feasibility and as per latest trends and techniques.

The approach towards rehabilitation of any building can be categorized in following steps and actions.

- Performing a Structural Audit of the building.
- Evaluating various retrofitting options, materials, feasibility and economy.
- Performing structural calculations and capacity demand ratio for structural members.
- Suggesting retrofitting/construction system and getting the rehabilitation of the building done.
- Post retrofitting tests on the building.

3.2.1 Rehabilitation of Buildings

1. Structural Audit

Structural Audit forms a preliminary step towards rehabilitation of buildings. Health assessment/structural audit of any existing structure, do determine whether its functionality is as per desired and acceptable. It ensures the existing structure is thoroughly inspected as per relevant codes, techniques and the serviceability of the structure is judged based on it. It is an activity where actual data related to civil structures is observed, measured, registered and conclusions are drawn. This is performed through all times by responsible designers, contractors and owners with almost identical objectives to check that the existing structures behave as intended. The Audit helps to understand critical areas to repair and enhance life cycle of building by suggesting preventive and corrective measures like repairs and retrofitting.

As per the Cooperative Housing Societies Bye-laws, structural Audit is also mandatory in India. It has to be performed once in 5 years for buildings aging between 15 to 30 years and every 3 years for buildings having age above 30 years.

Non-destructive tests which do not alter the original properties of the structural members are performed on the structure. The information on these tests is available in A.C.I. 228, IS 13311 (Part 1 and Part 2) 1992. Few of the widely used tests, but not limited to, for estimation of strength of concrete in place are proposed below.

- Rebound Hammer test
- Ultra Sonic Pulse Velocity
- Probe Penetration Rehabilitation of Buildings 335
- Pull Out
- Break Off
- Maturity Method
- Core Testing (ASTM 42) IS 516 & IS 1199
- Infrared Thermography
- X-Ray & Gamma Radiometric Methods
- Destructive tests that may be performed on the concrete are listed below.
- Gravimetric Technique (Weight Loss Method)

2. Approaches towards Retrofitting of Buildings

The engineering which involves in modifying the existing buildings for structural behaviour without hampering its basic intent of use is termed as retrofitting. It becomes necessary to improve the performance of structures including those facing loss of strength due to deterioration or which have crossed their anticipated lifespan. The realization of retrofitting depends on the authentic cause and measures adopted to prevent its further deterioration. This development includes repair, retrofit, renovation and reconstruction wherever required. A proper load path has to be analyzed by a structural engineer and a decision has to be taken if any additional member like shear walls, etc needs to be added.

The engineering analysis, design and construction of any necessary retrofitting must be carried out bearing in mind the following aspects:

- **Functionality Aspect:** The basic function/ operation of the structure should not be hampered.
- **Structural Safety Aspect:** The susceptibility of the structure to an earthquake event has to be within acceptable standards.
- **Importance Level Aspect:** Historic buildings with immense archeological importance are sometimes beyond the cost factor for retrofitting. Such structures have to be rehabilitated without changing its elegance.
- **Construction Methodology Aspect:** The retrofitting has to be performed using latest construction techniques that have the minimal impact on usual functioning of the buildings.
- **Economy Aspect:** The entire cost of construction has to be practical and logical towards extended life of the structure.
- **Skilled Labour Availability:** The retrofitting practices need unusual construction method and is highly technical job and calls for utmost care to implement it. A very skilled workmanship must be provided to instrument the suggested measures.

3.2.2 Different Retrofitting Options for Buildings

Based on the intensity of the repairs needed and calculations done, various retrofitting options listed below are used to enhance the structural strength. This is carried out under a strict supervision of a technical expert in the field.

- Replacement of structurally fragile concrete,
- Grouting and crack repair,
- Crack repairs and patch repairs,
- Replacement of carbonated concrete near steel reinforcement,

- Cleaning and passivating corroded steel reinforcement,
- Concrete overlays with normal low or highly fluid concrete, latex modified,
- Concrete and corrosion protection such as jacketing, etc.,
- Re-alkalization of carbonated concrete,
- Electrochemical removal of chloride from concrete, and
- Water proofing / protective coating.

Repair methods

The success of repair activity depends on the identification of the root cause of the deterioration of the concrete structures. If this cause is properly identified, satisfactory repairs can be done for the improvement of strength and durability, thus extending the life of the structure, is not difficult to achieve.

General procedure in the repair of distressed concrete structure:

1. Support the structural members properly as required.
2. Remove all cracked, spalled and loose concrete.
3. Clean the exposed concrete surfaces and steel reinforcement.
4. Provide additional reinforcing bars, if the loss in reinforcement is more than 10%
5. Apply shortcreting/polymer concrete for patch repair work and grouting for porous/honeycombed concrete.
6. Apply protective coatings over the exposed/repaired surface.

Guniting: Guniting is mechanically applied material consisting of cement, aggregates and water. The cement and sand are batched and mixed in the usual way and conveyed through a hose pipe with the help of compressed air.

A separate pipe line brings water under pressure and the water and cement aggregate mix are passed through and intimately mixed in a special manifold and then projected at high velocity to the surface being repaired. In good quality work, a density around 2100 kg/m^3 is achieved. For effective guniting, the nozzle should be kept at 60 cm to 150 cm from the work normal to the surface. Before guniting is applied, the old concrete surface is prepared properly, all the cracks treated and the new reinforcement fixed in position. Cracks wider than about 0.5 mm should be cut out and filled with hand-applied mortar or with gunite.

Repair for cracks:

(i) Stitching

(ii) Routing and sealing

(iii) Resin injection
(iv) Dry packing
(v) Polymer impregnation
(vi) Vacuum impregnation
(vii) Autogenous healing
(viii) Flexible sealing
(ix) Drilling and plugging
(x) Bandaging

Stitching
1. In this technique, the crack is bridged with U-shaped metal units called stitching dogs before being repaired with a rigid resin material.
2. A non-shrink grout or an epoxy resin based adhesive should be used to anchor the legs of the dogs.
3. Stitching is suitable when tensile strength must be re-established across major cracks.
4. Stitching dogs should be of variable length and orientation.

Benefits of Cracked Stitching
1. Quick, simple, effective and permanent.
2. The grout combination provides an excellent bond within the substrate.
3. Masonry remains flexible enough to accommodate natural building movement.
4. Non-disruptive structural stabilization with no additional stress

Routing and Sealing
1. This is the simplest and most common method of crack repair.
2. It can be executed with relatively unskilled labor and can be used to seal both fine pattern cracks and larger isolated cracks.
3. This involves enlarging the crack along its exposed face and sealing it with crack fillers.
4. Care should be taken to ensure that the entire crack is routed and sealed.

Resin Injection
1. Epoxy resins are usually selected for crack injection because of their high mechanical strength and resistance to most chemical environments encountered by concrete.
2. Epoxies are rigid and not suitable for active cracks.
3. This method is used to restore structural soundness of members where cracks are dormant or can be prevented from further movements.

3.3 GREEN BUILDING

3.3.1 Planning Concepts of Green Buildings or Eco-Housing

Eco-Housing: There is an urgent need to address the great challenges of our times: climate change, resource depletion, pollution, and peak oil. These issues are all accelerating rapidly, and all have strong links with the building industry. Eco-friendly construction can not only help to create a better outdoor environment, it can also help to build a healthier indoor environment. Green building is not only a wise choice for our future; it is also a necessary choice. The construction industry must adopt eco-friendly practices and materials that reduce its impacts, before we reach a point of irreversible damage to our life supporting systems. The industry needs to take its own initiative and find alternative ways to build, using green, renewable energy resources, and adopt non-polluting practises and materials that reduce, recycle and reuse, before it is too late.

A carbon footprint is used to calculate the amount of damage caused by an individual, household, institution or business to the environment through harmful carbon dioxide emissions. Reducing carbon dioxide emissions is seen as essential to sustaining the environment and can be achieved in two ways: **Reduction of Carbon Dioxide Emissions and Carbon Offsetting.**

There are many ways that companies and institutions can reduce carbon emissions. Here are just a few which may not only reduce carbon emissions but in turn improve overall efficiency of the houses.

- Enacting a recycling policy.
- Enacting and promoting a car-sharing scheme amongst its employees.
- Encouraging employees to walk or cycle to work.
- Educating employees in the need to reduce carbon emissions.
- Reducing the need for air travel.
- Reducing the use of electricity.
- Developing new methods of work and manufacturing that are less harmful to the environment.
- Other forms of carbon offsetting include investing in organizations that promote awareness of environmental issues and supporting sustainable technologies (such as solar or wind power).
- Use of locally available materials
- Use of daylight for sustainance
- Use of reclaimed materials
- Use of Environmentally Friendly, Non-Toxic Paint
- A Green Roof
- Use of insulating materials
- Adopting new developments: Environmentally Friendly Concrete

The list is endless; here few from the above said list are detailed in and the students may work out for the remaining areas on their own.

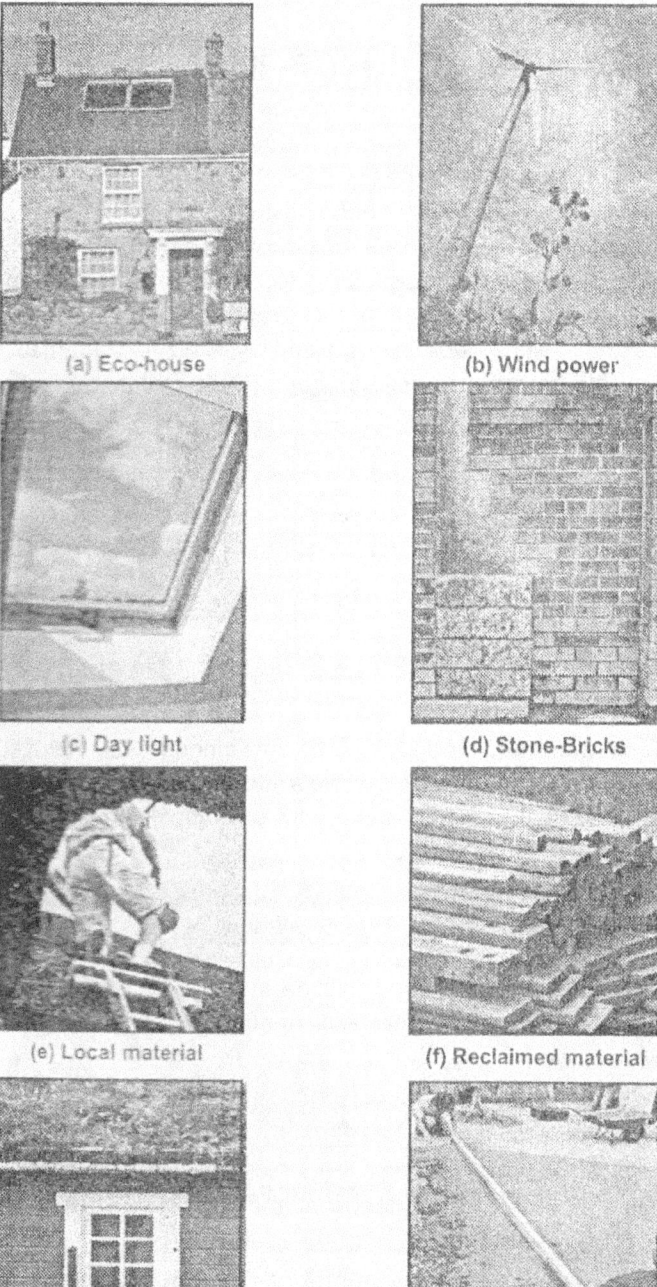

Fig. 3.1

Wind Power:

Wind generators are generating a lot of interest right now, offering the first small wind generator commonly available for the home. We need to dramatically reduce the emissions from the fuel and carbon we use, and wind as well as solar is one of the energy sources in plentiful supply, that we are learning to use.

Harnessing Energy From Wind:

Wind generators work by having their turbine blades, usually three, rotating in the wind, turning a copper coil inside a magnetic field, which in turn creates an electrical current. Clearly the stronger the wind the faster the blades will turn, hence the importance of siting the generator in a high, exposed place, where wind is continuous, or as continuous as can be expected.

Electricity created inside this unit, the current, can then be fed through the system directly into the grid, via a grid tie inverter, which converts the currents voltage.

Solar Energy:

- *Passive solar energy heating for cold climates, and passive solar cooling for hot humid climates.*
- *The term "Passive Solar Energy" means that basic physical concepts (such as sunshine, warm air rising, and cool air falling) are used to Heat and Cool a building, without the need for fans, water pumps, or other "active" mechanical equipment. Using solar radiation to Passively Heat Air and Water is very easy and inexpensive to do.*
- *Using the sun's solar energy for Cooling and Dehumidification in a hot humid climate, (where the night time air is too warm and contains too much water vapour to use for direct ventilation), is a challenging engineering problem.*

The Importance of Recycling:

Many people simply dispose of unwanted or used and consumed items without giving it much thought. They simply don't bother to consider the consequences of their actions. For example, things like batteries and electronics items often contain chemicals where, if they end upon a landfill site, they will eventually seep through the bottom and pollute the ground water. This results not only in the contamination of our water supply but also contamination of the soil in which we grow our food. Once in the food and water supply chain, these chemicals are impossible to get rid of so we are putting our own and future generations supplies of food and water and our own and future generations health at risk. Simply put, by not recycling, we are diminishing energy, water and other natural resources that mankind relies upon which is why we should get hold of a list of going green tips, which we can follow as well as doing some research on the green products which are available to us.

Lighting accounts for around 15% of the energy bill in most homes, and around 25% in commercial buildings. It is supplied by electrical power plants using fossil fuels, and is responsible for a significant percentage of carbon dioxide emissions, a leading cause of global climate change. Because of this, the building industry has targeted lighting as a key element in sustainable design, and there is now a global movement to develop and implement lighting solutions that meet people's needs and concerns, and address environmental regulations. One must concentrate upon the following factors.

Daylighting Design:

The most sustainable lighting is natural daylight. It is not only a free renewable resource but it also has well-documented health benefits. Careful architectural design is required to maximise natural light in a building while maintaining indoor temperature regulation and reducing direct light glare. The strategic placement of windows, skylights, light shafts, atriums and translucent panels in harmony with other building components, such that light is reflected evenly throughout internal spaces, is known as daylighting design.

Sunlight Transportation Systems:

An emerging new technology is that of sunlight transportation. Natural sunlight is collected on roof panels and transported into a building via fibre optic cables for distances upto 15 metres. These sunlight-piping systems can be used in combination with solar panels to integrate natural and artificial light systems, so that there is always light in the home.

Energy Efficient Light Bulbs:

The sustainable building industry is primarily focused on energy efficient lighting solutions. Standard light bulbs, known as incandescent bulbs, are known to be highly inefficient. Electricity is passed through a metal (tungsten) filament that heats to over 2000° celsius and glows to give off light. Only 10% of the electrical energy is converted to light; 90% is wasted as heat. Halogen bulbs are similar but instead have a small pocket of halogen gas that reacts with tungsten to produce light. They burn brighter, use less electricity and last twice as long as a standard bulb, but are still inefficient compared with other forms of bulbs.

Energy efficient light bulbs use significantly less energy than incandescent bulbs, and also last longer. There are two main kinds: Compact Fluorescent Lights and Light Emitting Diodes.

(a) Compact Fluorescent Lights (CFLs):

These are small versions of full fluorescent lights, and consist of a glass tube coated with phosphor, filled with gas and a small amount of mercury. Electricity jumps off electrodes on the end of each tube, and excites the mercury molecules to emit ultraviolet light. This excites the phosphor coating, which emits visible light that shines out of the tube. CFLs give off the same amount of light as incandescent bulbs, but they are upto 80% cooler, are four times more energy efficient (to replace a 60 watt incandescent, you only need a 15 watt CFL), last 10 times longer (upto 20,000 hours), and are responsible for the emission of 70% less carbon dioxide.

CFLs come in many different configurations and wattages, and are suitable for all lighting purposes. Although more expensive to buy than a standard bulb, they easily recover their costs in energy savings. On the downside, they contain trace amounts of mercury, which is hazardous to health and the environment. Care needs to be taken to ensure the glass tube doesn't break and that the bulbs are disposed of safely.

(b) Light Emitting Diodes (LEDs):

LEDs are small, solid light bulbs that are lit by the movement of electrons in a solid semi-conductor material as electricity is passed through it. This is also called 'solid state lighting', because it uses a solid material, as opposed to gas (CFL) or filament (incandescent). LEDs are extremely energy efficient, lasting over 100 times longer than incandescent bulbs, and upto 10 times longer than CFLs. They have low heat generation, low power requirements, and are highly durable because there is no filament or tube to break.

LED is a relatively new technology, and currently the bulbs are most suitable for track and recessed lighting, where a pointed light is required rather than radiated light. They are more expensive than CFLs, but energy savings over their lifetime means their cost is soon recouped. Because their power inputs are minimal, LEDs are readily combined with solar panels to provide reliable, energy efficient lighting day and night.

Use of Locally Available Materials:

Sustainable building is an essential aspect of widening efforts to conceive an ecologically responsible world. A building that is sustainable must, by nature, be constructed using locally sustainable materials: i.e. materials that can be used without any adverse effect on the environment, and which are produced locally, reducing the need to travel. There are key criteria that can be used to judge whether a material is sustainable or not:

- To what extent will the materials used in this building cause damage to the environment? When using locally sustainable materials it is essential that those materials are renewable, non-toxic and, therefore, safe for the environment. Ideally, they will be recycled, as well as recyclable.

- To what extent will a building material contribute to the maintenance of the environment in years to come? Alloys and metals will be more damaging to the environment over a period of years as they are not biodegradable, and are not easily recyclable, unlike wood, for example.
- To what extent is the material used locally replenishable? If the material is locally sourced and can be found locally for the foreseeable future, travelling will be kept to a minimum, reducing harmful fuel emissions.

Reclaimed Materials:

The construction industry is under increasing pressure to become sustainable. One way to address this is through the use of reclaimed materials. Reclaimed materials are those that have been previously used in a building or project, and which are then re-used in another project. The materials might be altered, re-sized, refinished, or adapted, but they are not reprocessed in any way, and remain in their original form. Materials that have been reprocessed and reused in the building industry are referred to as recycled materials.

Examples of materials that can be reclaimed include: bricks, slate roofing, ceramic tiles, fireplaces, doors, window frames, glass panels, metal fixtures and fittings, stairs, cobbled stones, steel sections and timber. A reclaimed material is often adapted for a different use, for example, a roof beam might be used as a mantelpiece. This is known as **re-purposing**.

Where to Find Materials:

The best place to source reclaimed materials is direct from a demolition or re-modelling project. Many of these projects carefully dismantle buildings in such a way that their materials can be sold and re-used. In the building trade this is known as **deconstruction**.

Reclaimed materials can also be sourced from salvage centres, reclamation yards and other specialist companies, who buy and sell materials that they have salvaged themselves from demolished sites. There are hundreds of salvage companies, some which deal only in high-end architectural materials, and others that are more like junkyards. Good quality, rare and heritage materials can be gleamed from salvage suppliers, and while purchasing can be more expensive than those sourced direct from a demolition site, there is a much wider choice of materials available on demand.

Reclamation in Sustainable Development:

Ongoing rapid development means that many historic buildings are being demolished to make way for new affordable housing and commercial space. Redirecting building materials from the waste stream of this process, and reusing them in other nearby projects is a critical component of sustainable development. There is a huge amount of construction waste, and the potential to reuse this to reduce landfill and new materials is enormous. When reclaimed materials are secured from an existing building site, the environmental impact is virtually zero. Even when they are sourced from far away, reclaimed materials are still the most environmentally friendly option for supplying materials to the building industry.

3.3.2 Salient Features of a Green Building

   (a) Minimal disturbance to landscapes and site conditions.
   (b) Use of recycled and eco-friendly building material.
   (c) Use of non-toxic and recyclable materials.
   (d) Efficient use of water with recyclable techniques.
   (e) Use of energy efficient and eco-friendly equipment.
   (f) Use of renewable energy.
   (g) Quality of indoor air for human safety and comfort.
   (h) Effective controls and building management systems.

The most important aspect is to consider many developmental alternatives and to explore opportunities to win-win design changes that further sustain building goals and reduce cost.

The efforts in this regard will start from selection of site.

In general one may consider the following points:

(a) **Use appropriate building sites:** As a general rule, promote sensitive infill consistent with local plans and infrastructure is environmentally preferable to create a new development requiring.

(b) **Preserve open space:** Incorporate the preservation of open spaces – undeveloped land and resource areas into building project while avoiding impact on previously undeveloped open spaces. If open spaces must be developed, consider donating an equivalent amount of land elsewhere to open space status.

(c) **Reduce sprawl:** Channelize the new building to previously developed areas with existing infrastructure wherever possible, while protecting green fields (natural or park areas) and preserving habitats. This is most relevant to developments in established suburban or urban environments. Even in rural areas, consolidating residential development through clustering which can produce vibrant communities with stores and services located within walking distance thereby reducing transportation needs and the potential for future sprawl patterns.

(d) **Develop brown fields:** (Rehabilitation of abandoned buildings and sites). A brown field is a real property, the expansion, redevelopment, or reuse of which may be complicated by the presence or potential presence of a hazardous substance, pollutant, or contaminant. Developing brown fields allows the cleanup and recycling of existing infrastructure while preventing degradation of undeveloped land.

(e) **Safeguard endangered species:** Avoid entirely any dry land or wet lands specifically designated as habitat for an endangered or threatened species.

(f) **Restore damaged environment:** Some building projects may provide the opportunity to restore damaged lands to a natural state, such as conservation of gravel parking lots to fields, wet lands or replanting trees or native grasses.

(g) **Design to optimize sun, wind and light:** The beneficial impacts of designing a building around its local climate and topography is to achieve desirable sun, wind and light patterns. Can be quite impressive, also one must take into account impact of building on its surroundings.

3.3.3 Site Integration

(a) **Enhance naturally occurring biodiversity:** To achieve this reconnect fragmented landscapes and establish continuous networks with other natural systems in and around site. Avoid major alterations, establish car free areas and develop foot traffic zones.

(b) **Minimize site disturbance:** Issues of concern include degradation of water quality through pollution or siltation, damaging soils through digging or mixing foreign materials etc. this can be minimized by proper site management plan.

(c) **Storm water management:** The problem arises because naturally porous vegetation is replaced with impervious surfaces like roads, parking lots etc. This causes far higher flows into local streams with high amounts of silt and potential pollutants from construction vehicles and building operations. Mitigate these problems by maximizing the use of porous surfaces or by capturing runoff.

(d) **Optimize transportation options:** This can be opted for maximizing convenience and minimizing transportation energy and time required by building users. Strategies include siting new buildings near public transport services, by promoting bicycles, covered bike racks etc. Parking lots can include spaces with electricity or natural gas recharging capacity in commercial buildings parking spots can be reserved for car pools.

(e) **Reduce heat islands:** These are responsible for creating detrimental impact on microclimate, human comfort and on animal habitat. It can be mitigated by providing shade from trees or roofs from highly reflective surfaces. Replace or line the constructed surfaces with vegetation or use star rated roofing material.

(f) **Reduce light pollution:** Reduce the intensity of external night lights, limit the height of the buildings and cover or partially shade the bright lights.

3.3.4 Benefits of Green Buildings

Environmental Benefits	Economic Benefits	Occupational Benefits
• Enhance and protect ecosystems and biodiversity • Improve air and water quality • Reduce solid waste • Conserve natural resources	• Reduce operating costs • Enhance asset values and profits • Improve employee productivity and satisfaction • Optimize life-cycle economic performance. • Reduces future liability. Increases retail sales	• Improves air, thermal and acoustics • Enhances occupant comfort and health • Reduces healthcare costs • Improves employee satisfaction and morale-less absenteeism and turnover

Green building materials are those with the least environmental impacts throughout their life cycle, whether measured in terms of energy used, scarce natural resources or air and water emissions. Reusing or recycling materials has substantial environmental benefits well beyond the weight of the material actually reused or recycled on site. Green building projects, like other building supplies, are required to meet the highest safety and performance requirements. The most significant benefits involve the reduced use of energy, reductions in air and water pollution during resource extraction and manufacturing and the safeguard of scarce natural resources.

Green Building Material Strategies:

- **Prepare a Green Building Product Selection Plan:**

    Excellent resources are available to assist with and the companies should discuss priorities with the contractors team at the earliest moment. While it is impractical to thoroughly evaluate every product alternative, it is reasonable to ask the contractor team to include green building products in the products considered at every stage.

- **Use of Salvaged Building Products:**

    Salvaged products like doors, framing, windows or plumbing can save costs and sometimes allow the use of high end or antique products that can greatly add to a building's ambience. They simultaneously keep old products out of the waste stream and they eliminate the need to manufacture new products. Deconstruction firms are beginning to compete effectively in some instances with demolition firms.

- **Use Recycled Content Building Products:**

  Recycled Content Products (RCP) must meet or exceed all the performance, health and safety requirements of other building products. Examples of products include lumber and carpet made from recycled plastics, cellulose installations made from recycled newsprint, aggregates made from recycled asphalt or glass, masonry blocks made from recycled glass and many more. For example, recycled plastic lumber made from 100% post consumer recycled plastics is available. This is suitable for 2×4 decking. Many other dimensions and products are available, such as 2×4 structural strength; 3/8" plywood sheet at prices comparable to the wood counterparts. These products are advertised as being maintenance free and come with a claim of no staining or rotting.

- **Use Locally Available Materials:**

  Each region produces a range of construction products unique to that region. Purchasing these products from the local suppliers rather than from distant resources can substantially save on shipment costs while greatly reducing their life cycle energy use. Depending on the region, materials like straw bales, earth or cob may be available which are appropriate for some residential buildings in certain climates with adequate rebar or other fortification to meet any applicable earthquake safety specifications.

- **Use Rapidly Renewable:**

  Rapidly renewable resources include agriculture-based materials like straw converted into pressed board products. Plastics can be made from agriculturally grown products. Boards can be made from sunflower seeds and wheat grass. Wool carpet is another example.

- **Use Certified Wood:**

  The smart wood program evaluates and recognizes forests managed according to sustainable principles. The Hoopa lumber is also certified by the Forest Stewardship Council (FSC). Criteria for certification include, ensuring the long term health and productivity of forests for timber production, wildlife habitat protection, clean air and water supplies, climate stabilization, spiritual renewal, and social benefits.

- **Use Structural Insulated Panels:**

  Structural Insulated Panels (SIPs) are high performance building panels that can be used in floors, walls and roofs, in both residential and commercial buildings. The panels are often made of Expanded Polystyrenes (EPS). SIPs are very strong, energy-efficient and cost effective. SIPs can reduce construction waste considerably and can be a very cost effective way of increasing the overall energy insulation of a building.

- **Commissioning of Green Buildings:**

  Commissioning is a systematic process – beginning in the design phase and extending through a typical period – of ensuring through documented variation, that all building systems perform interactively according to the contract documents, and that the faculty staff are properly trained and system documentation has been adequately provided.

Commissioning and Green Building design share three things in common:
(i) They both involve a systems approach to look at the buildings and its performance.
(ii) They both view buildings from a life-cycle perspective.
(iii) They both involve increased attention during the design phase to ensure that the design meets the owner and occupant needs.

Benefits of Green Buildings:

(I) Energy Savings:

Energy efficiency may be the foundation of green buildings. Buildings account for 36% of all energy use. Reducing energy use in buildings reduces the impacts proportionately. Increased efficiency also yields increased comforts, aesthetics, and productivity. Strategies used for energy saving result in a home or commercial space that are vastly more comfortable to live or to work in.

Energy saving strategies:

(A) Passive Solar Design:
- Optimize the site, design and orientation.
- Landscape to provide natural shade.
- Use natural daylight.
- Use natural heating and ventilation

(B) Energy Management Plan:
- Evaluate tradeoffs and minimize projected energy costs
- Train building occupants
- Track and optimize performance overtime
- Employ an energy management system and commissioning

(C) Energy Efficient Products:
- Use high performance thermal insulation
- Use high performance roofing and glazing
- Use high performance lighting
- Use high performance HVAC (Heating Ventilation and Air-Conditioning) systems.

(II) Waste Reduction:

Waste reduction is one of the two approaches used to conserve materials in green buildings. The other approach being the purchase of reused and recycled products. Waste reduction can focus on the construction site and can be part of an overall maintenance and operations plan. Rehabilitating buildings, reusing components of existing buildings or using salvaged building products may result in substantial cost saving, where it is a feasible option. They also have significant environmental benefits involving reduced use of energy, reductions in air and water pollution during resource extraction and manufacturing, and the safeguarding of scarce natural resources.

Waste Reduction Strategies:

    (a) Prepare and implement a construction waste reduction plan

    (b) Rehabilitate existing buildings

    (c) Demolition / deconstruction waste management

    (d) Design to facilitate recycling and reuse

    (e) Specify products that can be repaired or renovated instead of replacement

    (f) Specify environmentally preferable products and practices

(III) Health and Productivity Benefits:

There is growing recognition of the large health and productivity costs imposed by poor Indoor Environmental Quality (IEQ) in commercial buildings. This is not surprising as people spend 90% of their time indoors and the concentration of pollutants is typically higher than outdoors (ten to hundred times).

Following are some relevant attributes common in green buildings that promote healthier work environments. On an average 25-30% more energy efficient, much lower source emissions from measures such as better sitting, significantly better lighting quality, generally improved thermal comfort and better ventilation, commissioning use of measurement and verification, CO_2 monitoring to ensure better performance of systems such as ventilation, heating and air conditioning.

(IV) Indoor Air Quality:

Experience and research shows that these risks can be reduced or eliminated through the strategies discussed in this module. Like day lighting enhanced IAQ is a sustainable building strategy that can yield tangible benefits to users each and every day. The concept is responsible to increase the productivity at large.

IAQ Improving Strategies:

- Ensure adequate ventilation
- Designate indoor smoke free spaces
- Use low emitting building products
- Install controllable systems
- IAQ management plan

(V) Water Efficiency:

Water is the most vital of all resources for all living bodies. If the water conservation strategies are integrated with landscaping, industrial use etc. it will be an important step towards reducing the pressures on pure water supply.

Strategies to Achieve Water Efficiency:
- Water use management plan
- Indoor water conservation
- Outdoor water conservation (through rain water collection, sustainable landscape technique, high efficiency irrigation technique, innovative waste water management, use waterless urinals, use biological treatments).

Green Buildings in India:

The concept of GB is not new. Our ancestors worshipped the five elements of nature. Today through LEED (Leadership in Energy and Environmental Design), we are rediscovering the Indian ethos.

First GB in India: CII GODREJ GBC – PLATINUM RATING
ITC GREEN CENTER – GURGAON
WIPRO TECHNOLOGIES – GOLD RATING
GRUNDFOS PUMPS – CHENNAI- GOLD RATING
NEG MICON, CHENNAI

Standards followed: NBC guidelines, MoEF guidelines, CPCB norms, ENVIS norms etc

LEED Green Buildings Rating System-Certification Levels

Sr. No.	Credits	New building
1.	Energy and Atmosphere	17
2.	Indoor Environmental Quality	15
3.	Water Efficiency	5
4.	Sustainable Sites	14
5.	Materials and Resources	13
6.	Innovation and Accredited Professional Points	5
	Total	69

Rating	New building
LEED certified	26-32
LEED certified-silver level	33-38
LEED certified-gold level	39-51
LEED certified-platinum level	52-69

Through PMC Eco-Housing rating is set recently and if any building satisfies a particular level mentioned then many benefits will be given for the same like reduction in the Tax etc.

Science and Technology Park:
1. Science and Technology Park (Scitech Park) is one of the Science and Technology Entrepreneurship Development Parks (STEPs) promoted by National Science and

Technology Entrepreneurship Development Board (NSTEDB) of Department of Science and Technology, Government of India and University of Pune with an aim to convert **"Knowledge into Wealth"**.

2. Pune Municipal Corporation has appointed Scitech Park as the Certifying, Monitoring and Evaluating agency for Eco-housing certification of residential buildings.
3. One of Scitech Park's unique initiative is the Eco-housing Certification Program for certifying residential projects using world test practices adequately modified for application to different climate conditions.
4. **The Certification Criteria:**
   Climate specific
   Focus on Resource Conservation
   Site planning
   Environmental architecture
   Water management
   Eco-friendly building material
   Renewable energy
   Solid waste management
   Other innovative measures.

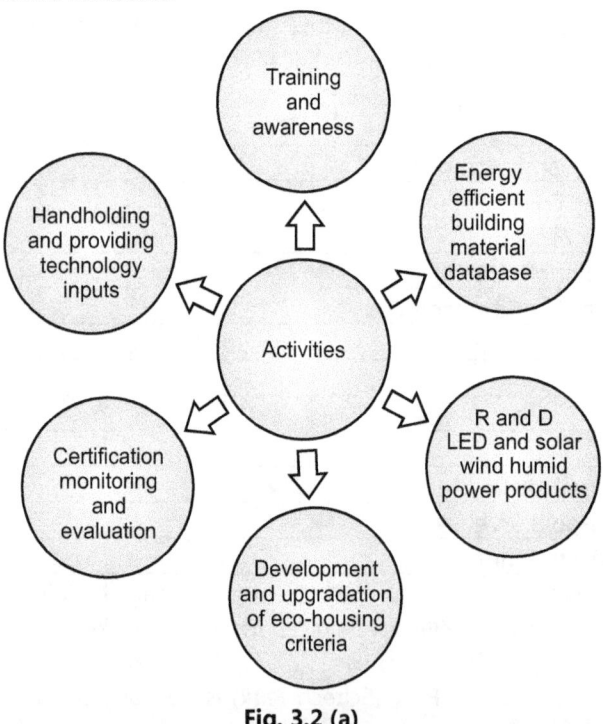

Fig. 3.2 (a)

5. **Climatic Zone Specific Criteria:** For the first time the certification criteria has been customized following different climatic zones of India which makes it more scientific.

   Hot and Dry

   Warm and Humid

   Composite

   Temperate

   Cold.

6. **Star Rating System:**

500 – 600	*
601 – 700	* *
701 – 800	* * *
801 – 900	* * * *
> 900	* * * * *

Design and Pre-construction phase

Construction phase

Post Construction phase

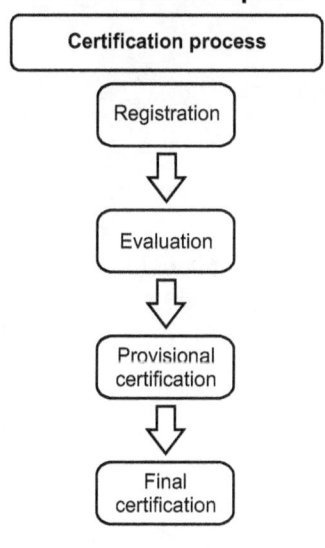

Fig. 3.2 (b)

Star Rating	Rebate in Total Premium	Rebate offered with Provisional Certificate
*	10%	5%
* *	20%	10%
* * *	30%	15%
* * * *	40%	20%
* * * * *	50%	25%

Star Rated Projects	Star
Nyati Environ, Phase I, II, III – M/s Nyati Builders	*****
Kumar Sublime-Bldg A & B M/s Kumar Builders	*****
Crossover County M/s Darode-Jog Lagad Venture	*****
Rohan Mithila, Plot B, C, D M/s Rohan Builders and Developers (I) Pvt. Ltd.	*****
Kool Homes – Solitaire M/s Kool Homes Group	***
Kool Homes – Arena M/s Kool Homes Group	***

3.3.5 Environmentally Friendly, Non-Toxic Paint

All paints contain three main components: pigment (colour), a binder (holds the paint together) and a carrier (disperses the binder). With many modern paints these ingredients are made using toxic chemicals that are harmful to both the environment and human health. Cadmium, lead and chromium are frequently used in pigments; and petrochemicals, solvents, benzene, formaldehyde and other volatile organic compounds (VOCs) are used in binders and carriers. Toxic, environmentally harmful, chemicals are also used in modern paints as preservatives, stabilisers, thickeners and driers.

VOCs are organic (carbon based) chemical compounds that evaporate easily in the atmosphere, and are known to be a major contributor to global climate change. Many of them are highly toxic and linked with numerous health problems such as respiratory disease, asthma, dizziness, headaches, nausea, fatigue, skin disorders, eye irritation, liver and kidney damage and even cancer. Modern chemical paints continue to emit VOCs many years after their application.

Increasing concerns about the impact of chemical paints on health and the environment have led to a growing market in non-toxic paints. Environmental regulations have forced conventional paint companies to significantly reduce their VOC content, and most of the large paint companies now offer one or more varieties of non-toxic paints. However, many of these still contain VOC solvents, chemical pigments and fungicides.

Eco-Labels for Paints:

Non-toxic paints are often called Low-VOC, No-VOC, VOC-Free, odourless, odour-free and green, natural or organic paints. There are no set standards for defining these labels, and they are widely misused for marketing purposes. To help consumers make informed decisions on their paint purchases, various ecological labels have been developed by different countries to indicate that the paint has fulfilled certain environmental requirements, in accordance with respective government regulations. These eco-labels can be found as logos on paint cans, and include the European Eco-Label, Blue Angel in Germany, and Green Seal and Green guard in the USA. In the UK, VOC labels are used, and indicate the content of VOCs using one of five classifications: Minimal (0-0.29%), Low, Medium, High and Very High (VOC content greater than 50%).

Low-VOC paints tend to use water as a carrier instead of petrochemical solvents, and so their emissions are minimal. Many conventional paints have achieved relatively low VOC levels. No-VOC or VOC-Free paints may still contain very low levels of VOCs in their pigments or additives. Although reducing VOC content is a move in the right direction, it is questionable whether either of these paint types can be considered non-toxic.

Natural Paints:

Natural paints are the only true non-toxic paint since they contain no VOCs, and are made from natural ingredients such as water, vegetable oils, plant dyes, and natural minerals. The main binders used in natural paints are: linseed oil (from flax seeds), clay, lime, and milk protein. Lime and milk paints give an authentic period look, and are often used in antique restoration projects. Chalk is used as an extender to thicken paint; turpentine (distilled from pine trees) is used as a solvent; essential oils from citrus fruits (d-limonene) are used as a solvent and fragrance; and natural mineral and earth pigments are used as colorants.

The main benefits of natural paints are:

- **Non-toxic:** No hazardous fumes or harmful effects on health. This is significant for allergy sufferers and chemically sensitive people who are unable to tolerate chemical paints.

- **Environmentally Friendly:** Use renewable resources; are biodegradable, can even be composted.

- **Micro-Porous:** Allow walls and surfaces to breathe, preventing condensation and damp problems, and reducing associated indoor allergens. They are also less prone to paint flaking, peeling and blistering.

3.3.6 Green Roofing

Plants have been used on roofs for thousands of years, from sod roofs in Europe to the hanging gardens of Babylon. But in the last 50 years this practice has evolved into what are now called green roofs, living roofs or eco-roofs. Green roofs are those that have been planted with specific vegetation using a well researched sustainable design methodology. They are an exciting new development in the sustainable building movement, and are gaining in popularity across the world.

Types of Green Roof:

While there is no standard classification for green roofs, they can be divided into two basic types:

- **Intensive Living Roofs:** These incorporate plants between 1 to 15 feet high, including shrubs and trees. They require deep levels of soil to support them and a weight loading roof. They support a high level of plant and wildlife diversity, but require ongoing maintenance and extensive irrigation. They are not suitable for most domestic buildings.

- **Extensive Living Roofs:** These incorporate low-lying plants from 2 to 6 inches high. They require only a few inches of soil to support them, and only need a low weight-loading roof. They are low maintenance and can be used for any kind of roof, including sheds, garages, houses, balconies, extensions and outhouses, and also commercial buildings.

Both types of green roofs can be used for flat or pitched roof construction. Flat roofs are the most common and the easiest to establish and maintain, but green roofs can have a pitch upto 45 degrees. With sloped roofs, there are design issues affecting drainage and soil loss that need to be carefully considered.

How to Construct a Green Roof?

A green roof system consists of layers that mimic natural processes and also protects the building and roof. The basic components are: a waterproof layer, root repellent membrane, filter cloth (to allow water to drain but prevent soil escaping), moisture blanket (to ensure enough water retention for plant life), drainage system (to drain excess water), soil substrate, seeds and plants. The soil is the growing medium and should be lightweight and free draining, but also be able to hold enough moisture for the plants to survive. Recycled aggregates such as crushed porous brick are often used in the soil substrate, with the added benefit of increasing its sustainability index.

Plants suitable for extensive green roofs are low growing, rapid spreading, drought-tolerant, have a fibrous root system (to protect roof membranes), low irrigation and nutrient requirements, low maintenance requirements, use native species, and are allergen-free. Short perennials, wild flowers and succulents such as sedum (stonecrop) are commonly used. To help cut down on planting time, impregnated sedum and wild flower mats are now commercially available. These can be rolled out directly onto the soil.

Living roofs can be designed to grow native plants that might otherwise become endangered, and to encourage a wide range of important wildlife including insect species such as butterflies, bees and beetles, and local birds.

Benefits of Green Roofs:

There are a number of social, economic and environmental benefits to green roofs, including:

- Increasing home energy efficiency - cooling in summer, insulation in winter.
- Filtering and cleaning toxins from both air and water.
- Reducing carbon dioxide emissions.
- Retaining rainwater before it evaporates, reducing the likelihood of flooding.
- Reducing urban temperatures and associated smog.
- Insulating against sound and noise.
- Preserving and enhancing biodiversity.

- Providing aesthetic appeal and 'green space' recreational opportunities.
- Using recycled materials like aggregates and plastic sheets.
- Biomass roofing is the use of plant materials to build roofs.

The Different Types of Biomass Roofing:

Although hundreds of different plants have been used to roof houses, these can be classified into two main types: thatch and wood tiles.

1. **Thatch**
   - All sorts of plants have been used for thatching in Britain: oats, reeds, broom, heather, bracken and various grasses. But today only three main thatching materials are used: water reed, wheat reed and long straw.
   - Water Reed is the most popular thatching material. Both water reed and wheat reed (actually a straw but cut with a binder and combed to give the appearance of reed) gives a compact and even texture when applied to a roof. This is in contrast with long straw (wheat straw that has been thrashed so that the ears and butts are mixed up together), which gives a shaggy, rounded appearance. The lifespan of thatch is around 30 to 50 years, although this varies widely depending on the skill of the thatcher, the pitch of the roof, the local climate conditions and the quality of the materials.
   - The technique for thatching is basically the same for all materials, first the thatch is fastened together in bundles about 25 inches in diameter. Each bundle is then laid down with the butt end facing outwards, secured together to the roof beams, and pegged in place with wooden rods. Successive layers are added on top of each other, working from the bottom of the roof up towards the top, with a final layer used to reinforce the ridgeline.
   - Thatch roofs can withstand high winds and heavy rains, provide good thermal insulation and are easy to repair. Thatch is light and needs only a simple support structure, and is flexible so can be used for any roof shape. On the downside, thatching is labour intensive and a certain level of skill is required. The materials can be expensive as reeds are increasingly imported from Europe to keep up with demand. Like all biomass materials, thatch is flammable which means that building restrictions may apply and home insurance can be high.

2. **Wood Tiles: Shingles and Shakes:**
   - Wood tiles have been used for roofs since medieval times in Britain. They are traditionally made by hand-splitting logs into small wedge shaped pieces, but today

most are manufactured by machine. There are two basic types: shingles, which are sawn, and shakes, which are split. Shakes are thicker and have a more rustic, rough look, whilst shingles are thinner and smoother. Both come in a variety of lengths and are made from the heartwood of unseasoned wood. Hardwood is best, with cedar being the most popular, although any straight-grained wood can be used. Split bamboo can also be used to create Spanish-style tiles, and are popular in some countries, but bamboo has the disadvantage of decaying fast in wet conditions unless chemically treated.

- Wood tiles are laid from the bottom of the roof to the top, with each row overlapping the previous one. A cap is placed at the roof ridge. Typically tiles are nailed onto wood strips spaced a few inches apart between the roof beams, to allow air to circulate and prevent decay.
- Wood tiles last between 25 - 50 years. Like thatch, they give good insulation and are flexible so can cover any roof shape. They are highly resistant to wind, heavy snow and hail, but must be regularly cleaned of vegetative debris. They are also flammable, and building regulations may prohibit their use in urban areas.

Is Biomass Roofing Sustainable?

The recognised need to use renewable resources has led to a revival of traditional, natural building methods, along with a growing market for biomass roofing. Thatch and wood tiles are not only aesthetically appealing, but are durable and biodegradable. But their sustainability value is diminished if the materials have been imported or produced and treated with chemicals. Biomass roofing is only a true sustainable solution if the materials are obtained from a local, renewable source, and are grown, harvested and manufactured in an environmentally sensitive way.

3.3.7 Use of Insulating Materials

Insulation is a key component of sustainable building design. A well insulated home reduces energy bills by keeping warm in the winter and cool in the summer, and this in turn cuts down carbon emissions linked to global climate change.

In terms of energy efficiency, investing in high levels of insulation materials for your home is more cost-effective than investing in expensive heating technologies. It is worth taking the time to choose the right materials in the context of whole building design.

Insulation materials are used in roofs, walls and floors. Solid wall structures such as stone, cob and adobe cannot be insulated, but they have good thermal mass to compensate. Timber frame homes need wall insulation in the form of batts (pre-cut sections that are designed to fit between stud walls), rolls or boards. Other types of construction such as brick or concrete insulate with spray foam, loose fill or rolls. It is far easier and cheaper to install insulation in the walls and floors of a new build home, than to retrofit an existing home. However, insulating roofs is easily achieved in any home using rolls or bags of loose fill.

Insulation materials work by resisting heat flow, measured by an R-value (the higher the R-value, the greater the insulation). This R-value varies according to material type, density and thickness, and is affected by thermal bridging, unwanted heat flow that occurs at joists, studs and rafter beams.

Conventional Insulation:

Conventional insulation materials are made from petrochemicals and include: fibreglass, mineral wool, polystyrene, polyurethane foam, and multi-foils. These materials are widely used because not only are they inexpensive to buy and install, but there is an assumption from the building industry that their performance ability is higher than the natural alternatives. On the downside, almost all conventional insulation materials contain a wide range of chemical fire retardants, adhesives and other additives, and the embodied energy in the manufacturing process is very high.

Natural Insulation Materials:

The green alternative to synthetic insulation is natural insulation. There are many different types available, including:

(a) Sheep's Wool:

This material usually needs to be treated with chemicals to prevent mite infestation and reduce fire risk, although some natural builders use it untreated with success. It has very low embodied energy (unless it is imported) and performs exceptionally well as an insulation material. Thermafleece is the most common commercial brand available.

(b) Flax and Hemp:

Natural plant fibres that are available in batts and rolls, and typically contain borates that act as a fungicide, insecticide and fire retardant. Potato starch is added to flax as a binder. Both materials have low embodied energy and are often combined in the same product. Examples include Isonat and Flax 100.

(c) Cellulose:

A recycled product made from newsprint and other cellulose fibre. It is one of the most favoured materials of natural builders because it can be blown into cavity walls, floors and roofs; used as a loose fill; and is also available in quilts, boards and batts. Like hemp and flax it contains borate as an additive. Products include: Warm cell and Eco-cell.

(d) Wood Fibre:

Made from wood chips that have been compressed into boards or batts using water or natural resins as a binder. It has very low embodied energy and uses by-products from the forestry industry. Examples include: Pavatex, Thermowall and Homatherm.

Expanded Clay Aggregate:

These are small fired clay pellets that expand at very high temperatures to become lightweight, porous and weight-bearing. They can be used in foundations as both an insulator and aggregate. They have excellent thermal insulation properties, but high embodied energy.

Insulating for a Better Environment:

Natural insulation products have many advantages over conventional materials. They are low impact, made from renewable, organic resources and have low embodied energy. They can be reused and recycled, and are fully biodegradable. They are non-toxic, allergen-free and can be safely handled and installed. They also allow for buildings to breathe by regulating humidity through their absorbent properties, and reducing problems of condensation. This keeps the indoor environment comfortable and protects any timber structures from rot.

Unfortunately, natural insulation materials are currently upto four times more expensive than conventional materials, which can be prohibitive to builders, architects and developers. But the environmental and health benefits of natural insulation materials far outweigh their costs, and growing consumer demand combined with government regulation, and rising oil prices will inevitably drive prices down. Despite the high price, natural insulation is an energy-efficient, healthy and sustainable choice for a better indoor and outdoor environment.

Use of New Techniques: A potentially sustainable new form of concrete has been recently created that might make it the most environmentally friendly type of building material.

Concrete in its traditional form is made from cement, mixed with a range of coarse aggregates such as gravel, limestone or granite, and some finer particle aggregates such as sand or fly ash.

These are mixed together with water, to form a quick drying bonded structure, which can easily be manipulated into many forms such as the surface of roads, or driveways or footings for structures. It is the most commonly used building material in the world - some estimate that in the region of 7 cubic kilometres of concrete are manufactured each year, and that there already is 1 cubic metre of concrete for every human on earth.

Unfortunately concrete is not an environmentally friendly material, either to make, or to use, or even to dispose of. To gain the raw materials to make this material, much energy and water must be used, and quarrying for sand and other aggregates causes environmental destruction and pollution.

Concrete is also claimed to be a huge source of carbon emissions into the atmosphere. Some claim that concrete is responsible for upto 5% of the world's total amount of carbon emissions, which contribute to greenhouse gases. This is created in the heat that is needed to create the raw cement - cement is burnt at high temperatures, and materials such as limestone must be burnt to create the high temperature.

A New Form of an Old Material:

Scientists at a British concrete manufacturer, the London-based Novacem, claim to have developed a new form of concrete that effectively absorbs large amounts of carbon dioxide as it hardens. Novacem's new version of concrete, uses a different raw material, magnesium sulphate, which requires much less heating. Novacem claim that each tonne of cement can absorb up to 0.6 tonnes of CO_2. This is opposed to figures that claim that each tonne of old style cement emits about 0.4 tonnes of CO_2.

Stones and bricks:

Stone is a beautiful natural material that can be cut to any size, and will enhance the exterior or interior of any building. A stone-clad building has a natural elegance to it, that gives it a timeless quality.

Brick can be made to any shape and most sizes, and because it is a man-made material, can be very flexible in its quality and potential uses. The use of red brick particularly can make a property very distinctive.

Weighing Up the Benefits of Both Materials:

Whether or not one material outweighs the other is not a straight-forward case; Stone needs to be quarried, which clearly has an environmental impact, dressed, and transported. Using locally quarried stone can offset some of this impact, or you might be lucky to have stone already on-site. Using stone from the site you are building which emulates the environment, and could be said to offset the impact of having to transport materials from further distances. It is also said that a stone-built building gives the effect of anchoring the building to the land, and into the local environment. Regional stone has its own distinctive colour, texture and quality.

However, both stone walling and cladding a wall with stone is a slow, laborious job, requires a lot of skill and patience that many enthusiastic self-builders may not have, and above all, it is highly physically demanding.

Stone buildings are also notoriously colder. They are great in hot climates where the thick stones keep the inside cool, but heat doesn't get effectively trapped by stone. Creating an insulation layer of either thin wood or a rendering of lime can help this.

Brick, on the other hand, takes as much resources from the land as stone, in the different components used.

Also the heating process to cook the brick has an environmental impact. There is much more opportunity to get exactly the type, texture, size and colour of brick you need to construct with, which is a big advantage. Unfortunately, the material is likely to come from further away, so bear in mind this important environmental impact of travel. If cost is the most important factor in design and construction of your project, brick is going to be the cheaper material to use. It is easier to use, and the skills involved in building with brick are less and easier to learn.

Using the Right Material for the Job:

These differences shown between the two materials show the unique possibilities of building with brick or with stone. It is possible, and quite common, to use a combination of brick and stone when designing and constructing a building. For example, using stone as a feature on an exterior wall, as a stone accent, or as a fascia, sets off a standard brick wall. Bearing in mind the sustainable element of the materials, comparing the impact of producing both, from a quarry or from a furnace, has to be specific to your project.

QUESTIONS

1. What is low cost housing? Give its materials.
2. Explain the various cost reduction methods for low cost housing.
3. What are repairs and rehabilitation of building?
4. Explain the methods of rehabilitation of buildings.
5. Explain the different retrofitting options for buildings.
6. What is green building?
7. Explain planning concepts of Green buildings or eco-housing.
8. What are the salient features of a green building?
9. Explain the features of site integration.
10. Give the benefits of green buildings.
11. Explain the star rating systems.
12. Write a note on: Environmentally friendly, Non-toxic paint.
13. What is green roofing? Explain types of green roofing.

14. Explain how to construct a green roof.
15. Give the benefits of green roofs.
16. Explain different types of biomass roofing.
17. Explain the use of insulating materials.

SECTION - II

Unit 4

PLUMBING SYSTEMS AND ELECTRIFICATION

4.1 PLUMBING SERVICES

A plumbing system includes the water supply and distribution pipes, plumbing fittings and traps, soil, pipes, vent pipes and antisiphonage pipes, building drains and building sewers including their respective connections, devices and appurtenances within the property lines of the premises and water treating or water using equipment.

4.2 WATER SUPPLY REQUIREMENTS FOR BUILDINGS

The requirements regarding water supply, drainage and sanitation for residences shall assume, that a minimum water supply of 200 litres per head per day is assured together with a full flushing system. In case of Lower Income Group (LIG) and Economically Weaker Sections of society (EWS), the minimum value of water supply may be reduced to 135 litres per head per day. Requirements of water supply for buildings other than residences are given in Table 4.1.

Table 4.1: Water Requirements for Buildings other than Residences

Sr. No.	Type of Building	Consumption per head per day
(1)	(2)	(3)
		litres
(i)	Factories where bathrooms are required to be provided	45
(ii)	Factories where no bathrooms are required to be provided	30
(iii)	Hospitals (including laundry) per bed:	
	(a) Number of beds not exceeding 100	340
	(b) Number of beds exceeding 100	450

contd. ...

(iv)	Nurses homes and medical quarters	135
(v)	Hostels	135
(vi)	Hotels (per bed)	180
(vii)	Offices	45
(viii)	Restaurants (per seat)	70
(ix)	Cinema halls, concert halls and theatres (per seat)	15
(x)	Schools:	
	(a) Day schools	45
	(b) Boarding schools	135

General Requirements of Plumbing System:

1. The plumbing work which is required to be carried out in a building should be executed only by a licensed plumber under the control of the authority and should be responsible to carry out all lawful directions given by the authority.

2. All premises intended for human habitation, occupancy or use should be provided with the supply of pure and wholesome water.

3. Plumbing fixtures, devices and appurtenances should be supplied with water in sufficient volume and at pressures adequate to enable them to function satisfactorily without undue noise under all normal conditions of use. There should be atleast a residual head of 0.018 N/mm² at the consumer's tap.

4. Plumbing system should be designed and adjusted to use the minimum quantity of water required for proper performance and cleaning.

5. Plumbing fixtures, installed in a building should be connected to a public sewer. If such a sewer does not exist near the building, suitable arrangements like septic tanks and soak pits should be made.

4.3 STORAGE OF WATER

In a building, provision is required to be made for storage of water for the following reasons:

1. To provide against interruptions in supply caused by repairs to mains,
2. To reduce the maximum rate of demand on the mains,

3. To tide over periods of non-supply in an intermittent supply system.

4. To maintain a storage for fire fighting requirement of the building (optional) minimum 10,000 litres.

As per I.S. 2065 – latest the storage capacity required, for premises occupied by tenements with common conveniences is calculated at the rate of 500 litres per tenement on each floor. For premises occupied as flats or blocks, the storage requirement is calculated as 8000 litres per tenement.

Reservoirs and tanks for reception and storage of water can be constructed of reinforced concrete, cast iron, galvanised mild steel plates. These tanks should be covered with a close fitting, dust tight, insect and fly-proof lid. These tanks are constructed either underground, above ground or above the building (overhead tanks). If the storage capacity required is more than 5000 litres, it is advantageous to arrange it in a series of tanks, so interconnected that each tank can be isolated for cleaning and inspection without interfering with the supply of water. The design of an underground storage tank is carried out with a provision for the draining of the tank when necessary.

The quantity of water to be stored is calculated by considering the following factors:

1. Supply rate, pressure and water supply hours to fill up the overhead storage tanks.
2. Frequency of replenishment of overhead tanks during 24 hours.
3. Regularity in water supply.
4. Types of building like public buildings, school buildings, hospitals etc.

The water supply system consists of municipal water supply mains, distributing pipes, consumer pipes, stopcocks, various types of taps, underground storage tanks, overhead reservoirs etc. Water is supplied to kitchen, bathrooms, W.C. etc. by service pipes and valves. The water supply arrangement in a multi-storeyed building is shown in Fig. 4.1.

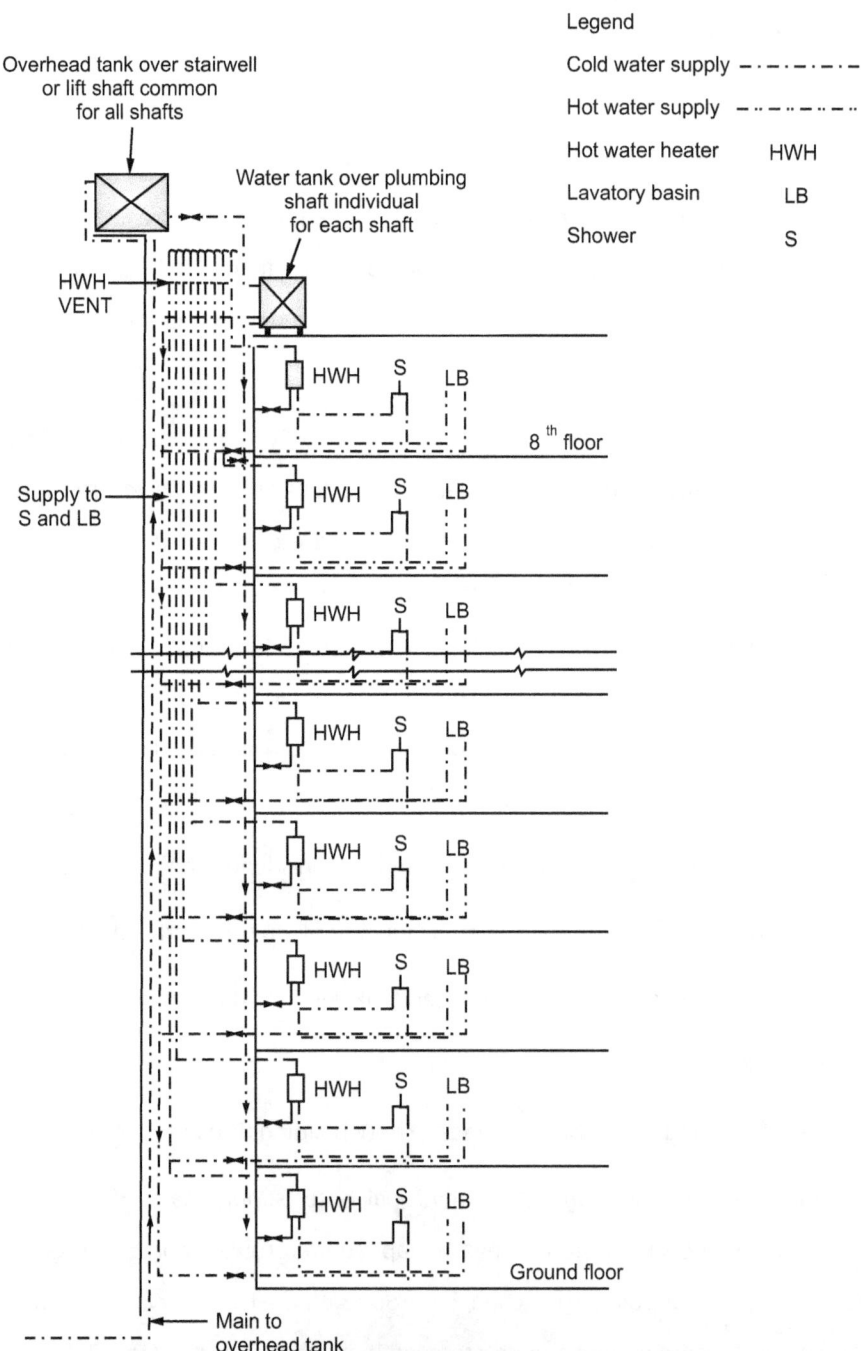

Fig. 4.1: Installation of water supply connections for 8-Storeyed Building

4.4 LAYOUT OF WATER SUPPLY AND DRAINAGE SYSTEM

Before commencing the plumbing work, a detailed layout showing the arrangements for water supply and drainage is prepared. The layout plan should contain location of service main water supply line, position of underground and overhead tanks, position of service connection depending upon various units of the building. It should also contain details regarding the drainage system which includes street sewer line, positions of manholes, inspection chambers, gully traps, drainage lines for sewage and sullage and rain water. The direction of flow should also be marked on this layout. A layout for water supply and drainage system for a multi-storeyed structure is shown in Fig. 4.2.

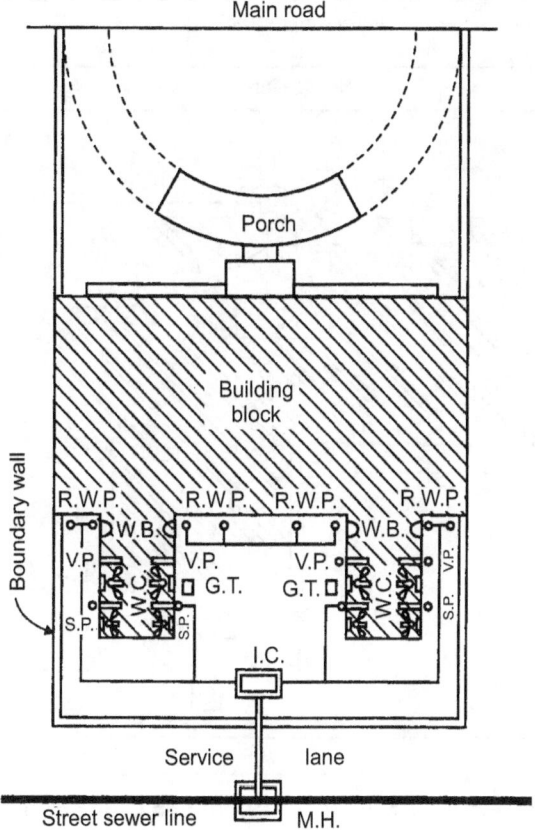

Fig. 4.2: Typical drainage layout plant of a terrace house drained at back

House Drainage Plans:

Before starting the plumbing work, it is most essential first to prepare the drainage plans. In the same way detailed drawings are prepared before the starting of the construction of buildings, the detailed drainage plans should also be prepared.

The following points should be kept in mind while preparing the drainage plans:

(i) The drains should be laid in such a way so as to remove the sewage quickly from the building. The quick removal is governed by the fall of the pipes. The drains should be laid at such a slope that self-cleaning velocity is developed in them. The following slopes are usually sufficient:

1 in 40 for	10 cm pipe
1 in 60 for	15 cm pipe
1 in 90 for	23 cm pipe

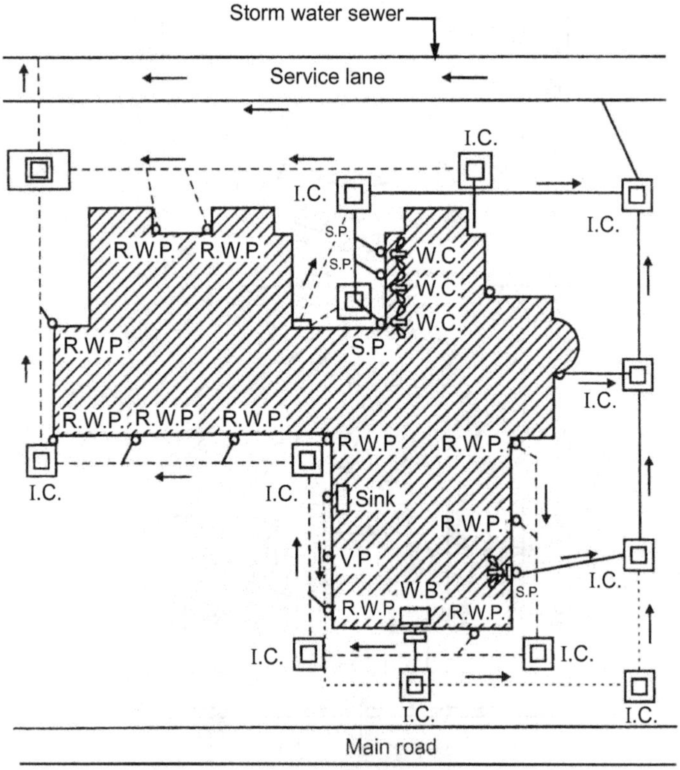

Fig. 4.3: Typical drainage layout of a large building

4.5 PLUMBING SYSTEM FOR WASTE WATER

The removal of any liquid by a system constructed for the purpose is called as drainage system. In designing a drainage system for an individual building, the aim is to provide a system of self cleaning conduits for conveyance of foul, a surface or subsurface waters.

And for the removal of such waste speedily and efficiently to a sewer or other outlet without risk of nuisance and hazard to people. The different types of wastes, which are required to be removed through the drainage system, include night soil (waste from W.C.), sullage from bath and kitchen and rain water collected over the building or on the premises. In the drainage system, generally, rain water is dealt with separately from sewage and sullage.

Following are the main systems of plumbing for the building drainage:

(a) Two-pipe System:
   (i) This is the most common system used in India. This method provides an ideal solution, where it is not possible to fix the fixture closely.
   (ii) All the drainage system should be properly ventilated on the house side. The ventilation pipe should be carried sufficiently high above the buildings. All the inspection chambers should provided with fresh air inlets.
   (iii) All the drains should be laid in such a way so as to ensure their safety in future.
   (iv) The drain should be laid in such a way that in future extension can be done easily if desired.
   (v) If the quantity of sewage flowing in a pipe is small, an automatic flushing tank may be provided on its top for flushing it.
   (vi) All the rain water pipes, sweeping from house and bath water should discharge over gully traps and should be disconnected from the drain.
   (vii) All soil pipes should be carried direct to the manholes without gully traps.

In this system, two pipes are provided. One pipe collects the foul soil and lavatory wastes, whereas the second pipe collects the unfoul water from kitchen, bathrooms, house washings, rain water etc. The soil pipes (pipes carrying the soil waste) are directly connected to the drain whereas the waste pipes (pipes carrying unfoul waste water) are connected through the gully trap. All the traps used in this system are fully ventilated.

(b) One-pipe System:

In this system, only one main pipe is provided which collects both the foul soil waste as well as unfoul waste from the buildings. The main pipe is directly connected to the drainage system. If this system is provided in multi-storeyed buildings the lavatory blocks of various floors are so placed one over the other, so that the waste water discharged from the different units can be carried through short branch drains.

All the traps of the W.C., basins, sinks etc. are fully ventilated and connected to the ventilation pipe.

(c) Single-stack System:

This is similar to single pipe system, the only difference being that no ventilation is provided even in the traps too.

(d) Single-stack Partially Ventilated System:

This system is in between the one pipe and single-stack system. In this system, only one pipe is provided to collect all types of waste water foul as well as unfoul. A relief vent pipe is provided for ventilating only the water closet-traps.

Now-a-days in modern multi-storeyed buildings one pipe system is becoming popular due to its low cost. C.B.R.I. Roorkee, after doing extensive research on this system, has recommended it in modern buildings. An analysis of this system showed that the flow from the appliance to the stack through branch is momentarily halted at the sharp change of flow of direction. Sometimes a plug of water is formed immediately at the junction, which depends upon the rate of change of discharge and the size of branch. This gives rise to unequal pressures at the seals for the lower floors of the building and sometimes this breaks the water seals of the sanitary appliances. C.B.R.I. has recommended the use of aerator and deaerator in the stack to increase its capacity.

The function of the **aerator** is to prevent the formation of the plugs of water in the vertical stack and to make a mixture of water and air of low specific gravity. The aerators are provided at every floor

   (a) For supply of water to various sanitary fittings.
   (b) For collection of waste water from the sanitary fittings.
   (c) For collection of rain water from the roofs, house and courtyard washings.

The fixing of sanitary appliances in the walls, floor and other places and their connected pipe works are to be done carefully for their proper functioning.

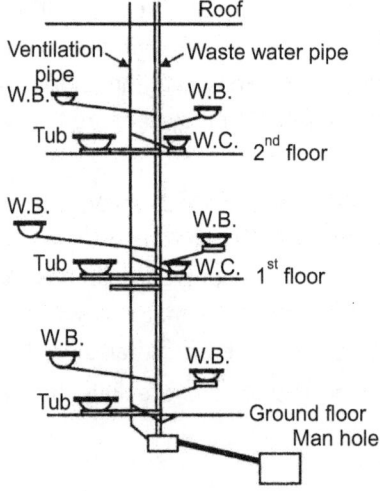

Fig. 4.4: Single stack partially ventilated system

Deaerators are provided at the foot of the stack to separate air and water to avoid excessive back pressure. Studies carried out by C.B.R.I. revealed that 100 mm diameter stack with these fittings can be safely used upto 15 storeys, whereas a single stack system without these fittings can be used only upto 5 storeys.

The two pipe system is costly as it requires much labour and material with antisyphonage pipe, as compared with single stack system of plumbing. No antisyphonage pipe is required. The single stack system is becoming popular in the modern building construction. The tests done by C.B.R.I. on 5 storeyed building show that there was no break of water seals. As it is the common practice in India to discharge the waste water from the sinks and wash basin to the floor trap, therefore, sanitary appliance carrying, unfoul waste water do not require deeper seals. 100 mm diameter stack with two appliances at each floor can be safely used upto 5 storeyed building.

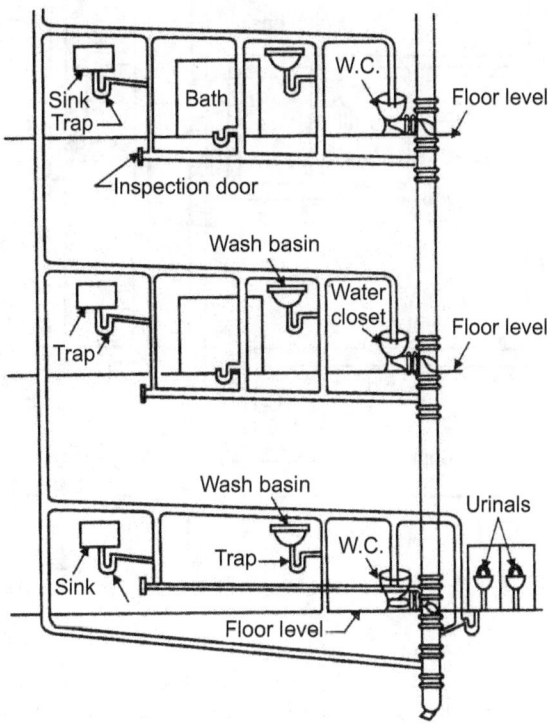

Fig. 4.5: Plumbing work of one-pipe system

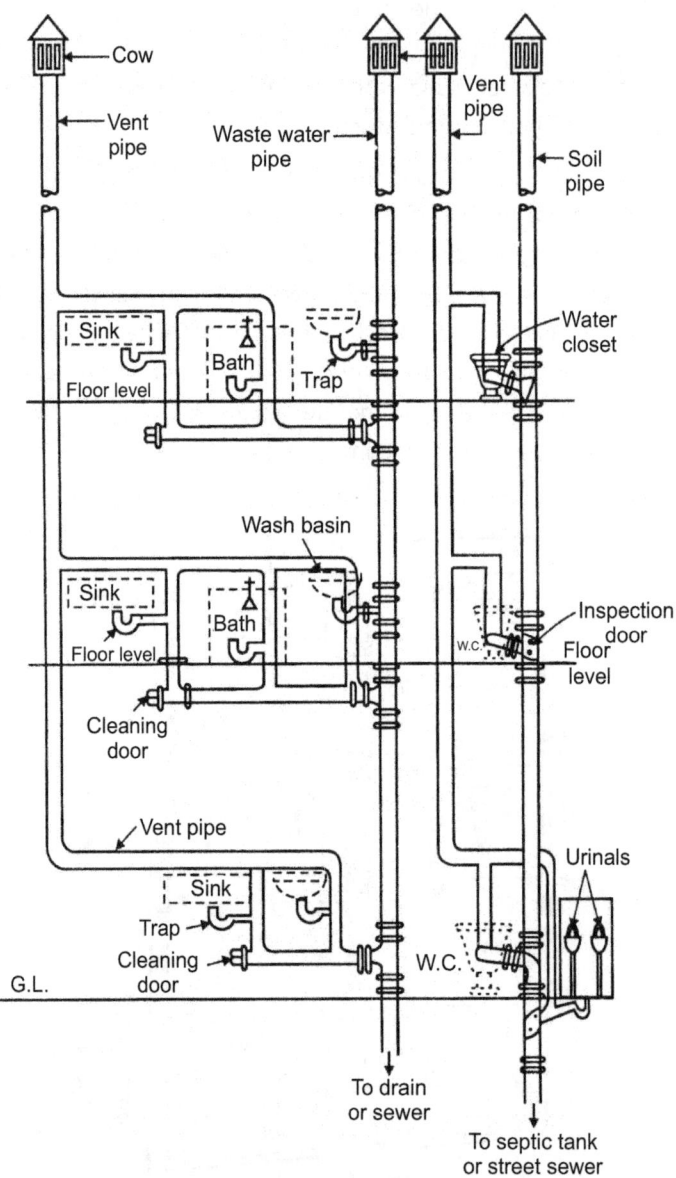

Fig. 4.6: Plumbing work of two-pipe system

Septic Tank: In the rural areas and the fringe areas of suburban towns and also in case of isolated buildings and institutions, hostels, hotel, hospital, school, small residential colonies, underground sewage system with complete treatment of sewage may be neither feasible nor economical. Under such cases septic tanks followed by subsurface disposal of effluent are provided. In the areas having porous soil, this method gives satisfactory results. The location of the septic tanks should be as far as possible away from the buildings, and should not be located in swampy areas or areas prone to flooding. In case of clayey, non-porous soils or where houses are closely spaced, suitably designed leading pits may have to be used, if septic tank cannot be avoided. The septic tank effluent should not be allowed into open drainage system, because it may cause health hazards, nuisance and mosquito breeking. If the facilities for connection to a sewer are available, the effluent from the septic tank should be connected to sewers.

Also it should be located at the lowest contour.

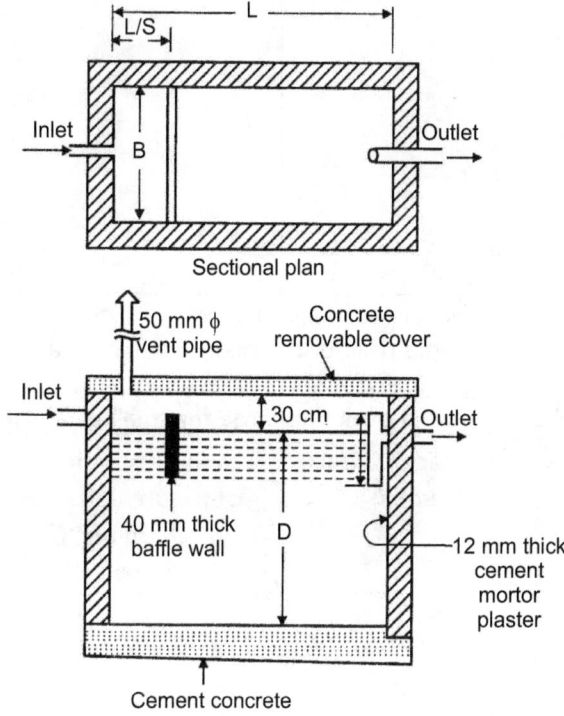

Fig. 4.7: Septic tank

Sewage Flow:

The maximum flow of sewage to the tank is based on the number of plumbing fixtures discharging simultaneously rather than the number of users and per capita waste water flow expected to reach the septic tank. For this purpose various sanitation appliances such as water closets, wash basins, bath etc. are equated in terms of fixture units as given in Table 4.2. A fixture unit is a standard receptacle which gives a discharge of 10 *l*pm when flushed.

Table 4.2: Fixture equivalents

Sanitary fixture	Equivalent fixture unit
1. Water closet	1.0
2. Bath	0.5
3. Wash basin/kitchen sink	0.5
4. Urinal with automatic flush	1.0
5. Urinal without automatic flush	0.5
6. Slope sink	1.0
7. Ablution tap	0.5
8. Dish washer	0.5
9. Combination fixture	1.0
10. Laboratory sink	2.0
11. Shower bath	1.0
12. Bath tub	2.0
13. Drinking fountain	0.5

Tables 4.3, 4.4 and 4.5 give the estimated number of fixture units and the number of fixture units that contribute to the peak discharge in small installations-residential colonies and hostels etc.

Table 4.3: Estimated peak discharge for small establishments

Number of users	Number of fixture units	Probable number of fixture units discharging simultaneously	Probable peak discharge *l*mp
5	1	1	10
10	2	2	20
15	3	2	20
20	4	3	30
25	5	4	40
30	6	4	40
35	7	5	50
40	8	6	60
45	9	6	60
50	10	7	70

Table 4.4: Estimated peak discharge for residential housing colonies

Number of users	Number of house holds	Number of fixture units	Probable peak discharge based on 60% fixture units discharging simultaneously in *l*pm
100	20	40	240
150	30	60	360
200	40	80	480
300	60	120	720

Table 4.5: Estimated peak discharge for casting establishments, boarding schools and similar establishments

Number of users	W.C.	Bath	Wash basin kitchen sink	Number of fixture units	Probable peak discharge based on 70% fixture units discharging simultaneously in *l*pm
50	6	6	6	12	84
100	12	12	12	24	168
150	19	19	19	38	266
200	25	25	25	50	350
300	37	37	37	74	518

Construction Details:

Following are the construction details of septic tanks:

(a) It is rectangular in plan, the length is usually 2 to 4 times the breadth.

(b) For smaller tanks liquid depth of 100 cm is provided, for larger tanks it may be upto 180 cm. Free board of 30-45 cm is provided above the level of liquid for fixing of pipes, scum, gases etc.

(c) An elbow pipe, usually T-pipe submerged to a depth of 15-25 cm below the liquid level is provided as inlet pipe. More number of inlet pipes may be provided for larger tanks.

(d) Single elbow or T-shaped outlet pipe is provided. It should also be submerged at least 15 cm below the liquid level. For very large tanks, weir type outlet similar to settling tanks are provided.

(e) In smaller tanks one baffle of hanging type is enough, the baffle is usually placed 20 to 30 cm from the inlet pipe and remains 15 cm above and 30 cm below the liquid level. Outlet baffle is provided only in large tanks, when weir type outlet is provided.

(f) Usually R.C.C. slab with C.I., manhole covers are provided.

(g) Ventilation pipe of usually 7.5 to 10 cm diameter of A.C. or C.I. is used for taking out the foul smells. Their tops are provided with cowls.

Table 4.6: The sizes of Septic Tanks as per I.S. 2470 (Part I) 1963

No. of Users	Length L	Breadth B	Liquid depth D min.	Liquid capacity to be provided	Free board min.	Sludge to be removed	Recommended interval of cleaning
	metre	metre	metre	m³	cm	m³	
1	2	3	4	5	6	7	8
5	1.5	0.75	⌈1.0 1.0 ⌊1.05	1.12 1.12 1.18	30 30 30	0.18 0.36 0.72	6 months 1 year 2 years
10	2	0.9	⌈1.0 1.0 ⌊1.4	1.8 1.8 2.52	30 30 30	0.36 0.72 1.44	6 months 1 year 2 years
15	2	0.9	⌈1.0 1.3 ⌊2.0	1.8 2.34 3.6	30 30 30	0.54 1.08 2.16	6 months 1 year 2 years
20	2.3	1.1	⌈1.0 1.3 ⌊1.8	2.53 3.3 4.55	30 30 30	0.72 1.44 2.88	6 months 1 year 2 years
50	4	1.4	⌈1.0 1.3 ⌊2.0	5.6 7.28 11.2	30 30 30	1.8 3.6 7.2	6 months 1 year 2 years

Design of Septic Tanks:

As septic tank is a settling-cum-digestion tank, it requires space for:

(i) Settling of the incoming sewage.

(ii) Digestion of the settled sludge.

(iii) Storage of digested sludge till it is taken out.

Design of space for settling: This is calculated for the average flow and detention period. Smaller tanks are designed on the basis of average flow and 24 hours detention period, while larger tanks are designed for 12 hours detention period.

Both surface area and detention of depth are important factors in the settling of flocculant particles such as sewage solids. For average Indian conditions at a temperature of 25°C, the surface area required will be 0.92 m^2 for every 10 $l$pm peak rate flow. This is based on 75% removal of sewage particles of 0.05 mm size and above with a specific gravity of 1.2. A minimum depth of sedimentation of 25-30 cm is necessary. The length of the septic tank is kept 2-4 times the breadth.

If only the discharge from the latrines flow is in the septic tank, the average flow per capita per day may be taken as 45 litres. On the other hand if all the waste water of the houses is to be treated in septic tank the average flow should be taken per capita per day depending on the water supply.

Design for digestion space: In the septic tank, the operation goes in natural way and there is no control over all it such as mixing, heating, etc. a provision of 0.0425 m^3 per capita should be done for it.

The fresh sludge stay in the tank should be long enough to undergo satisfactory anerobic digestion so that as much of the organic matter as possible may be destroyed and the sludge may become innocuous and suitable for dewatering or drying. The time required for digestion depends on the temperature. The per capita suspended solids entering the septic tank may be taken as 70 gm/day. Assuming that 60% of the solids are removed along with fresh sludge, of which 70% is volatile, with a solid content of 5% or moisture 95%, the volume of fresh sludge works out to 0.00083 m^3 /cap./day. Now considering that 2/4 of the volatile matter is destroyed of which 1/4 is mineralised during digestion and solid content of 13% in the digested sludge, the volume of the digested sludge works out to 0.0002 m^3/cap./day. The digestion zone contains both fresh and digesting sludge. Therefore, the digestion space should provide for the average volume of the mixture of fresh and digested sludge which works out to 0.000515 m^3/cap./day. Now based on the period of digestion, the capacity required for the digestion zone can be worked out. At 25°C, the capacity for sludge digestion works out to 0.032 m^3/capita.

Design of space for storage of digested sludge: The digested sludge produced per capita in different periods is as follows:

Period of Cleaning	Storage capacity
6 months	0.0283 m^3
1 year	0.049 m^3
2 years	0.0708 m^3
3 years	0.085 m^3

The design of space for storage of digested sludge is done on the basis of period of cleaning and the number of persons using the tank.

Adequate space should be provided in the septic tank for the storage of digested sludge and scum, otherwise their accumulation interferes with the efficiency of the tank by encroaching upon the space provided for sedimentation and digestion. A sludge storage capacity of 7.3 m³/100 persons for an interval of cleaning of one year is provided below the sedimentation zone.

Total Capacity: The tank should also provide for a free board of atleast 30 cm, which should be sufficient to include the scum depth above the liquid surface. Addition capacity for seed sludge is not required. Care should be taken to leave 25-50 mm depth digested sludge for seed purpose. When the cleaning is yearly, at 25°C for 10 persons the tank capacity shall be 2.15 m as per details below:

(i) Sedimentation = Probable Peak flow 320 lpm

Area required = $\dfrac{0.92 \ (m^2)}{10 \ (lpm)}$ = 1.84 m²

Provided a depth of 30, volume = 1.84 × 3 = 0.55 m³

(ii) Digestion space = 0.32 m³

(iii) Space for sludge storage = 0.73 m³

(iv) Space for free board including 0.25 m³
for seed sludge (1.84 × 0.3) = 0.055 m³

Total = 2.15 m³

A septic tank designed on the criteria given above normally provides a detention period of 24-48 hours, based on an average daily flow of sewage. But as the average daily flow varies so widely from one installation to another, detention period should not be considered as an important criteria for the design of septic tanks.

Example 9.1: *Design a septic tank for 50 users, assuming the rate of water supply as 60 litres/head/day.*

Solution: Assuming the detention period as 24 hours and the time of cleaning the sludge as 3 years.

Space required for setting = $\dfrac{50 \times 60}{1000}$

= 3.0 m³

Space required for design = 50 × 0.0425

= 2.125 m³

Space required for storage of sludge

$$= 50 \times 0.085$$
$$= 4.25 \text{ m}^3$$

Total space required $= 3.0 + 2.125 + 4.25$

$$= 9.375 \text{ m}^3$$
$$= (9.5 \text{ m}^3) \text{ say}$$

Providing free broad of 30 cm.

Provide the septic tank of $4 \times 1.4 \times 2.0$ metres.

Garbage Disposal Arrangement:

Refuse is all the solid and semisolid waste matter of a community except night soil. It can be broadly divided into two parts:

(1) Organic matter, (2) Inorganic matter.

The organic matter of the refuse is very offensive and creates health problems. The quantity and quality of refuse depends on various factors such as season, climatic condition, geographic location, habits of people, standards of living, etc. Garbage includes all sorts of putrescible waste obtained from hotels, restaurants, kitchens etc. Garbage should be handled carefully as flies, insects, rats etc. breed in it. Garbage decomposes very quickly and produces unpleasant odours. Garbage can be used after proper processing as fertilizer.

The garbage is stored in the houses, industries and business centres, temporarily in containers and it is dumped periodically in the refuse collection boxes or chambers provided along the streets for this purpose. In multi-storeyed buildings, refuse chute system is provided for collecting and transporting in a sanitary way.

This system has three components:

1. The chutes
2. Inlet hopper
3. Collection chamber.

Occupants of the building from successive floors drop their refuse into the inlets and the refuse is collected in the collecting chamber from where the refuse is cleared at suitable intervals. The inlet hopper is located in the passage near the kitchen or at the end of a common passage. Sufficient ventilation and lighting should be provided near the inlets. The collection chamber is provided at ground level for easy clearance.

4.6 VARIOUS TYPES OF PIPES

The pipes are available in several types and sizes. They may be classified into three groups according to the material used in their manufacturing.

- **Metallic Pipes:** The pipes such as CI Pipes, Steel pipes and GI Pipes.
- **Cement Pipes:** The pipes such as Cement Pipes, Asbestos Cement (AC) pipes, Cement Concrete pipes.
- **Plastic Pipes:** The pipes such as Un-plasticized PVC (UPVC) pipes, Polythene pipes (low density).

4.6.1 Metallic Pipes

Cast Iron (CI) Pipes

These pipes are mostly used in water supply. They are well suited for pressure and can withstand external load because of their thickness. The pipes are easy in manufacturing, layout and joining. These pipes are manufactured by vertical casting in sand moulds, horizontal casting in sand moulds and centrifugal casting (spun casting pipes).

CI pipes are heavy in weight. Therefore, transportation is costlier and they are not suitable for inaccessible places. Due to heavy weight these are generally made in short length. This increases layout and jointing cost. CI vertical casting pipes are not of very good quality and can be replaced by centrifugal casting (spun casting) pipes.

Steel Pipes

These pipes are extensively used for water supply. They are best suitable for long distance pipe lines of high pressure and provide satisfactory performance during service. These pipes have excellent mechanical properties and are ideally suited for welding. The pipes are made in length more than twice the length of CI pipes; which saves in transport, layout of pipe and joining cost. There is minimum damage to the pipes in transportation. The pipes being light in weight are used for large diameter pipe lines.

4.6.2 Cement Pipes

Main advantage of cement pipes in place of metallic pipes is their corrosion resistance. These pipes are bulky, heavy and require careful transportation and handling. The layout process of these pipes is costlier than steel pipes.

Asbestos Cement (AC) Pipes

These pipes are light in weight and easy in transportation and layout. They have smooth internal surface and are not affected by corrosion (rust). The pipes are extensively used for water supply systems. Holes can be drilled in these pipes. These pipes are not costlier.

4.6.3 Un-plasticized PVC (UPVC) Pipes

These pipes are rigid PVC pipes. They are light in weight, tough, resistant to chemical attack and large in length. Due to large in length the cost of handling is much whereas transportation and installation cost is less. Smooth internal surface of pipes provide less friction which results in saving of energy. These pipes are not suitable for the area which is very hot.

A trap is a device which is used to prevent sewer gases from entering the buildings. The traps are located below or within a plumbing fixture and retains small amount of water. The retaining water creates a water seal which stops foul gases going back to the building from drain pipes. Therefore all plumbing fixtures such as sinks, washbasins, bathtubs and toilets etc. are equipped with traps. This article tells you the features of traps, various types of traps and water seal.

A trap has the following features:

It may be manufactured as an integral trap with the appliance as in some models of European WC, or it may be a separate fitting called an attached trap, which is connected to waste or foul water outlet of appliances.

The traps should be of a self-cleansing pattern. Traps for use in domestic waste should be convenient for cleaning. A good trap should maintain an efficient water seal under all conditions of flow.

1. **Gully Trap:** These traps are constructed outside the building to carry waste water discharge from washbasin, sinks, bathroom etc. and are connected to the nearest building drain/sewer so that foul gases from sewer do not come to the house. These are deep seal traps, the depth of water seal should be 50 mm minimum. It also prevents the entry of cockroach and other insects from sewer line to waste pipes carrying waste water.

Fig. 4.8

2. **P Trap:** This trap is used with Indian water closet (ORISSA Pattern). The traps are made from cast iron or UPV sheet. This trap also has water seal and prevents entry of foul gases to the house.

Fig. 4.9

3. **Trap:** This trap is similar to P trap and is used for fixing water closets in toilets. The only difference between P trap and S trap is that P trap is used for outlet through the wall whereas S trap is used for outlet through the floor.

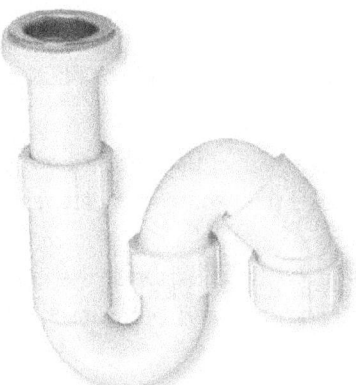

Fig. 4.10

4. **Floor Trap or Nahini Trap:** This trap is provided in the floor to collect waste water from washbasin, shower, sink and bathroom etc. These are available in cast iron or UPVC material and have removable grating (JALI) on the top of the trap. The minimum depth of water seal should be 50 mm.

5. **Intercepting Trap:** This trap is provided at the last main hole of building sewerage to prevent entry of foul gases from public sewer to building sewer. It has a deep-water seal of 100 mm.

6. **Grease Trap:** This trap is a device to collect the grease contents of waste and can be cleaned from the surface. This is generally used in food processing unit.

7. **Q Trap:** This trap is used in toilet under water closet. It is almost similar to S trap and is used in upper storey other than ground floor.

Water Seal: Water seal in a trap is the depth of water which should be removed from a fully charge trap before gases at atmospheric pressure may pass from the waste pipe through trap into a building. The tape is useless unless they retain their seals at all times. The seal may be broken due to air compressor, momentum and evaporation. The trap in fittings in range is liable to siphonic action and each trap should be ventilated.

4.7 RAIN WATER HARVESTING

Introduction: Every living organism requires air and water for survival mainly in addition to other parameters. We get air in abundance but as the availability of water totally depends upon rain.

We need water for the following reasons:

(i) Domestic uses such as drinking, cooking, bathing, washing, flushing toilets, cleaning utensils etc.

(ii) Agricultural practices.

(iii) Industrial use.

(iv) Other uses like – cleaning the roads, fire fighting, fountains etc.

Considering the asset and importance of water, towns, even in old ages, were developed nearby water bodies.

Initially the major percentage of population used to stay in rural areas but soon because of industrialization migration from rural to urban areas has set up in search of jobs. This phenomenal increase has pressurized the water supply in urban areas.

Even in the states like Assam where 1100 cm rainfall is observed, abundant surface runoff is responsible for inadequacy in water supply. Alongwith this in some of the areas there is depletion of water level because of many reasons. Bore wells already dug are becoming dry day by day.

In forthcoming years if we don't take proper steps for the resolution of the problem globally, we will face water scarcity. Future of water in India is in the hands of people, professionals, business sectors and the government.

Changes in atmospheric conditions, emission of CFCs, the interference of man in ecological/environmental activities is responsible for irregular and unbalanced rainfall. In turn to solve this problem we must store the rain water, recharge and replenish the water bodies. These are the only means by which sustainance for the water resources will be seen.

Need for Rain Water Harvesting:

Prior to industrialization and successive increased rate of urbanization, the natural filter for rain was the ground. This filter allows the penetration and hence the ground water was at substantial level. Continuous pumping of water for industrial use, domestic use etc., this level dropped down a lot. Also in urban areas specially, concrete pavements, foothpaths, parking area etc. were responsible for less filtration and more surface runoff leading finally towards sea.

Less deposition of water in this water bank below and more withdrawal for many activities are the keyfactors for this depletion of water. Hence, it is the responsibility of the mankind to increase this level. In this regard Rain Water Harvesting (RWH) is a very natural and cost effective solution which will improve the depleted water level.

Methods of RWH:

(i) Collection of rain water and utilization of the same.

(ii) Infiltration of the rain water into ground.

Aims:

(a) To control depletion of ground water level.

(b) To increase ground water table and its availability.

(c) To improve the quality of the ground water.

(d) To control the flow of sea water within the ground.

(e) To increase the availability of ground water as and when required at a particular place and particular time.

(f) To save the energy in turn.

Why RWH ?

1. To supply water and satisfy the increased demand.
2. To control floor in case of excessive rainfall.
3. To deposit rain water in water bank below ground.
4. To reduce contamination/pollution of ground water.
5. To improve the quality of ground water.
6. To control erosion of soil.

Advantages of RWH:

1. Self sustanaince in water availability.
2. Saving of energy.
3. Availability of soft water with high quality.
4. Less erosion of soil.
5. Cost effective techniques.

6. Easy employment of the technique.
7. It controls backflow of sea water.
8. It can be employed as a very effective tool in case of islands.

It is of utmost importance to study the geological characteristics of the land to adopt best possible technique in a particular area. Financial backing and the necessary support is given by National and State Government for RWH. Government of Maharashtra also has replenished RWH in the era of Chatrapati Shivaji on his forts.

Scope of RWH:

In Pimpri-Chinchwad region where the area is 171 sq. km, average annual rainfall is 600 mm. If this entire volume is stored we will get total volume of 1,02,600 million liters of water ($171 \times 1000 \times 1000 \times 0.6 \times 100$). That means 338 million liters of water will be available daily and the actual requirement of Municipal Corporation is 235 million liters, that means theoretically the availability is more than the requirement.

Considering the fact that if rainfall on 50% of terrace area is collected and stored then about 27 million liters per day which is around 12% of overall consumption per day.

Also the rain falling in agricultural land can be filtered through the soil layers which will improve ground water table and avoid soil erosion. The similar techniques are effectively employed by Shri. Anna Hajare in Ralegansiddhi, Shri. Popatrao Pawar in Hivare Bajar, Shri. Vijaykumar Kedia in Aurangabad, Shri. Rajendrasingh Jain in Rajasthan.

Roof top rain water harvesting: The quantum of rainfall collected from roof top is transferred to the tank by filtration and disinfected or filtered in ground to increase water table and then utilized as and when needed.

Following are the assets of roof top RWH:

1. Catchment area
2. Pipes
3. Filtration
4. Storage.

1. **Catchment Area:** Considering runoff coefficient for a particular area remaining part can be collected and stored, from terraces, roofs, footpaths etc.
2. **Pipes:** Normally used pipes for collection and transfer are PVC, Al, GI.
3. **Filtration:** The water collected from roofs is comparatively cleaner. But it is essential to filter it for the removal of soil particles, dust, floating objects etc. While recharging, water flowing from footpaths, roads, etc. it must be allowed to settle down in settling tank. Then this water is filtered.
4. **Storage:** After filtration the water is stored in water tanks above or below ground which are made up of RCC, bricks, stores, ferrocrete, PVC etc.

Recharging Technique: The types for recharging based on:

(a) Shallow structure: In this further classification is:
   (i) Pit method
   (ii) Trench method.

(b) Deeper Structure:
   (i) Bore wells
   (ii) Dug wells.

Details about Filters:

(i) Roof top water filter: Nearly 50,000 litres of water per annum can be stored or laid into borewell if the available roof is of area 1000 sq. ft. with annual rainfall of 600 mm.

Precautionary measures:

(a) Clean the roof carefully prior to rainy season.

(b) Do not allow the water to penetrate just after first fall.

(c) Filter can be cleaned by closing the valve infront of 'T' near borewell or tank and the water used for cleaning purpose is drained off from the 'T' closer to the roof side.

(d) For disinfection one may use TCL powder or potassium permanganate applied through 'T' section.

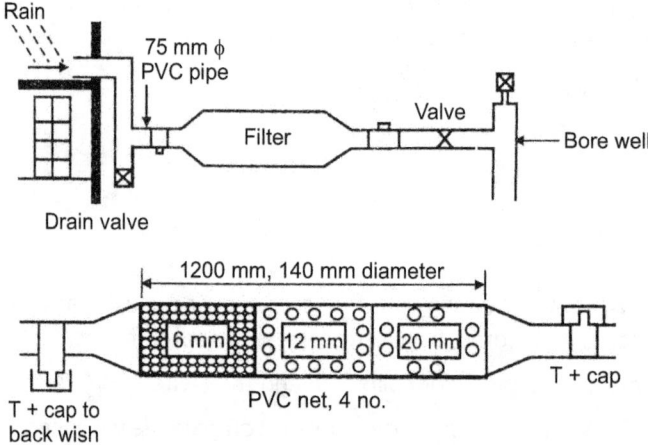

Fig. 4.11

(ii) Filter used in case of ferrocrete storage water tanks: Filtration tank is fitted above the ferrocrete water tank and filter medium is placed inside it. The water collected from top is collected from roof pipes and allowed to penetrate in the filter tank.

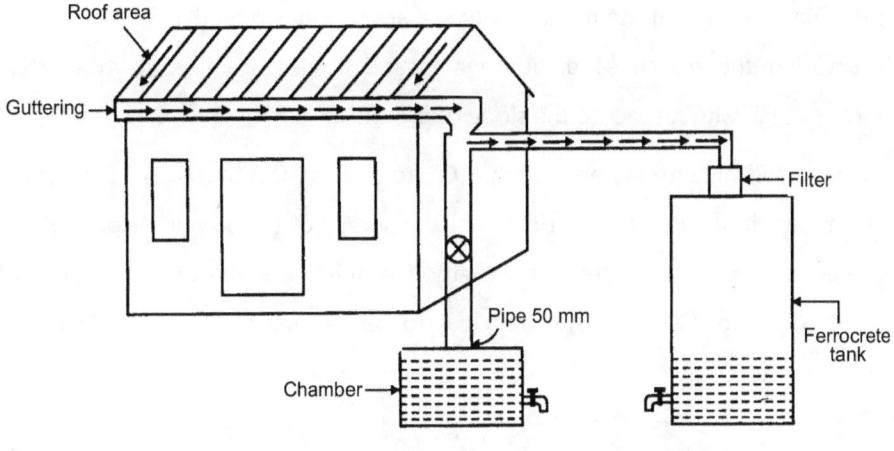

Fig. 4.12

Filter design will vary depending upon the available area and rainfall intensity.

Shallow Structure:

(a) Recharge pits: This is used for raising the shallow level ground water table. The dimensions for pit are $1 \times 1 \times 2$, $1 \times 1 \times 3$, $2 \times 2 \times 2$ or $2 \times 2 \times 3$ m^3 (or may be circular rectangular). After excavation the pit is filled with aggregates and stones. Care must be taken about the quality of water that will penetrate inside. It must be as clean as possible (i.e. avoid silted turbid water). The pit is to be cleaned periodically to remove silt. Normally this is to be adopted in case of 1000 sq. ft. roof top area. On the pit, grill is to be fitted to avoid any accident.

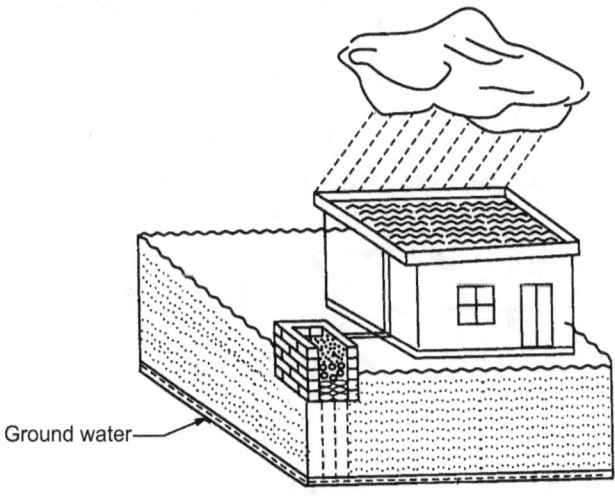

Fig. 4.13

(b) Recharge trench: If the top layers of soil are pervious then this method is preferred. After excavating the trench sand, aggregates and stones are filled with sand at top. The trench is at 90° with respect to the slope of ground.

Normally used dimensions are: width – 0.5 to 1.00 m, Depth 1.0 to 1.5 m and length 10 to 20 m; but these are finalized only after the survey of the area in respect of available area, rainfall, character of soil etc. This method is suitable when the available roof area ranges within 200 to 300 sq.m. The trench is to be cleaned frequently and grill is to be provided on the top.

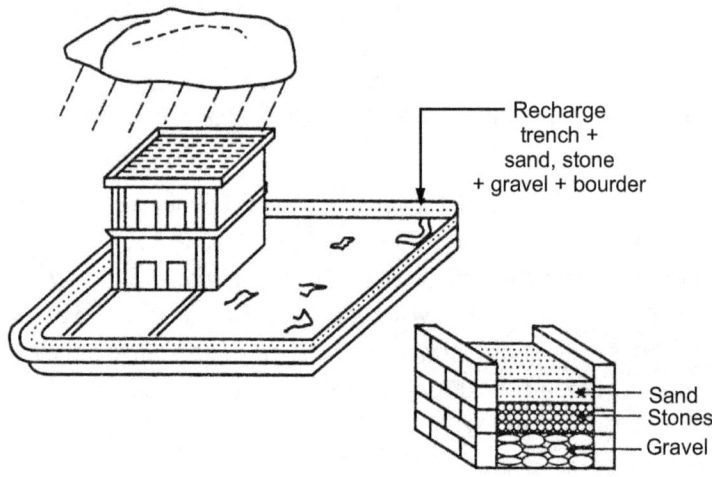

Fig. 4.14

Recharge well: If an old well is nearby any building then directly that well can be recharged by rain water collected from roof top after filtration.

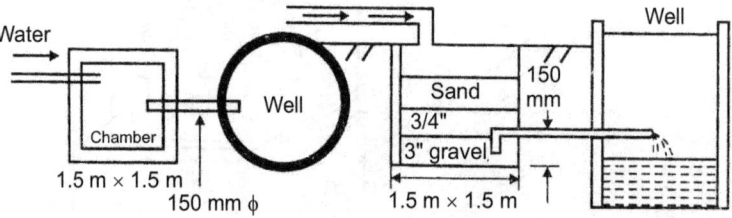

Fig. 4.15

Recharging the Borewell:

Sometimes in the borewell water is discharged through Ievas filters. But if the area available is more than the near borwell, a filter is provided and water is discharged.

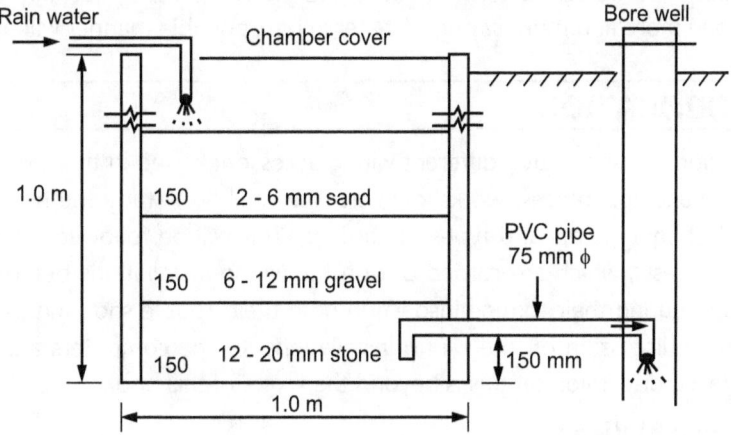

Fig. 4.16

Calculations:

Water quantity to be collected in one year (Q):

$$Q = A \times I \times R$$

where,
Q = Discharge in cu. m
A = Area in sq. m
I = Average annual rainfall in mm
R = Runoff coefficient

(GI sheets, clay tiles, slab = 0.8)

Available quantum of rainfall (in cu.m)

Rainfall mm	Roof top area (sq. m.)					
	50	60	70	80	90	100
500	20	24	28	32	36	40
600	24	28.8	33.6	38.4	43.2	48
700	28	33.6	39.2	44.8	50.4	56
800	32	38.4	44.8	51.2	57.6	64
900	36	43.2	50.4	57.6	64.8	72
100	40	48	56	64.0	72	80

Conclusion:

RWH is essentially to be employed because of increased demand of water. People participation, awareness and conscious efforts are the key factors for successful implementation of the technique. In addition to RWH, recycling techniques, if suitably considered, then more and more saving of water in best possible manner will be observed.

4.8 ELECTRIFICATION

In this section, we shall study different wiring accessories used in the wiring installations for residential buildings, offices, workshops, etc. We shall also study the needs of earthing for the electrical equipments and types of earthing. This will be followed by the discussion on the different tests, which are carried out on the wiring installations before they are put into service and during their routine inspection or in their trouble shooting. Finally, we shall have preliminary discussion on the wiring installations for the computers and their trouble shooting. Detailed discussion on this is beyond the scope of this book.

4.8.1 Types of Wires

Various types of wires are used for electrical wiring. The commonly used types are as follows:

(a) **V.I.R. (Vulcanised India Rubber) Wires:** This type of wire consists of a tinned conductor coated with rubber insulation. The thickness of rubber varies with the voltage for which the wire is designed i.e. 250 or 660 volts. This rubber insulation is not moisture or heat proof. Therefore, the conductor is further covered with protective cotton braiding saturated with heat and moisture resistant bitumen compound. For cleanliness and smoothness, it is finally finished with wax. These wires always have a single core. Because of their tendency to absorb the moisture quickly and the availability of other superior varieties at a cheaper cost, these wires are rarely used now-a-days.

(b) **C.T.S. (Cab Tyre Sheathed) / T.R.S. (Tough Rubber Sheathed) Wires:** In this, ordinary rubber insulated conductors are provided with an additional tough rubber sheath. Apart from providing extra insulation, this covering provides protection against moisture, chemical fumes and wear and tear. T.R.S. wires are available in single core, twin core and three core varieties.

(c) **Lead Sheathed Wires:** Similar to T.R.S. wires, in this variety also, ordinary rubber or paper insulated conductors are provided with an outer sheath of lead or lead alloy. It gives protection against moisture, atmospheric corrosion and wear and tear. These wires are available in single and multicore varieties. Being quite heavy and costlier, they are almost superseded by the C.T.S. / T.R.S. wires.

(d) P.V.C. (Poly Vinyl Chloride) Wires: These wires which are in most common use have conductors with P.V.C. insulation. P.V.C. is non-hygroscopic, tough, durable, resistant to corrosion and chemically inert, therefore, eminently suitable for general wiring work. P.V.C. insulation, being sufficiently tough to give mechanical protection, cotton taping or braiding is not essential as in the case of ordinary rubber insulated conductors. P.V.C. being a thermoplastic, softens at high temperature. Therefore, its use, where, extremes of temperatures are likely to occur, should be avoided. For example, it should not be used for giving connection to heating appliances.

(e) Weather Proof Wires: For outdoor service lines which are run at sufficient height and where the possibility of any one coming in contact with it is very small, costly wires like T.R.S. are not essential. Therefore, in such cases, weather-proof wires consisting of conductors with three braids of fibrous yarn, thoroughly saturated with a water-proof compound are used. These wires are cheap and at the same time, they are resistant to varying atmospheric conditions.

(f) Flexible Wires: These wires are normally used for pendant holders, household portable appliances such as heaters, irons, table lamps, etc. and wiring of temporary nature. The flexible wire normally consists of two separately insulated stranded conductors. The stranded conductors are used for flexibility and insulation used is either rubber or P.V.C. Cotton and silk braiding or T.R.S. sheathing is sometimes used in the case of rubber insulated conductors. Flexible wires are more commonly available in the parallel twin and twisted twin forms. The great advantage of flexible wire is the flexibility which makes the handling easy.

(g) Cables: Basically, a cable may be defined as a length of a single insulated conductor (solid or stranded) or two or more such conductors, each provided with its own insulation and put together. It may have in addition, an overall mechanical protective covering.

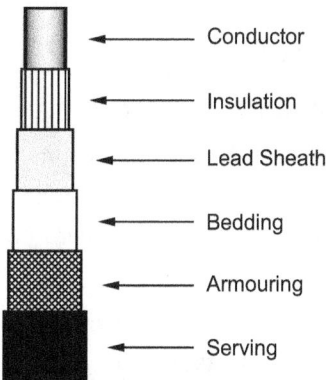

Fig. 4.17: General construction of the underground cable

The cables which are normally used by the supply undertakings for distribution purposes and which are laid along the wall poles are known as aerial cables. These cables are insulated with V.I.R. or P.V.C. or use varnish cambric. Being mechanically sound and weather proof, the V.I.R. and P.V.C. cables are mostly used for general outdoor works. Cables are also designed for underground laying and known as underground cables. Even though it is costly, an underground system of distribution is preferred in urban areas. Fig. 4.17 shows the general construction of the cable used for such a purpose. It consists of the following:

Conductor or Core: Each cable has one central core or a number of cores (2, 3, 3½ or 4) which are normally made up of tinned stranded copper or aluminium conductors. Stranding gives flexibility to the cable.

Insulation: Commonly used insulating materials are varnished cambric, vulcanised bitumen or impregnated paper. Impregnated paper is invariably used for high-voltage cables.

Metallic Sheath: Usually, a lead alloy or aluminium sheath is provided over the insulation for providing mechanical protection and preventing entry of moisture in the insulation which impairs its insulating property.

Bedding: The bedding consists of a layer of fibrous material like a paper tape compounded with jute or sometimes, a tape of strong coarse cloth of jute. It protects the metallic sheath against corrosion and from mechanical injury due to armouring.

Armouring: Armouring, usually consisting of one or two layers of galvanised steel wire or steel tape, is provided to protect the cable from mechanical injury while laying it and during the coarse of its use.

Serving: A layer of fibrous material like jute cloth is provided over the armouring to protect it from atmospheric conditions. This layer is known as serving.

4.8.2 Designation of Wires

The wires are normally specified in accordance with the following:

(i) **Types of Conductors:** Copper and aluminium conductors are most commonly used for wires. Even though the copper conductors are superior to aluminium conductors in almost all respects, due to their non-availability and exorbitant cost, they are rarely used now-a-days.

(ii) **Types of Wires:** Particularly this has reference to the insulation used e.g. V.I.R., C.T.S. / T.R.S., P.V.C., etc. Suitability of different types of wires for various applications has already been explained previously.

(iii) Sizes of Wires: The current flow through the wire causes heat proportional to the square of the current. Due to this heat, there is a limit to the current carrying capacity of the conductor of a given size. The insulation of the conductor also cannot withstand heat beyond a particular limit. Therefore, standards are laid down indicating the maximum values of currents which can be safely carried by the wires of various sizes with different insulations. Instead of referring to the wire sizes in terms of cross-sectional areas, they are designated by the gauge numbers assigned to them. The British standard Wire Gauge (Fig. 4.18) is commonly used in India.

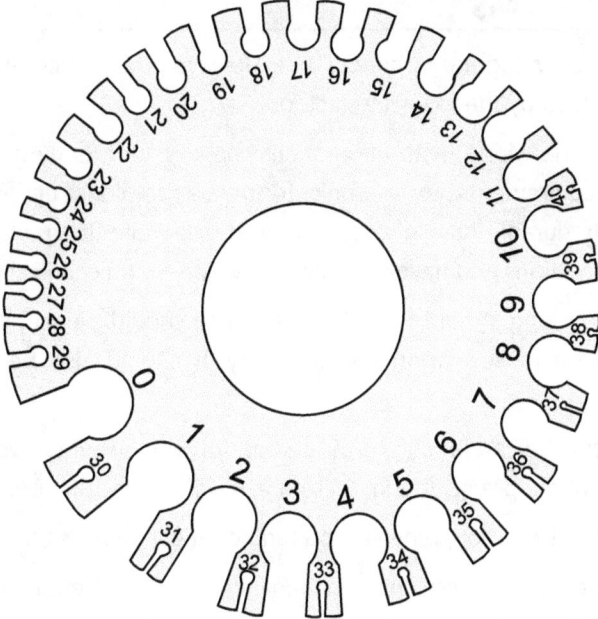

Fig. 4.18: Standard wire gauge

The smallest wire gauge is of No. 40 having a diameter of 0.1219 mm. The largest number of wire is 0,000,000 (named as seven zero) or written as 7/0, having a diameter of 12.7000 mm. Thus, it will be observed that the higher the number of wire gauge, the smaller is the diameter.

The wires used for ordinary house wiring purposes have single solid conductors, whereas, wires with higher capacities or flexible wires have stranded conductors for flexibility. Therefore, the sizes of wires are specified by the number of strands and their gauge number. For example, a wire of '1/18' size will have a single solid conductor of 18 SWG, whereas, a wire of '3/20' size will have three strands of 20 SWG.

In accordance with the new trend, now-a-days, the sizes of the wires are also denoted by cross-sectional area in square millimetres e.g. 1.5 sq. mm, 2.5 sq. mm, etc.

(iv) **Number of Cores:** Wires (cables) when used for some specific applications may have single, 2, 3, 3½ or 4 cores.

(v) **Voltage Grading:** It is the voltage to which the insulation of a wire can safely withstand. Wires are normally graded for 250 V or 660 V.

4.9 WIRING SYSTEMS

Several systems of wiring are in general use. However, the choice of the particular type of wiring will be decided by the following factors:

(i) **Durability:** The wiring installation should have a sufficiently useful life depending upon the requirements. For example, for permanent constructions, the wiring must be perfectly durable having a long span of useful life. It should withstand all odd weather conditions and have adequate provision for mechanical protection of wires.

(ii) **Safety:** The wiring should be quite safe. There should be no possibility of leakage or shock to a person using the electricity. It should also be free from the fire hazards.

(iii) **Appearance:** The careful choice of the type of wiring will always help in enhancing the beauty of the premises and, therefore, have architectural importance.

(iv) **Accessibility:** Extension, renewal or alteration must be possible.

(v) **Maintenance:** The lesser the maintenance required better is the system, as it reduces the maintenance cost. Fault finding must be easy and quick.

(vi) **Cost:** The system should be economical involving the less initial cost.

4.9.1 Various Systems of Wiring

The following systems of wiring are commonly used in actual practice:

(a) **Cleat Wiring:** This system employs V.I.R. or P.V.C. wires which are gripped between porcelain cleats with one, two or three grooves according to the requirements to accommodate a corresponding number of wires. These cleats are fixed by means of screws directly on to the wooden beams.

However, in case of brick and concrete walls, they are fixed with the help of rawl plugs or wood plugs (gutties) already cemented in the wall (Fig. 4.19).

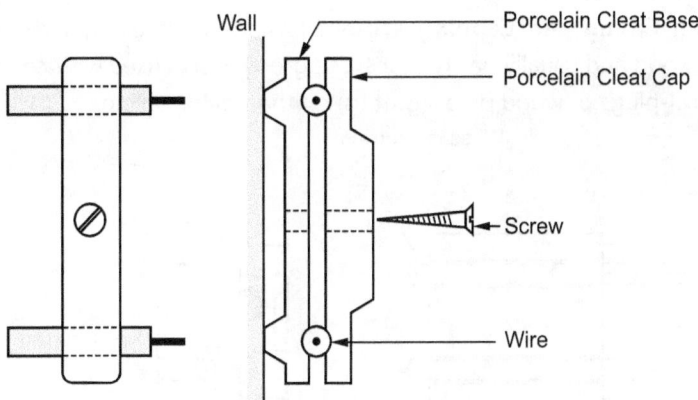

Fig. 4.19: Cleat wiring

Application: This system is rarely used at present, except for temporary work.

Advantages:

(i) Erection involves least skill.

(ii) One of the cheapest methods of wiring.

(iii) Installation and dismantling being very quick, the method is most suitable for temporary works.

(iv) The material can be fully recovered without any damage after dismantling the wiring when it is not required.

(v) Inspection, extension, renewal or alteration is very easy.

Disadvantages:

(i) Because of dirt and dust and sagging at some places, it looks shabby after some time.

(ii) Wires are easily damaged due to inadequate mechanical protection.

(iii) Since the wires are directly exposed to atmosphere, moisture impairs their insulation and chemical fumes, lime (used during white washing), etc. have a corrosive action on them.

(iv) Oil, smoke, etc. add to the possibilities of the fire hazards.

(v) Maintenance cost is high.

Because of the very serious disadvantages mentioned above, this type of wiring is not permitted for permanent jobs.

(b) Wooden Casing and Capping Wiring: Casing is a rectangular strip made from seasoned teak wood and usually has two or three grooves. It is fixed with countersunk wood screws using rawl-plugs or wood plugs (gutties) on the wall or ceiling.

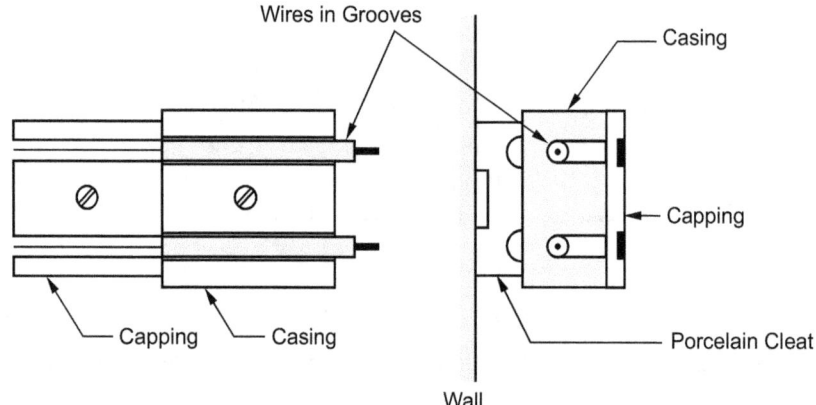

Fig. 4.20: Casing-capping wiring

Porcelain round cleats are used to keep the casing away from the walls or ceilings in order to protect it from dampness. The V.I.R. or P.V.C. wires are run in the grooves in a wooden casing. The casing is then finally covered at the top by a rectangular wooden strip of the same width as that of the casing. This strip known as capping, is then screwed to the casing (Fig. 4.20). The casing and capping are given a double coating of shellac varnish from inside and at the back. They are painted or varnished from the outside after erection.

Application: This system is now almost superseded by other types of wiring even though it was very popularly used for residential and commercial buildings in the early days. However, it is still in use for special situations and in places to fit in with the internal decorations of a room.

Advantages:

    (i) Gives good mechanical protection to the conductors.

    (ii) Neat appearance.

    (iii) Installation and repairs are easy in comparison with conduit wiring.

Disadvantages:

    (i) The system is costly since it involves highly skilled labour.

    (ii) Wood being inflammable, it is quite susceptible to fire hazards.

    (iii) Inspite of coating with varnish, it cannot be used in damp situations.

(c) Metal Sheathed or Lead Sheathed Wiring: This system employs rubber or paper insulated conductors with a lead sheath.

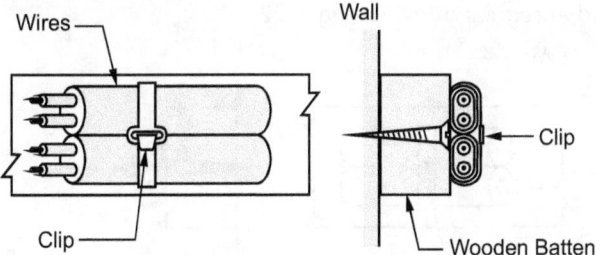

Fig. 4.21: Lead sheathed wiring

These wires are run on the wooden battens fixed to the brick or concrete walls by means of screws and rawl plugs or wood plugs. The metal clips spaced at regular intervals are used to clamp the wires to the batten (Fig. 4.21).

The lead sheath is efficiently earthed to provide a safety against the metal sheath becoming alive and to avoid electrolytic action due to leakage current on it.

Application: This system is also superseded by the C.T.S. system, but still preferred in damp situations as on ships.

Advantages:

(i) Neat appearance.

(ii) Lead sheath provides protection against fires, high temperature, moisture and to some extent against mechanical injuries. Due to this feature, this type of wiring can be used for outdoor work.

(iii) It is particularly suitable in damp situations.

Disadvantages:

(i) Lead sheathed wires are costly.

(ii) The lead sheath is to be effectively earthed to avoid any possibility of electrical shocks and to prolong the life of the lead sheath which otherwise is reduced due to the electrolytic action of leakage current.

(iii) Sharp bends sometimes cause breaking of the lead cover.

(d) Tough Rubber Sheathed (T.R.S.) or Cab-Tyre Sheathed (C.T.S.) Wiring: This wiring is similar to lead sheathed wiring except that C.T.S. or T.R.S. wires are used in place of lead sheathed wires.

Initially the wooden battens are fixed to the brick or concrete walls by means of screws and rawl plugs or wood plugs. The wires are run on these battens and clamped with the help of metal clips spaced at regular intervals (Fig. 4.22).

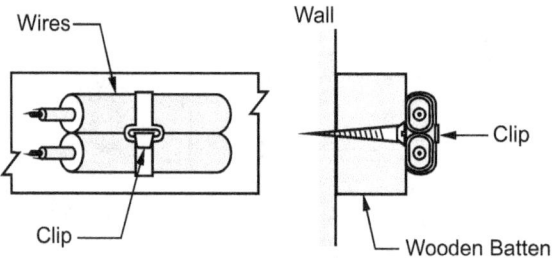

Fig. 4.22: T.R.S. / C.T.S. wiring

Application: It is most widely used for indoor wiring for houses, shops, offices, etc.

Advantages:

(i) Neat appearance.

(ii) Tough rubber sheath or cab tyre sheath gives good mechanical protection and is unaffected by moisture, chemical fumes, paint or wet plaster.

(iii) Being cheaper, more rapid and easier to erect than the wooden casing-capping and lead sheathed wiring, it is the most widely used system of surface wiring.

Disadvantage: It should not be used for outdoor work where wiring is exposed to sun as it cannot withstand much heat.

(e) Conduit Wiring: In this system, V.I.R. or P.V.C. wires are run through black enamelled or galvanised metallic tubing called conduits.

Types of conduits: The following two types of conduits are normally used for this type of wiring.

(i) **Thin Wall Conduits:** These are the light gauge iron conduits with a seam along its length. The seam may be an open type with no mechanical adhesion between its two edges as in split conduits or sometimes these edges are brazed together which makes the conduits damp proof. Friction tight slip fittings are normally used to join conduit ends.

(ii) **Rigid Conduits:** These are the heavy gauge iron conduits either solid drawn or with welded seam. The ends of conduit length and various fittings to join them are always threaded. These conduits being more costly, are normally used for all medium pressure (250 to 600 volts) circuits and in places where a good degree of mechanical protection and absolute protection from moisture is required.

Types of Conduit Wiring: Depending upon whether the conduits are laid inside the walls or supported on the walls, there are two types of conduit wiring:

(i) **Surface Conduit Wiring:** In this method, conduits are fixed on the walls by means of saddles screwed to rawl plugs or wood plugs embedded in the wall. In damp situations, these conduits are spaced apart from the wall surface by small wooden blocks fixed below the pipe at regular intervals as illustrated in Fig. 4.23.

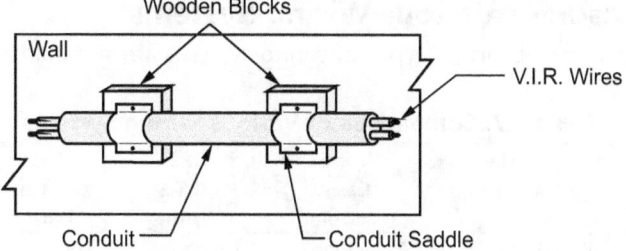

Fig. 4.23: Surface conduit wiring

(ii) **Concealed Conduit Wiring:** This method employs heavy gauge rigid conduits burried under wall plaster. Such wiring is used in cases where beauty is the main consideration irrespective of cost.

In both the above types, it is essential that the whole length of the conduit piping is kept at earth potential by proper earthing.

Wiring of the Conduits: The drawing in method of wiring the conduit is most commonly adopted. After planning the layout carefully, the conduits are erected in position with a number of draw-in (or inspection) fittings provided along the length. Then V.I.R. or P.V.C. wires are drawn through the conduits by means of a steel draw wire. In order that the wires may be easily pulled, they are sometimes rubbed with French chalk.

Application: Surface conduit wiring is mainly used for all indoor and outdoor wirings of permanent nature for light and power e.g. in godowns, workshops and public buildings. The concealed type is preferably used in public buildings, offices, shops and houses for its nice appearance.

Advantages:
  (i) Very long life.
  (ii) Provides good protection against mechanical injury, moisture and fire hazards.
  (iii) Neat appearance. Particularly, the concealed type of conduit wiring adds to the beauty of the building.
  (iv) Less maintenance.

Disadvantages:
(i) Most costly system of wiring.
(ii) Erection requires highly skilled labour and time.
(iii) Repairs, particularly with concealed wiring are difficult and take long time.
(iv) In the absence of earth continuity on all conduit joints, there is the possibility of an electrical shock.
(v) If proper precautions are not taken to file sharp edges of the conduits, there is possibility of damage to the wire insulation.

4.9.2 Comparison of Various Wiring Systems

Comparative aspects of various types of wiring systems are summarized in the following Table 4.7.

Table 4.7: Comparison of Various Wiring Systems

Sr. No.	Particulars	Cleat Wiring	Wooden Casing Capping	T.R.S./ C.T.S. Wiring	Lead Sheathed Wiring	Conduit Wiring
1.	Durability of life	Short	Fairly long	Long	Long	Very long
2.	Mechanical protection	Poor	Good	Fair	Good	Very good
3.	Appearance	Shabby	Neat	Neat	Neat	Good particularly with concealed type
4.	Possibility of fire hazards	Rare	More than in other types	Rare	Rare	Nil
5.	Protection from dampness	Nil	Poor	Good	Very good	Poor with split conduits. However, fair with rigid conduits.
6.	Type of labour required	Semi-skilled	Highly skilled	Skilled	Skilled	Highly skilled
7.	Cost	Low	Medium	Medium	Costlier than casing capping or C.T.S. wiring	High
8.	Application	For temporary installations	General indoor wiring in houses, shops, offices. Superseded by C.T.S./ T.R.S. wiring	Most widely used in indoor wiring for houses, shops, offices	Used only in damp situations	Concealed type for all public buildings, offices, shops and houses. Surface conduit wiring for godowns, workshops and public buildings.

4.10 WIRING INSTALLATIONS

The power to the wiring installation is tapped from the low-voltage distribution line known as the *distributor*. The wires supplying power from the distributor to the wiring installation are known as *service mains*. As an illustration, Fig. 4.24 shows the layout of a typical wiring installation for a small house.

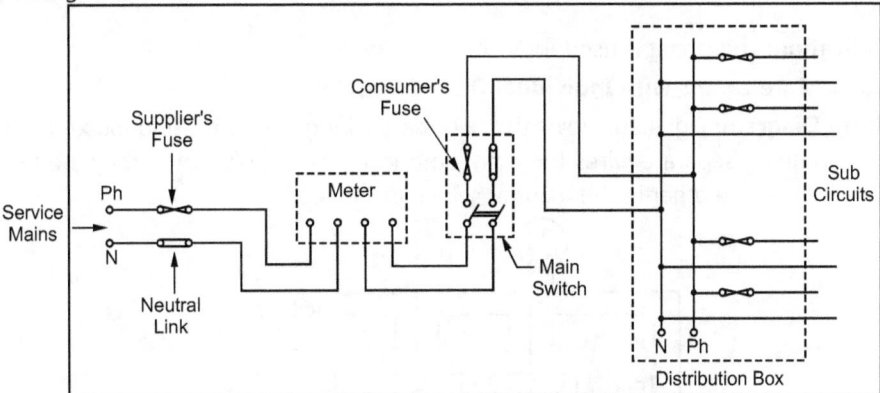

Fig. 4.24: Domestic wiring installation

The supply is a single phase a.c. and brought in through the supply company's sealed fuse box and meter to the consumer's main switch. From the main switch, supply is given to the distribution box which feeds the various sub-circuits. Two separate meters may be provided, one for lighting (with 5 amperes capacity) and the other for power (with 15 amperes capacity). For the sub-circuit supplying lighting load, the number of points connected (i.e. lamps, tubes, fans, etc.) should not exceed 10 and the total load should not be more than 800 watts. For sub-circuit supplying power to appliances such as heaters, electric irons, single-phase motors, etc. the number of points connected in one sub-circuit should not exceed two and the total load should not be more than 3000 watts.

4.11 SIMPLE WIRING DIAGRAMS

In general, the house wiring involves various types of circuits for lamps, fans and other devices controlled from one or more points depending upon the requirements. Wiring diagrams for few of the commonly used circuits are discussed below:

(a) Control of One Lamp by Means of One Single-Pole Switch:

Wiring Diagram: For controlling the lamp L, a single-pole switch A is introduced in its circuit as shown in Fig. 4.25.

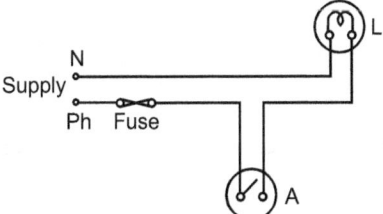

Fig. 4.25: Wiring diagram for control of one lamp by one single-pole switch

The live or phase wire is always connected to the lamp holder through the switch, whereas, neutral is connected directly to it. All the accessories such as a single-pole switch, lamp holder, etc. are always fitted on the teak-wood round blocks.

Working: When the switch is turned on, a full-supply voltage is applied across the lamp terminals and the lamp glows. Thus, the lamp can be independently controlled by the single-pole switch.

Application: The circuit is used for single room wiring.

(b) Two or More Lamps with Individual On-off Control:

Wiring Diagram: Fig. 4.26 shows the necessary wiring diagram using *looping-in system*. Instead of running separate wires for each lamp from the supply point, they are looped in from one lamp to the other in the manner shown in Fig. 4.26.

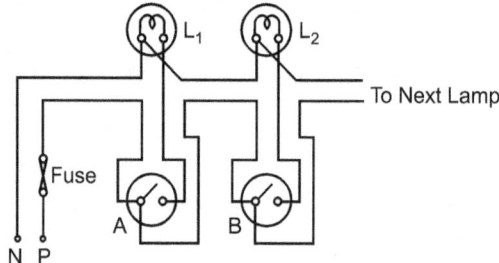

Fig. 4.26: Two or more lamps with individual on-off control

Working: In this case, it will be observed that the position of any switch does not affect the working of other lamps and thus, each lamp is controlled independently by its own switch.

Application: This system is commonly used in domestic wiring as it saves length of wire and other wiring material and avoids the soldered joints.

(c) Control of One Lamp, One Wall Socket and One Fan with Individual On-off Control:

Wiring Diagram: Fig. 4.27 shows the necessary wiring diagram using looping-in system.

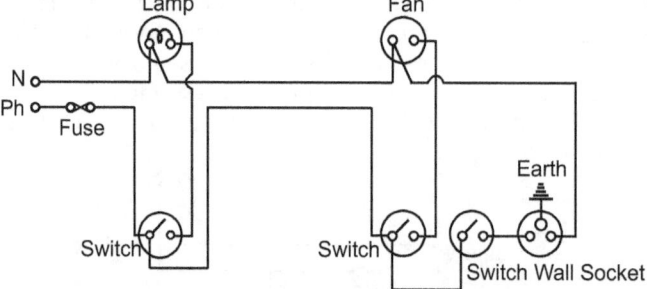

Fig. 4.27: Wiring diagram for the control of one lamp, one wall socket and one fan

Working: Fig. 4.27 is self-explanatory.

Application: This system is commonly used in house wiring.

(d) Control of Two Lamps, Two Wall Sockets and Two Fans with Individual On-off Control:

Wiring Diagram: Fig. 4.28 shows the necessary wiring diagram using looping-in system.

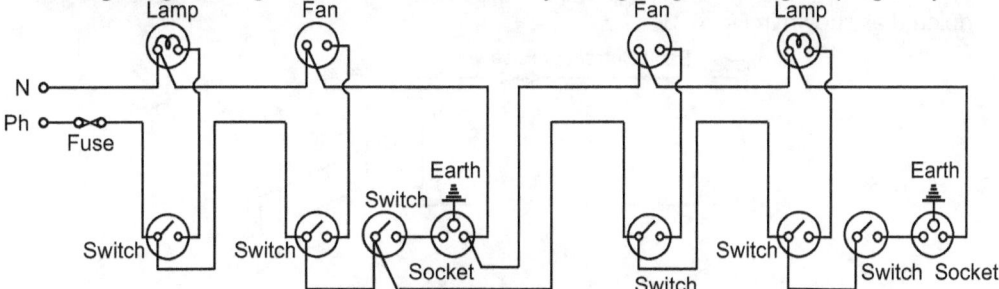

Fig. 4.28: Wiring diagram for the control of two lamps, two wall sockets and two fans with individual on-off control

Working: Fig. 4.28 is self-explanatory.

Application: This system is commonly used in house wiring.

4.12 NECESSITY OF EARTHING

In order to ensure safety in electrical installations, it is essential that all metal casings containing conductors (e.g. conduits, the frames of the motors and other appliances) must be connected to the general mass of earth, supposed to be at zero potential, by a wire of negligible resistance. This is generally known as *earthing* or *grounding*.

To understand the utility of such earthing, consider a non-earthed piece of metal-cased appliance such as a heater connected to the supply (Fig. 4.29).

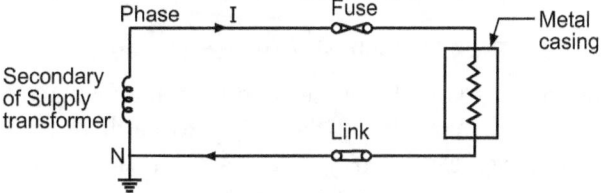

Fig. 4.29: Non-earthed appliance connected to supply

If a fault develops causing contact between the conductor and the casing, the casing becomes live with respect to earth by acquiring a potential equal to that of the phase wire (Fig. 4.30).

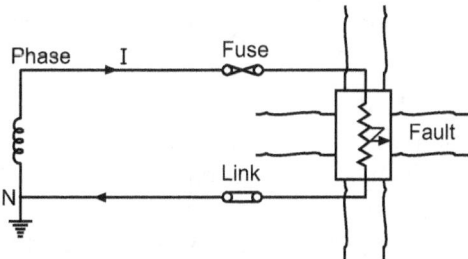

Fig. 4.30: Fault with non-earthed appliance

If the casing is standing on an insulating or partially insulating surface, there will be no leakage current and the appliance continues to operate. But this state of affairs is highly dangerous. When a person touches the metal casing of the appliance, a circuit to earth is completed as shown in Fig. 4.31.

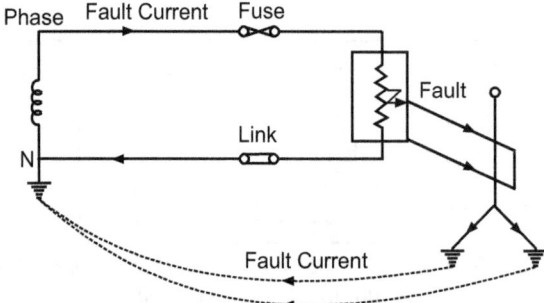

Fig. 4.31: Faulty non-earthed appliance giving an electric shock

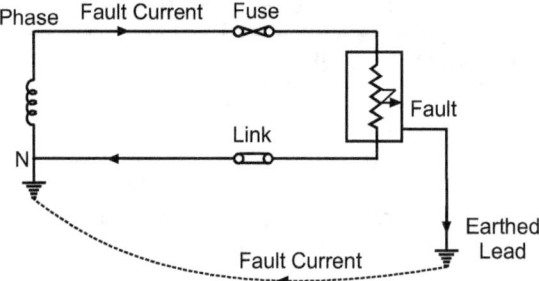

Fig. 4.32: Fault with earthed appliance

The fault current flows through the phase conductor, the fault and the person to earth. In this condition, the person completing the circuit to earth receives an electric shock. If, however, the casing is well earthed (Fig. 4.32), its potential cannot rise appreciably and immediately upon occurrence of a severe type of fault, a large current flows through the earth lead, back to the earthed neutral point, blowing the fuse and disconnecting the appliance from the supply. This isolation of the appliance not only makes it safe from the point of view of electric shock but also saves it from further damage. However, to achieve this, a fuse must be provided in the live wire only and not in the neutral wire.

Methods of Earthing:

Any metal plate, pipe, rod, other conductor embedded in earth and which makes an effective electrical connection with the general mass of earth is known as *earth electrode*. For small installations such as residential buildings, one electrode is sufficient, in addition to the earth connection through the overhead or underground service connection. For larger installations including substations, several electrodes connected together in parallel are to be provided.

Depending upon the type of electrode used, following are the commonly used methods of earthing:

(a) Plate Earthing: In this method as illustrated in Fig. 4.33, the earth wire is securely bolted to the earth plate either of copper (minimum size: 60 cm × 60 cm × 3.18 mm) or of galvanized iron (minimum size: 60 cm × 60 cm × 6.35 mm) burried in the ground to the depth of 3 m.

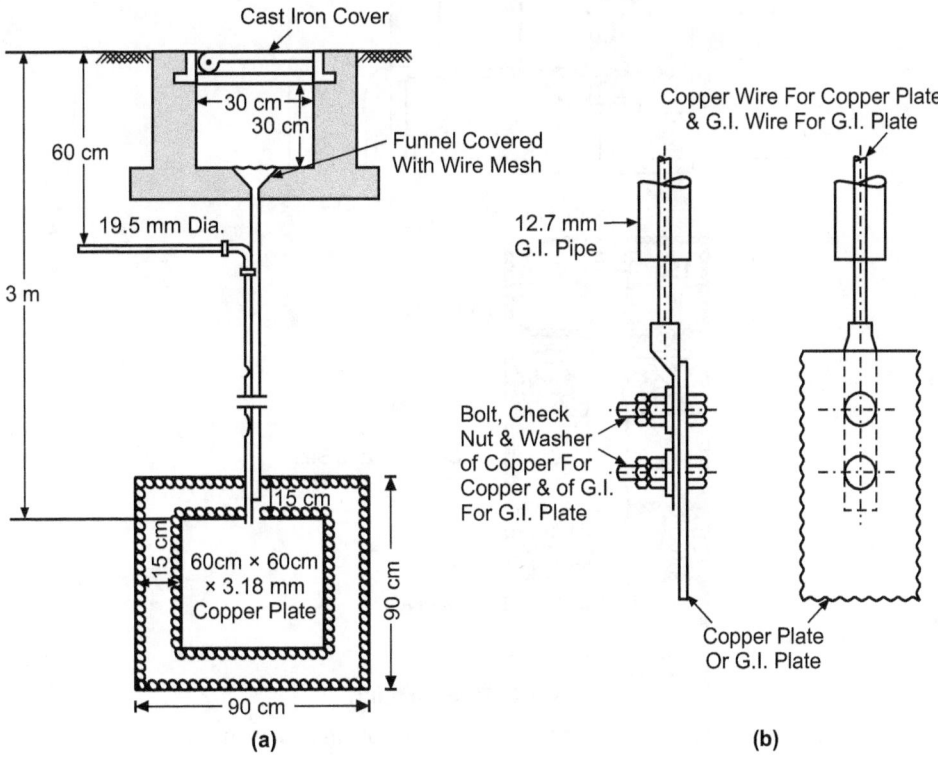

Fig. 4.33: Plate earthing

The plate is kept in vertical position and is embedded in an alternate layer of coke and salt, each with a minimum thickness of about 15 cm. The layers of coke and salt help to reduce the earth resistance. A galvanized iron pipe fitted with funnel at the top is provided to pour salty water in the pit of earth plate from time to time in the summer season when the moisture content in the soil reduces to a large extent.

(b) Pipe Earthing: In this method (Fig. 4.34), the galvanized iron pipe of not less than 38.1 mm diameter and 2 m in length for ordinary soil and 2.75 m for dry and rocky soil is embedded vertically in the ground to work as earth electrode. The depth at which the pipe should be burried in the ground depends upon the soil condition. The earth wire is fastened to the top section of the pipe with nut bolts. The pit area around the galvanized iron pipe is filled with alternate layers of salt and broken pieces of coke or charcoal. A funnel is fitted to the galvanized iron pipe at the top to pour salty water in the pit of earth electrode from time to time in the summer season as mentioned in the case of plate earthing.

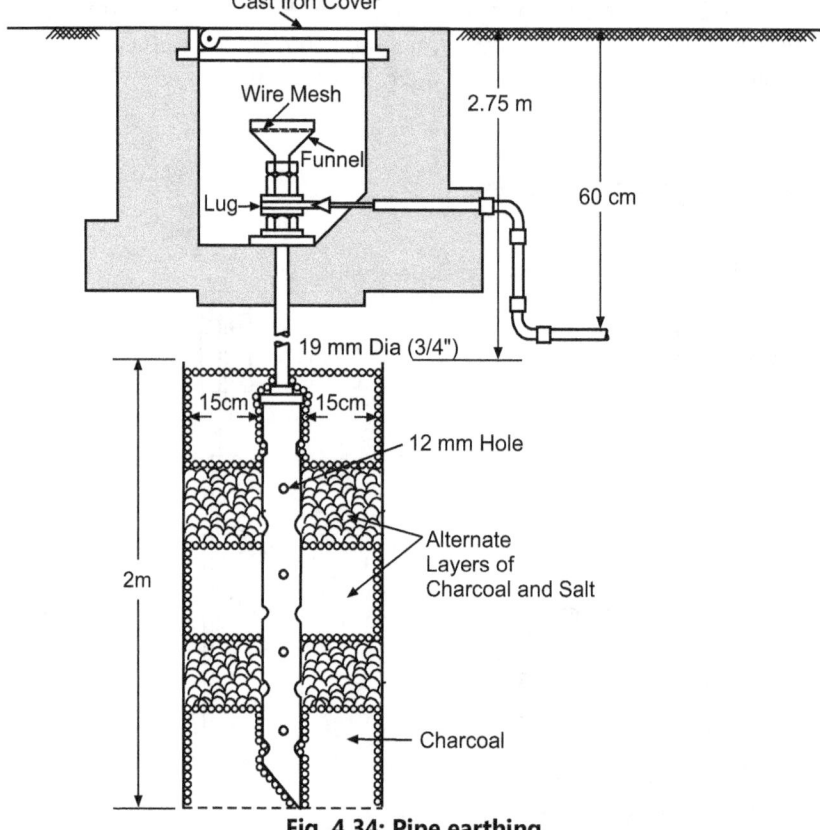

Fig. 4.34: Pipe earthing

In this method, the earth wire connection with galvanized iron pipe being above the ground level, it can be easily checked for carrying out continuity tests as and when desired. It is an advantage of this method over the plate earthing.

4.13 FIRE RESISTANCE IN BUILDING

Fire is an essential and integral part of our daily life but any misuse or accident in the use of fire can precipitate disaster.

Fires in buildings are nearly always man-made, resulting from error or negligence.

In olden times, dwellings were mostly timber - framed construction with thatched roofs, and within the walled townships overcrowding, narrow lanes, overhanging eaves and indiscriminate use of combustible materials provided all the necessary ingredients for the conflagrations which followed.

Towards the end of the nineteenth century, it was possible to construct large multi-storeyed buildings, the structural elements of which were of non-combustible materials. However, even today, inspite of using the most modern techniques of construction and fire resistant materials, fires still occur and cause a lot of damage to property and life.

Several rules and regulations have been drafted by government bodies to ensure the nature and quality of fire protection and safety accorded to a building.

The main purpose of fire safety legislation is:

1. To impose a level of fire safety, such that it is unlikely that people occupying a building would suffer injury in the event of an unwanted fire.
2. To protect the community at large from the consequences of a fire in an individual building.

Building regulations assume that if certain components of fire safety can be identified and suitable standards applied to particular building types, a satisfactory level of fire safety will be achieved.

It is assumed that if the purpose, for which buildings will be generally used, can be determined; then buildings used for a similar purpose can be classified as a particular building type. This method assumes that each building of a particular type will:

(i) have the same fire loading,

(ii) be of similar geometry,

(iii) experience a similar fire scenario and

(iv) be exposed to a fire of similar severity.

Hence, the standards for components of fire safety can be prescribed for building types.

Thus, building classification becomes a factor in risk determination.

Fire Safety

"Fire Safety is defined a person in or adjacent to a building will be exposed to an unacceptable fire hazard as a result of the design and construction of the building".

In simpler terms, fire safety is the reduction of the potential for harm to life as a result of fire in buildings. Although the potential for being killed or injured in a fire cannot be completely eliminated, fire safety in a building can be achieved through proven building design features intended to minimize the risk of harm to people from fire to the greatest extent possible. Designing a building to ensure minimal risk or to meet a prescribed level of safety from fire is more complex than just the simple consideration of what building materials will be used in construction of the building.

4.14 CLASSIFICATION OF BUILDINGS BASED ON OCCUPANCY

All buildings are classified according to the use or the character of occupancy into the following groups:

Group	
A	Residential
B	Educational
C	Institutional
D	Assembly
E	Business
F	Mercantile
G	Industrial
H	Storage
J	Hazardous

Group A: Residential Buildings:

These include any building in which sleeping accommodation is provided for normal residential purposes, with or without cooking or dining.

For example, residential houses, apartments, lodging and boarding houses, hotels, hostels, etc.

Group B: Educational Buildings:

These include buildings for schools, colleges or day care purposes involving assembly for instruction and education.

Group C: Institutional Buildings:

These include hospitals and sanatoria; homes for the aged, the convalescent and orphans; buildings for jails, prisons, mental hospitals, etc.

Group D: Assembly Buildings:

These are buildings in which groups of people congregate or gather for amusement, recreation, social and religious activities and also for activities related to travel.

For example, theatres, assembly halls, auditoria, exhibition halls, museums, gymnasiums, restaurants, places of worship, dance halls, clubs, passenger stations and terminals of air, surface and marine public transportation services, stadia, etc.

Group E: Business Buildings:

These are buildings which are used for transaction of business, for keeping of accounts and records, professional establishments, service facilities, etc.

For example, city halls, town halls, court rooms, libraries, offices, banks, laboratories, research establishments, etc.

Group F: Mercantile Buildings:

These are buildings which are used as shops, stores, market; for display and sale of merchandise.

Group G: Industrial Buildings:

These are buildings in which products or materials of all kinds are fabricated, assembled, manufactured or processed.

Group H: Storage Buildings:

These are buildings used primarily for the storage or sheltering of goods, wares or merchandise (except those that involve highly combustible materials or explosives), vehicles or animals.

For example, warehouses, cold storage, truck and marine terminals, garages, grain elevators, barns and stables.

Group I: Hazardous Buildings:

These include buildings which are used for storage, handling, manufacture or processing of highly combustible or explosive materials or products which are liable to burn rapidly and/or produce poisonous fumes or explosions.

For example, storage under pressure of acetylene, hydrogen, natural gas, ammonia, etc.

Storage and handling of highly inflammable materials or liquids, rocket propellants, etc.

Manufacture of artificial flowers, synthetic leather, ammunition, explosives, fire crackers, match sticks, etc.

4.15 FIRE LOAD

The term fire load is used to describe the heat energy which could be released per square metre of floor area of a compartment or storey by the combustion of the contents of the building and any combustible parts of the superstructure itself.

$$\text{Fire load} = \frac{M \times C}{A} \text{ in kJ/m}^2$$

where,

M = Mass of combustible materials in the compartment or storey, in kg

C = Calorific value of materials, in kJ/kg

A = Floor area, in m².

Building regulations have adopted a grouping system, which is a grading of occupancies based on assumed fire loadings. The grouping of buildings is then used as a determinant in establishing the desirable fire-resisting characteristics of the elements of the structure of the building.

Thus, it is seen that the concept of fire loading attempts is to relate the combustible contents of a building to the potential severity of a fire in that building and consequently to the fire-resisting capabilities of the elements of the structure.

Broadly, the buildings are classified into the following three groups depending upon the fire load.

Building hazard classification	Fire load in kJ/m²
Low hazard group	0 - 49
Medium hazard group	50 - 100
High hazard group	> 100

Certain rules and regulations have been framed by government bodies, which direct that all the buildings must statisfy certain requirements which contribute individually and collectively, to the safety of life from fire, smoke, fumes and panic arising from fire.

The following are some of the general requirements:

- Every building must be restricted in its height above the ground level regarding the number of storeys, depending upon its occupancy and type of construction.
- Open spaces around or inside a building must conform to the requirements of local development control rules and general building requirements.
- For high rise buildings (height more than 15 m), the following additional requirements must be considered.
    (a) The width of the main street on which the building abuts should not be less than 12 m.
    (b) The road should not have a dead end.
    (c) Compulsory open spaces around the building must not be used as parking spaces.
    (d) Adequate passageways and clearances required for fire fighting vehicles to enter the premises must be provided at the entrance, the width of such an entrance should not be less than 4.5 m. If an arch or a covered gate is constructed; it should have a clear head room of not less than 5 m.
- Fire detecting and extinguishing systems must be provided as per accepted standards according to the type of occupancy.
- All buildings depending upon the occupancy, use and height, should be protected by wet riser, wet riser-cum-down comer, automatic sprinkler installation, high pressure water spray or foam generating system etc. as per accepted standards.
- Static water storage tanks: A satisfactory supply of water for the purpose of fire fighting should always be available in the form of an underground static storage tank with its capacity specified for each building.

- Automatic sprinklers can be installed in basements used as carparks; departmental stores, shops of area more than 750 m²; godowns and warehouses on all floors of the buildings other than residential buildings, if the height of the building exceeds 45 m.
- Air conditioning and ventilating systems should be so installed and maintained as to minimise the danger of fire, smoke or fumes spreading from one floor to another or from outside into any occupied building or structure.
- For buildings over 15 m in height, fire lifts should be provided with a minimum capacity of 8 passengers and thus should be fully automated with emergency switches at ground level.

4.16 FACTORS INFLUENCING FIRE DEVELOPMENT

The growth and development of a fire depend to a great extent on the geometry and ventilation of the enclosure containing fire.

A fire usually starts because a material is ignited by a heat source. The development of a fire within an enclosure depends on the following factors:

- The item first ignited is sufficiently inflammable to allow a flame to spread over its surfaces.
- The heat flux from the first ignited item is sufficient to irradiate adjacent materials which in turn begin to burn.
- Sufficient fuel exists within the enclosure; otherwise, the fire may simply burn itself out.
- The fire may burn very slowly because of a restricted supply of oxygen as in the case of a well sealed room and may eventually smoother itself.
- If there is sufficient fuel and oxygen available, the fire may totally involve the entire enclosure.

4.17 PATTERN OF FIRE

The pattern of every fire is different but the majority pass through the following stages.

Flashover is the rapid involvement of an enclosure's combustible contents as they ignite almost simultaneously. Thus, it is the time when the flames cease to be localised and flaming can be observed throughout the whole enclosure. **Flashover** is, in fact, the transition from the growth period to a steady state of combustion, or a fully developed stage in fire development.

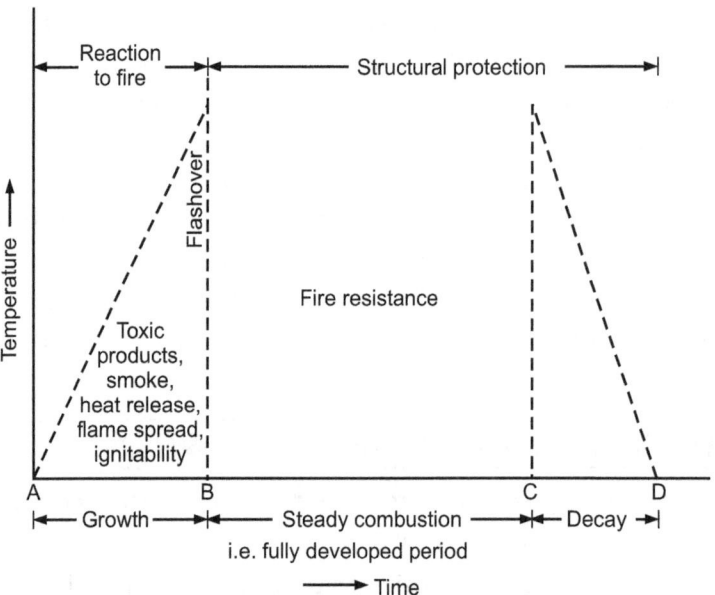

Fig. 4.35: Different phases of fire

The period A - B is known as the growth period. It is essentially the pre-flashover period during which the temperatures in the enclosure are relatively low and chances of escape are relatively high.

At B, the fire progresses rapidly through flashover to the fully developed stage upto C. During this period all the combustibles in the compartment are burning and the temperature within the enclosure is highest.

At C, the steady combustion period ends, the temperature begins to fall and C - D is the decay period.

Though the temperatures during the growth period are low, the duration of the growth period is very important as it determines the time available for escape and for the effective operation of the emergency fire fighting services.

4.18 FIRE SEVERITY

It may be defined as the destructive potential of a fire i.e. the potential impact that a fire in a given enclosure will have upon the structural and constructional components which form the enclosure and its components. Hence, fire severity has a direct relation to the structural performance in terms of a component's fire-resisting capabilities. Therefore, the fire resistance offered by a component during the fully developed stage of a fire is extremely important in evaluating the extent of fire severity.

4.19 FIRE RESISTANCE

If a fire burns unnoticed and uncontrolled in a building, the building elements can be subjected to very high temperatures. The temperature levels and the duration of heating are dependent upon a number of factors related to the design of the building and its contents. If the building elements can withstand this exposure without the building becoming unstable or suffering collapse and without the fire spreading unrestrictedly, they are considered to have adequate fire resistance.

Thus, **fire resistance** can be defined as the ability of an element of building construction to withstand the effects of fire for a specified period of time without loss of its fire separating and load bearing functions. Therefore, a structural component should be able to:

1. endure a fire without collapse,
2. prevent the penetration of flame,
3. resist the spread of fire by conduction through the component or by radiation from the face of the component not exposed to the fire.

The factors which determine the level of fire resistance of structural components are:

1. Type of occupancy,
2. Height of the building,
3. Floor area of the storey or compartment,
4. Cubic capacity of the building or compartment and
5. Location of the component

   i.e. (a) ground or upper storey

   (b) basement.

Unit: The fire resistance of a building or its structural elements is expressed in hours against a specified test load which is expressed in $kcal/m^2$ and against a certain intensity of fire.

The types of construction according to fire resistance are classified into four categories, namely, type 1, type 2, type 3 and type 4.

Table 4.8 gives the fire resistance ratings for various types of construction for structural elements.

Table 4.8: Fire resistance ratings of structural elements (in hours)

Structural Element		Type of Construction			
		Type 1	Type 2	Type 3	Type 4
1. Exterior walls	Bearing	4	2	2	1
Fire separation less than 3.7 m	Non-Bearing	2	$1\frac{1}{2}$	1	1
Fire separation of 3.7 m or more but less than 9 m	Bearing	4	2	2	1
	Non-Bearing	$1\frac{1}{2}$	1	1	1
Fire separation of 9 m or more	Bearing	4	2	2	1
	Non-Bearing	1	1	1	1
2. Fire walls and party walls		4	2	2	2
3. Fire separation assemblies		4	2	2	2
4. Fire enclosures of exit ways, hallways and stairways		2	2	2	2
5. Shaft other than exit ways, elevator hoist ways		2	2	2	2
6. Exit way access corridors		1	1	1	1
7. Vertical separation of tenant spaces		1	1	1	1
8. Dwelling unit separations		1	1	1	1
Non-bearing partitions		← At least half an hour →			
9. Interior bearing walls, bearing partitions, columns, girders, trusses (other than roof trusses) and framing	Supporting more than one floor	4	2	2	2
	Supporting one floor only	3	$1\frac{1}{2}$	1	1
	Supporting a roof only	3	$1\frac{1}{2}$	1	1
10. Structural members supporting walls		3	$1\frac{1}{2}$	1	1

contd. ...

		3	$1\frac{1}{2}$	1	1
11. Floor construction, including beams		3	$1\frac{1}{2}$	1	1
12. Roof construction, including beams, trusses and framing arches and roof deck	5 m or less in height to lowest member	2	$1\frac{1}{2}$	1	1
	More than 5 m but less than 6.7 m in height to lowest member	1	1	1	1
	6.7 m or more in height to lowest member	0	0	0	0

In relation to fire, the building materials can be classified into two categories - combustible and non-combustible. Combustible materials are those that catch fire themselves and contribute to the growth of fire. e.g. wood, fibre board, straw board curtains, apparel, etc.

Non-combustible materials are those that do not catch fire, but after being exposed to fire for some time, loose their inherent qualities. They may loose their shape and load carrying capacity and yield, thus resulting in the collapse of the structure e.g. steel, stone.

4.20 SOME COMMON CONSTRUCTION MATERIALS

1. **Timber:** Though timber catches fire and is a combustible material, it has the ability to offer resistance to fire for a period of time. It gets charred, on exposure to fire and this coating of char on timber surface functions as an insulating material and slows down the process of combustion. However, on prolonged exposure to fire, it undergoes total combustion.

2. **Stone:** Stone is a non-combustible material but has very little fire resisting properties. Granite, when exposed to fire, breaks into pieces. Limestone and marble get calcined. Compact sandstone can withstand fire to some extent.

3. **Bricks:** Well burnt bricks have good fire resisting properties and may withstand temperatures upto $1200°C$.

4. **Iron and Steel:** Though iron and steel are non-combustible materials, they are very good conductors of heat. They expand, get wrapped and loose their shape under exposure to prolonged fire. Thus, a steel structural component may yield under heat resulting in collapse of the structure.

5. **Concrete:** Concrete, in general, is a good fire-resistant material, but this resistance will depend to a large extent on the type of aggregates used. However, RCC structure with a good cover to reinforcement offers good resistance to fire.
6. **Glass:** Glass is a good fire resisting material because of its low thermal conductivity. However, it cannot tolerate sudden changes in temperature.
7. e.g. When it is exposed to extreme heat in the event of a fire, and the fire is doused with water, glass may crack. Reinforced glass has better fire resistance.
8. **Asbestos Cement:** Asbestos cement is an excellent fire resisting material. It is a combination of fibrous material and cement and is largely used in the construction of fireproof partition walls and roofs.

4.21 FIRE RESISTANT CONSTRUCTION

Walls and Columns: Fire ratings of some types of constructions for walls are given in the following tables. Specifications of materials should be so selected; as to give these ratings.

Table 4.9: Masonry walls: Solid (Required to resist fire from one side at a time)

Nature of Construction and Materials	Minimum Thickness (mm), Excluding any finish, for a fire resistance (Hours) of									
	Load Bearing					Non-load Bearing				
	1 hr.	$1\frac{1}{2}$ hrs.	2 hrs.	3 hrs.	4 hrs.	1 hr.	$1\frac{1}{2}$ hrs.	2 hrs.	3 hrs.	4 hrs.
1. Reinforced* cement concrete	120 (25)	140 (25)	160 (25)	200 (25)	240 (25)					
2. Unreinforced cement concrete	150	175	–	–	–					
3. No-fines concrete with: (a) 13 mm cement/sand or gypsum/sand (b) 13 mm lightweight aggregate gypsum plaster						150 150	150 150	150 150	150 150	150 150
4. Bricks of clay: (a) Without finish (b) With 13 mm lightweight aggregate gypsum plaster	90 90	100 90	100 90	170 100	170 100	75 75	90 90	100 90	170 90	170 100
5. Bricks of sand lime: (a) Without finish (b) With 13 mm lightweight aggregate gypsum plaster	90 90	100 90	100 90	190 100	190 100	75 75	90 90	100 90	170 90	170 100

contd. ...

6. Blocks of concrete:										
(a) Without finish	90	100	100	–	–	75	90	100	140	150
(b) With 13 mm lightweight aggregate gypsum plaster	90	90	90	100	100	75	75	75	90	100
(c) With 13 mm cement/sand or gypsum/sand						75	90	90	100	140
7. Blocks of lightweight concrete:										
(a) Without finish	90	100	100	140	150	75	75	75	125	140
(b) With 13 mm lightweight aggregate gypsum plaster	90	90	90	100	100	50	63	75	75	75
(c) With 13 mm cement/sand or gypsum/sand						75	75	75	90	100
8. Blocks of aerated concrete:										
(a) Without finish	90	100	100	140	180	50	63	63	75	100
(b) With 13 mm lightweight aggregate gypsum plaster	90	90	100	100	150					

*Walls containing at least 1 percent of vertical reinforcement.   ( ) Minimum thickness of actual cover to reinforcement.

Table 4.10: Masonry walls, hollows (Required to resist fire from one side at a time)

Nature of Construction and Materials	Minimum Thickness (mm), Excluding any finish, for a fire resistance (Hours) of:										
	Load Bearing					Non-load Bearing					
	1 hr.	1½ hrs.	2 hrs.	3 hrs.	4 hrs.	½ hr.	1 hr.	1½ hrs.	2 hrs.	3 hrs.	4 hrs.
1. Bricks of clay:											
(a) Without finish	170	170	170	200	200	75	100	100	170	170	200
(b) With 13 mm lightweight aggregate gypsum plaster	100	100	170	170	170	75	75	90	100	100	170
2. Blocks of concrete:											
(a) Without finish						90	125	125	140	140	150
(b) With 13 mm cement/sand or gypsum/sand	190	200	200	–	–	90	125	125	140	140	140
(c) With 13 mm light weight aggregate gypsum plaster						75	90	90	100	125	125
3. Blocks of light weight concrete:											
(a) Without finish	100	100	100	–	–	75	90	90	100	140	150
(b) With 13 mm cement/sand or gypsum/sand						75	75	75	100	140	140
(c) With 13 mm light weight aggregate gypsum plaster						63	63	75	75	90	100

Table 4.11: Framed construction, load bearing
(Required to resist fire from one side at a time)

Nature of construction and materials / Timber studs at centres not exceeding 600 mm, faced on each side with	Minimum thickness (mm) of Protection for a fire resistance of 1 hr.
1. Plasterboard layers with joints staggered, joints in outer layer taped and filled – Total thickness for each face	25
2. One layer of 12.7 mm plasterboard with a finish of lightweight aggregate gypsum plaster.	13
3. Metal lath and plaster, thickness of plaster: (a) Sanded gypsum plaster (metal lathing grade) (b) Lightweight aggregate gypsum plaster	 22 13

Table 4.12: Framed construction, non-load bearing
(Required to resist fire from one side at a time)

Nature of construction and materials/ Steel or Timber frame at centres not exceeding 600 mm, facing on both sides of	Stud Construction	Minimum thickness (mm) of Protection for a fire resistance of 1 hr.			
		$\frac{1}{2}$ hr.	1 hr.	$1\frac{1}{2}$ hrs.	2 hrs.
(A) Dry lining with materials fixed direct to studs (without plaster finish):					
1. One layer of plasterboard with taped and filled joints	Timber or steel	12.7			
2. Two layers of plasterboard with joints staggered, joints in outer layer taped and filled – Total thickness for each face	Timber or steel	19	25		
3. One layer of asbestos insulating board with transverse joints backed by fillers of asbestos insulating board not less than 9 mm thick or by timber	Timber Steel	9 12			
4. One layer of wood wool slabs	Timber	25			
5. One layer of chipboard or of plywood	Timber or steel	18			
(B) Lining with materials fixed direct to studs, with plaster finish: 1. Plasterboard of thickness:					
(a) With not less than 5 mm gypsum plaster finish	Timber or steel	9.5			
(b) With not less than 13 mm gypsum plaster finish			12.7		
(C) Wet finish: 1. Metal lath and plaster, thickness of plaster: (a) Sanded gypsum plaster (b) Lightweight aggregate gypsum plaster	 Timber or steel Timber Steel	 13 	 13 13	 19 	 15

Table 4.13: Encased steel columns, 203 mm × 203 mm
(Protection applied on four sides)

Nature of construction and materials	Minimum thickness (mm) of protection for a fire resistance of				
	1 hr.	$1\frac{1}{2}$ hrs.	2 hrs.	3 hrs.	4 hrs.
(A) Hollow protection (without an air cavity over the flanges):					
1. *Metal lathing with trowelled lightweight aggregate gypsum plaster	13	15	20	32	–
2. Plasterboard with 1.6 mm wire binding at 100 mm pitch, finished with lightweight aggregate gypsum plaster not less than the thickness specified:					
(a) 9.5 mm plasterboard	10	15			
(b) 19 mm plasterboard	10	13	20		
3. Asbestos insulating boards, thickness of board:					
(a) Single thickness of board, with 6 mm cover fillets at transverse joints		19	25		
(b) Two layers, of total thickness				38	50
4. Solid bricks of clay composition or sand lime, reinforced in every horizontal joint, unplastered	50	50	50	75	100
5. Aerated concrete blocks	60	60	60		
6. Solid blocks of lightweight concrete	50	50	50	60	75
Hollow protections (with an air cavity over the flanges)					
(B) Asbestos insulating board screwed to 25 mm asbestos battens	12	19			
(C) Solid protections					
1. Concrete, not leaner than 1 : 2 : 4 mix (unplastered):					
(a) Concrete not assumed to be load bearing, reinforced †	25	25	25	50	75
(b) Concrete assumed to be load bearing	50	50	50	75	75
2. Lightweight concrete, not leaner than 1 : 2 : 4 mix (Unplastered) concrete not assumed to be load bearing, reinforced †	25	25	25	40	60

* So fixed or designed, as to allow full penetration for mechanical bond.

† Reinforcement shall consist of steel binding wire not less than 2.3 mm in thickness, or a steel mesh weighing not less than 0.5 kg/m^3. In concrete protection, the spacing of that reinforcement shall not exceed 200 mm in any direction.

Table 4.14: Framed external walls load bearing
(Required to resist fire from one side at a time)

Nature of construction and materials	Minimum thickness (mm) of Protection for a fire resistance of 1 h
Timber studs at centres not exceeding 600 mm with internal linings of plaster board layers with joints in outer layer taped and filled, total thickness of plasterboard	31

Table 4.15: Reinforced concrete columns

Nature of construction and materials		Minimum dimensions (mm), excluding any finish for a fire resistance of					
		$\frac{1}{2}$ hr.	1 hr.	$1\frac{1}{2}$ hrs.	2 hrs.	3 hrs.	4 hrs.
1. Fully exposed	Width	150	200	250	300	400	450
	Cover	20	25	30	35	35	35
2. 50 percent exposed	Width	125	160	200	200	300	350
	Cover	20	25	25	25	30	35
3. One face exposed	Thickness	100	120	140	160	200	240
	Cover	20	25	25	25	25	25

Table 4.16: Concrete beams

Nature of construction and materials		Minimum dimensions (mm), excluding any finish for a fire resistance of					
		$\frac{1}{2}$ hr.	1 hr.	$1\frac{1}{2}$ hrs.	2 hrs.	3 hrs.	4 hrs.
1. Reinforced concrete (simply supported)	Width	80	120	150	200	240	280
	Cover	20	30	40	60	70	80
2. Reinforced concrete (continuous)	Width	80	80	120	150	200	240
	Cover	20	20	35	50	60	70
3. Prestressed concrete (simply supported)	Width	100	120	150	200	240	280
	Cover	25	40	55	70	80	90
4. Prestressed concrete (continuous)	Width	80	100	120	150	200	240
	Cover	20	30	40	55	70	80

Table 4.17: Encased steel columns, 203 mm × 203 mm
(Protection applied on four sides)

Nature of construction and materials	Minimum thickness (mm) of protection for a fire resistance of				
	1 hr.	$1\frac{1}{2}$ hrs.	2 hrs.	3 hrs.	4 hrs.
(A) Hollow protection (without an air cavity over the flanges):					
1. *Metal lathing with trowelled lightweight aggregate gypsum plaster	13	15	20	32	–
2. Plasterboard with 1.6 mm wire binding at 100 mm pitch, finished with lightweight aggregate gypsum plaster not less than the thickness specified:					
(a) 9.5 mm plasterboard	10	15	20		
(b) 19 mm plasterboard	10	13			
3. Asbestos insulating boards, thickness of board:					
(a) Single thickness of board, with 6 mm cover fillets at transverse joints		19	25		
(b) Two layers, of total thickness				38	50
4. Solid bricks of clay composition or sand lime, reinforced in every horizontal joint, unplastered	50	50	50	75	100
5. Aerated concrete blocks	60	60	60		
6. Solid blocks of lightweight concrete Hollow protections (with an air cavity over the flanges)	50	50	50	60	75
(B) Asbestos insulating board screwed to 25 mm asbestos battens	12	19			
(C) Solid protections					
1. Concrete, not leaner than 1 : 2 : 4 mix unplastered):					
(a) Concrete not assumed to be load bearing, reinforced †	25	25	25	50	75
(b) Concrete assumed to be load bearing	50	50	50	75	75
2. Lightweight concrete, not leaner than 1 : 2 : 4 mix (Unplastered) concrete not assumed to be load bearing, reinforced †	25	25	25	40	60

* So fixed or designed, as to allow full penetration for mechanical bond.

† Reinforcement shall consist of steel binding wire not less than 2.3 mm in thickness, or a steel mesh weighing not less than .5 kg/m^3. In concrete protection, the spacing of that reinforcement shall not exceed 200 mm in any direction.

Every opening in the wall should be protected by a fire resisting door having a fire rating of not less than 1 hour.

In load bearing structures, bricks are preferred to stones because of their fire resisting properties. In framed structures, RCC frames are better than structural steel frames.

In RCC frame work the reinforcement should have proper cover to prevent it from being exposed to fire.

Partition walls also should be of fire resisting material such as hollow concrete blocks, bricks, reinforced glass, asbestos cement board, etc.

All walls should be plastered with fire resisting mortar.

The use of inflammable surface finishes on walls (including external facade of the building) and ceilings affects the safety of the occupants of a building. Such finishes tend to spread the fire and even though the structural elements may be adequately fire resistant, serious danger to life may result. Therefore, the finishing materials used for various surfaces and decor should not add to the spread of fire and in addition should not generate toxic fumes and smoke.

Floors and Roofs:

The fire ratings of some floors are given in the following tables. The specifications of materials should consider these ratings.

Table 4.18: Concrete floors

	Nature of construction and materials		Minimum Dimensions (mm), Excluding any finish for a fire resistance of:					
			$\frac{1}{2}$ hr.	1 hr.	$1\frac{1}{2}$ hrs.	2 hrs.	3 hrs.	4 hrs.
1.	Reinforced concrete (simply supported)	Thickness	75	95	110	125	150	170
		Cover	15	20	25	35	45	55
2.	Reinforced concrete (continuous)	Thickness	75	95	110	125	150	170
		Cover	15	20	20	25	35	45

Table 4.19: Concrete floors: Ribbed open soffit

	Nature of construction and materials		Minimum Dimensions (mm), Excluding any finish for a fire resistance of:					
			$\frac{1}{2}$ hr.	1 hr.	$1\frac{1}{2}$ hrs.	2 hrs.	3 hrs.	4 hrs.
1.	Reinforced concrete (simply supported)	Thickness	70	90	105	115	135	150
		Width	75	90	110	125	150	175
		Cover	15	25	35	45	55	65
2.	Reinforced concrete (continuous)	Thickness	70	90	105	115	135	150
		Width	75	80	90	110	125	150
		Cover	15	20	–	35	45	55

**Table 4.20: Timber floors -
Any structurally suitable flooring of timber or particle boards**

Nature of construction and materials 37 mm (minimum) timber joists with a ceiling of	Minimum thickness (mm), of protection for a fire resistance of:	
	$\frac{1}{2}$ hr.	1 hr.
1. Timber lathing and plaster, plaster of thickness	15	
2. Metal lathing and plaster, thickness of plaster for:		
(a) Sanded gypsum plaster (metal lathing grade)	15	
(b) Light weight aggregate gypsum plaster	13	19
3. One layer of plaster board with joints taped and filled and backed by timber	12.7	
4. Two layers of plaster board, with joints staggered, joints in outer layer taped and filled total thickness.	25	
5. Two layers of plaster board, each not less than 9.5 mm thick, joints between boards staggered and outer layer finished with gypsum plaster	5	
6. One layer of plaster board not less than 9.5 mm thick, finished with:		
(a) Sanded gypsum plaster	13	
(b) Lightweight aggregate gypsum plaster	15	
7. One layer of plasterboard not less than 12.7 mm thick, finished with:		
(a) Sanded gypsum plaster	15	
(b) Lightweight aggregate gypsum plaster	13	
8. One layer of asbestos insulating board with any transverse joints backed by fillets of asbestos insulating board not less than 9 mm thick, or by timber	12	

RCC floors are most suitable for fire resistance. Flat roofs are preferred to sloping or pitched roofs. A surface covering, of non-combustible and non-toxic material, should be laid directly on the incombustible floor. Flooring materials like concrete tiles and ceramic files are quite suitable.

Linings or false ceilings should not be encouraged in buildings.

In some cases, requiring provision of skylights, monitor lights or north lights in the roofs; glazings should be of glass in metal frames with a fire rating of minimum half an hour.

Staircase: All internal staircases must be of fire resisting materials such as RCC stairs. It should be constructed as a self contained unit and should be completely enclosed.

4.22 MEANS OF ESCAPE

The present method of providing means of escape from buildings is by observing specifications and rules i.e. rules that have evolved through time and are deemed to provide a satisfactory escape route.

The main objective of the provision of a means of escape is that the occupants should be able to reach a place of safety unharmed, in the event of a fire occurring.

A place of safety is normally associated with an area outside the building away from the threatened space. It may also be a protected corridor, a protected staircase or a place of refuge within the buildings.

Places of refuge are necessary in very tall buildings because the evacuation of these buildings may take two hours or more. Refuge floors may be provided every six or eight floors up the building, depending on the nature of occupancy, so that occupants of the fire floor, floors below the fire and above the fire can be evacuated to a place of safety.

Evacuation Time:

This is the time taken for a person to go from any occupied part of the building to a place of safety. Ideally this should be 2 – 3 minutes, but evacuation time will vary according to a person's speed of travel depending upon his age and general physical condition.

In fact, 2 - 3 minutes evacuation criterion is derived from studies which conclude that such a time is reasonable for people in a stressful situation, before panic conditions develop. Thus, it is highly desirable to evacuate people before a state of irrational behaviour starts.

In multistoreyed buildings, where this evacuation time of 2 – 3 minutes cannot be achieved, places of safety must be provided within the building.

Travel Distance:

Travel distance is the distance to be traversed in order to reach a place of safety from which dispersal can take place. This place of safety can be a protected escape route, an external escape route or a final exit.

A range of travel distances is given in the following table; varying relative to purpose, grouping and particular situation.

Table 4.21: Travel distance for occupancy and type of construction

Sr. No.	Group of occupancy	Construction types	
		1 and 2 (m)	3 and 4 (m)
1.	Residential	22.5	22.5
2.	Educational	22.5	22.5
3.	Institutional	22.5	22.5
4.	Assembly	30.0	30.0
5.	Business	30.0	30.0
6.	Mercantile	30.0	30.0
7.	Industrial	45.0	30.0
8.	Storage	30.0	30.0
9.	Hazardous	22.5	22.5

The travel distance to an exit from the dead end of a corridor should not exceed half the distance specified in the above table, except in educational, assembly and institutional occupancies, in which case it should not exceed 6 m.

These distances have been established by experience over many years and give guidance for particular applications. However, the distance to be travelled must be related to the risk involved i.e. the rapidity of flame and smoke spread. When a fire is in the growth stage, a great deal of smoke can be produced and this smoke can move, on occasions, more quickly than normal walking pace. It is, therefore, essential that travel distances can be such that persons can reach a place of safety before smoke-logging of the means of escape occurs.

Exit Requirements:

Entrances, exits and circulation areas are provided in all buildings for normal use. Means of escape considerations should utilize existing arrangements wherever possible.

An exit may be a doorway, corridor, passageway to an internal staircase, external staircase, verandah or terrace which has access to the street or to the roof of a building or a refuge area. An exit may also include a horizontal exit leading to an adjoining building at the same level. Lifts and escalators are not considered as exits.

The primary consideration should be with regard to the sufficiency of existing exits in terms of:

(i) disposition,

(ii) width and

(iii) number.

(i) Disposition: The position of exits as a means of escape in the case of a fire is absolutely critical. Exits should be clearly visible and the routes to reach the exit should be clearly marked and signs should be posted to guide the population of the floor concerned.

Exits should be so arranged, that they may be reached without passing through another occupied unit. They should also be located in such a way that the prescribed travel distances are not exceeded.

(ii) Width: It is essential while designing that bottlenecks i.e. areas where congestion will occur, are avoided. Thus, corridors should not become narrower as they approach a storey exit or staircase. No obstructions should be kept in the corridors which will reduce the effective width of the corridors.

Building codes have specified a unit of exit width of 50 cm to measure the capacity of any exit. A clear width of 25 cm is counted as an additional half unit. Clear widths less than 25 cm should not be counted for exit widths.

The following table gives the number of occupants discharged per minute in a single file through different exits.

Table 4.22: Occupants per unit exit width

Sr. No.	Group of occupancy	Number of occupants		
		Stairways	Ramps	Doors
1.	Residential	25	50	75
2.	Educational	25	50	75
3.	Institutional	25	50	75
4.	Assembly	40	50	60
5.	Business	50	60	75
6.	Mercantile	50	60	75
7.	Industrial	50	60	75
8.	Storage	50	60	75
9.	Hazardous	25	30	40

A width of 50 cm is not acceptable in practice. Hence the national building code has specified that:

(a) Every exit doorway must have a minimum width of 100 cm and a minimum height of 200 cm.
(b) No door, when opened, should reduce the required width of a stairway or landing to less than 90 cm.
(c) Landing width of the stairway must be equal to at least the width of the door.
(d) Width of exit-corridor and passageways should not be less than the required aggregate width of exit doorways leading from them in the direction of travel to the exterior.
(e) Minimum width of stairs in residential buildings should be 1.0 m and in public buildings 1.5 m, as per NBC.
(f) Width of a straight flight in a fire escape stair should not be less than 75 cm and in case of a spiral fire escape, its diameter should not be less than 150 cm.

(iii) Number: Every building meant for human occupancy must be provided with exits sufficient to permit safe escape of occupants, in case of fire or other emergency.

All buildings which are 15 m or more in height and all buildings used as educational, assembly, institutional, industrial, storage and hazardous occupancies, having area more than 500 m^2 on each floor must have a minimum of two staircases.

4.23 FIRE DETECTING SYSTEMS

One method of increasing escape potential and reducing fire casualties would be the introduction of fire-detection systems as a component of escape route design, linked to a warning alarm system which would alert the occupants of a building to the presence of fire.

Various types of fire detectors are available for installation in buildings intended for different occupancies. Fire detectors may respond to the generation of heat, smoke and flames and accordingly there are heat detectors, smoke detectors and flame detectors.

4.24 FIRE EXTINGUISHING SYSTEMS

The method of extinguishing fire will depend on the building type, building occupancy and the nature of hazard. The following are some of the fixed fire extinguishing systems:

(a) Automatic water sprinkler system,

(b) Automatic high velocity water spray or emulsifying system,

(c) Fixed foam installation, and

(d) Carbon dioxide fire extinguishing system.

An automatic sprinkler system consists of an arrangement of pipes at a regular spacing under the ceiling or the most hazardous part of the building. This network of pipes is supplied with water from the fire tank pumps at regular intervals, depending upon the hazards. These sprinkler heads contain a fusible plug which is designed to open at a predetermined temperature. Thus, the heat of the flame raises the temperature of the nearest sprinkler to its operating point and it opens up, releasing a flow of water under pressure and dousing the fire beneath. To avoid unnecessary damage due to water, the sprinkler system can be provided with a water flow alarm to sound at some fire alarm headquarters.

QUESTIONS

1. What is plumbing services?
2. Explain the water supply requirements for buildings.
3. Write a note on storage of water.
4. Explain the layout of water supply and drainage system.
5. Explain the plumbing system for waste water.

6. What are types of pipes?
7. Write a note on metallic pipes, cement pipes and unplasticized PVC pipes.
8. What is rain water harvesting? Give its need, scope.
9. Explain the different types of wires.
10. Explain the designation of wires.
11. Explain the factors for deciding wiring systems.
12. Explain the various systems of wiring.
13. Give the comparison of various writing systems.
14. Write a note on wiring installations.
15. Explain the simple wiring diagrams.
16. Explain the necessity of earthing.
17. Explain fire resistance in building.
18. How does fire occur in buildings? What is the purpose of fire safety legislation?
19. How are buildings classified? How does the classification become a factor in risk determination?
20. What is fire load? What are the general requirements which contribute to safety from fire?
21. What factors influence fire development in a building?
22. What is the pattern generally followed by a fire in a building?
23. What is fire resistance of a building element? What factors determine the level of fire resistance?
24. How would you plan means of escape in the event of a fire in a building?
25. Discuss different types of fire-detecting systems.
26. Explain the methods of extinguishing an accidental fire in a building.
27. Explain fire grade.
28. Explain the term fire load. How do you determine it?
29. Compare fire resisting properties of timber and concrete.
30. Explain the terms: (a) Fire load (b) Evacuation time (c) Travel distance
31. What are different fire extinguishing systems? Explain any one in detail.
32. Write a note on fire escape elements.
33. Compare fire resisting properties of: (a) Concrete (b) Store
34. What exit requirements are to be provided in a public building to escape from fire.
35. State commonly adopted fire extinguishing services. Describe any one in detail?
36. What is fire hazard? How will you carry on fire resisting construction?
37. Explain points to be observed for making walls and columns fire resistant.
38. What is fire load and how fire safety is achieved?
39. How would you plan means of escape in the event of fire in a building?
40. Discuss important considerations in fire protection.
41. State the various fire resistant materials that can be used for walls and floors.

■■■

Unit 5
HEAT, VENTILATION AND AIR CONDITIONING SYSTEMS IN BUILDING

5.1 VENTILATION

5.1.1 Introduction

Our body produces heat continuously during its metabolic activity of converting the food we eat into living matter and energy required for doing work. Only some 20% of the energy produced is utilized by the body, the remaining 80% is to be dissipated as surplus heat from the system.

Heat may also be gained by the body from the environment by the following processes:

(i) Conduction by contact with warmer objects,

(ii) Absorption of heat from warmer enveloping air and,

(iii) Radiation by exposure to heat rays from the sun or hotter objects in the vicinity.

Dissipation of excess of heat, generated by metabolic activity and heat gained by the body, is very essential in order to maintain the intestinal temperature or deep body temperature constant around 37°C.

Excess body heat can be dissipated by conduction, convection, radiation and evaporation.

Heat loss by *conduction* depends upon the temperature gradient between the skin temperature and colder objects in contact with the skin.

Heat loss by *convection* is due to heat transmission from the body to the cooler air surrounding it. The heat loss increases with a faster rate of air movement around the body.

Heat loss by *radiation* is governed by the temperature difference between the skin and the objects surrounding it (but not touching it).

Heat loss by *evaporation* depends on the humidity of surrounding air and on the amount of body moisture available for evaporation. Low humidity of ambient air promotes a greater rate of evaporation.

To maintain the heat balance of the body, excess of heat generated and gained by the body must be equal to the heat lost by the body.

In a hot environment, the heat acquired is more than the heat lost; blood circulation to the skin increases and skin temperature increases. If heat acquisition continues, the body sweats or perspires to prevent continued rise in skin temperature. In this condition, air movement close to the skin will reduce heat stress by dissipating heat from the body by evaporation of the sweat, particularly when the relative humidity is high and air temperature is near body temperature.

People consume oxygen, by inhaling air and exhale carbon dioxide. An average person, depending on his activity, inhales about 0.5 to 5 m³/hr. In a closed environment, oxygen content is reduced and the carbon dioxide content is increased by man's presence. [Biologically the limit for comfortable existence is 0.5% CO_2 content by volume but a 0.15% increase is perceptible, because of the discomfort caused.]

The content of carbon dioxide in air rarely exceeds 0.5 to 1%. Body smells, fumes and vapours produced by a variety of processes such as combustion from the kitchen and other heating appliances, smoking etc., result in vitiating the air.

Hence, a supply of fresh air is required to supply oxygen to the human body and to maintain carbon dioxide concentration in the air within safe limits; for the control of odours, for the removal of products of combustion or other contaminants in air and to provide such a thermal environment as will assist in the maintenance of heat balance of the body in order to prevent discomfort and injury to health of the occupants.

Ventilation may be defined as *'the process of removing vitiated air from an enclosed space and supplying fresh air, either by natural or artificial means'*.

5.1.2 Comfort Factors for Ventilation

Where no products of combustion or other contaminants are to be removed from air, the amount of fresh air required for dilution of inside air to prevent vitiation of air by body odours depends on the air space available per person and the degree of physical activity. The amount of air requirement increases with decrease in air space per person and it may vary from 20 to 30 m³ per person per hour.

Requirement of air for different occupancies may be expressed in terms of air changes per hour which indicate the replacement of air in an occupancy by fresh air, expressed as the number of times such replacement is effected in an hour.

The following values of air changes are recommended by the National Building Code of India, based on the maintenance of required levels of oxygen, carbon dioxide and other air quality parameters and for the control of body odours when no products of combustion or other contaminants are present in the air.

Table 5.1

Space to be ventilated	Air changes per hour
Assembly Halls / Auditoria	3 – 6
Bed Rooms / Living Rooms	3 – 6
Bath Rooms / Toilets	6 – 12
Cafes / Restaurants	12 – 15
Cinema halls / Theatres	6 – 9
Class Rooms	3 – 6
Factories (Medium metal work)	3 – 6
Garages	12 – 15
Hospital wards	3 – 6
Kitchen (Common)	6 – 9
Kitchen (Domestic)	3 – 6
Laboratories	3 – 6
Offices	3 – 6

Air change per hour: It is the volume of outside air allowed into a room in terms of the number of room volumes exchanged, in one hour.

Thermal comfort is that condition of thermal environment, in which a person can maintain a bodily heat balance at normal body temperature without perceptible sweating.

Air movement is necessary in hot and humid weather for body cooling. A certain minimum desirable wind speed is needed for achieving thermal comfort at different temperatures and relative humidities.

As per the National Building code of India, the following wind speeds are recommended:

Case 1: Applicable to sedentary work in offices and other places having no noticeable sources of heat gain.

Table 5.2: Desirable wind speeds in m/s for thermal comfort conditions

Dry bulb temperature in °C	Relative Humidity (percentage)						
	30	40	50	60	70	80	90
28	×	×	×	×	×	×	×
29	×	×	×	×	×	0.06	0.19
30	×	×	×	0.06	0.24	0.53	0.85
31	×	0.06	0.24	0.53	1.04	1.47	2.10
32	0.20	0.46	0.94	1.59	2.26	3.04	H
33	0.77	1.36	2.12	3.00	H	H	H
34	1.85	2.72	H	H	H	H	H
35	3.20	H	H	H	H	H	H

× - None, H - Higher than those acceptable in practice

Case 2: In somewhat warmer conditions such as in godowns and machine shops where work is of lighter intensity and higher temperatures can be tolerated without much discomfort, minimum wind speeds for just acceptable warm conditions are given in the following Table 5.3.

Table 5.3: Minimum wind speeds in m/s for just acceptable warm conditions

Dry bulb temperature in °C	Relative Humidity (percentage)						
	30	40	50	60	70	80	90
28	×	×	×	×	×	×	×
29	×	×	×	×	×	×	×
30	×	×	×	×	×	×	×
31	×	×	×	×	×	0.06	0.23
32	×	×	×	0.09	0.29	0.60	0.94
33	×	0.04	0.24	0.60	1.04	1.85	2.10
34	0.15	0.46	0.94	1.60	2.26	3.05	H
35	0.68	1.36	2.10	3.05	H	H	H
36	1.72	2.70	H	H	H	H	H

× - None, H - Higher than those acceptable in practice

For normal industrial working activity for a worker with light clothing, the wet-bulb temperature may not exceed 29°C and a minimum air velocity of 30 m/min. may be provided.

In relation to the dry bulb temperature, the wet bulb temperature of air in the work room, as far as practicable, should not exceed that given in the following Table 5.4.

Table 5.4

Dry bulb temperature in °C	Maximum wet bulb temperature in °C
30	29.0
35	28.5
40	28.0
45	27.5
50	27.0

The industry should not allow thermal conditions to go beyond the above limits, for more than one hour continuously.

Efficiency decreases with the rise in dry bulb temperature for a given wet bulb temperature attained and efforts should be made to bring down the dry bulb temperature as much as possible. Long exposures to temperatures of 50°C dry bulb and 27°C wet bulb may prove dangerous.

[**Note: Dry bulb temperature:** It is the temperature of air, read on a thermometer, taken in such a way as to avoid errors due to radiation.

Wet bulb temperature: The steady temperature finally given by a thermometer having its bulb covered with gauge or muslin moistened with distilled water and placed in an air stream of not less than 4.5 m/s.]

5.1.3 Various Systems of Ventilation

There are two systems of ventilation:
I. Natural system
II. Mechanical system.

Natural Ventilation:

It is achieved by natural means through windows and ventilators.

Natural ventilation may be achieved by:
1. **Wind effect** which depends on the direction and velocity of wind outside and sizes and disposition of openings.
2. **Stack effect** arising from difference in air temperature or vapour pressure between inside and outside the room and the difference in height between the inlet and outlet openings.

1. **Ventilation due to Wind Effect:**

The general direction of prevailing winds is made use of, as far as possible, in the location of openings in buildings, for natural ventilation.

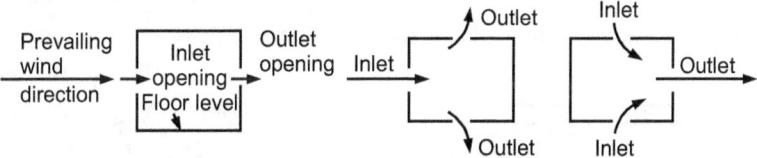

Fig. 5.1: Movement of wind through buildings

At the stage of planning itself, *orientation* of buildings with respect to the wind direction could gain some advantage in ventilation and removal of heat from inside buildings, so that the inside temperature is kept close to, if not lower than, the ambient temperature.

General Rules for Location of Windows:
1. Inlet openings in the building should be well distributed and should be located on the windward side at a low level and outlet openings should be located on the leeward side near the top, so that the incoming air passes over the occupants.

2. When outlets also serve as inlets, they should be at the same level.
3. Inlet openings should not, as far as possible, be obstructed by buildings, trees, signboards etc.
4. If inlet and outlet openings are of nearly equal areas, then greater flow per unit area of openings is obtained.
5. If only one wall of a room is exposed to the outer atmosphere, it is better to provide two small windows in the wall than to provide one large window.
6. As per the National Building Code of India, the minimum area of openings, excluding doors should not be less than,
    (a) One-tenth of the floor area for dry hot climate,
    (b) One-sixth of the floor area for wet hot climate,
    (c) One-eighth of the floor area for intermediate climate,
    (d) One-twelfth of the floor area for cold climate.

2. Ventilation due to Stack Effect:

Natural ventilation by stack effect occurs when air inside a building is at a different temperature than air outside. Thus, in heated buildings or in buildings wherein hot processes are carried out and in ordinary buildings during summer nights and pre-monsoon periods, the inside temperature is higher than that of outside, in which case, cool air will tend to enter through openings at low level and warm air will tend to leave through openings at high level. It would, therefore, be advantageous to provide ventilators as close to the ceiling as possible.

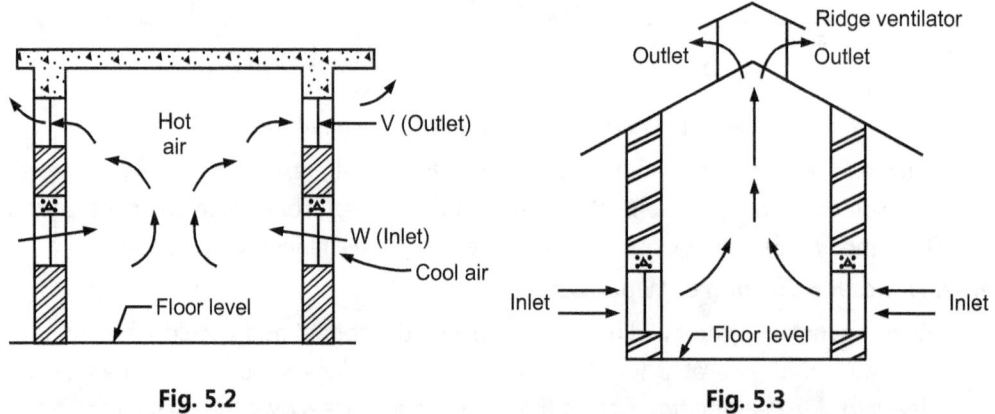

Fig. 5.2   Fig. 5.3

Calculation of Window Areas / Rate of Ventilation in Case of:

1. Ventilation due to Wind:

Based on the wind speed and angle of incidence of wind on the openings in buildings, the quantity of air through ventilating openings by wind action is given by,

$$Q = KAV$$

where,
- Q = Rate of air flow, in m³/h
- A = Free area of inlet openings, in m²
- V = Velocity of wind, in m/h
- K = Coefficient of effectiveness of openings.

The effectiveness of the openings, K, depends on the direction of the wind relative to the openings and on the ratio between the areas of inlet and outlet openings. It also depends on the ratios of larger openings to the smaller openings.

When inlet openings and outlet openings are equal in area,

Value of K = 0.6 for winds perpendicular to openings and K = 0.3 for winds at an angle less than 45° to the openings.

Example 5.1: *Calculate the area of openings required for ventilating a living room of size 5 m × 4 m × 3 m in dry hot climate, if the wind is blowing at a velocity of 7.5 km/h perpendicular to the openings.*

Solution: According to the table of number of air changes for different occupancies (Table 5.1) for a living room the number of air changes required is 3 to 6 per hour.

Assuming minimum 3 air changes/hour.

The volume of fresh outside air required in m³/h.

= (Number of air changes/h) × (Volume of the room in m³)

Hence, Q (m³/h) = 3/h × (5 m × 4 m × 3 m)

Also, Q = KAV, Q = 180 m³/h, V = 7,500 m/h and

Assuming K = 0.6 for winds perpendicular to openings,

180 m³/h = 0.6 × A × 7500 m/h

$$A = \frac{180 \text{ (m}^3\text{/h)}}{0.6 \times 7500 \text{ (m/h)}} = 0.04 \text{ m}^2 \text{ (minimum)}$$

As per National Building Code, for dry hot climate, the minimum area of opening

$$= \left(\frac{1}{10}\right)^{th} \text{ of floor area}$$

$$= \frac{1}{10} \times (5 \times 4) \text{ m}^2 = 2 \text{ m}^2$$

Hence, required area of opening is 2 m².

(Here the local bye-laws should also be considered).

2. Ventilation due to Stack Effect:

Ventilation due to convection effects arising from temperature difference between inside and outside air is given by

$$Q = KA\sqrt{h(t_i - t_o)}$$

where,
- Q = The rate of air flow, in m³/h
- A = Free area of inlet openings, in m²
- h = Vertical distance between inlets and outlets, in m
- t_i = Average temperature of indoor air at height h, in °C
- t_o = Temperature of outdoor air, in °C
- K = Constant (usually 7) governed by the difference in elevation and temperature gradient between inlet and outlet openings

Example 5.2: *The internal dimensions of a factory building are 30 m × 20 m × 10 m (height).*

The number of air changes required per hour are 3, the indoor temperature is 36°C and outdoor temperature is 30°C. Find the area of openings required, if the distance between the inlet and outlet openings is 6 m.

Solution: Volume of fresh outside air required in m³/h

$$Q = (\text{Number of air changes/h}) \times (\text{Volume of the room in m}^3)$$

$$Q = \frac{3}{h} \times (30 \times 20 \times 10) \text{ m}^3 = 18{,}000 \text{ m}^3/\text{h}$$

Also

$$Q = 7 \times A \times \sqrt{h(t_i - t_o)}$$

i.e.

$$18{,}000 \text{ m}^3/\text{h} = 7 \times A \times \sqrt{6(36-30)}$$

Therefore free area of inlet openings,

$$A = \frac{18000}{7 \times 6}$$

$$= 429 \text{ m}^2$$

Ventilation of Industrial Buildings:

The volume of air required for ventilation of industrial buildings varies with the nature of manufacturing processes, height of buildings etc.

The supply of air from outside becomes necessary in an industrial building to remove contaminants as well as to remove heat generated.

The volume of air required for removal of heat should be calculated by using both sensible heat and latent heat.

(i) Volume of Air Required for Removing Sensible Heat: Increase in sensible heat is said to occur, when there is a direct addition of heat in a building, given off by various sources; namely, the sun, manufacturing processes, machinery, occupants etc.

The volume of outside air to be provided for removing sensible heat is calculated from

$$Q_1 = \frac{2.9768\ K_s}{t}$$

where, Q_1 = Quantity of air, in m³/h
K_s = Sensible heat gained, in W
t = Allowable temperature rise, in °C.

Temperature rise refers mainly to the difference between the air temperatures at the outlet (roof exit) and at the inlet openings for outside air.

Table 5.5: Allowable temperature rise values for industrial buildings

Height of outlet opening, m	Temperature rise, °C
6	3 to 4.5
9	4.5 to 6.5
12	6.5 to 11

(ii) Volume of Air Required for Removing Latent Heat: An increase in latent heat is said to take place when there is an increase in the humidity of the enclosure due to the addition of water vapour emitted by humans and from various manufacturing processes.

Therefore, if the latent heat gained from the manufacturing processes and occupants is known and a suitable value for the allowable rise in the vapour pressure is assumed, then the volume of air required for removing the latent heat is given by

$$Q_2 = \frac{4127.26 \times K_l}{h}$$

where, Q_2 = Quantity of air, in m³/h
K_l = Latent heat gained, in W
h = Allowable vapour pressure difference, in mm of mercury.

In majority of cases, sensible heat gain will far exceed the latent heat gain.

Mechanical Ventilation:

When natural ventilation is not sufficient for providing the required thermal environment, mechanical ventilation may have to be resorted to.

Mechanical ventilation may be achieved by means of ceiling fans, exhaust fans, positive ventilation or a combination of exhaust and positive ventilation.

- **(i) Ceiling Fans:** These are generally provided in non-industrial occupancies and serve the purpose of creating air movement. They are, however, effective only over limited areas.

- **(ii) Exhaust/Vacuum System:** It consists of mechanically removing the used air, thus creating a zone of low pressure and letting fresh air find its way in through grills and openings.

    For removing used air, exhaust fans are provided in walls on one side of the building or in the attic and roof to draw large volumes of air through the building. These fans are usually of propeller type, since they operate against little or no resistance. Adequate inlet openings should be provided on the opposite walls to let the fresh air come inside the building.

- **(iii) Plenum System or Positive Ventilation:** In this system, fresh air is supplied into a room by mechanical means and the used air is allowed to leave through the grills and ventilators.

    Positive ventilation is provided by centrally located supply fans which are usually of the centrifugal type or sometimes axial flow type, since this application requires duct work with a wide range of satisfactory and quiet operation against high pressure. The air from such centrally located fans are supplied to individual rooms through these ducts. The ductwork should be air-tight and should be properly designed to allow smooth flow of air.

    Unit ventilators may be provided for individual rooms and may be placed against the outside wall. Both the central system as well as unit ventilators, besides ventilating, may also carry out the function of cooling the incoming air by evaporation or the use of cooling coils.

- **(iv) A Balanced System:** It involves both supplying and removing of air by mechanical means. The exhaust system will remove ventilated air from inside and positive ventilation will supply fresh air from outside to replace the air driven out by the exhaust system. Hence, a balanced system has the advantage of providing better control conditions and better distribution of air over the entire area of occupancy, particularly in big buildings. This system consists of supplying sufficient volumes of air in proportion to heat load generated in the respective areas, at suitable velocities, at the required areas through duct work and by extracting used air in the return ducts in proportion to the supplied air quantities and recirculating the air or a part of it after properly mixing it with cool fresh air.

(v) Air Conditioning: Air conditioning may be provided where the desired temperatures and humidities cannot be obtained by mere ventilation.

Air conditioning is the process of treating air so as to control simultaneously its temperature, humidity, purity and distribution to meet the requirements of the enclosed space.

5.2 AIR CONDITIONING

5.2.1 Necessity

In rapidly developing cities, land area available for construction of houses is progressively reducing and the cost of construction, particularly in busy localities, is steadily increasing. It is no longer possible to construct independent houses, economically, conforming with specific conditions of aspects and orientation; in order to derive maximum benefits from natural light and ventilation. Also regional or local parameters such as temperature and humidity may be inclement and not contributory to creature comfort. Hence, in congested housing complexes and also in houses in regions of extremely hot, humid, cold or polluted environment, conditioning of air is desirable to maintain living comfort and well-being of inmates.

The following are the functions of a modern heating, ventilating and air conditioning system for a building:

1. Control of air temperature at desired values at all times by heating or cooling,
2. Control of air humidity (water vapour content) by humidification or dehumidification,
3. Control of air movement at a desirable velocity,
4. Introduction of outside air as required,
5. Control of air quality by removal of particles of dust and gaseous pollutants,
6. Control of sound produced by the air conditioning system itself.

5.2.2 Purpose

Air conditioning is used for two purposes, for providing comfort to people in a living space or a working space or for control of a process. Comfort refers to supply of conditioned air that provides satisfaction to people in terms of creature comforts. Process control refers to air conditions, that are required to carry out or improve some operations of a process. For example, Textile industry requires dry bulb temperature of about $25^{\circ}C$ and relative humidity of 50 - 85%. Rubber industry requires dry bulb temperature of $25^{\circ} - 35^{\circ}C$ and relative humidity of 25 - 50%.

5.2.3 Comfort Air Conditioning

Design Conditions: Cooling load calculations are usually based on inside and outdoor conditions of temperature and humidity.

Table 5.6: Inside design conditions for summer

Sr. No.	Optimum conditions		Maximum conditions	
	Dry bulb temp. °C	Wet bulb temp. °C	Dry bulb temp. °C	Wet bulb temp. °C
(1)	(2)	(3)	(4)	(5)
(i)	23.3	19.4	25.9	21.8
(ii)	23.9	18.4	26.1	21.6
(iii)	24.4	17.6	26.7	20.9
(iv)	25.0	16.8	27.2	20.1
(v)	25.6	16.0	27.8	19.4
(vi)	26.1	15.2	28.3	18.8
(vii)	–	–	28.9	18.1
(viii)	–	–	29.4	17.5

Table 5.7: Inside design conditions for winter

Sr. No.	Optimum conditions		Maximum conditions	
	Dry bulb temp. °C	Wet bulb temp. °C	Dry bulb temp. °C	Dry bulb temp. °C
(1)	(2)	(3)	(4)	(5)
(i)	21.4	17.8	18.3	15.0
(ii)	21.7	17.3	18.9	13.4
(iii)	22.2	16.4	19.4	12.0
(iv)	22.8	15.3	19.7	10.8
(v)	23.3	14.4	–	–
(vi)	23.6	13.4	–	–

Inside conditions are those that provide comfort (Table 5.6 and Table 5.7).

Outside design conditions are based on dry bulb and wet bulb temperatures for summer months for different cities in India, based on a 10 years data (Table 5.8). Based on the outside design conditions and required comfort conditions inside, the amount of heat to be removed and the change in humidity can be calculated. This would require a certain rate of movement of air (Table 5.9).

Comfort Factors for Air conditioning:

For comfort air conditioning, dry bulb and wet bulb temperatures may be adopted as given in the following Table 5.8.

Table 5.8: Outside design conditions for summer

City	Temperature, °C							
	Dry Bulb				Wet Bulb			
	1%	2.5%	5%	10%	1%	2.5%	5%	10%
Ahmedabad	42.8	41.7	40.7	39.5	27.6	27.2	26.9	26.4
Amritsar	42.5	41.5	40.3	38.4	27.9	26.9	26.3	25.3
Bhopal	41.7	40.8	39.8	38.5	25.3	24.8	24.4	23.8
Mumbai	34.5	33.8	33.6	32.8	28.4	28.0	27.8	27.4
Kolkata	39.5	38.3	37.4	35.6	29.3	29.2	28.8	28.4
Coimbatore	36.7	35.9	34.9	33.7	28.3	27.4	26.7	25.9
Delhi	43.0	41.9	41.4	40.3	28.1	27.2	26.4	25.8
Hyderabad	39.5	38.7	37.9	36.7	25.3	24.4	23.9	23.5
Jodhpur	43.5	42.5	41.3	40.0	27.9	27.2	26.5	25.8
Lucknow	42.8	41.9	41.0	39.5	28.3	27.7	27.2	26.5
Chennai	39.2	37.8	36.9	35.5	28.5	28.2	27.8	27.4
Nagpur	42.9	42.0	41.1	39.9	27.5	26.2	25.6	25.1
Patna	42.4	41.1	39.9	38.3	28.1	27.8	27.4	27.1
Roorkee	42.5	41.4	40.6	39.2	27.8	26.9	26.1	25.6
Trivendrum	32.9	32.4	31.8	31.0	27.2	26.9	26.7	26.4
Vishakhapatnam	38.4	37.0	36.0	35.1	30.4	29.7	29.3	28.8

As far as possible, thermal shock of more than 11°C should be avoided.

Adequate movement of air should be provided in an air conditioned enclosure. Air velocities in the zone between floor level and 1.5 m level should be 0.25 m/s in the case of comfort air conditioning. Air velocity in excess of 0.5 m/s in this zone should be avoided.

The total minimum outside fresh air introduced into an enclosure by an air conditioning plant or unit is related to the number of occupants in the enclosure at any time, whether they are smokers or non-smokers and to the cubic contents of the enclosed space as per the following Table 5.9.

Table 5.9: Minimum fresh air requirements

Sr. No.	Applications	Smoking	Air requirement in m^3/min.		Per m^2 of floor area
			Recommended	Minimum	
(1)	(2)	(3)	(4)	(5)	(6)
(i)	Apartments	Some	0.56	0.28	–
(ii)	Banking space	Occasional	0.28	0.21	–
(iii)	Board rooms	Very heavy	1.40	0.56	–
(iv)	Department stores	None	0.21	0.14	0.015
(v)	Directors rooms	Very heavy	1.40	0.84	–
(vi)	Drug stores	Considerable	0.28	0.21	–
(vii)	Factories	None	0.28	0.21	0.03
(viii)	Garages	–	–	–	0.30
(ix)	Hospitals:				
	(a) Operating rooms (all fresh air)	None	–	–	0.60
	(b) Private rooms	None	0.84	0.70	0.10
	(c) Wards	None	0.56	0.28	–
(x)	Hotel rooms	Heavy	0.84	0.70	0.10
(xi)	Kitchens:				
	(a) Restaurant	–	–	–	1.20
	(b) Residence	–	–	–	0.60
(xii)	Laboratories	Some	0.56	0.42	–
(xiii)	Meeting rooms	Very heavy	1.40	0.84	0.38
(xiv)	Offices:				
	(a) General	None	0.42	0.28	–
	(b) Private	Some	0.70	0.42	0.08
		Considerable	0.84	0.70	0.08
(xv)	Restaurants:				
	(a) Cafeteria	Considerable	0.34	0.28	–
	(b) Dining room	Considerable	0.42	0.34	–
(xvi)	Retail shop	None	0.28	0.21	–
(xvii)	Theatre	None	0.21	0.14	–
		Some	0.42	0.28	–
(xviii)	Toilets (exhaust)	–	–	–	0.60

The above table is to be used only when the contamination of the air in the conditioned enclosure results solely from respiratory and other physiological activities of occupants or due to their smoking.

5.2.4 The Cooling Load

The interior of a building, gains heat from a number of sources. If the temperature and humidity of the rooms are to be maintained at a comfortable level, heat must be extracted to offset these heat gains. The net amount of heat that is removed is called the **cooling load**.

The gross room heat gain is the rate at which heat is being received in the room at any time. This heat gain is made up of the following components from many sources:

1. Conduction through exterior walls, roof and glass.
2. Conduction through interior partitions, ceilings and floors.
3. Solar radiation through glass.
4. Lighting.
5. People.
6. Equipment and furniture.
7. Heat from infiltration of outside air through openings.

Heat gains can be classified into two groups: Sensible and latent heat gains.

(a) Sensible heat gains result in increasing the air temperature.

(b) Latent heat gains are due to addition of water vapour, thus increasing humidity.

Items 1 through 4 are solely sensible heat gains, items 5 and 7 are partly sensible and partly latent, item 6 can be either sensible or latent or both depending on the type of equipment and the process carried out.

Procedure for Calculating Cooling Load for a Building:

1. Select inside and outside design temperatures from Tables 5.6, 5.7 and 5.8.
2. Use building plans to measure dimensions of all surfaces through which there will be external heat gain for each room.
3. Calculate areas of all these surfaces.
4. Select heat transfer coefficient for each material.
5. Calculate the heat gain through structure i.e. through walls, roof, ceiling and floor by using the following equation

$$Q = U \times A \times ETD$$

where,

Q = Sensible heat gain, in kcal/h

U = Overall heat transfer coefficient between the adjacent and conditioned space, in kcal/h $\times$ m² $\times$ °C

A = Area of the separating section concerned, in m²

ETD = Equivalent temperature difference between outdoor and indoor, in °C

6. Calculate heat gain through glass.
   Radiant energy from the sun passes through transparent materials such as glass and becomes a heat gain to the room. Its value varies with time, orientation, shading and storage effect. The net heat gain can be found from the following equation
   $$Q = SHGF \times A \times SC \times CLF$$
   where,
   - Q = Net solar radiation heat gain through glass, in kcal/h
   - $SHGF$ = Solar heat gain factor, in kcal/h-m²
   - A = Area of glass, in m²
   - SC = Shade coefficient
   - CLF = Cooling load factor for glass

7. Calculate heat gain from people. This consists of two parts-sensible heat and latent heat resulting from respiration.
   Following equations may be used
   $$Q_S = q_s \times n \times CLF$$
   and
   $$Q_L = q_L \times n$$
   where,
   - Q_S = Sensible heat gain
   - Q_L = Latent heat gain
   - q_s = Sensible heat gain per person
   - q_L = Latent heat gain per person
   - n = Number of people
   - CLF = Cooling load factor for people

8. Heat gain from equipment may be found directly from the manufacturers.

9. Find the heat load from outdoor air and ventilation using the following equations.
   $$Q_S = V \times (t_o - t_i) \times \rho_a \times S_a$$
   and
   $$Q_L = V \times (W_s - W_i) \times \rho_a \times C$$
   where,
   - Q_S = Sensible heat gain
   - Q_L = Latent heat gain
   - V = Volume of outdoor air, in m³/h
   - t_o = Outdoor dry bulb temperature, in °C
   - t_i = Indoor dry bulb temperature, in °C
   - ρ_a = Density of air
   - S_a = Specific heat of dry air
   - W_s = Outdoor humidity ratio, kg of moisture per kg of dry air
   - W_i = Indoor humidity ratio, kg of moisture per kg of dry air
   - C = Constant approximating the average kilocalories released in condensing one kg of water vapour from air

10. Add heat gains due to supply ducts, leakage in ducts, heat gain due to supply fans etc.
11. Calculate required supply air conditions. All the heat gains must be offset by supplying air at a temperature and humidity low enough so that it can absorb these heat gains. The supply air takes care of removing both sensible and latent heat gains. In order to find the outside air load, psychrometric charts are used. The psychrometric chart is a graphical representation of the properties of atmospheric air.

5.2.5 Various Components of Air Conditioning System

Any air conditioning system has the following basic components:
1. Heating,
2. Humidifying,
3. Filtering and cleaning,
4. Circulating,
5. Dehumidifying and
6. Cooling.

Depending upon the season, there are two types of air conditioning systems - (a) winter air conditioning, and (b) summer air conditioning.

(a) Winter Air Conditioning:

In winter, if the air in a building is to be maintained at a comfortable temperature, heat must be furnished to the air in the rooms. This is because there is a continuous heat loss to the outdoor surroundings, that is at a lower temperature. If this loss of heat is not replenished, the room temperature will fall rapidly. Also if the air is very dry, certain amount of moisture will have to be added to the air. Therefore, during winter, heating and humidifying equipment is used.

Heating of air may be done by using radiators.

Humidifying devices provide a means of turning water into water vapour and mixing this vapour with air in the occupied space.

This can be done by many methods:
1. Exposing a large surface of water to air being humidified, or
2. Spraying atomised water into air being humidified.

The simplest spray system passes water directly from the city water system through spray nozzles which break the water up into very small droplets. The spray humidifiers are followed by elimination plates so arranged that when the air passes over these plates, the droplets of water are removed from air.

Humidification is important because, a dry atmosphere causes dry skin which may lead to dermititis in the form of flaking or scaling of the skin; breathing dryness and loss of moisture from hygroscopic materials such as wood, natural fibres and most foods.

A simple flow diagram of the operations carried out in the winter air conditioning system can be shown as follows:

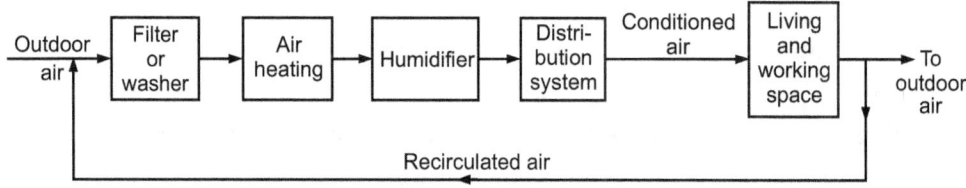

Fig. 5.4: Winter air conditioning

(b) Summer Air Conditioning:

In summer, in order to maintain the room air at a comfortable temperature, there must be continuous removal of heat from the room to offset the heat gains from the surroundings. The equipment that removes this heat is called a cooling system.

Cooling of air is done by several methods:
1. by mechanical refrigeration.
2. by using ice.

In mechanical refrigeration, air is passed over cooled surfaces of metal coils which contain a volatile refrigerant.

In ice system of air conditioning, cooling is done by melting ice, this is a practical method for theatres and public halls that have short operating houses and relatively high peak loads. Since, mechanical refrigeration equipment is expensive for short periods, ice can be used.

In a cooling cycle, the dry bulb temperature of the air is lowered. When this happens, the relative humidity increases. Some moisture must be removed to make this air comfortable. Excess humidity will cause condensation on window panes. Also, the rate of evaporation of perspiration being low, causes a wet and clammy feeling to the occupants. Very humid atmosphere also encourages the growth of several types of fungi and other micro-organisms. Therefore, dehumidification is carried out to remove the excess moisture.

Dehumidification may be done by two methods:
1. Dehydrating the air with chemicals or
2. Cooling the air below dew point, then removing the excess moisture by condensing it on a cooled surface. The air is then reheated to the desired temperature with dry heat.

In general, air filtering and circulating equipment are the same for both winter and summer air conditioning.

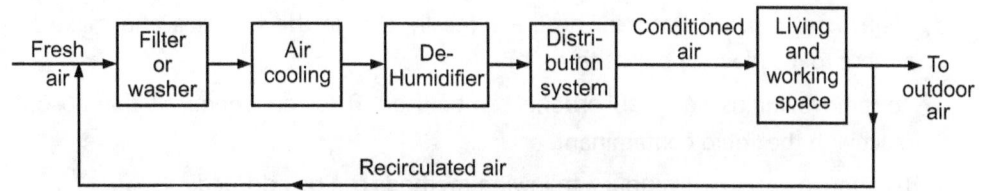

Fig. 5.5: Summer air conditioning

Air Cleaning:

Cleaning the air is a very important part of air conditioning.

Air contaminants include solids, liquids, gases and vapours. Efficient air conditioning systems will remove 75 to 95% of these contaminants.

Suspended solid particles are of the following three types:

(a) **Dust** which can have its origin in animal, vegetable or mineral matter.

(b) **Fumes** formed from materials that are ordinarily solids, but have been put into a gaseous state usually by an industrial or chemical process.

(c) **Smoke** caused by incomplete combination, consists of solid particles carried into the atmosphere by the gaseous products of combustion.

Liquid contaminants include the following:

(a) **Mists:** These small liquid particles are mechanically ejected into the air by splashing, mixing or atomizing.

(b) **Fogs:** These are small liquid particles formed by condensation.

Gaseous contaminants include carbon monoxide, sulphur oxides, nitrogen oxides and hydrocarbons.

The air cleaning devices must also be able to remove pollen, bacteria and moulds from the air.

Removal of solid contaminants can be done by using any of the following methods:

(i) centrifuging force for large particles,

(ii) washing the air for particles that can be wetted,

(iii) screens to block the larger particles.

(c) **Adhesives:** These are filters made of various fibres - glass, cotton, synthetic material and aluminium.

Fibres of adhesive filters are coated with adhesive liquid or oil. Air is forced to pass over these filters and the dust particles stick to the adhesive surface. When these filters get chocked with clogged dust over a period of time, they may either be washed and reused or replaced.

(d) Electrostatic precipitators: These electrically charge the particles and make them adhere to a surface of opposite charge.

To remove liquids, liquid absorbents can be used. These are chemicals that absorb or react with the liquid contaminant.

To remove gases and vapours, following methods can be adopted:

(i) **Condensation:** Cool the contaminant gas to its dew point and remove as a liquid.

(ii) **Chemical reaction:** Pass the gas through a chemical which will remove the gas as a reaction product.

(iii) **Dilution:** Mix the gas with air.

(iv) **Adsorption:** Pass the gas over an adsorbent (e.g. activated carbon).

5.2.6 Air Distribution System

To deliver air to the conditioned space, air carriers are needed. These carriers are called ducts. They are made of steel, aluminium alloy or some non-combustible material such as clay or asbestos cement.

Ducts work on the principle of air pressure difference. Air will flow from a higher pressure area to a lower pressure area.

There are three types of ducts:
1. Conditioned air ducts,
2. Recirculating air ducts,
3. Fresh air ducts.

Ducts may be round, square or rectangular in cross-section.

They should be made substantially air-tight throughout and should have no openings other than those required for proper operation and maintenance of the system.

5.2.7 Various Systems of Air Conditioning

1. Room Air Conditioner:

It is also called unitary air conditioner and it is popular in moderate climates.

This consists of an encased assembly designed as a self contained unit, primarily for mounting in a window or through the wall or as a console. It consists of a compressor, heat exchangers and air handling system installed in one cabinet. It is designed essentially to provide free delivery of conditioned air to an enclosed space, room or zone. It includes a prime source of refrigeration for cooling and dehumidification and means for circulation and filtering of air. It also includes means for exhausting air. It may also include means for heating, humidifying or inducting fresh air. It is factory assembled. No ducts are needed for air distribution.

2. **Packaged Air Conditioners:**

   Packaged air conditioning units come with all the needed equipments in a single cabinet and are suitable for offices, banks, shops, residences and some plants.

   Window units are available upto a limited capacity. Large packaged units have ductwork for fully automatic room conditioning that is too large for one outlet.

3. **Central Air Conditioning System:**

   A central air conditioning system has all the major items of equipment like filters, air washers, fans and refrigeration machinery in one centrally located space, removed from the area to be conditioned. The conditioned air is distributed to the desired spaces through a network of ductwork.

Advantages of a Central Air Conditioning System:

   (i) The space occupied by the equipment need not be very valuable. The equipment can be located in the basement of a large building.

   (ii) For a large conditioning load, the equipment may cost less.

   (iii) The maintenance and inspection of a central system does not disturb the people in the conditioned areas.

   (iv) The exhaust air can be returned and partly reused with obvious savings in heating and refrigeration.

5.3 DESIGN OF BUILDINGS FOR DIFFERENT CLIMATIC CONDITIONS

Climate is a state of the atmospheric environment over a stretch of time, of nearly the same or comparable weather conditions. For example, regions with tropical climates are places where the annual mean temperature is not less than 20°C. It is combined of temperature, rainfall and wind. To make climate as an intrinsic paradigm of design, various climatic parameters such as radiation, air temperature, humidity and wind speed have to be understood both in terms of their content and application in the process of design.

Global Climatic Factors:

Major factors influencing global climates are:

1. **Quality of Solar Radiation Received by the Earth:** Ultra-violet, visible light and infrared energy distribution, which varies with altitude due to the filtering effect of the atmosphere.

2. **Inclination of the Earth's Fixed Axis of Rotation:** With respect to the earth's elliptical orbit around the sun governing seasonal changes.

3. **The "Earth-sun" Geometrical Relationship at any Stage of the Earth on its Orbit Around the Sun:** Governing the amount of solar radiation received by a unit area on the earth's surface.

4. **The Earth's Thermal Balance:** Between the total amount of sun's heat absorbed by the earth and the total amount of heat lost by the earth by long wave radiation, by evaporative cooling and convection air cycles.
5. **Winds:**
   (i) Trade winds - generated by earth's thermal forces and "coriolis force", which causes slippage at the boundary layer between the earth and its atmosphere, resulting in the experience of a wind blowing in a direction opposite to the direction of earth's rotation.
   (ii) Mid latitude westerlies,
   (iii) Polar winds, etc.

5.3.1 Elements of Climate

The following parameters constitute elements of a climate:

1. **Temperature:**

   The temperature of the air is measured in $°C$. True air temperature is measured by a dry bulb mercury thermometer in the shade (inside a louvered wooden box) at a height of about 1.5 m above the ground.

   Five values of temperature are important for design work.

   (a) **Monthly Mean Temperature:** This is the average temperature of daily averages taken for each month, each daily average temperature being taken between each day's minimum and maximum temperatures.

   (b) **Monthly Mean Maximum:** This is the average of daily maximum temperatures of a full month.

   (c) **Monthly Mean Minimum:** This is the average of daily minimum temperatures of a full month.

   (d) **Monthly Extreme Maximum:** This is the highest temperature recorded during any day in the month.

   (e) **Monthly Extreme Minimum:** This is the lowest temperature recorded during any day in the month.

2. **Humidity:**

   (a) **Absolute Humidity (AH):** This is the actual amount of moisture present in an unit mass or unit volume of air, g/kg or g/m^3.

   (b) **Saturation Point Humidity (SH):** This is the maximum amount of moisture, the air can hold at a given temperature, g/kg or g/m^3.

   (c) **Relative Humidity (RH):** This is the ratio of absolute humidity to saturation point humidity at a given temperature, expressed as a percentage. Relative humidity indicates evaporation potential. It is necessary for design to establish monthly mean maximum and monthly mean minimum relative humidity values for each month of an year.

(d) Vapour Pressure: This is the partial pressure of water vapour present in the air (N/m^2). (The relationship of DBT, WBT, AH, RH and vapour pressure is shown by the psychrometric chart)

3. **Precipitation:**
This is the term used for all forms of water (rain, snow, hail, dew, mist, frost) deposited from the atmosphere, mm/hour, mm/day or mm/month.

4. **Driving Rain:**
This is intense rain accompanied by a strong wind. The driving rain index (m^2/s), is the product of annual rainfall (m) and annual average wind velocity (m/s). This expresses the degree of exposure causing penetration of rain into building structures. An index below 3 m^2/s indicates the structure is sheltered. Between 3 and 7 m^2/s indicates the exposure of the structure is moderate. More than 7 m^2/s indicates the exposure is severe.

5. **Sky Conditions:**
These are governed by the presence or absence of clouds. Generally, two observations are made everyday and the portion of the sky covered is expressed as a percentage. The information is used for the design of roofs and overhangs.

6. **Solar Radiation:**
Solar radiation incident on a surface is recorded as an instantaneous intensity and is expressed in joules per m^2 of the surface during one second (J/m^2 × s) or watt per m^2 of the surface (W/m^2). For design, hourly average intensities must be known for a typically high and a typically low radiation day of each year.

7. **Wind:**
Wind velocity is measured by an anemometer or a pitot tube and wind direction is measured by a wind vane.

An anemograph gives continuous data of wind velocity and changes in direction.

8. **Special Characteristics:**
Special occurrences such as hail - storms, squalls, earthquakes, tornadoes, hurricanes, dust - storms etc. which affect human comfort and cause structural damage need observation and recording as to their intensity and frequency.

9. **Vegetation:**
Vegetation influences climate, even as climate determines the type of vegetation that can grow in a region. Vegetation is an important element in the design of out-door spaces and selection of shady areas and glare-free locations.

Site Climate:
Every city, town, zone or construction site may have its own climate more or less different from the climate indicated for the region, because of immediate surrounding physical and environmental conditions. It is essential for the designer to identify the characteristics of the area allotted for construction and prepare plans which would maximize the beneficial aspects and minimize the effects of adverse factors constituting the local site climate.

The following factors influence site climate:

1. **Local Factors:**

   Topography: Elevation, openness, ground slope, undulations of the site, hill top or basin area, etc.

   Land: Natural or built-up, soil characteristics, depth of groundwater and its seasonal movement.

   Existing objects: Trees, fences, walls, neighbouring structures, etc.

2. **Normal Air Movement in Open Country:**

   Day Time Effect: Ground is heated by solar radiation. Layers of air closest to the ground get heated up and start rising up. Air temperature decreases with increase in altitude. So cooler air descends to the ground to replace hot air moving up.

   Night Time Effect: After sunset, particularly on clear nights, the ground becomes cooler than the air above. The direction of heat flow is reversed from the air to the ground.

3. **Temperature Inversion:**

   At a site surrounded by high-rise buildings, air temperature shows little or no decrease with height or as sometimes happens - because of heat radiation from surrounding high building tops, an actual increase in temperature with height may occur. There will be no vertical air movement. This condition is known as temperature inversion and is undesirable. High concentrations of air-pollutants remain stagnant at ground level and increase the load on air-conditioning units.

4. **Humidity:**

   Day Time Effect: Relative humidity decreases close to the ground, as air gets warmed and moves up, rate of evaporation increases which produces a cooling effect.

   Night Time Effect: Especially on a clear night, when the air is still, as the lowest layer of air cools, its relative humidity increases. With further cooling, humidity reaches saturation point and excess moisture starts settling out in the form of dew.

5. **Precipitation:**

   A site on the windward slope of a hill can receive more rainfall than a site on the leeward slope. High rise buildings also serve as hill slopes diverting moist hot air with particulates upwards, which after entering cooler zones undergo condensation and result in cloud bursts, so often experienced in coastal cities.

6. **Solar Radiation:**

   The intensity of solar radiation at the site is influenced by the slope and orientation of the site. The effect of site slope is more at higher latitudes and much less at the equator.

If the solar radiation is incident on vegetation at and around the site, there is a considerable reduction in the intensity of solar heat, but a stone or concrete building receiving solar heat can reach a temperature much higher than the surrounding air.

7. **Air Movement:**

Ground wind speeds can be reduced by thick fences or walls surrounding the site. Sites at crests of hills experience great wind movement. Sites in depressions and valleys, not facing winds, experience little air movement. Sea shore sites may receive sea breezes which may lower the maximum temperature by nearly 10°C although rise in humidity will be undesirable.

8. **Vegetation:**

The moderating effect of vegetation on site climate can never be underestimated. Outdoor landscaping at the site, which includes even the lightest plant cover, is important in the context of air temperature control, regulation of humidity, radiation and dust absorption and maintenance of high oxygen content in the air.

Main Climatic Zones of India:

India is a country with wide variations in climate. There are regions which are extremely hot as Kutch in Gujrat, and there are regions which are extremely cold as upper reaches of Himalayas. Thus, based on climatic data, country can be divided into the following seven climatic zones:

- Hot and dry
- Hot and humid
- Warm and humid
- Moderate
- Cold and cloudy
- Cold and dry
- Composite.

The main determining factors for the classification of the climatic zones, air temperature and relative humidity predominantly influence heat exchange between the human body and the surroundings. The two other factors, viz. solar radiation and precipitation also influence building design.

5.4 COMFORT STANDARDS AND SAFETY MEASURES

The task of the designer is to create the best possible indoor climate (it is not feasible to regulate outdoor conditions). The environment that produces thermal comfort depends on temperature, humidity, air movement, etc. To some extent, thermal comfort also depends on personal or individual reactions.

Body temperature depends on the balance between heat production and heat loss. Heat resulting from the breakdown of food elements in the body (metabolism) maintains the body temperature well above that of the surrounding air in a cool or cold environment. Under normal conditions of rest, the body temperature is maintained within a normal range of 38 to 39°C. Therefore, heat production by the body must be balanced by the heat loss. When the body is at work, the body temperature may rise, say by about 0.5°C. The thermal load, to which a body is subjected in a hot environment, is the sum of the environmental load and the heat from metabolism.

Due to exchange of heat between environment and body, physical sensation of warmth or cold is felt by the body. This sensation of warmth or cold can be expressed by:

(i) **Dry Bulb Temperature:** It is the true temperature of moist air at rest; errors due to radiation are avoided.

(ii) **Effective Temperature:** This combines into a single value the thermal effect of dry bulb temperature, humidity and movement of air, and is assumed to express the sensation of warmth or cold felt by the human body. The numerical value of the index for any given combination of conditions is the temperature of still saturated air which would induce an identical feeling of warmth. The effective temperature is generally applicable to warm atmospheres when heat - radiation effects are not significant; the scale of effective temperature makes too much allowance for humidity at low temperature and too little at higher temperature.

However, attempts have been made to apply corrections to effective temperature due to radiant heat. For this purpose, the black globe temperature is substituted for dry bulb temperature in the determination of the effective temperature scale; this corrected temperature is called the Corrected Effective Temperature (CET). For Indian conditions for various climatic zones, the effective temperature for comfort is between 21°C to 24°C and the values can vary by ± 3°C. Values beyond these limits will lead to discomfort.

5.4.1 Heat Exchange

1. Body Heat Exchange:

The thermal balance of the body depends on the amount of heat produced by the body (metabolic heat) and how it is lost at the surface of the body. Clearly if the body is not to overheat or overcool, then the heat lost at the surface must be the same as the heat produced by the metabolism [Fig. 5.6 (a) and (b)]. This thermal balance can be expressed by an equation. If the heat gain and heat loss factors are:

Gain: Met = metabolism (basal and muscular)

                  Cnd = conduction (contact with warm bodies)

                  Cnv = convection (if the air is warmer than the skin)

                  Rad = radiation (from the sun, the sky and hot bodies)

Loss: Cnd = conduction (contact with cold bodies)
        Cnd = conduction (contact with warm bodies)
        Cnv = convection (if the air is warmer than the skin)
        Rad = radiation (from the sun, the sky and hot bodies)

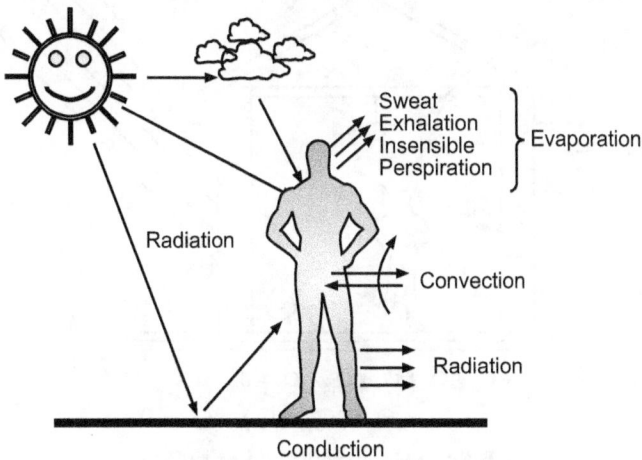

Fig. 5.6 (a): Body heat exchange

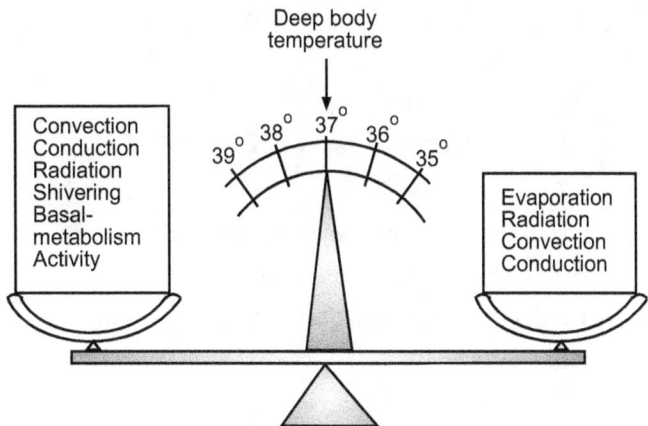

Fig. 5.6 (b): Thermal balance of the body

2. Heat Exchange of Buildings:

It is established by the laws of heat transfer that *when a temperature difference between the inside and outside or different parts of the building exists, it results in exchange of heat from the hotter to colder zones.* The rate of heat flow from one part to the other depends on the capacity of the building material or building unit such as wall, floor, roof, doors, windows, etc. The building is considered as a defined unit and its heat exchange processes with the outdoor environment is examined here.

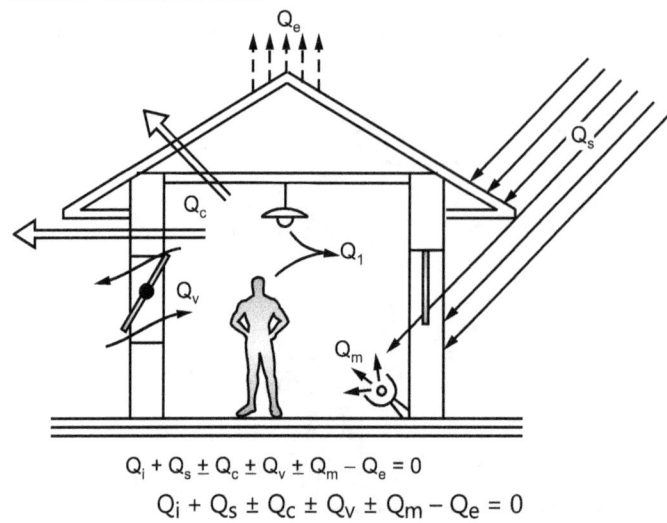

$$Q_i + Q_s \pm Q_c \pm Q_v \pm Q_m - Q_e = 0$$
$$Q_i + Q_s \pm Q_c \pm Q_v \pm Q_m - Q_e = 0$$

Fig. 5.6 (c): Heat exchange of buildings

Heat exchange can take place by following ways:

Conduction:

(a) **Conduction** of heat may occur through walls either inwards or outwards, the rate of which will be denoted as Q_c.

$$Q_c = A \times U \times \Delta T$$

where, Q_c = Conduction heat flow rate in 'W'

A = Surface area in m²

U = Transmittance value in W/m² °C

ΔT = Temperature difference.

(b) **Radiation through windows:** Radiation through glazed windows will be,

$$Q_s = A \times I \times \theta$$

where, A = Area of window in m²

I = Radiation heat flow density in W/m²

θ = Solar gain factor of window glass.

(c) **Convection:** Convection heat flow rate between the interior of a building and the open air, depends on the rate of ventilation, i.e. air exchange. The rate of ventilation heat flow is described by the equation,

$$Q_v = 1300 \times V \times \Delta T$$

where, Q_v = Ventilation heat flow rate, in W
1300 = Volumetric specific heat of air, J/m³ °C
V = Ventilation rate, in m³/s
ΔT = Temperature difference, °C

$$\text{Ventilation rate (V)} = \frac{N \times \text{Room volume}}{3600}$$

N = Number of air changes per hour

(3600 is the number of seconds in an hour)

(d) Internal heat gain: This may result from the heat output of human bodies, lamps, motors, and appliances. This is denoted by Q_i.

(e) Heating and cooling: There may be a deliberate introduction or removal of heat (heating and cooling) using some form of outside energy supply. The heat flow rate of such mechanical controls may be denoted as Q_m.

(f) Evaporation: If evaporation takes place on the surface of the building (e.g. roof pool) or within building (human sweat or water in a fountain) and the vapours are removed, this will produce cooling effect, the rate of which will be denoted as 'Q_e'.

$$Q_e = 666 \times \text{kg/hr.}$$

as the latent heat of evaporation of water around 20°C is approximately 2400 kJ/kg, this gives,

$$2400 \times 1000 \text{ J/hr.} = \frac{24 \times 10^5}{3600} \text{ J/sec.} = 666 \text{ W}$$

The estimation of evaporation rate is more difficult task and it can rarely be done with any degree of accuracy (except under mechanically controlled conditions), as it depends on many variables, such as available moisture, humidity of the air, temperature of the moisture itself and of the air and velocity of the air movement.

The thermal balance, i.e. the existing thermal condition is maintained if,

$$Q_i + Q_s \pm Q_c \pm Q_v \pm Q_m - Q_e = 0$$

If the sum of this equation is less than zero (negative), the building will be cooling and if it is more than zero, the temperature in the building will increase.

5.4.2 Heat Loss Calculation

The purpose of heat loss calculation is usually for the design of a heating installation. Heat loss rate for a condition which is the coldest for 90% of the time is calculated. The heating installation is then designed to produce heat at the same rate.

Under less severe conditions, the installation can work with a reduced output. Colder conditions in the remaining 10% of the time normally occur in short spells and may be bridged by the thermal inertia of the building and by an 'overload capacity' of the installation.

The calculation method is best illustrated by a simple example:

Example 5.3: *A 6 ×6 m and 2.5 m high office is located on an intermediate floor of a large building, therefore, it has only one exposed wall facing south, all other walls adjoining rooms kept at the same temperature ; $T_i = 20°C$, $T_o = -1°C$.*

The ventilation rate is three air changes per hour. Four 100 W bulbs are in continuous use to light the rear part of the room, which is used by four clerical workers.

The exposed 6 × 2.5 m wall consists of a single glazed window, 1.5 × 6 m = 9.0 m², U = 4.48 W/m² °C, and a clinker concrete spandrel wall, 200 mm, rendered and plastered, 1 m ×6 m = 6 m², U = 1.35 W/m² °C.

Calculate the heat loss for heating installation.

Solution:

$$\text{Temperature difference } (\Delta T) = 20°C - (-1°C) = 21°C$$
$$Q_c = (9.0 \times 4.48 + 6 \times 1.35) \times 21$$
$$= (40.32 + 8.1) \times 21$$
$$= 1016.8 \text{ W}$$

The volume of the room is $6 \times 6 \times 2.5 \text{ m} = 90 \text{ m}^3$

Thus, the ventilation rate is:

$$\text{Ventilation rate} = \frac{N \times \text{Room volume}}{3600}$$
$$= \frac{90 \times 3}{3600}$$
$$= 0.075 \text{ m}^3/\text{s}$$

$$\therefore \quad Q_v = 1300 \times 0.075 \times 21$$
$$= 2047.5 \text{ W}$$

The four light bulbs and four persons produce:
$$Q_i = 4 \times 100 + 4 \times 140 = 400 + 560 = 960 \text{ W}$$

As no solar radiation and no evaporative loss are considered, the thermal balance equation is
$$Q_i - Q_c - Q_v + Q_m = 0$$

Substituting the calculated values, we get,
$$960 - 1016.8 - 2047.5 + Q_m = 0$$
$$Q_m = 2104.3 \text{ W}$$

The heating installation should provide heat at this rate, or, rounded up, at the rate of 2.1 kW.

5.4.3 Heat Gain Calculation

Example 5.4: *Heat gain is usually calculated for the purposes of air conditioning design. It is obvious that this installation should cope with the warmest conditions at its peak capacity. Again, the highest temperature for 90% of the time is taken as 'design outdoor temperature' and a solar radiation intensity is taken on similar grounds.*

The above example will be used, except
$T_o = 26\ °C$ *and the incident radiation (l)* $\quad = 580\ W/m^2$

Absorbance of the wall surface, $\quad a = 0.4$
Surface conductance, $\quad f_a = 10\ W/m^2\ °C$
Solar gain factor for window, $\quad \theta = 0.75$
Calculate heat for design of air-conditioning.

Solution:

Temperature difference (ΔT) = 26°C − 20°C = 6°C for conduction through the window and for ventilation heat flow, but for the opaque surface, the solar temperature must be found as

$$T_s = 26 + \frac{I \times a}{f_a}$$

$$= 26 + \frac{580 \times 0.4}{10} = 26 + 23.2 = 49.2°C$$

Thus, for the spandrel wall,

$$\Delta T = 49 - 20°C = 29°C$$
$$Q_c = (9.0 \times 4.48 \times 6) + (6 \times 1.35 \times 29)$$
$$= 241.9 + 234.9 = 476.8\ W$$
$$Q_s = 9.0 \times 580 \times 0.75 = 3915\ W$$
$$Q_v = 1300 \times 0.075 \times 6 = 585\ W$$
$$Q_i = \text{(as before)} = 960\ W$$

No evaporation loss is considered, thus the thermal balance equation is

$$Q_i + Q_s + Q_c + Q_v + Q_m = 0$$

Substituting the calculated values, we get,
$$960 + 3915 + 476.8 + 585 + Q_m = 0$$
$$5936.8 + Q_m = 0$$
$$\therefore \quad Q_m = -5936.8\ W$$

The air conditioning system must be capable of removing heat at this rate, or rounded up, 6 kW.

5.4.4 Definitions of Terms

The definitions of the following terms should be well understood to study the effects of heat transfer and thermal insulation behaviour of the material and building components:

1. **Thermal Conductivity (k):** The thermal conductivity of a material is the amount of heat that will flow through an unit area of material, of unit thickness in one hour, when the difference of two temperatures is maintained at 1°C. It is expressed as $\frac{kcal\ cm}{m^2\ h\ °C}$. Values of k for various building and insulating materials are given in Table 5.1.

2. **Thermal Resistivity (1/k):** This is the reciprocal of thermal conductivity and is denoted by 1/k.

3. **Thermal Conductance (c):** It is the thermal transmission of a single layer structure per unit area divided by temperature difference between the hot and cold faces. It is expressed as $\frac{kcal}{m^2\ h\ °C}$. The values of thermal conductance of air gaps of different thickness are given in Table 5.10.

4. **Thermal Resistance (R):** It is the reciprocal of thermal conductance. For a structure having plane parallel faces, thermal resistance is equal to thickness (L) divided by thermal conductivity.

$$R = \frac{L}{k}$$

It is expressed as $\frac{m^2\ h\ deg.\ C}{kcal}$.

The usefulness of this quantity is that when heat passes in succession through two or more components of the building unit, the resistance may be added together to get the total resistance of the structure.

5. **Surface Coefficient (f):** It is the thermal transmission by convection, conduction or radiation from unit area of the surface, for unit temperature difference between the surface and the surrounding medium. It is expressed as $\frac{kcal}{m^2\ h\ deg.\ C}$.

6. **Surface Resistance (1/f):** It is the reciprocal of surface coefficient, and is expressed as $\frac{m^2\ h\ deg\ C}{kcal}$.

7. **Total Thermal Resistance (R_T):** The total thermal resistance is the sum of the surface resistances and the thermal resistance of the building unit itself. Thus,

$$R_T = \left(\frac{1}{f_o} + \frac{1}{f_i}\right) + R_1 + R_2 + R_3 + ...$$

where, f_o = Outside surface conductance
f_i = Inside surface conductance

Values of $\frac{1}{f_o}$ for walls and roofs may be taken as 0.0515. Values of $\frac{1}{f_i}$ for walls may be taken as 0.125 and that for roofs as 0.171.

$R_1, R_2, R_3, ...$ = Thermal resistance of different materials.

The total thermal resistance is expressed as $\frac{m^2 \, h \, deg. \, C}{kcal}$.

8. **Thermal transmittance (U):** Overall thermal transmittance is the thermal transmission through unit area of the given building divided by the temperature difference between the air or other fluid on either side of the building unit in 'steady state' conditions. *It is reciprocal of total thermal resistance* and is expressed as $\frac{kcal}{m^2 \, h \, deg. \, C}$. Thermal transmittance differs from 'thermal conductance' in so far as temperatures are measured on the two surfaces of material or structure in the latter case and in the surrounding air or other fluid in the former. The conductance is a characteristic of the structure whereas the transmittance depends on conductance and surface coefficients of the structure under the conditions of use. The recommended values of thermal transmittance are given in Table 5.11. The value of thermal transmittance of a structure serves as a guide for thermal insulation and the value of thermal transmittance can be brought down to the required level by adding thermal insulating material in the structure.

9. **Thermal damping (D):** It is expressed by the equation,

$$D = \frac{T_o - T_i}{T_o} \times 100$$

where, T_o = Outside temperature range
T_i = Inside temperature range

Thermal damping or decreased temperature variation is a characteristic dependent on the thermal resistance of the materials used in the structure.

10. **Thermal time constant (T):** It is the ratio of heat stored to thermal transmittance of the structure.

$$T = \frac{Q}{U}$$

where, Q = Quantity of heat stored.

For *homogeneous* wall or roof, thermal time constant may be calculated from the following expression:

$$T = \frac{Q}{U} = \left(\frac{1}{f_o} + \frac{1}{2k}\right) L\rho c$$

where, f_o = Surface coefficient of outside surface
k = Thermal conductivity of the material
L = Thickness of the component
ρ = Density of the material
c = Specific heat of the material.

For composite wall or roof, T may be obtained from the following expression:

$$T = \Sigma \frac{Q}{U} = \left(\frac{1}{f_o} + \frac{L_1}{2k_1}\right)(L_1 \rho_1 c_1)$$
$$+ \left(\frac{1}{f_o} + \frac{L_1}{k_1} + \frac{L_2}{2k_2}\right)(L_2 \rho_2 c_2)$$
$$+ \left(\frac{1}{f_o} + \frac{L_1}{k_1} + \frac{L_2}{k_2} + \frac{L_3}{2k_3}\right)(L_3 \rho_3 c_3)$$

Also temperature drop, $\Delta t_1 = \left(\frac{R_1}{R_T}\right) t_i - t_o$

Table 5.10: Values of thermal conductivity (k) for different building materials and insulating materials

Material (1)	Density (2)	Thermal Conductivity (k) $\frac{\text{kcal cm}}{\text{m}^2 \text{ h deg. C}}$ (3)
(a) Building Materials:		
1. Cement mortar (1 : 3)	1.648	81.8
2. Brick-work common	1.92	69.7
3. Asbestos cement sheeting	1.52	24.8
4. Timber (various)	0.48 to 0.72	12.4
5. Dense concrete (1 : 2 : 4)	2.288	136.4
6. Cinder concrete (1 : 4)	1.406	59.5
7. Glass (i)	2.64	65
(ii)	2.35	70
(iii)	2.24	94
8. Roofing felt	0.80	49.6
9. Asphalt	2.24	105.2
10. Slate	2.72	161.2
11. Stone (i) Granite	2.64	252.0
(ii) Limestone	2.18	131.5
(iii) Sand stone	2.00	111.5
12. Terrazzo	2.43	136.3

contd.

(b) Insulating Materials:

1.	Gypsum board (with a layer of hessian cloth)	0.939	35.0
2.	Asbestos cement board	0.616	14.3
3.	Asbestos cement board	1.008	31.0
4.	Cork slab	0.192	3.78
5.	Gasket cork sheet	0.304	4.76
6.	Exfoliated vermuculite (loose)	0.264	5.99
7.	Mineral wool blanket	0.192	3.35
8.	Glass wool	0.189	3.47
9.	Soft board (wood fibre board)	0.249	4.09
10.	Wall board (wood fibre board)	0.262	4.65
11.	Insulating board (laminated bitumen bounded wood fibre board)	0.342	4.77
12.	Chip board	0.432	5.89
13.	Chip board (perforated)	0.352	5.83
14.	Foam plastic	0.024	2.73
15.	Foam glass	0.160	4.79
16.	Foam concrete	0.224	4.44
17.	Foam concrete	0.704	12.83
18.	Saw dust	0.188	4.40

Table 5.11: Values of surface conductances for various wind velocities

Sr. No.	Wind Velocity	Position of Surface	Direction of Heat Flow	Surface Conductance (for non-reflective surface) kcal/m^2 h deg. C
(1)	(2)	(3)	(4)	(5)
1.	Still air	(i) Horizontal	Up	7.96
		(ii) Sloping 45°	Up	7.81
		(iii) Vertical	Horizontal	7.13
		(iv) Sloping 45°	Down	6.44
		(v) Horizontal	Down	5.27
2.	Moving air 24 km/hr.	Any position	Any direction (for winter)	29.29
3.	Moving air 12 km/hr.	Any position	Any direction (for summer)	19.53

Table 5.12: Values of Thermal conductances for air gaps (IS: 3792 - 1966)

Sr. No. (1)	Thickness of Air Gaps (2)	Thermal Conductance kcal/m² h deg. C (3)
1.	Closed space, 1.88 cm wide or more:	
	(i) Bounded by ordinary building material	4.88
	(ii) One or both sides faced with reflective insulation	2.44
2.	Closed space, 0.62 cm wide:	
	(i) Bounded by ordinary building material	7.52
	(ii) One or both sides faced with reflective insulation	4.88
3.	Open space, 1.88 cm wide or more	7.52
4.	Closed space, 1.88 cm minimum, one face corrugated	5.44
5.	Closed space between plane and corrugated surfaces in contact	9.76

Table 5.13: Recommended thermal transmittance (U) values

Surface	Thermal Transmittance Value in kcal/m² h deg. C
1. External walls	1.0
2. Ground floor	1.0
3. Roof and top floor ceiling:	
(i) Bungalows, flats and houses in which the rooms on the top floor are generally heated.	1.0
(ii) Houses in which the rooms on the top floor are unheated or only occasionally heated.	1.5

5.4.5 Units Related to Heat Transfer

The physical units for expressing these coefficients are a little complicated and require explanation, particularly, inter-conversion between the imperial and metric system.

(a) Units of Heat:

Calorie: Heat required to raise the temperature of 1 g of water through 1°C.

British Thermal Unit (Btu): Heat required to raise the temperature of 1 lb of water through 1°F = 252.0 cal.

Celsius Heat Unit (Chu): Heat required to raise the temperature of 1 lb of water through 1°C = 453.6 cal.

(b) Mechanical Equivalent of Heat:

1 calorie at 20°C = 4.1868 J
1 W = 1 J
1 J = 0.2388 cal

(c) Interconversion of Units:

Unit		Equivalent
Energy	1 Btu	0.2519968 kcal, or 1055.06 J or 2.93071×10^{-4} kWh
Intensity of heat flow rate	1 Btu/ft² h	3.15459×10^{-4} W/cm²
Thermal conductance	1 Btu/ft² h°F	5.6783×10^{-4} W/cm² deg. C
Thermal conductivity	1 Btu in./ft² h°F	1.44228×10^{-3} W/cm⁻³ W/cm deg. C

5.4.6 Temperature Gradient

The internal temperature attained in the hottest month is dependent on the amount of solar radiated heat received. It is also governed by the conditions influencing loss of heat from the internal space, by conduction and ventilation to the open air and due to the speed with which the internal structure absorbs and releases heat. Large heat gains occur due to incorrect orientation and large openings. In short, the internal temperature for a given amount of solar radiation will depend on:

- The value of thermal transmittance (U value) of construction;
- The area of room surfaces exposed to open air so that the large surface areas would release large amounts of heat;
- The rate of ventilation; and
- Rate at which the structure absorbs and releases heat.

Example illustrates the procedure for the temperature gradient across a cross-section of a wall and a roof due to thermal conductivity of the materials of construction per unit area.

5.4.7 Planning for Thermal Comfort

The objective of planning a building and the orientation of their components is to reduce solar radiation which would contribute to thermal comfort. For this purpose, the path of the sun with respect to the latitude of the place during the year should be known, particularly the diurnal variation of the sun during the hot months. Effects of shadow throw of neighbouring buildings should also be found out.

Shading devices for exposed walls and windows have to be provided, these are explained below:

(a) Orientation:

Orientation has to be considered for several situations. Fresh or new layouts of neighbourhoods offer scope for getting maximum benefits from orientation. A site in a built-up area has to take into account several constraints, such as existing buildings, existing roads, etc.

Table 5.14: Sunshine hours on vertical walls facing different directions for different latitudes

Latitude	April 16 and August 27						May 16 and July 28						June 22					
	North		South		East		North		South		East		North		South		East	
	h	m	h	m	h	m	h	m	h	m	h	m	h	m	h	m	h	m
9° N	12	18	–		6	09	12	30	–		6	15	12	40	–		6	20
13° N	7	08	5	16	6	12	12	44	–		6	22	12	54	–		6	47
17° N	5	18	7	14	6	16	12	56	–		6	28	13	10	–		6	35
21° N	4	20	8	18	6	19	9	40	3	28	6	34	13	26	–		6	43
23° N	4	00	8	42	6	21	8	32	4	44	6	38	13	36	–		6	45
27° N	3	32	9	16	6	24	7	12	6	19	6	45	19	38	4	14	6	56
31° N	3	14	9	42	6	28	6	24	7	20	6	52	18	20	5	50	7	05
35° N	3	20	10	02	6	32	5	56	8	04	7	00	17	36	6	56	7	16

The temperature of a structure is raised by direct penetration of the sun's rays through openings and indirectly by absorption, conductance and radiation of heat by walling and roofing. To reduce this, efforts can be made to eliminate the penetration of the sun's rays and by protecting as many exposed facades of the building as possible.

Information on the path of the sun through solar diagrams, can be analysed to get further details on the actual direct sun on different walls of a building in a day. For instance sunshine hours on the north, south and east walls for different latitudes for certain typical dates are given in Table 5.14.

From this table, it is seen that as the northern latitudes increase, the number of hours of direct sun on the north wall decreases except on June 22. Conversely, for south facing walls, the duration of sunshine increases. On the east and west walls, the duration is almost the same for all latitudes.

Therefore, protection of northern walls in northerly latitudes can be less rigorous than that of the southern wall in summer. However, in the extreme north latitudes, longer duration of sunshine in the southern facade is an advantage in winter.

The eastern and western facades receive nearly equal amounts of daily solar radiation throughout the year because of almost the same duration of exposure. The only difference is that on the eastern side the building is comparatively cool after a cool night and the indoor temperature is low. So the effect of direct penetration of the sun's rays has a reduced effect on temperature indoors, except if the eastern side is glazed. On the other hand, in the western facade, the indoor temperature is already high in the afternoon and the sun's rays further increase it. The heat on the western facade can be minimized by reducing the area of the facade or by providing thermal insulation on the exterior or by shading this facade by verandahs, creepers, plants, etc.

The preparation of solar diagrams would be of help in deciding on the aspects of orientation, particularly with regard to the location and height of shading devices in relation to the altitude of the sun.

The word "shadow throw" indicates the actual line of the shadow when a pin is fixed on a wall; if the sun is to the right and above the horizontal level of the pin, the shadow will be to the left of the pin and also inclined to the vertical. The horizontal component of the shadow is called the horizontal shadow throw; the vertical component of the shadow is the vertical shadow throw. The vertical shadow is always downwards; the horizontal shadow throw could be to the right or left of the pin (or sunshade) depending on the time of the day.

(b) Cold Climate: In the case of cold climate as in hill stations and northern latitudes of Kashmir, orientation should be so as to increase the inside temperature during winter months.

(c) Temperate Climate: In areas where the climate is temperate like in Bangalore, where generally the mean day temperature is between $20°C$ to $30°C$, the problem of orientation of building for solar radiation does not arise. However, other considerations such as glare, humidity, prevailing winds etc. may come in.

(d) Hot and Very Hot Region: In hot and very hot regions (mean maximum temperature of $30°C$ or more) the maximum day temperatures occur in the months of April to June between 2 PM to 5 PM. The sun would be on the western side and the exact altitude could be found from the solar diagram for different months of the year. In general, in north India, the afternoon sun is W-S-W and the altitude is not high during these hours. Hence, it is difficult to provide for protection against the sun through shading devices.

(e) Hot Dry and Hot Humid Regions: The diurnal range of temperature gives important information regarding local climate for orientation purposes. A difference of $8°C$ and more between the daily mean maximum and minimum temperatures would suggest a dry climate. If the maximum temperature is above $30°C$, the conditions would be hot and dry. In such a condition, protection of openings against direct incidence of sunlight is very essential; evaporative cooling brings relief. On the other hand, if the difference is less than $8°C$, the conditions signify hot and humid climate. For these conditions, the provision of ventilation with large openings opposite to the walls facing the prevailing wind directions can help.

5.4.8 Thermal Insulation of Buildings

When there is difference in temperature of inside of a building and outside temperature, heat transfer takes place from areas of higher temperature to those of lower temperature. This transfer of heat may take place by any or more of the three methods namely, conduction, convection and radiation. In colder regions, when the buildings are internally heated and where outside temperature is cool, it is necessary to check this heat loss of the building. Similarly in very hot regions, when buildings are internally cooled and the outside temperature is unbearably warm, it is essential to check the entry of heat from outside into the building. The term thermal insulation is used to indicate the construction or provisions by way of which transmission of heat from or in the room is retarded. The main objective of thermal insulation is to conserve a constant heat or temperature inside the building, irrespective of temperature changes outside.

5.4.9 General Principles of Thermal Insulation

Thermal insulation of buildings works on the following general principles:
1. The materials used in the building should have a low heat conductivity, that is a high degree of heat resistance per unit of thickness. In other words, the materials having adequate heat insulation value, should be used.
2. The thermal resistance of the material directly varies with its thickness and hence, the material should be installed in an adequate, thickness depending upon the insulation desired.
3. The provision of air spaces or open spaces in different types of construction, like cavity, walls etc. and also in materials for roofs, ceilings etc. offers very good insulation against heat transmission.
4. The thermal resistance of the building in general and doors and windows in particular, depends on its orientation with respect to the movements of sun. The building should be so located that there is minimum transfer of solar heat during the day in summer and there is maximum transfer of solar heat during the day in winter.
5. Thermal insulation to some extent can be achieved by adopting general measures such as use of sun-shading devices like sun-breakers etc. increasing the height of ceiling (about 1 to 1.3 m above the occupant height), increase the height of parapet walls when the altitude angle of the sun is low; etc.

5.4.10 Means of Thermal Control

The objective of thermal control can be stated briefly as follows:
1. When cold discomfort conditions prevail;
   (a) to prevent heat loss,
   (b) to utilize heat gain from the sun and internal sources,
   (c) to compensate for any net loss, by heating which uses some form of energy supply.
2. When hot discomfort conditions prevail;
   (a) to prevent heat gain,
   (b) to maximize heat loss,
   (c) to remove any excess heat by cooling which uses some form of energy supply.
3. When conditions vary diurnally between hot and cold discomfort;
   (a) to even out variations,
   (b) (i) in cold phase and (ii) in the hot phase (as above),
   (c) to compensate for both excesses by a flexible heating-cooling system.

Objectives listed under (a) and (b) in each group can be achieved by structural or constructural (passive) means, item (c) in each group is the task of mechanical or energy based (active) controls.

5.4.11 Thermal Insulation of Roofs

Insulation Standards: Indian standard, IS : 3792 - 1966 recommends that no roof should have an overall thermal transmittance of more than 2.00 kcal/m² h deg. C. It is also recommended that the roof should not have a thermal damping less than 75% (or thermal time constant less than 20 hours). The relationship between *thermal damping* and *thermal time constant* is given by the limiting curves given in Fig. 5.7.

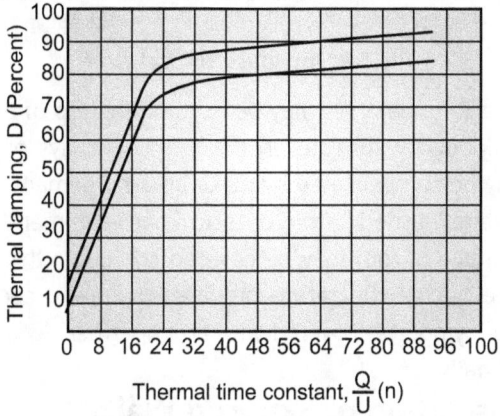

Fig. 5.7: Limiting curves showing relation between D and $\frac{Q}{U}$

Methods: Heat gain through roofs may be reduced by adopting the following methods:

1. **Application of heat insulating materials:** Heat insulating materials may be applied externally or internally to the roofs. In case of external application, heat insulating material may be laid over the roof but below a water-proof course. In case of internal application, heat insulating material may be fixed by adhesive or otherwise on the underside of roofs from within the rooms. False ceiling of insulating material may be provided below the roof with air gaps in between, as shown in Fig. 5.8.

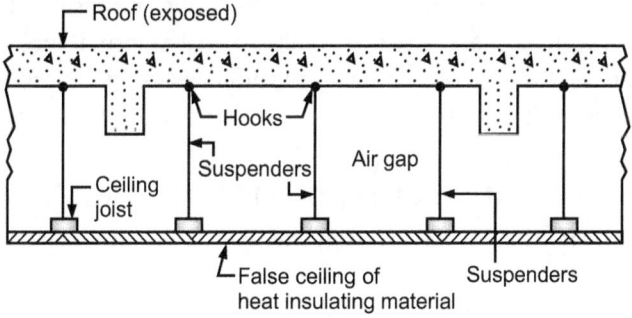

Fig. 5.8: Suspended false ceiling

2. For flat roofs, external insulation may also be done by arranging asbestos cement sheets or corrugated galvanised iron sheets on bricks as shown in Fig. 5.9.

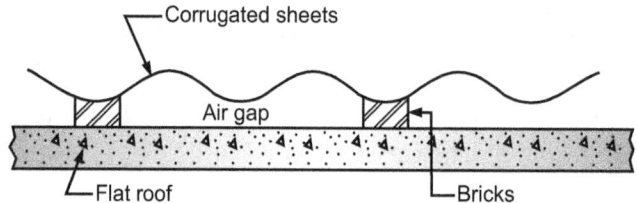

Fig. 5.9: Air space for flat roof

3. Shining and reflecting materials may be fixed on the top of the roof.
4. Roofs may be flooded with water in the form of sprays or otherwise. Loss due to evaporation may be compensated by make up arrangements.
5. Roofs may be white-washed before on-set of each summer.
6. Top exposed surface of roof may be covered by 2.5 cm thick layer of coconut pitch cement concrete. Such a concrete is prepared by mixing coconut pitch with cement and water. After laying, it is covered with an impermeable layer and then allowed to dry for 20 to 30 days.

5.4.12 Thermal Insulation of Exposed Walls

Insulation standards: IS : 3792 - 1966 recommends that no exposed wall should have an overall thermal transmittance of more than 2.2 kcal/m² h deg. C. It is also recommended that the wall should not have a thermal damping less than 60% (or thermal time constant less than 16 hours).

Methods: Heat insulation of exposed walls may be achieved by the following ways:
1. The thickness of wall may be increased.
2. Cavity wall construction may be adopted, for external walls.
3. The wall may be constructed out of suitable heat insulating material, provided structural requirements are met.
4. Heat insulating materials may be fixed on the inside or outside of the exposed wall, in such a way that the value of overall thermal transmittance is brought within desired limits. In the case of external application, overall water-proofing is essential.
5. Light-coloured white-wash or distemper may be applied on the exposed side of the wall.

5.4.13 Thermal insulation of Exposed Doors and Windows

In dealing with heat insulation of exposed windows and doors, suitable methods should be adopted to reduce:
(a) Incidence of solar heat, and
(b) Reduction of heat transmission.

(a) **Reduction of Incidence of Solar Heat:** This may be achieved by any one of the following means:
   (i) External shading, such as louvered shutters, sun breakers chhajjas, and
   (ii) Internal shading, such as curtains and venetian blinds.
(b) **Reduction of Heat Transmission:** Where glazed windows and doors are provided, reduction of heat transmission may be achieved by providing insulating glass or double glass with air space or by any other suitable means.

SOLVED EXAMPLES

Example 5.5: *Compute the thermal transmittance (U) value for a 30 cm thick brick outside wall provided with 15 mm thick cement plaster on both the sides.*

Solution: (Refer Fig. 5.10)

From Table 5.14,

$k_1 = 81.8$

$k_2 = 69.7 \quad \dfrac{\text{kcal cm}}{\text{m}^2 \text{ h deg. C}}$

$k_3 = 81.8$

where, k = thermal conductivity

$L_1 = 1.5$ cm; $L_2 = 30$ cm;

$L_3 = 1.5$ cm

$\therefore \quad R_1 = \dfrac{L_1}{k_1} = \dfrac{1.5}{81.8} = 0.0183$

$R_2 = \dfrac{L_2}{k_2} = \dfrac{30}{69.7} = 0.430$

$R_3 = \dfrac{L_3}{k_3} = \dfrac{1.5}{81.8} = 0.0183$

For walls,

$\dfrac{1}{f_i} = 0.125$ and,

$\dfrac{1}{f_o} = 0.0515$

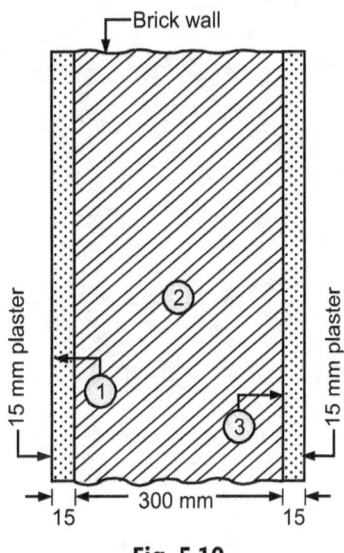

Fig. 5.10

$$R_T = \dfrac{1}{f_o} + \dfrac{1}{f_i} + R_1 + R_2 + R_3$$

$= (0.0515 + 0.125) + 0.0183 + 0.430 + 0.0183$

$= 0.643$

Hence, $U = \dfrac{1}{R_T}$

$= \dfrac{1}{0.643}$

$= 1.55 \dfrac{\text{kcal}}{\text{m}^2 \text{ h deg. C}}$

Example 5.6: *What will be the modified value of U if an air gap of 5 cm is introduced between two halfs of the brick wall of Example 5.5, as shown in Fig. 5.11?*

Solution:

$k_1 = k_5 = 81.8 \quad \dfrac{\text{kcal cm}}{\text{m}^2 \text{ h deg. C}}$
$k_2 = k_4 = 69.7$

$L_1 = L_5 = 1.5 \text{ cm}; \; L_2 = 15 \text{ cm} = L_4$

For 5 cm air gap,

adopt $C_3 = 5.35 \dfrac{\text{kcal}}{\text{m}^2 \text{ h deg. C}}$

$R_1 = \dfrac{L_1}{k_1} = \dfrac{1.5}{81.8} = 0.0183 = R_5$

$R_2 = \dfrac{L_2}{k_2} = \dfrac{15}{69.7} = 0.215 = R_4$

$R_3 = \dfrac{1}{C_3} = \dfrac{1}{5.35} = 0.187$

where,   C = Thermal conductance for air gap

Also, for wall,

$\dfrac{1}{f_i} = 0.125 \text{ and } \dfrac{1}{f_o} = 0.0515$

∴ $R_T = R_1 + R_2 + R_3 + R_4 + R_5$

$= (0.0515 + 0.125) + 0.0183 + 0.215 + 0.187 + 0.215 + 0.0183$

$= 0.8301$

Hence, $U = \dfrac{1}{0.8301}$

$= 1.20 \dfrac{\text{kcal}}{\text{m}^2 \text{ h deg. C}}$

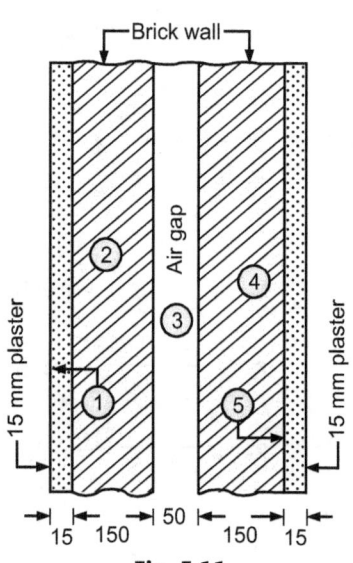

Fig. 5.11

Example 5.7: *What will be the U value of the wall of Example 5.5, if a 3.0 cm thick layer of foam plastic is introduced on one face, between brick wall and cement plaster?*

Solution: From Table 5.14.

$k_1 = k_4 = 81.8$

$k_2 = 69.7 \dfrac{\text{kcal cm}}{\text{m}^2 \text{ h deg. C}}$

$k_3 = 2.73$

Also, $L_1 = 1.5 \text{ cm} = L_4$

$L_2 = 30 \text{ cm}; L_3 = 3.0 \text{ cm}$

$R_1 = \dfrac{L_1}{k_1} = \dfrac{1.5}{81.8} = 0.0183 = R_4$

$R_2 = \dfrac{L_2}{k_2} = \dfrac{30}{69.7} = 0.430$

$R_3 = \dfrac{L_3}{k_3} = \dfrac{3.0}{2.73} = 1.09$

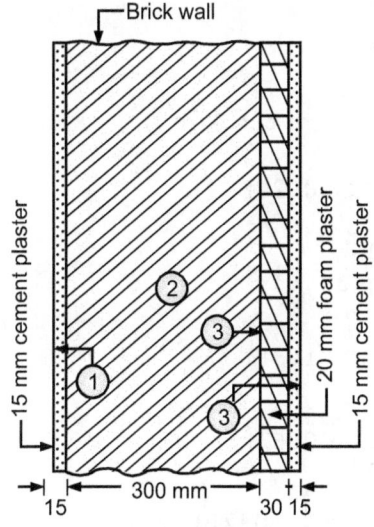

Fig. 5.12

For wall, $\dfrac{1}{f_o} = 0.0515$ and $\dfrac{1}{f_i} = 0.1250$

∴ $R_T = \left(\dfrac{1}{f_o} + \dfrac{1}{f_i}\right) + R_1 + R_2 + R_3 + R_4$

$= (0.0515 + 0.1250) + 0.0183 + 0.430 + 1.09 + 0.0183 = 1.73$

∴ $U = \dfrac{1}{R_T} = \dfrac{1}{1.73} = 0.58 \dfrac{\text{kcal}}{\text{m}^2 \text{ h deg. C}}$

Example 5.8: Compute the U value for a R.C.C. slab, 15 cm thick, insulated with 5 cm thick foam, plastic and finished with 4 cm thick brick tiles on the top and 2.0 cm thick cement plaster on the bottom.

Solution: (Refer Fig. 5.13)

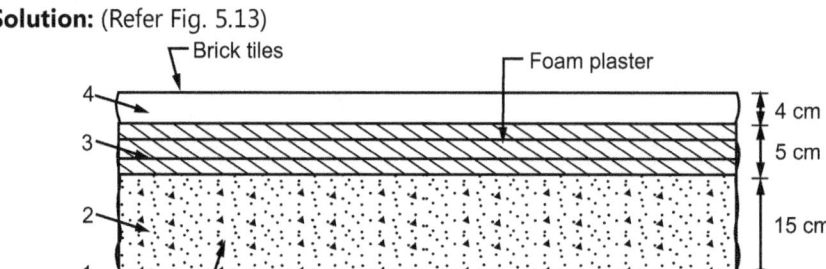

Fig. 5.13

From Table 5.14, we have,

$k_1 = 81.8$
$k_2 = 136.4$
$k_3 = 2.73$ $\dfrac{\text{kcal cm}}{\text{m}^2 \text{ h deg. C}}$
$k_4 = 69.7$

$L_1 = 2.0$ cm; $L_2 = 15$ cm; $L_3 = 5$ cm; $L_4 = 4$ cm

$\therefore \quad R_1 = \dfrac{L_1}{k_1} = \dfrac{2.0}{81.8} = 0.0244$

$R_2 = \dfrac{L_2}{k_2} = \dfrac{15}{136.4} = 0.1099$

$R_3 = \dfrac{L_3}{k_3} = \dfrac{5}{2.73} = 1.8315$

$R_4 = \dfrac{L_4}{k_4} = \dfrac{4}{69.7} = 0.0574$

For roofs, $\dfrac{1}{f_o} = 0.0515$ and $\dfrac{1}{f_i} = 0.1710$

$\therefore \quad R_T = \left(\dfrac{1}{f_o} + \dfrac{1}{f_i}\right) + R_1 + R_2 + R_3 + R_4$

$\qquad = (0.0515 + 0.1710) + 0.0244 + 0.1099 + 1.8315 + 0.0574$

$\qquad = 2.246$

$\therefore \quad U = \dfrac{1}{R_T} = \dfrac{1}{2.246} = 0.445 \dfrac{\text{kcal}}{\text{m}^2 \text{ h deg. C}}$

Example 5.9: *Compute thermal time constant (T) for the wall of Example 5.5.*

Solution:

(i) For plaster,

$$L_1 = 1.5 \text{ cm} = 0.015 \text{ m}$$
$$k_1 = 0.818 \text{ kcal m/m}^2 \text{ h deg. C}$$
$$\rho_1 = 1648 \text{ kg/m}^3$$
$$c_1 = 0.22 \text{ kcal/kg deg. C}$$

$\therefore \quad L_1 \rho_1 c_1 = 0.015 \times 1648 \times 0.22 = 5.438 = L_3 \rho_3 c_3$

$$\frac{L_1}{k_1} = \frac{0.015}{0.818} = 0.0184 = \frac{L_3}{k_3}$$

$$\frac{L_1}{2 k_1} = 0.0092$$

(ii) For bricks,

$$L_2 = 30 \text{ cm} = 0.30 \text{ m}$$
$$k_2 = 0.697 \text{ kcal m/m}^2 \text{ h deg. C}$$
$$\rho_2 = 1920 \text{ kg/m}^3$$
$$c_2 = 0.20 \text{ kcal/kg deg. C}$$

$\therefore \quad L_2 \rho_2 c_2 = 0.30 \times 1920 \times 0.20 = 115.2$

$$\frac{L_2}{k_2} = \frac{0.30}{0.697} = 0.430$$

$$\frac{L_2}{2 k_2} = 0.216$$

$$T = \sum \frac{Q}{U} = \left(\frac{1}{f_o} + \frac{L_1}{2 k_1}\right)(L_1 \rho_1 c_1)$$
$$+ \left(\frac{1}{f_o} + \frac{L_1}{k_1} + \frac{L_2}{2 k_2}\right)(L_2 \rho_2 c_2)$$
$$+ \left(\frac{1}{f_o} + \frac{L_1}{k_1} + \frac{L_2}{k_2} + \frac{L_2}{2 k_2}\right)(L_3 \rho_3 c_3)$$

$= (0.0515 + 0.0092) \times (5.438) + (0.0515 + 0.0184 + 0.216) \times (115.2) + (0.0515 + 0.0184 + 0.430 + 0.216)(5.438)$

$= 0.33 + 32.93 + 3.89$

$= 37.15$

Example 5.10: *Determine the temperature gradient for the cavity wall shown in Fig. 5.14. Outside temperature is 40°C and inside temperature is 25°C.*

Solution: From Table 5.14.

$k_1 = k_5 = 81.8$ $\dfrac{\text{kcal cm}}{\text{m}^2 \text{ h deg. C}}$
$k_2 = k_4 = 69.7$

$L_1 = L_5 = 1.5$ cm
$L_2 = L_4 = 15.0$ cm

For 5 cm air gap,

$C_3 = 5.35$ kcal/m² h deg. C

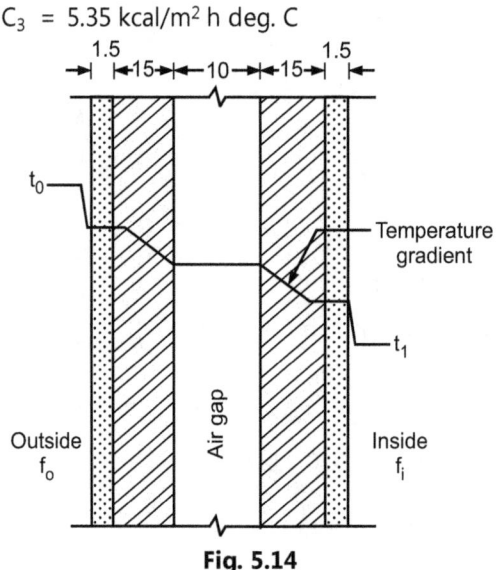

Fig. 5.14

(a) Calculation of 'R' values

1. R_1 (for plaster) = $\dfrac{L_1}{k_1} = \dfrac{L_5}{k_5} = \dfrac{1.5}{81.8} = 0.0183 = R_5$

2. R_2 (brick wall) = $\dfrac{L_2}{k_2} = \dfrac{15}{69.7} = 0.215 = R_4$

3. R_3 (for air gap) = $\dfrac{1}{5.35} = 0.187$

4. Also, for wall, $\dfrac{1}{f_i} = 0.125$ and $\dfrac{1}{f_o} = 0.0515$

∴ $R_T = \left(\dfrac{1}{f_o} + \dfrac{1}{f_i}\right) + R_1 + R_2 + R_3 + R_4 + R_5$

= (0.0515 + 0.125) + 0.0183 + 0.215 + 0.187 + 0.215 + 0.0183
= 0.8301

(b) Temperature drop between individual elements is as below:

Drop in temperature (t_{1-2})

$$= \frac{\Delta T}{R_T} \times R \text{ of element, where } \Delta T = 15°C \text{ and } R_T = 0.8301$$

$$= \frac{15}{0.8301} \times R \text{ of element}$$

$$= 18.07 \, R$$

∴ 1. Drop in temperature from outside air to surface

        = 18.07 × 0.0515

        = 0.93°C   ∴ drop is from 40°C to 39.07°C

2. Drop in temperature across plaster

        = 18.07 × 0.0183

        = 0.33°C   ∴ drop is from 39.07°C to 38.74°C

3. Drop in temperature across brick wall

        = 18.07 × 0.215

        = 3.88°C   ∴ drop is from 38.74°C to 34.85°C

4. Drop in temperature across air gap

        = 18.07 × 0.187 = 3.38°C   ∴ drop is from 34.85°C to 31.47°C

5. Drop in temperature across brick wall

        = 18.07 × 0.215 = 3.88°C   ∴ drop is from 31.47°C to 27.59°C

6. Drop in temperature across plaster

        = 18.07 × 0.0183

        = 0.33°C   ∴ drop is from 27.59°C to 27.26°C

7. Drop in temperature from inside surface to inside air

        = 18.07 × 0.125 = 2.25°C

∴ drop is from 27.26°C to 25.01°C (close to 25°C)

Fig. 5.14 shows temperature gradient line.

5.5 SOUND INSULATION

5.5.1 Introduction

Hearing is one of the man's most important communication channels, perhaps only second to vision. But, whilst the eyes can be shut when there is too much light or an unwanted scene not be viewed, the ears are open throughout life to unwanted noises as well as to wanted sounds. Protection, if necessary, will have to be provided in the environment.

Unwanted sound reaching the ears is called *noise*. It may be due to frequency of sound or intensity of sound or both. Noise due to high frequency sound is more unpleasant than noise due to low frequency sounds. Noisy conditions not only result in uncomfortable living conditions. Fatigue, inefficiency and mental strain, but prolonged exposure to such conditions may cause temporary deafness or nervous breakdown.

5.5.2 Effects of Noise

The effects of noise on man can be divided into two categories: (a) psychological and (b) physiological, and for most purposes, can be considered under the following headings:

1. Causing annoyance or dissatisfaction.
2. Affecting communication.
3. Causing damage to hearing.
4. Leads to fatigue and decreases the efficiency of persons.
5. Causing permanent changes in the normal functioning of human organism, resulting in Deterioration in mental and/or physical health.
6. It takes away essence of music and speech.

5.5.3 Comfort Standards

The comfort factors controlling noise are the acceptable noise levels in working interiors and sound insulation between rooms in the same building against air borne noise and impact noise.

Acceptable Indoor Noise Levels:

These noise levels are those which will neither cause uncomfortable conditions nor damage the acoustics of the building. Acceptable noise levels depend upon:

(a) nature and type of noise
(b) time of fluctuations of noise
(c) background noise, and
(d) type and use of building.

The acceptable noise levels inside buildings from the point of view of comfort, economy and practical considerations recommended in India are given in Table 5.15.

Table 5.15: Acceptable indoor noise levels

Sr. No.	Type of Building	Noise Level (dB)
1.	Radio and TV studios	25 - 30
2.	Music room	30 - 35
3.	Hospital and auditoria	35 - 40
4.	Apartments, hotels and homes	35 - 40
5.	Conference rooms, small offices and libraries	35 - 40
6.	Court rooms and class rooms	40 - 45
7.	Large public offices, banks and stores	45 - 50
8.	Restaurants	50 - 55
9.	Factories	55 - 60

5.5.4 Properties of Sound

(a) Characteristics of Sound:

There are three characteristics of sound:

1. Intensity and loudness of sound
2. Frequency or Pitch
3. Quality or timbre.

1. Intensity and Loudness of Sound:

Intensity of sound is defined as the amount or flow of wave energy crossing per unit time through a unit area taken perpendicular to the direction of propagation. Mathematically, the intensity at a point is proportional to the square of the amplitude of vibration of the point, i.e. $I \propto A^2$; whereas, **loudness** of a sound corresponds to the degree of sensation depending on the intensity of sound and the sensitivity of ear drums, and does not increase proportionally with intensity but more nearly to its logarithm, i.e. $L \propto \log I$. Thus, intensity of sound is purely a physical quantity, of which is independent of ear of listener. Loudness, on the other hand, is the degree of sensation which depends upon characteristics of ear and the listener.

2. Frequency or Pitch of Sound:

It is defined as the number of cycles which a sounding body makes in each unit of time. It is that characteristic by which a shrill sound can be distinguished from a grave one, even though the two sounds may be of the same intensity. The sensation of pitch depends upon the frequency with which the vibrations succeed one another at the ear; the greater the frequency, the higher the pitch and lesser the frequency, lower the pitch. The frequency scale covers a wide range varying from 20 cycles per second to 1500 cycles per second. If the frequency of sound is below 20 cycles per second, then effect of sound is lost (one can't hear such a sound).

3. Quality or Timbre:

The **quality** of a sound is that characteristic which enables us to distinguish between two notes of same pitch and loudness played on two different instruments or produced by two different voices. A study of vibration curves of various musical instruments has shown that notes emitted by them are seldom pure. They contain some fundamental tones of frequency 'n' and additional tones of frequencies 2n, 3n, 4n etc. called overtones.

The quality of sound is determined by the number of overtones present along with the fundamental frequency of the wave and also their intensities.

5.5.5 Measurement of Sound

The range of variation of intensity is very high. The loudest and almost painful sound is about 10^{13} times the intensity of sound which is just audible by the human ear. If I_1 and I_0 represent the intensities of two sounds of a particular frequency and L_1 and L_0 are their corresponding measures of loudness, we have,

$$L_1 = K \log_{10} I_1$$

and

$$L_0 = K \log_{10} I_0$$

The difference in loudness of the two, technically known as intensity level 'L' between them, is given by

$$\boxed{L = K \log_{10} \frac{I_1}{I_0}}$$

In the above equations, K is the constant depending upon the units of measurements. When K = 1 (unity), the difference in loudness is expressed in *bels*, a unit named after A. G. Bel. This unit is rather large. Hence, a shorter practical unit called *decibel* (written as dB) equal to $\frac{1}{10}$ of bel, is used. Thus, the intensity level is expressed as,

$$L = 10 \log_{10} \frac{I_1}{I_0} \text{ dB}$$

If L = 1 dB, we have,

$$L = 10 \log_{10} \frac{I_1}{I_0}$$

or

$$\log_{10} \frac{I_1}{I_0} = \frac{1}{10}$$

$$\frac{I_1}{I_0} = 1.26$$

i.e., a 26 per cent change in intensity alters the level by one decibel. This is practically the smallest change in intensity level that the ear can ordinarily detect.

Also, when $I_1 = 100 I_0$
we get, $L = 10 \log_{10} 100 = 10 \log_{10} 10^2 = 20$ dB
Similarly, when $I_1 = 1000 I_0$,
we have $L = 10 \log_{10} 1000 = 10 \log_{10} 10^3 = 30$ dB.

Table 5.16: Rating of intensity of sound

Common Sound	Intensity level (dB)		Threshold of Feeling
	Range	Average	
1. Threshold of audibility.		0	Very very faint
2. Rustle of leaves, whisper, sound proof room.	0 – 20	10	Very faint
3. Quiet living room, private office, quiet conversation, average auditorium.	20 – 40	30	Faint
4. Noisy home, average office (acoustically treated), average conversation, quiet radio etc.	40 – 60	50	Moderate
5. Noisy office, average street noise, average radio, average factory.	60 – 80	70	Loud
6. Noisy factory area, loud street noise, police whistle, truck unmuffled, train sound.	80 – 100	90	Very loud
7. Thunder, artillary, aeroplane motors, pneumatic hammers etc.	100 – 120	110	Deafening
8. Loudest sound due to pneumatic drills, or aeroplane at a distance of 4 m.	120 – 140	130	Pain and discomfort

Thus, we learn that when two sounds differ by 20 dB, the louder of them is 100 times more intense and when they differ by 30 dB, the louder one is 1000 times more intense.

To build a scale of loudness, we have to fix its zero. The loudness corresponding to the threshold of hearing is the zero of this scale; while 130 dB is the threshold of painful hearing.

The sound pressure corresponding to the threshold of hearing is about 0.0003 dynes/sq. cm and that corresponding to threshold of pain is about 300 dynes/sq. cm. Table 5.16 gives the rating of intensity of sound, in decibels.

5.5.6 Behaviour of Sound in Enclosures

When sound is generated in a room, the distance between the source and the walls is so small that there is little or no reduction due to distance. When the sound waves strike the surfaces of a room, three things happen:

(i) Some of the sound is *reflected* back in the room.

(ii) Some of the sound energy is *absorbed* by the surfaces and listeners.

(iii) Some of the sound waves set on the walls, floors and ceiling vibrating and are thus *transmitted* outside the room.

The amount of sound *reflected* or *absorbed* depends upon the surfaces, while the sound *transmitted* outside the room depends upon *sound insulation* properties of the surfaces.

5.5.7 Reflection of Sound

Sound waves get reflected from a large uniform plane surface in the same manner as that of light waves, the angle of incidence being equal to angle of reflection, as shown in Fig. 5.15. The reflection of sound has certain virtues in acoustics, such as the enhancement of loudness and enrichment of total quality of sound. The following characteristics of reflection of sound waves are noteworthy:

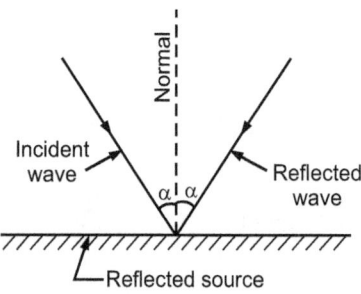

Fig. 5.15: Reflection of sound waves

1. Reflection of sound waves follow practically the same laws as that of reflection of light. However, this may not be true in some exceptional cases, hence great caution should be exercised while applying these laws.

2. The reflected wavefronts from a flat surface are also spherical and their centre of curvature is the image of source of sound [Fig. 5.16 (a)].

3. Sound waves reflected at a convex surface are magnified and are considerably bigger [Fig. 5.16 (b)]. They are attenuated and are therefore weaker. Convex surfaces may be used with advantage to spread the sound waves throughout the room.

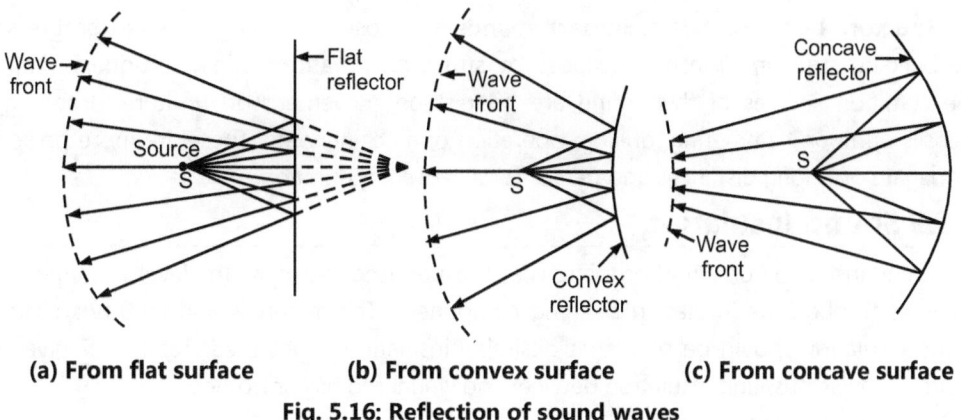

(a) From flat surface   (b) From convex surface   (c) From concave surface

Fig. 5.16: Reflection of sound waves

4. The sound waves reflected at a concave surface are considerably smaller [Fig. 5.16 (c)]. The waves are most condensed and therefore amplified. The concave surfaces may be provided for the concentration of reflected waves at certain points.

5.5.8 Noise Classification

From the origin point of view, noises may be of two types:

(a) Outdoor noises,

(b) Indoor noises.

Outdoor noises are caused by road traffic, railways, aeroplanes, lifts, moving machinery, machines in nearby factory or building etc.

Indoor noises are those which are caused either in the same room or in the adjacent room. These are due to conversation of people, moving of people or furniture, crying of babies, playing of radios or other musical instruments, operations of cisterns and water closets, noise of type writer, banging of door, etc.

Noise may be alternatively classified as follows:

(a) Air borne noises or sounds.

(b) Structure borne noises or impact noises or sounds.

Air borne sounds are those which are generated in air and which are transmitted in air directly to human ear. Such a sound travels from one part of the building to the other, or from outside of the building to inside by (i) openings such as doors, windows, ventilators, key holes etc. or by (ii) forced vibrations set up in walls, ceilings etc. Air borne noise possesses less power, continues for a long duration and is confined to places near its origin.

Structure borne sounds or **impact sounds** are those which originate and progress on the building structure. These are caused by structural vibrations originated due to impact. The common sources of this sound are: foot steps, movement of furniture, dropping of utensils on floor, hammering, drilling, operation of machinery etc. These are more powerful, propagate over long distances and persist for a very shaft duration.

5.5.9 Sound Insulation

Sound insulation or sound proofing is a measure used to reduce the level of sound when it passes through the insulating building component. The materials and methods used for sound insulation should be such that desirable insulation is obtained. Table 5.17 gives the desirable levels of sound insulation between individual rooms (air borne).

Table 5.17: Sound insulation between individual rooms

Sr. No.	Situation	Overall insulation in dB
1.	Between living room in one house or flat and the living room and bed rooms in another.	50
2.	Elsewhere between houses or flats.	40
3.	Between one room and another in the same house or flat.	30
4.	Between teaching rooms in a school.	40
5.	Between one room and another room in an office.	30
6.	Between one ward and another ward in a hospital: (a) Normal wards. (b) Extra–quiet special wards.	40 45

For Impact Noise: The floor of a room immediately above a living room or bed room should have impact insulation which should be able to reduce the noise by 15 dB in addition to the insulating value of base concrete and by around 20 dB in the case of normal timber floor construction.

5.5.10 Noise Control

The levels of desired sound insulation, for different types of buildings and between the individual rooms or apartments of a building, can be achieved by the following constructional measures of noise control and sound insulation:

1. Wall insulation (i.e. Vertical barriers)
2. Floor and ceilings insulation (i.e. Horizontal barriers)
3. Windows and doors.
4. Insulating sanitary fittings.
5. Machine mounting or insulations of machinery.

1. Wall Insulation:

Walls and partitions are the vertical barriers to noise. Their proper design and construction may insulate the sound to the desired level. To achieve this objective, the following methods of wall construction can be adopted:

Table 5.18: Typical insulation values for different types of walls

Type of Construction	Approx. Weight in kg/m²	Average TL in dB
1. One brick thick (i.e. 20 cm) wall	485 – 490	50
2. One and a half brick thick (i.e. 30 cm) wall	705 – 710	53
3. Cavity wall having two leaves each of half brick thickness (i.e. 10 cm) with 5 cm cavity.	485 – 490	50 – 53
4. Cavity wall having two 10 cm thick leaves of clinker block with 5 cm cavity.	310 – 312	50
5. Half brick wall with 13 mm thick plaster on both sides.	268 – 270	45
6. 20 cm thick hollow dense concrete block wall with 13 mm thick plaster in both sides.	185	45
7. Partition wall made with gypsum wall board fixed on timber frame work.	68 – 70	45
8. 76 mm thick hollow clay block wall with 13 mm thick plaster on both sides.	108 – 110	36

(a) Rigid homogeneous walls: A rigid wall consists of stone, brick or concrete masonry construction, wall plastered on one or both the sides. The sound insulation offered by these rigid walls depends upon their weight per unit area. The sound insulation thus increases with the increase in the thickness of the wall. Because of the logarithmic variation between weight and transmission loss, such a construction becomes highly uneconomical and bulky after a certain limit. In this type, sound is transmitted through the holes and cracks and space left due to badly fitted doors and windows.

The degree of insulation offered by different types of partition walls is shown in Table 5.18.

(b) Partition walls of porous materials: The partition walls are made of porous materials, may be rigid or flexible in nature. In case of partitions of rigid porous materials such as concrete masonry, cinder concrete etc., the sound insulation increases about 10% higher than the non-porous rigid material. However, partition walls of non-rigid porous materials such as felt, mineral wool etc. offer very low sound insulation, though they can be used in combination with rigid materials with added advantage.

(c) Double wall partition: A double wall partition, shown in Fig. 5.17 consists of plaster boards or fibre boards or plaster on laths on both the faces, with sound absorbing blanket in between. Staggered wooden studs are provided as support, though their number should be a minimum. A double wall construction is thus a partition wall of rigid and non-rigid porous materials.

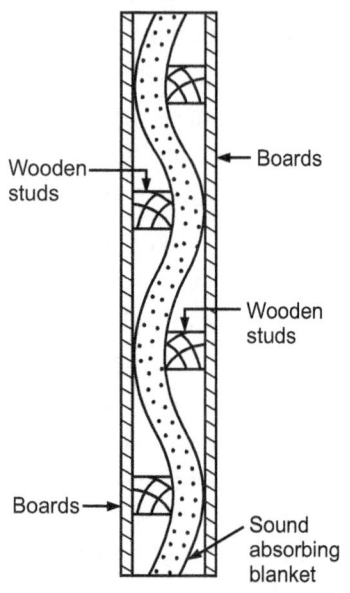

Fig. 5.17: Double wall partition

(d) Cavity wall construction: This is an ideal construction from the point of view of sound proofing, as shown in Fig. 5.18. The gap between the two leafs of the wall may be left air-filled or else filled with some resilient material, like quilt etc. well suspended in the gap. The two faces of the wall may be fixed with celotex or other insulating board. The width of cavity should be atleast 5 cm and the two wall leaves should be tied by use of only light butterfly wall ties.

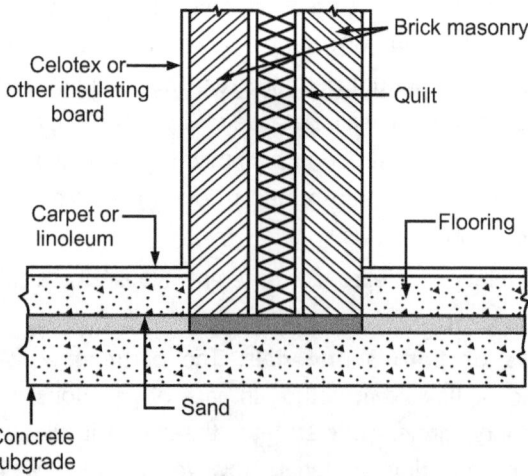

Fig. 5.18: Cavity wall or double wall construction

Table 5.19 gives typical insulation values of various types of walls.

2. Floors and Ceilings Insulation: Horizontal Barriers:

Insulation or floors and ceilings act as horizontal barriers to both air borne as well as impact sounds. Normally, the rigid construction materials used for floors and ceilings offer excellent insulation against air borne noise, but they do not function well for impact or structure borne sounds. Hence, the objective of sound proofed floors and ceilings is aimed at offering good insulation against impact sounds, and this can be achieved by the following constructional features.

(a) Use of resilient surface material on floors: In this method, over the massive and rigid construction of floor slabs, a surface larger of resilient materials such as linoleum, insulation board, cork, asphalt mastic and carpet etc. are employed. By this method, insulation against impact noises to an extent of 5 to 10 dB over a bare concrete floors can be obtained. The softer the materials used, greater would be the insulation value.

(b) Providing a floating floor construction:

(i) **Concrete floors:** This is an additional floor constructed and isolated or floated from the existing concrete floor by means of a resilient material and therefore, does not let the impacts and consequent vibration to be transmitted to the room below. It also provides useful improvement in the insulation fair borne sounds. The cement concrete used may be about 5 cm thick which is poured over a resilient material like quilted mineral or glass wool. It is important that a water proof paper be used in between and both the quilt and paper lapped so as to prevent concrete from getting through (Fig. 5.19).

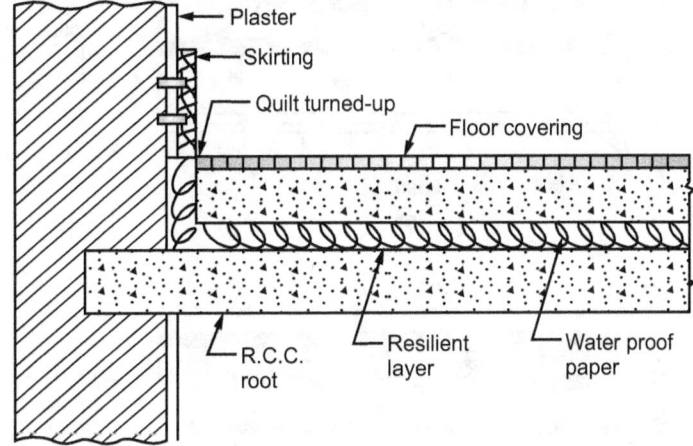

Fig. 5.19: Concrete floor floating construction

(ii) **Wooden floors:** In case of floors constructed of wooden joints, the problem of sound insulation becomes more difficult, particularly in the presence of heavy mechanical impact sounds. Fig. 5.20 shows the methods of insulating such existing floors, while Fig. 5.21 shows new timber floors, employing mineral or glass wool quilt for isolation purposes. Resilient mountings may be used to obtain even more satisfactory results. A further improvement in the insulation of such floors is achieved by employing a pugging or deadening material in the air space between the wood joists. Either sound absorbent type materials like mineral wool or other materials like sand or ashes may be used, the latter are more effective because of the fact that the efficiency of pugging depends on the weight of the material used. In order to obtain useful improvement, at least 100 kg/m² of sand pugging is usually employed. Mineral wool pugging (at least 15 kg/m²) is used mainly in conjunction with thin walls of 10 cm thickness or less.

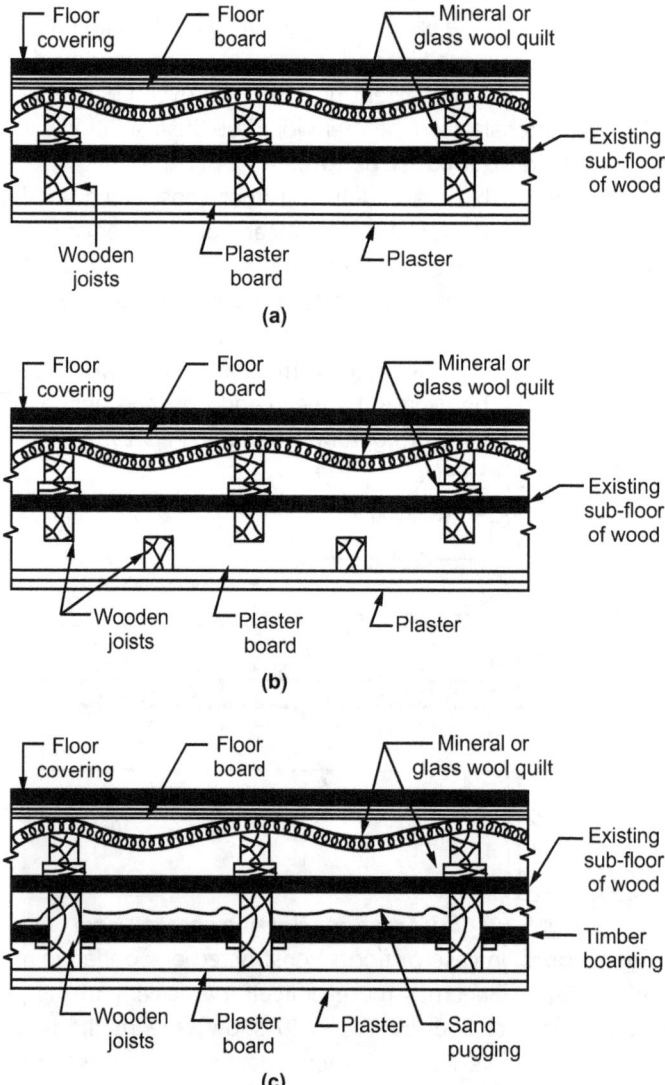

Fig. 5.20: Existing timber floors, floating construction

(c) By providing a suspended ceiling with air space: This type of construction helps to improve the insulation of both air borne and structure borne sounds by attenuating and isolating them from room below. Typical constructions for wooden floors are shown in Fig. 5.21. For solid floors, metal hangers of acoustic clips may be used to support the ceiling below, as shown in Fig. 5.22. The extent of improvement effectively depends upon the weight of the ceiling as well as on the structural rigidity with which it is connected to the solid or wooden floor. Thus, the higher insulation could be achieved by using a very heavy ceiling which is arranged to be independent of the floor by supporting it on resilient mountings.

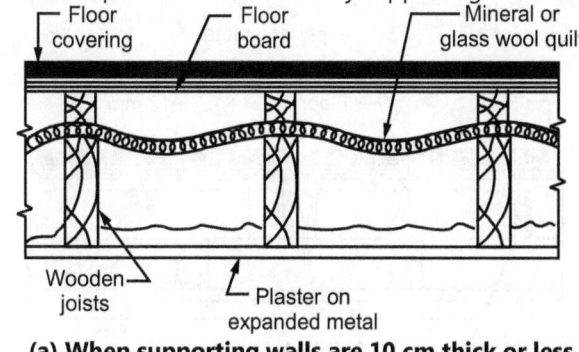

(a) When supporting walls are 10 cm thick or less

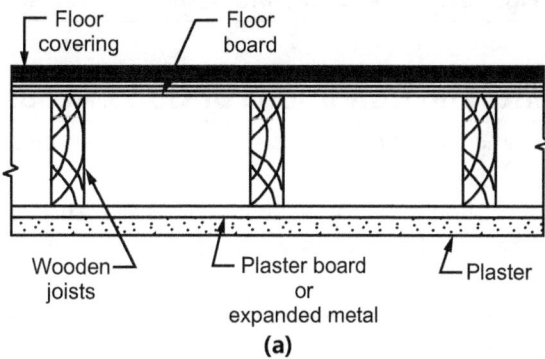

(b) When supporting walls are 20 cm thick or more
Fig. 5.21: New timber floors, floating construction with pugging

(a)

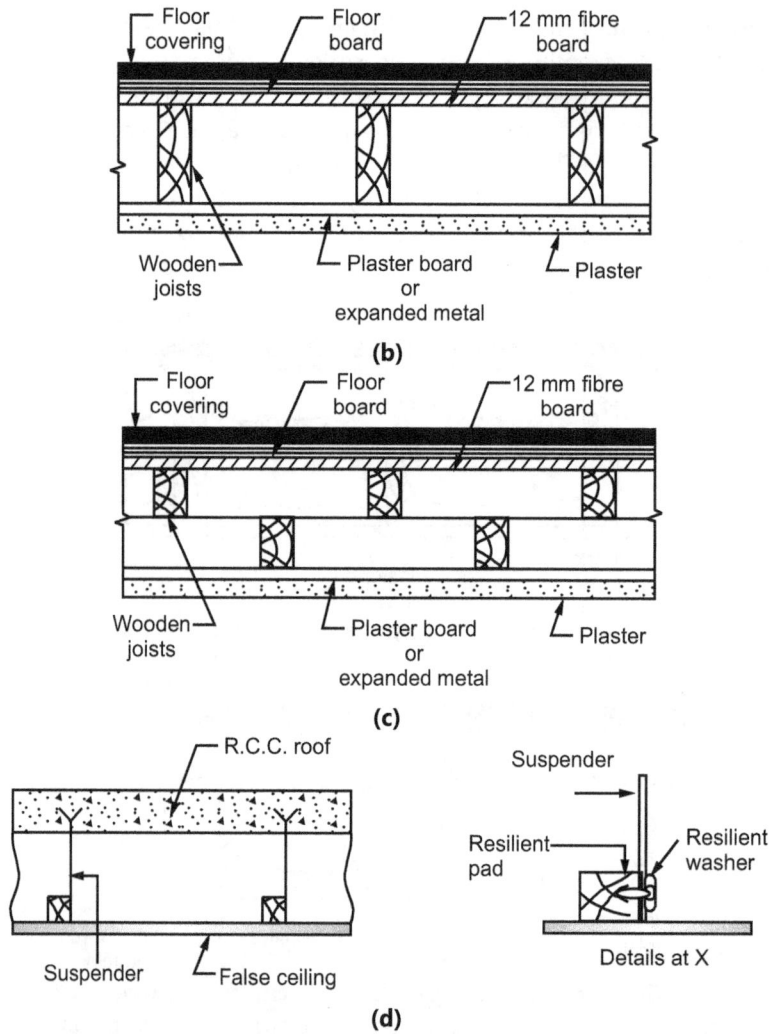

Fig. 5.22: Timber floors with suspending ceiling

5.6 ACOUSTICS

5.6.1 Requirements and Conditions of Good Acoustics

The following requirements and conditions should be fulfilled by a building having good acoustics:

- The initial sound should be of adequate intensity such that it can be heard throughout the hall. For halls of big size suitable sound amplification system should be installed.
- The sound produced should be evenly spread over the entire area so that sound foci and dead spots are avoided.

- The boundary surfaces should be so designed that there are no formation of echoes.
- The boundary surfaces of the hall should be properly designed so that the desired reverberation time is achieved and unwanted sound is absorbed. The absorbent materials should be distributed evenly over the wall surface of the hall.
- In case of conference halls, the acoustics of the halls should be so designed as to ensure proper conditions for listening, assuming that a person may speak or listen from anywhere in the hall.
- In the case of music halls, the treatment should be such that the initial sound reaches the audience with the same intensity and frequency.
- All noises (i.e. unwanted sounds) whether originating from outside or inside of the hall, should be reduced to such an extent that they do not interfere with the normal hearing of music or speech.

5.6.2 Sound Absorption

When a sound wave strikes a surface, a part of its energy is absorbed by friction. The sound generated in an auditorium or a hall is absorbed in four ways: (i) in the air, (ii) by the audience, (iii) in furniture and furnishing, and (iv) at the boundary surfaces such as floors, ceilings, walls etc.

(i) **Absorption in air:** This is mainly due to the friction between the oscillating molecules when sound wave travels through it. However, this absorption is extremely small.

(ii) **Absorption by audience:** Sound energy absorbed by the clotting of the audience. Room acoustics change perceptibly by the number of audience present. Also, absorption is more in winter, than in summer, because of heavy clottings.

(iii) **Absorption in furnitures and furnishings:** Furnitures, curtains, carpets etc. also absorb sound energy to a fairly good extent.

(iv) **Absorption by boundary surfaces:** When sound waves strike the boundary surfaces such as walls, floors, ceilings, absorption takes place due to the following factors: (a) Penetration of sound into porous materials, (b) Resonant vibration of panel materials, (c) Molecular damping in soft absorbing materials; and (d) Transmission through structures.

5.6.3 Sound Absorbents or Acoustical Materials

Special materials used on boundary surfaces for achieving good acoustical requirements of design by increasing their absorption are known as *absorbents*. The sound reducing effect of an absorber depends upon its area as well as on the efficiency of the materials and is indicated by a sound *absorption coefficient*. The term absorption coefficient is used to express the percentage of the incidence of sound that can be absorbed by a material.

An open window is considered to have 100% absorption as it does not interfere with the free passage of the entire sound. The *open window* has a coefficient of absorption as unity and hence the absorbing capacity of all other materials is compared with this open window unit as a standard. This open window unit is also called a *sabin*, named after the scientist who established the unit. The absorption capacity of sound and hence absorption coefficient, depends upon the frequency of incident sound. In general, low density materials have higher absorption coefficient at higher frequencies than at low frequencies. Table 5.19 gives absorption coefficient of commonly used building materials and furnishings.

Table 5.19: Absorption coefficients for building material and furnishings

Sr. No.	Materials	Absorption Coefficient at		
		125 c/s	500 c/s	2000 c/s
	(a) Hangings and floorings:			
1.	Carpet, lined.	0.10	0.25	0.40
2.	Carpets, unlined.	0.08	0.15	0.25
3.	Cotton fabric, 475 g/m² draped to half its area.	0.07	0.49	0.66
4.	Draperies, velours 610 g/m²	0.05	0.35	0.38
5.	Draperies, as above draped to half their area.	0.14	0.55	0.70
6.	Stage curtain.	0.19	0.20	0.23
7.	Linoleum or concrete floor.	0.02	0.03	0.04
8.	Floor, wood on solid.	0.12	0.09	0.09
9.	Floor, wood boards on timber frame.	0.25	0.13	0.15
	(b) Masonry and building materials:			
10.	Brick wall 40 cm thick.	0.02	0.03	0.05
11.	Plaster on wall.	0.03	0.02	0.04
12.	Ceiling, 50 mm plaster of paris suspended from trusses.	0.08	0.05	0.04
13.	Plyboard on 75 mm air space.	0.30	0.10	0.05
14.	Wood veneer 10 mm thick on 50 × 75 mm wood studs at 40 cm centre to centre.	0.11	0.12	0.10
15.	Glass against solid surface.	0.03	0.03	0.02
16.	Marble.	0.01	0.01	0.01
	(c) Audience, chairs etc.:			
17.	Audience seated in fully upholstered seats (per person).	0.18	0.46	0.51
18.	Chair, upholstered seat with spring.	–	0.16	0.071
19.	Seat (unoccupied) fully upholstered (per seat).	0.16	0.40	0.44
20.	Wood veneer seat and back.	–	0.023	–

Table 5.20: Absorption coefficients of indigenous acoustical materials

Sr. No.	Materials	Thickness (mm)	Density (g/cm^2)	Absorption Coefficient at 125 c/s	500 c/s	2000 c/s
1.	Fibrous (acoustic) plaster	20	0.1	–	0.30	0.50
2.	Compressed fibre board:					
	(a) Unperforated.	12	–	0.24	0.3	0.2
	(b) Perforated uniformly over part depth (rigid backing).	12.7	0.3	0.06	0.55	0.67
	(c) Perforated randomly over part depth (rigid backing).	12.7	0.3	0.15	0.52	0.76
3.	Compressed wood particle board:					
	(a) Perforated (rigid backing)	12.7	0.37	0.04	0.36	0.78
	(b) Perforated (rigid backing)	19.1	0.34	0.05	0.61	0.91
	(c) Perforated and painted (rigid backing)	12.7	0.40	0.05	0.40	0.82
	(d) Perforated and painted (rigid backing)	19.1	0.38	0.10	0.62	0.74
4.	(a) Wood wool board.	25	0.4	–	0.20	0.60
	(b) Wood wool board (50 mm from wall)	25	0.4	–	0.35	0.35
5.	Mineral glass wool quilts and mats.	25	0.06	0.09	0.17	0.50
6.	Bonded and compressed mineral/glass wool tiles.	50	0.04	0.12	0.26	0.44
7.	Composite units of perforated hard board backed by perforated fibre board.	25	0.4	0.25	0.5	0.65
8.	(a) Mineral/glass wool with scrim mat (rigid backing)	25	0.08	0.29	0.85	0.84
	(b) Mineral/glass wool with scrim mat (rigid backing)	50	0.08	0.57	0.99	0.95
	(c) Mineral/glass wool with scrim mat faced with perforated (10% open area) hard board (rigid backing).	25	0.08	0.06	0.99	0.49
9.	Miscellaneous:					
	(a) Straw board.	13	0.24	–	0.30	0.35
	(b) Straw board spaced 50 mm from wall.	13	0.24	–	0.35	0.30
	(c) Composite panel: 5 mm perforated plywood, 50 mm mineral wool and 22 mm cement asbestos (suspended from the trusses).	–	–	0.36	0.95	0.67
	(d) Composite panel: 5 mm perforated plywood, 50 mm mineral wool and 22 mm hard board (suspended from trusses)	–	–	0.47	0.20	0.09

5.6.4 Classification of Sound Absorbents or Acoustical Materials

The sound absorbent or acoustical materials can be broadly classified into four groups:

1. **Porous Absorbents:** Absorption in porous materials is mainly due to the frictional losses which occur when the sound waves cause to and fro movement of the air contained in the material. However, their materials absorb sound mainly in the higher frequencies. Their efficiency depends upon porosity, the resistance to air flow through the materials and the thickness. Examples of absorbents under this category are rock wool, glass silk, wood wool, curtains and other soft furnishings; drilled fibre boards and acoustics plaster.

2. **Resonant Panels:** These are semi-hard materials in the form of porous fibre boards which absorb the sound by damping the sympathetic vibrations in the panels, caused by sound pressure waves of appropriate frequency, by means of air space behind the panel. These panels absorb sound only at lower frequencies, over a comparatively narrow frequency band ranging from 50 to 200 cycles. The frequencies, at which panels vibrate, depend upon their weight and depth of air spaces behind them.

3. **Cavity Resonators:** These cavity resonators consist of a container or chamber with small opening in which absorption takes place by the resonance of the air in the container which causes loss of sound energy. They can be designed to absorb sound of any frequency.

4. **Composite Type-Absorbents:** There are a comparatively recut developments, combining the functions of all the above three absorbents. It consists of a perforated panel fixed over an air space containing porous absorbent. The perforations in the panel should form at least 10% of the total area to allow the porous materials to absorb sound at higher frequencies.

5.6.5 Requirements of a Good Acoustic Material

1. It should have high coefficient of absorption.
2. It should be efficient over a wide range of frequencies.
3. It should be relatively cheap and easily available.
4. It should give pleasing appearance after firing.
5. It should be self supporting and should efford easy fixing.
6. It should be fire resistant.
7. It should have sufficient structural strength.
8. It should be heat insulating and non-hygroscopic.
9. It should be durable and should not be liable to attack by insects, vermits, termites etc.

5.6.6 Acoustical Defects

To achieve perfect acoustic conditions, in practice, one has to remove or minimise all the defects in acoustics by considering suitable intensity of sound and an acceptable level of reverberation. These defects, which require due consideration for improving the acoustical conditions, are described as follows:

1. Formation of echoes,
2. Reverberation,
3. Sound foci,
4. Dead spots,
5. Insufficient loudness,
6. Exterior noise nuisance or outdoor noise effects.

1. Formation of Echoes: An *echo* is produced or formed when the reflected sound wave (from surface of walls, roofs, ceilings etc.) reaches the ear just when the original sound from the same source has been already heard. Thus, there is repetition of the sound.

The formation of echoes normally happens when the time lag between the two voices or sounds is about $1/17^{th}$ of a second and the reflecting surfaces are situated at a distance greater than 15 m. The defect usually occurs when the shape of the reflected surface is curved with smoother character. Echoes cause disturbance and unpleasant hearing. *Multiple echoes* may also be heard when a sound is reflected from a number of reflecting surfaces suitably placed, such as two parallel cliffs.

The remedy of this defect is to select the proper shape of the auditorium and surfaces, and to use the rough and porous materials for interior surfaces to disperse the energy of echoes.

2. Reverberation: It has been generally noticed that in public halls and auditoriums, the sound persists even after the source of sound has stopped. This persistence of sound is called reverberation. It is due to multiple reflections in an enclosed space. Reverberation is a familiar phenomenon in cathedrals and new halls/rooms without furniture, where even after sound source stops, the reverberation is heard even upto 10 seconds. A certain amount of reverberation is desirable, specially for giving richness to music, but too much reverberation is undesirable.

The time during which the sound persists is called the *reverberation time* of sound in the hall. It is the period of time in seconds, which is required for sound energy to decay or diminish by 60 dB after the sound source has stopped.

The remedy of this defect lies in selecting a correct time of reverberation known as *optimum time of reverberation*, which can be achieved by suitably using the absorbent or acoustical materials for different reflecting surfaces.

Sabine's Expression for Reverberation Time:

Prof. W.C. Sabine (1868–1919) of Hardward University studied the whole subject of architectural acoustics, particularly with reference to reverberation time. He found experimentally that the reverberation time of a room varies inversely as the effective surface area and directly as the volume of the room. He also showed that this time is independent of the position of the source and the listener and the shape of the room.

As the result of the experiments, he established the following expression for reverberation time:

$$t = \frac{0.16\,V}{\alpha_1 s_1 + \alpha_2 s_2 + \alpha_3 s_3 \ldots} \qquad \ldots (5.1)$$

or

$$t = \frac{0.16\,V}{\sum \alpha s}$$

$$= \frac{0.16\,V}{A} \qquad \ldots (5.2)$$

where,

t = Reverberation time in seconds

V = Volume of the room in m^3

$\alpha_1, \alpha_2, \alpha_3 \ldots$ = Absorption coefficient of individual units (i.e. walls, floors, ceilings, etc.) See Table 5.19.

$s_1, s_2, s_3 \ldots$ = Areas of individual absorbing surfaces

A = Total absorption power.

The total *absorbing power* is expressed in m^2 sabines.

Fig. 5.21 is also used to calculate the total absorption to be provided, in order to achieve any desired time of reverberation.

Table 5.21 gives the relation between reverberation time and the acoustics of a room.

Table 5.21: Reverberation time and acoustical quality

Reverberation time in seconds	Acoustics
0.50 to 1.50	Excellent
1.50 to 2.00	Good
2.00 to 3.00	Fairly good
3.00 to 5.00	Bad
Above 5.00	Very bad

Table 5.22 gives the optimum reverberation time and audience factors for acoustical design.

Table 5.22: Optimum reverberation time

Type of Building	Optimum Reverberation Time (seconds)	Audience Factor
1. Cinema theatres	1.3	Two-thirds
2. Churches	1.8 to 3	Two-thirds
3. Law courts, committee rooms, conference halls	1 to 1.5	One-third
4. Large halls	2 to 3	Full
5. Music concert hall	1.6 to 2	Full
6. Parliament house, Assembly hall, Council chamber	1 to 1.5	Quorum
7. Public lecture hall	1.5 to 2	One-third

Indian Standard Code IS : 2526–1963 recommends to use Fig. 5.23 for the determination of reverberation time for various size of enclosed space and for various purpose/use of the space.

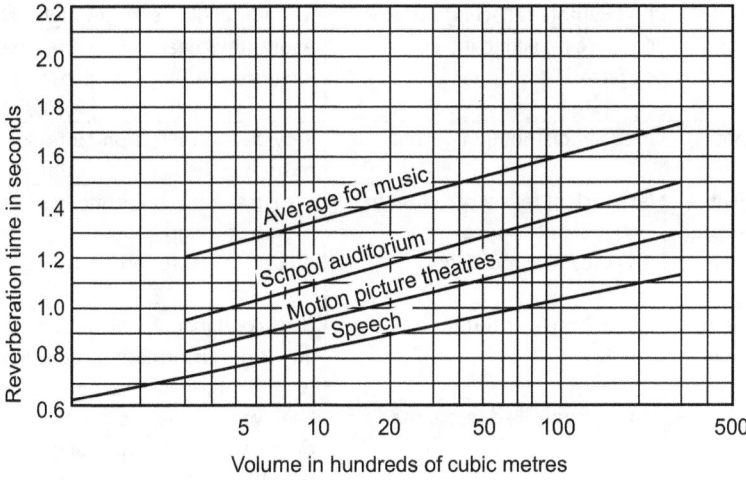

Fig. 5.23: Optimum reverberation time at 500 cycles for different types of rooms as a function of room volume

3. Sound Foci: When the interior surfaces are concave, the reflected sound waves concentrate at certain spots and produce sound of large intensity. Then spot of higher sound intensity are known as sound foci. They can be removed by avoiding concave interiors or by providing absorbent materials on focusing areas.

4. Dead Spots: This defect is an outcome of the formation of sound foci. Because of high concentration of reflected sound at sound foci, there is deficiency of reflected sound at some other points. These points are known as dead spots, where sound intensity is so low that it is insufficient for hearing. This defect can be removed by installation of suitable diffuser so that there is even distribution of sound in the hall.

5. Insufficient Loudness: This defect is caused due to lack of sound reflecting flat surface near the sound source and excessive sound absorption treatment in the hall. The defect can be removed by providing hard reflecting surface near the source and by adjusting the absorption of the hall so as to get optimum time of reverberation. When the length of hall is more, it may be desirable to install loud speakers at proper places.

6. Exterior Noise and Outdoor Nuisance: This defect is caused mainly due to poor sound insulation and partly due to poor planning and this results into bad acoustics. The exterior noise nuisance is carried inside the hall or auditorium through loose door, ventilator and window openings. This defect can be corrected or rectified by providing adequate insulation against sound for various components of the hall and through proper planning in relation to the surroundings.

Table 5.23: Summary of common acoustical defects in auditoriums and conference halls and recommended remedies

Sr. No.	Defect	Cause	Recommendations for	
			New Design	Existing Building
1.	Excessive Reverberation	Insufficient absorption	Add absorbents.	
2.	Echoes	(a) Unsuitable shape (b) Remote reflecting surfaces	Avoid unsuitable shape. Make offending surfaces highly absorbent.	
3.	Sound foci	Concave reflecting interior surfaces	Avoid curvilinear interiors.	Alter shape or use absorbents on focussing areas.
4.	Dead spots	Irregular distribution of sound	Provide even diffusion of sound.	Introduce suitable diffusers.
5.	Insufficient sound volume	(a) Lack of reflections close to source to sound (b) Excessive absorption	Disperse hard reflecting surfaces about the source of sound. Adjust absorption to give optimum reverberation.	
6.	Colouring of sound quality	(a) Selective absorption (b) Uncontrolled resonance	Use combination of absorbents to obtain uniform absorption coefficient over the required frequency range. Use wood panel absorbents which resonate over a wide frequency range and fix these on battens provided at irregular intervals. Adopt rigid construction with studs etc.	
7.	High back-ground noise	Poor sound insulation, badly fitting doors and windows or noisy air-conditioning systems.	Select construction with requisite sound insulation; provide proper fitting doors and windows with requisite sound insulation. Reduce noise from air-conditioning equipment by isolating the machine and/or treatment or plant room etc.	

5.6.7 General Principles and Factors in Acoustical Design

Following is the list of general planning principles and factors which are important for good acoustical conditions in a building. (Refer Article 5.29 for details)

1. Site selection and planning
2. Dimensions (size)
3. Shape
4. Seats and seating arrangement
5. Treatment of interior surfaces
6. Reverberation and sound absorption.

5.6.8 Acoustics for Various Types of Buildings

Following practical cases of buildings which deserve acoustical treatment from designer or planner will be described in short under this head.

(A) Cinema Theatres for Sound Films:

The following special considerations should be made in the acoustical design and planning of the cinema theatres:

1. **Site selection and planning:** A noise survey of the area should be made and the site selected should be in quietest surroundings as otherwise elaborate and expensive construction may be required to provide requisite sound insulation. Depending on the ambient noise level of the site, orientation, layout and structural design should be arranged to provide necessary noise reduction so that the background noise level of not more than 40 to 45 dB is achieved within the hall.

2. **Dimensions (Size):** The size should be fixed in relation to the number of audience required to be seated, and in proportion to the intensity of sounds to be generated. The floor area of the theatre should be calculated on the basis of 0.6 to 0.9 m^2/person. The height of the hall is determined by such considerations as ventilation, presence (or absence) of balcony and type of performance etc. The ceiling of the theatre should be splayed type with a slight upward slope towards the rear-side. Total volume should be designed on the basis of 4.0 to 5.0 m^3/person.

3. **Shape:** The shape is extremely important in the acoustical design since it is a governing factor in correcting defects like echoes, sound foci, dead spots etc. A fan shaped plan with diverging side walls has been considered to be the best (Fig. 5.24).

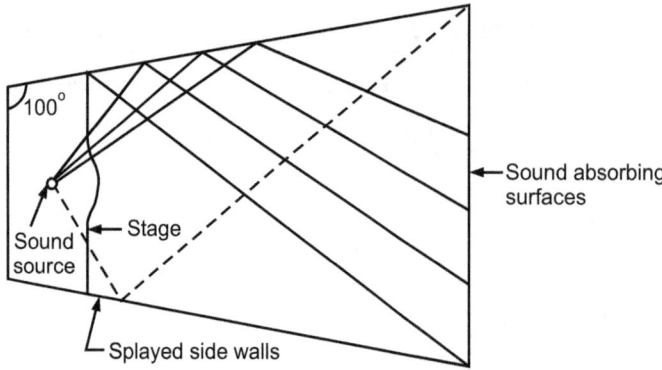

Fig. 5.24: Fan shaped plan of favourable reflection from sides

4. **Seats and seating arrangement:** The seats should be arranged in concentric arcs of circles drawn with the centre located as much behind the centre of the curtain line as its (curtain line) distance from the auditorium rear wall.

    - The angle subtended with horizontal at the front most observer by the highest object should not exceed 30°.
    - On this basis, the distance of front row works to about 4.5 m or more for cinema theatres.
    - The width of a seat should be between 45 to 56 cm.
    - The back to back distance of chairs in successive rows of seats shall be at least 85 cm.
    - If extra comfort is required, a higher spacing may be provided which shall vary between 85 to 106 cm.
    - Seats should be staggered sideways in relation to those in front so that a listener in any row is not looking directly over the head of the person in front of him.

5. **Other points:**

    (a) The surface near the source of sound should be polished hard and reflecting than those of distant or rear walls of absorbent material.

    (b) The echo defect should be prevented at any cost, particularly by avoiding curved surfaces and using sound absorbing materials on the rear walls.

    (c) Optimum reverberation time as per Table 5.21 should be attained finally after acoustical analysis and treatment for connection.

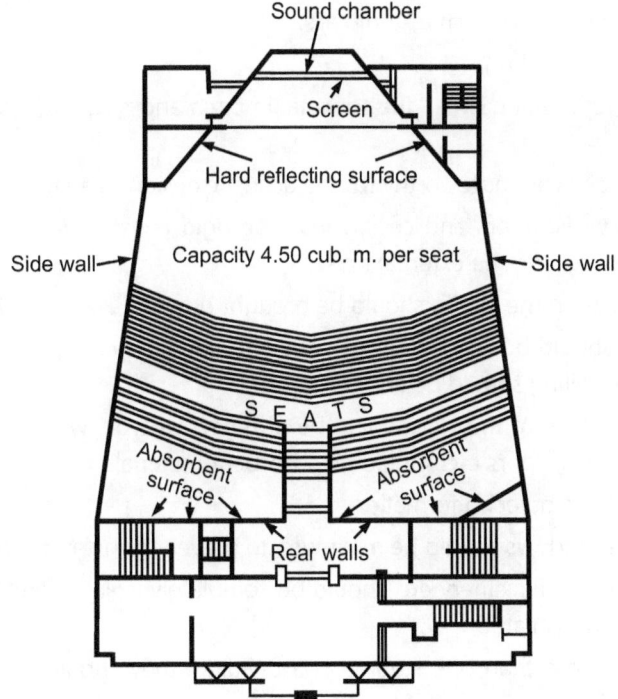

Fig. 5.25: A plan of a typical cinema theatre

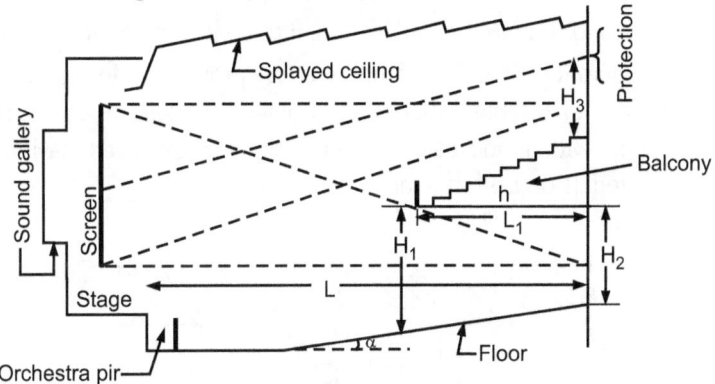

Fig. 5.26: Longitudinal section of a typical auditorium or a cinema theatre

$\alpha \approx 8°$; $L_1 > 2 H_1$; $L_2 > L/3$; $H_2 < 3$ m; $H_3 < 2.3$ m

(B) Radio-Broadcasting Studios:

A studio is a big room or a hall where sound is picked up by a microphone, and is either recorded or broadcast. It includes radio-broadcasting station, television station and sound-recording studio.

The basic requirements of such a studio are:

(i) Perfect sound proofing.

(ii) Variable reverberation time, due to variable pitch and frequency of sound produced then.

The following points are noteworthy for the acoustic design of a studio:

1. The studio walls, floors and ceiling must be rigid-construction so as to completely insulate and exclude the external noise.
2. The noise level in the studio should be brought down to 20 to 30 dB.
3. The studio should be rectangular in plan with ratio of height, breadth and length as 2 : 3 : 5. The ceiling should be flat.
4. The outer surface of the wall should be of reflective type, while the interior surfaces of walls, ceilings, floors etc. should be absorbent materials.
5. There should be no echo formation.
6. Provision of windows should be minimum, to prevent transfer noise from outside.
7. Air conditioning machinery etc. should be completely isolated and their noise should be completely insulated.
8. If there are more than one studios in a building, they should preferably be on the same floor. Two studios should not be located one above the other, there should be a gap of atleast one floor.
9. Heavy curtains and draperies should be used to control the reverberation time.
10. Variable reverberation time can be obtained by providing hinged panels or shutters, with one surface of rotable panel of absorptive material and the other of reflective material. Panels with hinge at the centre may also be used having two different absorbent materials on both the faces. (Fig. 5.27)

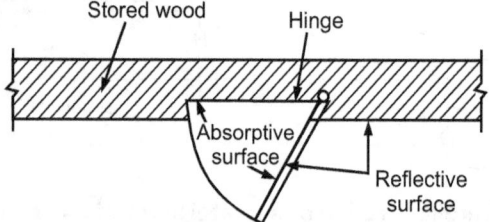

Fig. 5.27: Hinged panels on shutters in studio walls

11. Reverberation time can also be varied by providing rotable cylinders in the ceiling of the studio. Each cylinder or drum has three sectors, provided with three different absorptive materials. The cylinders can be rotated by rack and pinion arrangement, thus getting the required units of absorption for the desired reverberation time.

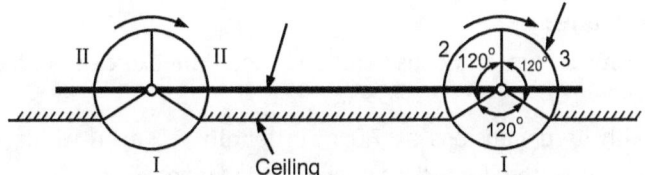

Fig. 5.28: Rotable cylinders in studio-ceiling

(C) Open Air Theatres:

Open air theatre has no side walls or barriers and hence there is no reverberation. In acoustical design of open air theatre, following points require special attention:

- The selection of the site for an open air theatre should be done very carefully considering the topographical, meteorological and acoustical properties of all available locations for the theatre. The question which is most important is the acoustical considerations thought in the selection of the site.
- The average noise level should not exceed 40 dB for a satisfactory site of a theatre.
- The slope of the seating area should not be less than about 12 degrees for good audibility and visibility.
- A properly designed orchestra shell is a must for an open air theatre. This is required for two purposes viz.
    (a) The reflective power of the shell raises the average sound level throughout the area uniformly, and
    (b) The shell enables the stage performers to hear each other more easily.
- A sound amplification system should be provided especially where the strength of audience will be more than 600.
- The direction of wind at the time of programme is an important factor in either helping or obstructing the passage of sound.

(D) Public Lecture Halls:

The following precautions should be taken in acoustic design of a public lecture hall:

- The optimum reverberation time should not exceed 1.5 seconds, even for large halls.
- The volume per seat should be between 3 and 4 m^3.
- The hard reflecting surface on the back and around the dias or stage, including slightly outwards, should be provided.
- The rear walls facing against the dias or platform should be treated with absorbing materials.

(E) Class Lecture Rooms:

The following precautions and considerations should be exercised in the acoustic design of the class rooms:

- A room with its dimensions as 7.0 m in length, 8.5 m in width, 4 m in height is considered satisfactory for a class of about 40 students.
- The noise level should be kept or brought down to 40 dB.
- The optimum reverberation time should be between 0.75 seconds at frequencies of 500 to 2000 c.p.s. and 9 seconds at frequency of 125 c.p.s.
- The volume per seat should be kept as small as possible, usually 12 m^3 or less.
- The audience should be seated near the lecture platform and seats may be arranged elevating upwards from near the platform.
- The walls and ceilings should be properly designed to give favourable reflections of sound.
- The amount of absorptive material to be used for each class room for achieving optimum time of reverberation depends upon the room size, purpose, capacity and age of the students. Hence, a class room of children having less absorption on their account, requires more absorptive material to be used for the walls and the ceiling than that would be required in rooms for adults.

5.7 SOUND LEVEL MEASUREMENTS

The human ear responds to sounds in a complex way. There is really no simple relationship between the physical measurement of sound pressure levels and an individual's perception regarding the loudness of sounds. To a certain extent, the perception of relative loudness is subjective and depends on the individual's opinion. But one physical characteristic of sound (other than amplitude) that is known to have a definitive effect on the perception of loudness is the pitch, or frequency of the sound wave.

Experiments have shown that the average person with normal testing will perceive a high-pitched sound to be louder than a low-pitched sound, even though both sounds have exactly the same intensity of SPL. For example, a sound with SPL = 70 dB at a frequency of 1000 Hz is usually perceived as being louder than a 70 dB sound at a frequency of 100 Hz. In fact, a sound with a frequency of 100 Hz must have an SPL of about 76 dB for it to be judged equally as loud as a 1000 Hz sound with an SPL of 70 dB. A higher pressure level (that is, more energy) is needed at the lower frequency for the average person to perceive the same loudness, because the human ear is somewhat inefficient in detecting low-pitched sounds.

Because sounds are of the same SPL intensity, but varying frequencies are not perceived as being of equal loudness or volume, a method that allows meaningful and consistent sound or noise–level measurements is needed. One way to accomplish this is to use a chart showing equal loudness contours, as depicted in Fig. 5.29.

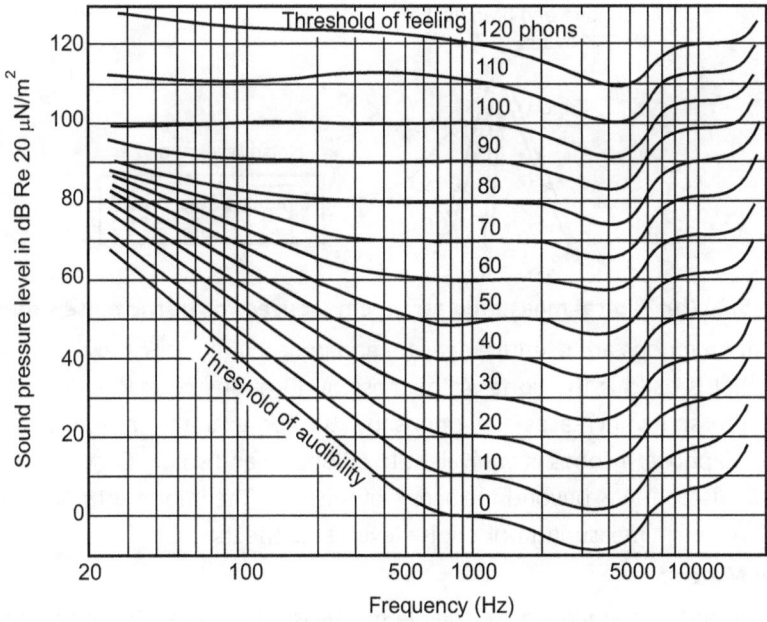

Fig. 5.29: Equal loudness contours in phons

The contour curves represent loudness or sound levels called **phons**. At a frequency of 1000 Hz, the reference pitch, sound pressure levels are the same as sound levels; both are expressed in terms of decibels. Consider, for example, a listener with normal hearing who hears a 100 Hz tone with an SPL of 70 dB. What loudness does the listener perceive? Enter the chart on the bottom axis at 100 Hz and follow the vertical line upward to a point at the 70 dB value for SPL; the closest contour curve is labelled 60. In other words, the sound will be judged to have a loudness of 60 phons. Using the same contour, it can be seen that a person hearing a 65 dB SPL sound 200 Hz would perceive the same loudness, that of 60 phons.

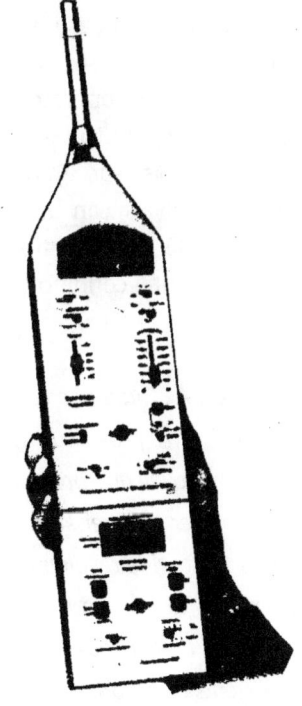

Fig. 5.30 (a): Typical hand–held sound level meter

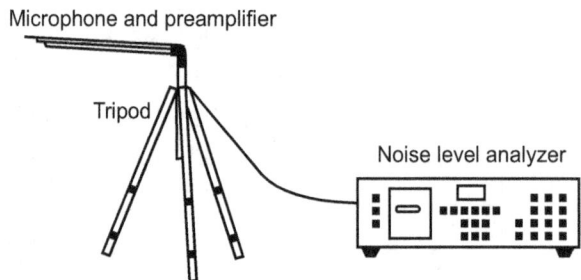

Fig. 5.30 (b): Typical measuring arrangement used for traffic noise surveys

Many other methods are used to measure apparent loudness. For example, another unit of loudness that is used is the **sone**. A loudness of 40 phons corresponds to 1 sone; each doubling of the sones increases the phons by 10. For example, a sound of 2 sones is equivalent to 50 phons, 4 sones is equivalent to 60 phons, and so on. Other units are used, as well, but a full discussion is beyond the scope of this text. The important point to note is the complexity involved in measuring both noise levels and effects.

Sound Level Meters:

Many electronic instruments are available for measuring noise. The basic components of a typical noise meter includes a microphone, an amplifier, a frequency filter, and a readout device. The readings or measurements are called sound levels and take into account the variation of perceived noise or loudness with frequency. Some noise surveys can be conducted with a battery-operated, hand-held, sound level meter, as shown in Fig. 5.30 (a). If noise measurements are to be made at one location over a relatively long period of time, such as for a traffic noise survey, meters can be mounted on a tripod, and a recording device and a frequency analyzer can be added to the system. (b) Noise meters generally cover a range of 20 to 180 dB. The selection of noise–measuring instruments depends on the type of noise, the environmental conditions and the general purpose of the survey.

SOLVED EXAMPLES

Example 5.11: *A studio has clear dimensions of length = 12 m, breadth = 8 m and height = 5 m. The ceiling is provided with acoustical tiles having absorption coefficient of 0.25. Curtains in heavy folds are provided on one of the short walls (absorption coefficient 0.5). The absorption power of other surfaces of the studio may be considered as 6.0 m^2 sabines.*

It is desired to provide revolving panels in the studio such that the time of reverberation can be varied from 0.80 to 1 second. Calculate the following:

(a) Absorption units needed with each time of reverberation.

(b) Coefficients of absorbent materials on both the faces of the revolving panel.

(c) Area of wall panel.

Solution:

(a)

Surface	Area in m²	Absorption coefficient per m³	Absorption units in m² – Sabines
Acoustical tiles	96	0.25	24
Curtains in heavy–folds	40	0.50	20
Other surfaces	–	–	6.0
		Total	50

Volume of room = 12 × 8 × 5 = 480 m³

Now, $$T = \frac{0.16\,V}{A}$$

or $$0.80 = \frac{0.16 \times 480}{A}$$

or $$A = \frac{0.16 \times 480}{0.80}$$

$$= 96 \text{ m}^2\text{–Sabines}$$

∴ Extra absorption units required

$$= 96 - 50 = 46 \text{ m}^2\text{–Sabines}$$

when $T = 0.80$

Then, $$T = \frac{0.16\,V}{A}$$

or $$1 = \frac{0.16 \times 480}{A}$$

or $A = 0.16 \times 480 = 73.6$ m²–Sabines

∴ Extra absorption units required

$= 96 - 73.6$
$= 22.4$
$\approx 23 \text{ m}^2 - \text{Sabines}$

when, $T = 1.00$

(b) From the number of extra absorption units worked out in (a), it is clear that the ratio of coefficients of absorbent materials on both the faces of the revolving panel should be equal to 2. Hence, provide hairfelt with coefficient of absorption as 0.60 on one face of the panel and perforated compressed fibreboard with coefficient of absorption 0.30 on the other face of the panel.

(c) ∴ Area of revolving panel $= \frac{46}{0.6} = 76.67$ m²

or, Area of revolving panel $= \frac{23}{0.3} = 76.67$ m².

Example 5.12: *An auditorium is rectangular in shape. The length is 40 m, breadth is 30 m and height is 10 m. The inner surfaces of the auditorium are covered by the following materials:*

1. Cement plaster – 1400 m²
2. Concrete floor – 1200 m²
3. Curtains – 200 m²
4. Celotex ceiling – 1200 m²

The capacity of the auditorium is 2000 seats. Determine the following:

(a) *Number of absorbing units and time of reverberation when there is (i) no audience, (ii) an audience of 1200 persons and (iii) full audience.*

(b) *Number of extra absorbing units required to obtain a reverberation time of 1.3 seconds when capacity of audience is 900 persons.*

(c) *Co-efficient of absorbing material, if the area available for fixing the absorbing material is 1800 m².*

Solution:

(a)

Surface	Area or No.	Absorption coefficient m² or per No.	Absorption units in Sabines
Plaster	1400	0.02	28
Concrete	1200	0.03	36
Ceiling	1200	0.10	120
Curtains	200	0.40	80
Seats	2000	0.02	40
			Total 304

Now the absorption power in m² – Sabines of an adult is 0.46. Hence, net increase in absorption power of room due to presence of one person is obtained by deducing absorption power of seat from that of a person.

∴ Net increase in absorption power per person

$$= 0.46 - 0.02$$
$$= 0.44$$

The absorption units of the auditorium with different capacity of audience will be as follows:

Audience	Absorption unit when room is empty	Absorption units of audience	Total absorption units in m² Sabines
NIL	304	–	304
900	304	396	700
1200	304	528	832
2000	304	880	1184

Now, Volume of auditorium $= 40 \times 30 \times 10$
$$= 12{,}000 \text{ m}^3$$

The time of reverberation for various capacity of audience is worked out by using Sabin's equation

$$T = \frac{0.16\, V}{A}$$

For no audience, $T = \dfrac{0.16 \times 12000}{304} = 6.32$ seconds

For 1200 audience, $T = \dfrac{0.16 \times 12000}{832} = 2.30$ seconds

For full audience, $T = \dfrac{0.16 \times 12000}{1184} = 1.62$ seconds

(b) $T = \dfrac{0.16\, V}{A}$

or $1.3 = \dfrac{0.16 \times 12000}{A}$

or $A = \dfrac{0.16 \times 12000}{1.3} = 1477$ m² – Sabins.

Absorption power of room when audience consists of 900 persons is 700 m² – Sabines.

∴ Extra absorption units required
$$= 1477 - 700$$
$$= 777 \text{ m}^2 - \text{Sabine}$$

(c) Coefficient of absorbing material
$$= \frac{777}{1800} = 0.43$$

QUESTIONS

1. Explain with a neat diagram summer air-conditioning.
2. Explain with diagram winter air-conditioning.
3. Explain briefly the working principles of comfort air-conditioning.
4. Explain with sketches wind effects and stack effects.
5. What are the circumstances in which mechanical system of ventilation is adopted?
6. Explain in details Natural system of ventilation.
7. State different methods of mechanical ventilation. Explain only one in detail.
8. Explain with sketches various units of an air-conditioning system.
9. Differentiate between summer and winter air-conditioning.
10. Differentiate between:
    (a) Natural and Artificial ventilation.
    (b) Humidification and Dehumidification.
11. Define noise pollution. Enlist various effects of noise pollution.
12. What are different acoustical defects? Explain any one in detail.
13. Describe the various methods adopted in achieving noise control.
14. Explain:
    (a) Sabine's formula
    (b) Sound foci and Dead spots.
15. How would you control noise at the stage of planning of a building?
16. What are the courses of excessive reverberation and formation of echoes? How do you correct for the optimum time of reverberation?
17. Explain briefly the characteristics of an audible sound.

■■■

Unit 6
PAINTS AND PLASTERS

6.1 INTRODUCTION

Building finishes include plastering, pointing, white washing, colour washing, painting, varnishing, distempering etc. The main objective of finishing the surface is to protect the surface from atmospheric agents like rain water, wind, temperature etc. and to improve the appearance of the surface. Various techniques are employed to cover the surface. These different types of building finishes are described in various articles of this chapter.

6.2 PAINTS AND PAINTING

Paints are thick fluid materials which are applied over the surfaces of wood work, metal work etc. to provide a thin coating. The process of application of paints is called as painting.

Objects of Paintings:
1. To protect wood from decaying effects.
2. To prevent corrosion in metals.
3. To protect the surface from harmful effects of atmospheric agencies.
4. To give decorative and attractive appearance to the surfaces and to make it pleasant.
5. To render surfaces hygienically safe and clean.
6. To provide healthy condition to live in.

6.2.1 Requirements of Good Paint

1. It should have good spreading or covering power i.e. it should cover maximum area with minimum paint. The cost of painting depends upon covering power of the paint.
2. It should have good consistency so that it can be applied easily and freely on the surface with the help of brush.
3. It should be harmless to the user.
4. The paint should be cheap.
5. It should form a thin uniform film on the painted surface. The film should be hard and durable.

6. It should adhere properly to the surface.
7. The paint should dry within 24 hrs. after application, but should not dry too rapidly.
8. The painted surface should not get affected by atmospheric agencies such as rain, heat, wind etc.
9. The paint should give attractive, decorative and pleasant appearance to the surface.
10. The colour of the paint should be retained for long time.
11. After painting, paint should not show signs of brush marks, shrinkage marks or cracks on the painted surface.
12. It should have good fire and moisture resistance.

6.2.2 Ingredients of a Paint

Following are the ingredients of a paint:
1. A base
2. An inert extender or filler
3. A vehicle or carrier
4. A drier
5. A solvent or thinner
6. A colouring pigment.

1. **Base:** A base is a solid substance of a metallic oxide in a fine state of division. It forms the main body of the paint and performs following functions.
   (i) To provide opaque coating which hides the surface to be painted.
   (ii) To make a coating film of paint resistant against abrasion and prevent formation of shrinkage cracks.

Sr. No.	Type of base	Properties and Uses
1.	White lead	Cheapest base and commonly used for ordinary painting work, forms base for lead paint, has great covering power, protective qualities and workability, very poisonous, available in powder and paste form, suitable for wood work painting but not recommended for painting iron work as it does not provide resistance against rusting.

contd. ...

2.	Red lead	It is a oxide of lead which is base for lead paints, got excellent properties of rust prevention, toughness and durability. It is available in powder and paste form. Dries very fast and can be used as a drier. Used for steel work and as a priming coat for wood work.
3.	Zinc white or Zinc oxide or Zinc sulphate	It is a base for zinc paint. It is non-poisonous, transparent, smooth and does not get affected by sulphur fumes. It has got good binding and spreading properties. It is costlier than white lead and less durable and workable. The zinc white film is very hard, brittle and has tendency to crack.
4.	Iron oxide	It is the base for all iron paints. The tink of this base varies from yellowish to brown to black. It is used for the priming coat on structural steel work. It is very effective in preventing rusting of steel. It is cheap and durable and mixes rapidly with the vehicle oil.
5.	Titanium white	It is a oxide of titanium which is bright white in colour. It is non-poisonous and not affected by heat, light or chemicals. It forms opaque coating. It has high oil absorption capacity, high elasticity and great covering properties. It is used as under coat in case of enamel paints.
6.	Aluminium powder	It is the base for all aluminium paints. It is impervious and maintain moisture in the wood which reduces warping and cracking of wood. It is used as a priming coat to new wood work.
7.	Lithopone	It is a white substance attained by mixing in equal quantities zinc sulphide and barium sulphate and processing under controlled condition. It is cheap and has good covering capacity. Since it changes colour when exposed to sunlight it is used as a priming coat for interior work.

2. **Vehicles:** It is a liquid substance which is used to keep solid ingredients in suspensions. It performs the following functions:
   (a) It imparts adhesive property to paint by acting as a binder for solid ingredients.
   (b) It helps the ingredients to spread evenly on the surface to be painted.
   (c) Because of vehicles, paint develops an elastic and protective film on the surface after drying.

Following are commonly used vehicles and their properties and uses.

Sr. No.	Type of vehicle	Properties and Uses
1.	Linseed oil	It is commonly used as a vehicle in all oil paints and is extracted from flax seeds. After oxidizing it gets thicker. Linseed oil is clear, pale, transparent, brilliant odourless. It is used in different forms as follows.
	(a) Raw linseed oil	It is thin, odourless, transparent and brilliant. It dries very slowly and therefore used for interior painting work.
	(b) Boiled linseed oil	It is obtained by boiling the mixture of 10% drier like red lead or litharge and raw linseed oil. It is thicker and darker as compared to raw oil and dries rapidly. But has got lesser penetration power and elasticity. It is basically used for exterior painting work.
	(c) Pale boiled linseed oil	It has got properties similar to boiled oil but it is not dark in colour. It can be used for light or white coloured paints. It is suitable for painting plastered surface and metal work.
	(d) Double boiled linseed oil	It has quick drying properties but it is very thick and requires turpentine for thinning purpose. It is colourless and transparent. It is used for painting external work.
	(e) Stand oil	It is obtained by heating linseed oil. It dries slowly and gives clean, durable and shining finish.
2.	Tung oil	It is used for superior work as it has got properties superior than linseed oil.
3.	Poppy oil	It is obtained from poppy seeds. It dries very slowly. It is expensive. The colour lasts for longer period. Its raw quality is not suitable for painting work and is mixed with some other materials. It is used for making delicate, light coloured paints.
4.	Nut oil	It is obtained from ordinary walnuts. It is colourless, cheap, quick drying. But less durable. Hence, it is used for temporary painting work for white or light coloured paints.

3. **Extenders or Inert Filler or Adulterants:** These are the cheap inert materials used to alter properties of paints. Their functions are as follows:
   (a) They reduce cost of the base and the cost of painting work.
   (b) They keep other ingredients in suspension.
   (c) They change weight of the paint and reduce rapid setting of paint.
   (d) They increase durability of the paint.
   (e) They reduce shrinkage and cracking of paint.

The commonly used extenders are Baryte (barium sulphate), Silica, Lithopone, Whiting, Charcoal, Gypsum, Silicate of magnesia, Alumina etc. They should not be used in excess because in that case paint looses its original character and becomes weak.

4. **Drier:** It is a metallic compound and acts as a catalyte and accelerates the process of drying of the paint. It absorbs oxygen from atmosphere and oxidizes the vehicle to become thicker. It adversely affects colour and elasticity of the paints. It is not used in final coat of paints. Various patented driers are available in the market. They are either oil driers or paste driers. Types of oil driers are litharge, magnesium dioxide, magnesium borates. Paste driers are compounds of lead, cobalt, manganese which are mixed in inert fillers and ground with linseed oil.

5. **Thinner or Solvent:** It is liquid which is added to the paint to obtain derived consistency so that the paint can be applied easily on the surface. It helps the paint to penetrate through the porous surface. It improves spreading properties of paint. It evaporates after application and surface becomes more even and smooth. For oil paints Turpentine is generally used as a thinner. It is inflammable, volatile and colourless liquid. It gets affected by weather and should be used for interior work. White spirit and naptha are also used as thinner in place of turpentine.

6. **Colouring Pigments:** It is added in white paints to get different shades of colour when the desired colour of paint is different from the colour of base. The white, black and other dark shades of paints are obtained by selecting base of specific colours. The other desired shade may be obtained by using single or combination of colouring pigments.

Table 6.1: Colouring pigments for paints

Sr. No.	Desired colour of paint	Pigment used
1.	Blue	Indigo blue, pursian blue, cobalt blue, ultramarine blue
2.	Brown	Burnt umber, raw umber, burnt sienna
3.	Black	Lamp black, ivory black, graphite, vegetable black
4.	Green	Chrome green, copper sulphate, emerald green, green earth
5.	Yellow	Chrome yellow, raw sienna, yellow ochre, zinc chromate, barium chromate
6.	Red	Cormine, red lead, vermilion red, venetian red, Indian red

6.2.3 Types of Paints

There are different types of paints available in the market in different forms and in different colour shades. The selection of the paint is governed by various factors such as nature of material required to be painted, nature of surface, properties of paints, climatic conditions etc. Following are the types of paints used for painting work:

1. **Aluminium Paint:** This type of paint is produced by mixing aluminium powder in quick drying spirit or slow drying oil. After application of paint spirit or oil evaporates leaving behind a coating of aluminium powder on the surface. Aluminium paint is used for painting wood work, metal work, hot water pipes, gas tanks, electricity poles, storage tanks etc.

   It has got the following qualities:
   (a) It protects iron and steel from corrosion.
   (b) It has high electric resistance.
   (c) It has good weather resisting and water proofing properties.
   (d) Because of its shining colour it is visible in darkness.
   (e) It has high spreading capacity.
   (f) It offers resistance against effects of marine water.

2. **Anticorrosive Paints:** This type of paint is used to protect structural steel work against the adverse effects of weather, fumes, acids, corrosive chemicals etc. This paint is used for external work. It is very cheap, lasts for longer period and black in colour.

3. **Asbestos Paint:** This paint mainly consists of fibrous asbestos as one of the ingredients. It is used for stopping leakage of metal roofs and painting gutters, spouts, flashing etc. This paint is used as damp proof coat over the outer surface of the basement walls. This paint resists effects of water, acid and steam. This paint protects metal fittings from rusting.

4. **Bituminous Paint:** These paints are produced by dissolving bitumen or tar in naptha or petroleum. This paint is black in colour but colour can be modified by adding certain coloured pigments. These paints are alkali resistant and have high covering capacity. These paints are used for painting structural steel work under water.

5. **Bronze Paint:** This paint is produced by mixing aluminium bronze or copper bronze in suitable vehicle. This paint is reflective in nature hence used for painting radiators. The paint is used for painting internal and external metallic surfaces.

6. **Cellulose Paint:** It is prepared from celluloid sheets, nitro cotton and photographic films. This paint hardens by evaporation of thinner unlike other types of paint which get hardened by oxidation. This paint dries very quickly and provides flexible, hard and smooth surface. The painted surface can be washed and cleaned very easily. The paint remains unaffected under very hot and cold conditions and also when the surface comes in contact with hot water, smoke or acidic atmosphere. This paint is superior than other types of oil paints and therefore used for painting aeroplanes, cars and other superior work.

7. **Cement Paint:** The base of cement paint is white or coloured cement. This paint is available in various shades and in powder form. Cement paint has better water proofing qualities. It has good strength, hardness, density and durability. It offers excellent decorative appearance to the surface. This paint can be used for painting plastered surfaces, concrete surfaces, corrugated iron sheets etc.

8. **Emulsion Paint:** The main ingredient of this type of paint is a vehicle polyvenyl acetate or synthetic resins such as chlorinated rubber. This paint can be applied easily. It has got excellent alkali resistance. This paint dries very quickly and has good workability and high durability. The painted surface can be cleaned by washing with water.

9. **Enamel paint:** This paint is obtained by mixing metallic oxide (white lead or zinc white) with petroleum spirit having resinous matter in solution form. Different colouring pigments are added to get desired colour. This paint dries slowly and produces a very hard, impervious, glossy, elastic, smooth and durable film over the surface being painted. It is not affected by water, steam, acids, alkalies and other atmospheric agents. It can be used for external as well as internal surfaces.

10. **Plastic Paint:** This paint has various types of plastics as base material. Plastic paints are available in market in variety of shades and under different trade names. This paint is attractive, quick drying and has good covering power. This paint is used for painting commercially important buildings.

11. **Rubber Paint:** This paint is prepared by dissolving synthetic resins in suitable solvents. This paint dries quickly and little affected by moisture, atmosphere, sunlight, alkalies etc. This paint is cheap and can be used for painting cement or lime plastered surfaces.

12. **Silicate Paint:** It is produced by mixing calcium and finely ground silica with various materials. It produces a very hard and durable film on painted surface. It has good qualities of adhesion and there is no action of alkalies. It can be applied to brick work, plastered and concrete surfaces.

13. **Oil Paint:** These paints are made with one of the bases and pigments, described earlier, mixed with linseed oil. They are generally applied in three coats.
    (a) A thin coat of priming after the surface is prepared.
    (b) The second or undercoat is of the same material as used for finishing coat.
    (c) The final coat is usually of white zinc mixed with linseed oil and some pigment. A little turpentine is also added to accelerate drying of the paint. Each coat is applied only when the previous coat is fully dried.

6.3 PLASTERING

Plastering is the covering with material of various composition applied either externally or internally to walls, partitions of leth, ceiling etc. to cover rough walls and uneven surface of a building. The thin covering is known as **plaster**.

Plastering is done by plastic mortar obtained by mixing some binding material with fine aggregate and water in suitable proportion. The binding material used may be lime, cement or mud.

6.3.1 Objectives of Plastering

1. To provide an even smooth, regular, clean and durable finished surface.
2. To resist the atmospheric influences particularly the infiltration of rain.
3. To conceal the defective workmanship.
4. To fill the joints formed in masonry work.
5. To cover inferior quality materials.
6. The internal plaster provides a smooth surface which does not allow dust, dirt and vermin to lodge on it.
7. To prepare satisfactory base for decorating the surface by the application of white or colour wash, distemper or paint.

The requirements of an ideal plaster are:

1. It should be smooth, non-absorbant, reasonably sound deadening, flame retarding, washable and not affected by rise or fall in temperature.
2. The plaster should not shrink while drying and setting.
3. It should adhere firmly to the surface and should provide the surface with required decorative effect and durability.

6.3.2 Selection of Type of Plaster

The following factors affect the selection of plaster to be used:

1. Availability of binding materials
2. Desired durability
3. Desired finishing
4. Atmospheric conditions to which plaster is subjected.
5. Whether the plaster is to be used on exterior surfaces or interior surfaces.

Types of Plaster:
1. Mud plaster
2. Cement plaster
3. Lime plaster
4. Special type of plasters.

1. **Mud Plaster:** This is the cheapest type of plaster which is generally used for construction in villages. Mud plaster consists of well tampered clay, cow dung, chopped straw and sand. The earth should be free from roots, grass, organic matter and stone pebbles. The earth is mixed with ample quantity of water and left to season for about a week. Chopped straw, hay or hemp is added to the prepared earth at the rate of about 30 kg/m^3. The mixture is converted into a homogeneous mass by working it up and down.

   The surface is prepared by knocking off projections, racking out joints, wetting with water etc. and then vertical screeds are formed so as to act as thickness gauges. Mud plaster is now applied between screeds by dashing the mortar against the prepared surface in a thickness of 12 mm. Before starting plastering, the surface to be plastered should be wetted thoroughly. Dashed mortar against the walls is then finished by means of a straight edge and wooden float. After 24 hours of setting, but before drying of the plaster of the first coat, the second coat is applied in thickness of 6 mm.

   The plaster is not cured but the surface is treated with fine white earth, cow dung and cement.

2. **Cement Plaster:** It is an ideal coating for external surfaces. It is suitable for damp conditions. The plastering includes two stages:
   (i) Preparation of surface for plastering, ground work for plaster;
   (ii) Application of cement mortar on surface.

   (i) **Preparation of surface for plastering:** For good plaster it is essential that plaster covering should have proper bond or adhesion with the surface of masonry to be plastered and therefore preparation of the background for plastering is very important. It is done in the following steps:

   All mortar joints of wall to be plastered are left rough and projecting which provide key or hold to the plaster. All the joints and surfaces are cleaned with wire brush. This process is very essential to obtain a good key of the plaster with the wall surfaces. Oil and grease spots should be removed either by brushing or scrapping. All cavities and holes in the surface to be plastered are filled up properly. The projections more than 12 mm on the surface are removed. The area to be plastered is washed and kept wet.

   (ii) **Ground work for plaster:** In order to maintain uniform thickness of the plaster, the screeds or bands are formed. On the prepared wall surface by fixing dots (patches of plaster 150 mm × 150 mm). These dots are applied horizontally and vertically at a distance of about 2 m over the surface to be plastered. The two dots lying in the vertical plane are checked for verticality by means of plumb bob. After fixing the dots the vertical strips of mortar are formed between the dots. These screeds act as gauges for maintaining even thickness of plaster being applied. Now the surface to be plastered is ready for applying plaster.

(iii) Application of cement mortar on surface: Cement plaster consists of an uniform mixture of cement and clean coarse sand with suitable quantity of water. The proportion of cement to fine aggregate may vary according to the requirements of the plaster. But generally the ratio is 1: 3 or 1: 4. To produce mortar, these materials are thoroughly mixed in dry condition and water is added in the dry mix. In mortar, consistency of mix is very important. Cement plaster may be done in one coat or two coats as illustrated in Fig. 6.1.

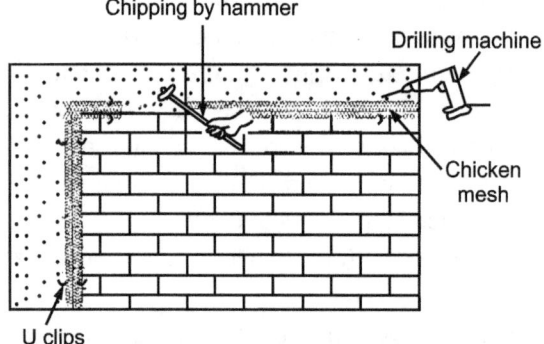
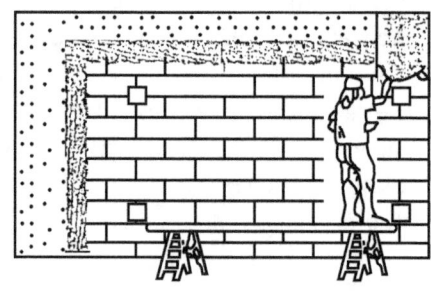

(1) It is essential to fix chicken mesh near the junction of concrete and stone/brick work before plastering to reduce cracks in plaster

(2) Prepare cement mortar of (1: 4) mix and apply layer of cement mortar of 10 to 12 mm thickness

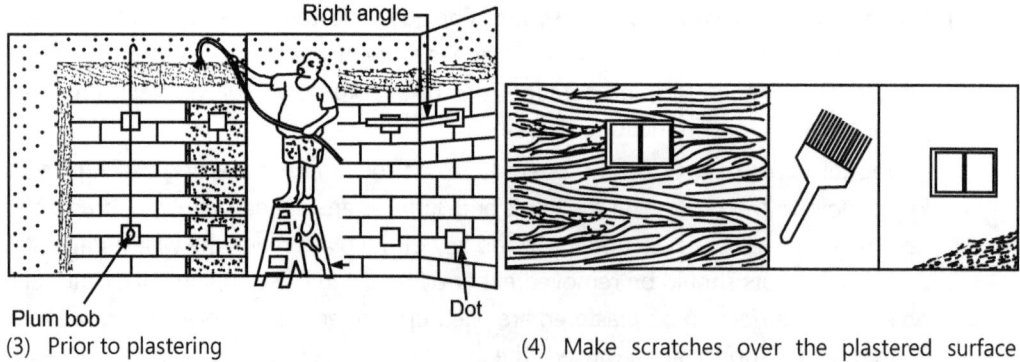

(3) Prior to plastering

(4) Make scratches over the plastered surface before it becomes too hard, so as to have good grip of the final coat over the previous coat

(5) Level with aluminium float

(6) Excess water present in mortar can be mopped by use of sponge

Fig. 6.1: Procedure to be adopted while plastering

First coat or rough coat: Surface is well raked and cleaned off loose dust and well water before plastering. After preparing the surface as explained earlier and the mortar is dashed against the surface. Between the screeds, the surface of mortar when it is plastic, is levelled with the help of float and straight edges and finally finished with trowels. If second coat is to be applied, the surface of the first coat is not polished but roughened with scratching tool to produce key to the second coat of plaster. Second coat is applied after a lapse of 2 days. The thickness of second coat is normally 3 mm. The mortar that is used for second coat, consists of cement and very fine sand in proportion of 1: 2. The finished plaster with one coat or two coats is cured by spraying water for atleast 7 days.

3. **Lime Plaster:** Lime plastering is the process of covering the surface with lime mortar. In lime plaster, fat lime is normally used. Hydraulic lime slakes very slowly which results into blisters on the plaster surface. The lime mortar, generally, consists of lime and sand in the proportion of 1: 1. The mixture is thoroughly ground in mortar mills to produce a uniform plaster mix. To improve the strength of the mortar, sometimes a small quantity of cement is added. The sand used is clean, coarse and free from deleterious matters. The plaster may be applied in one, two or more coats. The first coat has an average thickness of about 12 mm on brick or ashlar masonry and 20 mm on Rubble masonry. The first coat is applied by dashing the lime mortar between the screeds. It is then finished with the help of floats. The first coat is left exposed to air for a period of 2 days to set before applying the second coat.

The second coat which is called as floating coat is applied after preparing the surface of the first coat. The surface is prepared by sweeping it clean off any dust or loose particles and spraying water. The second coat is spread uniformly with trowels. It is pressed and finished with straight edge to obtain the desired finish. The thickness of the second coat, generally, is kept between 6 - 9 mm. The third coat is applied after 5 - 6 days of the second coat. The mortar for finishing coat consists of cream of white or fat lime (NEERU) mixed with fine sand in the proportion of 1: 2. The mortar is well rubbed with wooden float and finally finished with trovel to obtain desired surface. The surface is allowed to dry for 24 hrs. and then it is well watered for about a week. The thickness of the final coat is kept nearly 3 mm.

4. **Special Type of Plasters:** The special type of plasters are used to obtain a specific finish. Following are the details of some of the special plasters:

   (i) Water proof plaster: This type of plastering is done with the help of mortar which is prepared by mixing one part of cement, two parts of sand and fine alum at the rate of 12 kg/m^3 of sand. Water having 75 gm/lit. of soap is used as mixing water. The application of plaster is similar to that of lime or cement plaster.

   (ii) Stucco plaster: This type of plaster is provided on external face and internal face of the wall. This is a decorative plaster which provides attractive surface. Stucco plastering is done in three coats and the total thickness is 25 mm. The first coat which is called as scratch or rough coat, functions to bond with the wall. The second coat which is called as final coat or brown coat provides desired shape to the surface. The last coat which is known as finishing coat provides required texture, smoothness and decorative appearance to the surface. The composition of stucco plaster is different for interior and exterior surfaces.

   (a) For exterior walls: In this case, the mortar for the first coat consists of 1 : 3 cement and sand to which about 10% of hydrated lime by weight is added. After preparing the surface in the usual manner, the first coat is applied in the thickness of 12 mm. After drying of first coat, second coat having thickness of 9 mm with same composition as the first coat is applied. After drying of second coat the third coat which is 3 mm in thickness is applied. The mortar used for the third coat is made up of cement and sand in proportion of 1 : 2 or $1 : 2\frac{1}{2}$.

   To give desired shade to the finish, white or coloured cement is used in place of gray cement.

   (b) For interior walls: For internal stucco plastering the first coat consists of ordinary lime plaster 13 mm thick. The second coat of lime plaster which is richer is applied in thickness of 9 mm. After drying of second coat the final coat is applied in thickness of 3 mm. The mortar consists of finest lime and well powdered white stone. The final coat is first polished with linen cloth containing moist chalk and then with oil and chalk. Finally, the surface is finished smooth and brightened by rubbing only with oil.

   All the coats in the stucco plastering are cured for sufficient time to attain sufficient strength and hardness.

(iii) Plaster of paris: It is obtained from gypsum which is a naturally occurring material. When gypsum is heated to a certain temperature, water of crystallization gets removed leaving behind a very fine powder of plaster of paris. When water is added in this powder, it sets immediately therefore, when plaster of paris is used for plastering purpose, the setting time is increased by adding certain salts, some burnt ash and fine sand. The dry mix of plaster of paris and sand is prepared on a platform. Small quantity of this mix is taken in a pan and suitable quantity of water is added. This plaster is applied within 5 minutes after addition of water. This type of plaster produces very good smooth finish with sharp edges and corners. This plaster is not used for external surfaces.

External finishes of plaster: Depending upon the desired appearance, cost and degree of maintenance, the external walls are given different finishes.

Following are some of the commonly adopted external wall finishes:

(i) **Smooth Cast Finish:** This finish provides a levelled and smooth surface. The mortar used for final coat consists of 1: 3 cement and fine sand. The plaster is worked with wooden float.

(ii) **Rough Cast Finish:** In this type, the mortar is produced with 1 part of cement, $1\frac{1}{2}$ parts of fine sand and 3 parts of coarse sand with appropriate quantity of water.

This mixture is dashed against prepared plaster surface with the help of large trovel and finished rough with wooden flat. Rough cast finish is waterproof, durable and resistant to cracking and crazing. This type of finish is used for buildings which are subjected to heavy rainfall and high winds.

(iii) **Pebble Dash Finish:** In this type of finish, a coat of plaster having thickness 13 mm (with 1 : 3 cement and sand proportion) is applied. Clean pebbles of size varying from 10 - 20 mm are dashed on the first coat when it is plastic. On setting, dashed pebbles remain held in position. The pebbles are slightly tapped or pressed into the mortar with a wooden float. This type of finish is suitable for buildings which are subjected to heavy rainfall and high winds.

(iv) **Sand Faced Finish or Sponge Finish:** This type of finishing is carried out in two coats, base coat and final coat. The base coat of cement mortar (1 cement: 4 coarse angular sand) is applied in a thickness not less than 12 mm. This coat is cured for a week and then second coat is applied. The thickness of second coat is about 8 mm and the mortar consists of cement and fine sand in the proportion of 1 : 1. The second coat, when it is still wet is worked with sponge so that equal and uniform sand grain appear on surface. The surface is cured for about two weeks.

(v) Depeter Finish: This is a kind of rough cast finish. In this type of finish, final coat of 13 mm thickness is applied as in the case of pebble dash finish. Over this coat, while it is still wet gravel or different coloured flints are pressed with hand. Therefore, it is possible to have beautiful patterns and design on the surface by selecting materials of different colours.

(vi) Scrapped Finish: This type of finish is produced by allowing the final coat to stiffen for some time and then scrapping so as to remove surface skin. Different types of scrapping tools are used to obtain different types of scrapped finishes. The final coat is 12 mm thick and thickness of 3 mm is scrapped by scrapping tools. Scrapping helps in exposing the aggregate inside the final coat. This scrapped surface presents a rough surface with exposed aggregate and texture depending upon the grading of aggregate used in final coat. This finish is not liable to crack.

(vii) Textured Finish: In this type of finish, it is possible to produce various ornamental patterns and beautiful designs by working with suitable tools on freshly laid final coat of stucco plastering. This type of finish has advantages similar to rough cast finish.

6.4 POINTING

The joints on the face of stone or brick masonry are roughly filled in, while the walls are being raised. Pointing is the art of finishing the mortar joints in the exposed masonry with suitable cement or lime mortar, to protect the joints from weather effects and also to improve the appearance of building structure. Plastering involves use of mortar and labour and therefore it is costlier. The mortar joints are weak parts of the masonry and therefore they need protection from rain water, sunrays and snow. Pointing is comparatively a cheaper method of protecting the joints.

Mortar for Pointing: Pointing is done in lime mortar or cement mortar or sometimes in composite mortars.

Lime Mortar: The lime mortar for pointing is produced by grinding fat lime and sand in a mortar mill.

Cement Mortar : The cement mortar which is used for pointing is produced by mixing together cement and clean sand in the proportion of 1 : 2 or 1 : 3.

Composite Mortar : Composite mortar is produced by mixing cement, lime and sand in the proportion of 1 : 2 : 9 or 1 : 1 : 6.

Method of Pointing: Pointing is done in the following stages.
1. All the mortar joints in the masonry are raked out to a depth of 10 - 15 mm with the help of pointing tools.
2. Dust and loose mortars are thoroughly cleaned.
3. The joints and the surface are washed with clean water and kept wet for some time.
4. Mortar is taken in small pans and the joints are filled up with small trowel by pressing it into the joints to form a close contact with the old mortar joints. The joints are left - flush, sunk or raised depending upon the requirements.
5. Excess mortar is scrapped away.
6. The finished work is cured for 3 - 4 days in case of lime mortar and for 10 days when cement mortar is used.

6.4.1 Types of Pointing

Pointing is classified according to the shape of finishing. The type of pointing is decided considering the type of masonry, nature of building structure and the desired effects of finish.

1. **Flush Pointing:** In this type of pointing, joints are raked and they are finished flush with the face of the brick masonry. The edges are properly trimmed. It is the simplest type of pointing which is extensively used in masonry work. This pointing does not give good appearance but it is very durable and it does not allow dust, dirt or water to lodge over it.
2. **Cut or Weathered or Struck Pointing:** In this pointing, the face of pointing is not kept vertical but it is kept inclined. The upper edge of pointing plaster is pressed inside the masonry by about 10 mm and lower edge is finished level with the face of masonry. This type of pointing is mostly used for brick work particularly for finishing horizontal joints.
3. **Recessed Pointing:** In this type of pointing, finished face of pointing mortar is kept vertical but inside the wall surface with the help of suitable tool. This type of pointing is suitable for facing work of good texture bricks and superior quality mortar.
4. **Keyed, Rubbed or Grooved Pointing:** In this type of pointing, the recked joints are filled up flush with the face of the wall and semi-circular notches are formed by a special tool. This type of pointing is commonly used as it improves the appearance of the wall.
5. **Tuck Pointing:** In this type, the mortar is pressed in the joints and finished flush with the face of the wall. When the mortar is still wet a rectangular groove (5 mm width and 3 mm depth) is formed at the centre of joints. This groove is filled with white

lime putty and small quantity of silver sand by keeping it slightly projecting outside the finished surface of the pointing plaster. This type of pointing gives attractive appearance but the fillet part is not very durable.

6. **Vee Pointing:** In this type of pointing either 'V' - shaped grooves are engrowed in the finished surface of the pointing plaster when it is still green or by projecting the 'V' - shape of the pointing face outside the wall surface.

7. **Beaded Pointing:** This type of pointing gives very good appearance but it is difficult to maintain. The raked joints are filled up with mortar and finished flush with the face of the wall and then bead is formed by a steel rod having concave edge in the middle of joints.

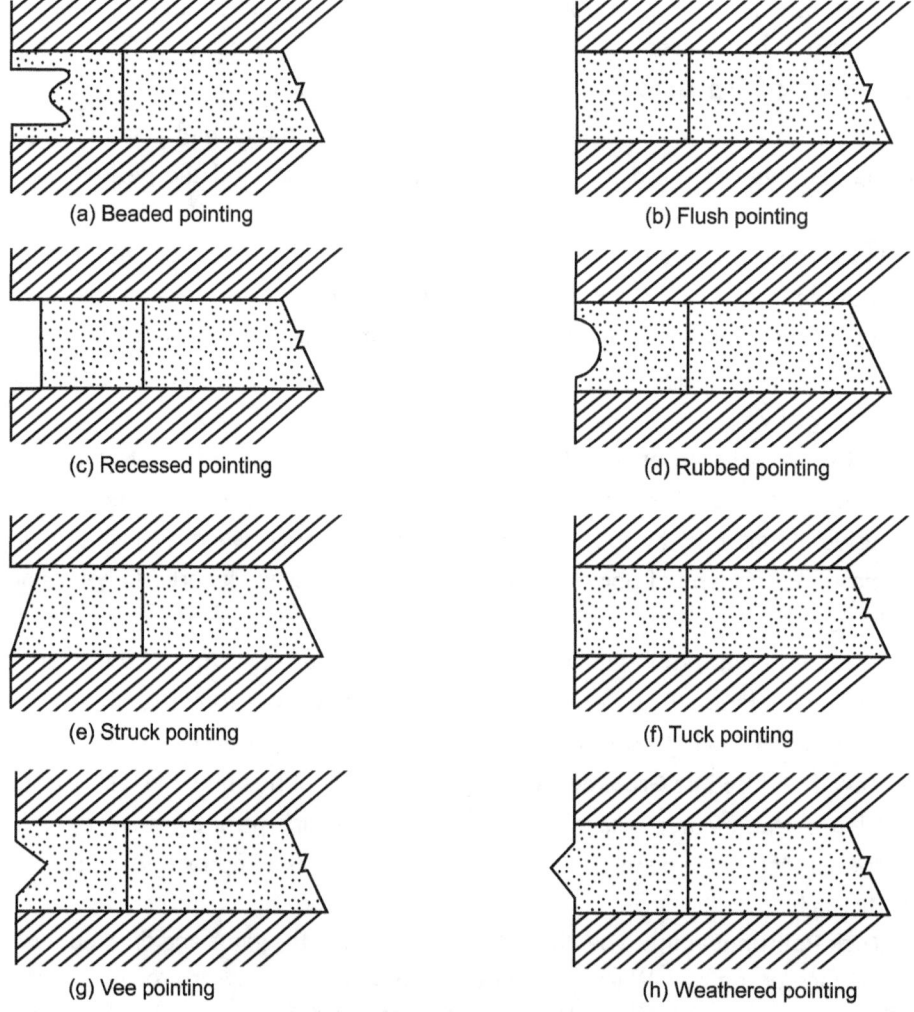

Fig. 6.2: Different types of pointing

6.5 WHITE WASHING

It is a process of giving wash covering to the plastered or pointed surface. In case of white washing a wash of slaked lime mixed with water is applied. Sometimes other ingredients like gum, rice water, common salt etc. are added to improve the properties of the lime.

White washing includes the following operations:
1. Preparation of white wash
2. Preparation of surface for white wash
3. Application of white wash.

1. **Preparation of White Wash:** The material required for white washing is fat lime or shell lime. Unslaked lime lumps are mixed with water and the mixture is thoroughly stirred with the help of bamboo. The lime is allowed to get fully slaked for about 24 hrs. After 24 hrs. it is stirred up with a pole and additional water is added until it attains the consistency of thin cream. This mixture is then screened through a clean coarse cloth. Clean gum is dissolved in hot water at the rate of 4 kg/m^3 of thin cream. The dissolved gum is added to the slaked lime solution. Sometimes alum, common salt or rice water are used in place of gum. To prevent the glare effect due to white wash sometimes copper sulphate at the rate of 4 kg/m^3 of thin cream is added. Gum or rice water is used to improve adhesive properties of white wash.

2. **Preparation of Surface:** Before applying white wash, the surface to be white washed should be made thoroughly dry. If the surface is new, it should be thoroughly cleaned, brushed and made free from mortar droppings or any other loose materials. If the surface is very smooth, the white wash will not stick to it and therefore, the surface should be rubbed with sand paper to ensure proper adhesion of white wash. In case of white washing the old surface again, all loose materials and scales should be scrapped off. The old loose white wash is removed by rubbing with sand paper. All holes in the wall, irregularities of surface should be filled with lime putty well in advance, so that the surface is dry before white washing. If there are oil or grease spot on the surface, they should be rubbed with sand paper and should be given a coat of mixture of rice water and sand, so that the white wash can stick to the surface. If the surface is discoloured because of smoke (as in case of kitchens) the surface should be washed with wood ash and water or Multani earth (yellow earth).

3. **Application of White Wash:** After preparing the surface the white wash is applied in one coat, two coats or three coats. In case of new surfaces three coats of white wash are required and for old surfaces one or two coats of white wash are sufficient. The

white washing is done with the help of a jute brush. For each coat one stroke is given from top to bottom and the other from bottom to top over the first stroke and one stroke from the right and other from left over the first stroke. Each successive stroke of brush should slightly overlap the preceeding stroke. If only one or two strokes of white wash are to be applied the last coat should be applied with horizontal strokes of the brush. Each coat should be allowed to dry before applying the next coat. The finished dry surface of white wash should be smooth and even and it should not come off readily on fingers when rubbed.

6.6 COLOUR WASHING

The application of colour wash is similar to white wash. A colour wash is prepared by adding certain colouring pigments in suitable quantities in the prepared white wash to obtain desired shade of the finished colour wash. While using different types of coloured pigments it should be ensured that the colouring pigment is not affected by the presence of lime. Before applying colour wash on new surfaces, a coat of white wash should be applied. This coat acts as a primary coat.

Following Table 6.2 shows various types of colour wash and the materials required to be mixed in the white wash.

Table 6.2: Types of colour wash and materials required to be mixed in the white wash

Type of colour wash	Materials mixed in white wash
1. Buff colour wash	Multani mitti
2. Green colour wash	Solution of boiled mango bark and copper sulphate
3. Blue colour wash	Burnt coconut shells
4. Slate colour wash	Lamp black and copper sulphate
5. Yellow colour wash	Yellow earth
6. Pink colour wash	Vermillion

6.7 DISTEMPERING

It is a process of applying wash on the surface. But the surface obtained by distempering is much more superior as compared to the surface obtained by white washing or colour washing. The process of distempering is easy and less costly as compared to the process of painting.

1. **The Composition of Distempers:** A distemper is composed of a base, glue or casein as binder water as carrier or thinner and suitable quantities of colouring pigments. Distemper is termed as a water paint having whiting as base and water as carrier.

Distempers are available in the market in a variety of shades under different trade names in the form of either powder or paste. Distempers are required to be mixed with hot water before use.

Different forms of distempers are:

(i) White distempers

(ii) Coloured distempers

(iii) Oil bound distempers

(iv) Casein paints.

All the manufacturers of distempers supply complete directions as how to use their products. These guidelines should be strictly followed to get the best results.

2. **Process of Distempering:** It includes:

   (i) Preparation of surface

   (ii) Application of priming coat

   (iii) Application of coat of distemper.

   (i) The Surface for Distempering is Prepared in the Following Manner: If the receiving surface is rough, it should be made smooth by rubbing with sand papers. The surface should be perfectly dry before applying the distemper. If the surface is damp the distemper coat gets spoiled. If new plaster surface is to be distempered it should be allowed to dry for atleast 2 months. The newly lime plastered surface should be washed with a dilute sulphuric acid and left for 24 hrs. and then wall should be thoroughly washed with clean water. The new cement plaster surface should be washed with solution of zinc sulphate and should be allowed to dry. If the surface is having efflorescence patches they should be wiped clean with dry cloth before applying the prime coat. In case of distempering old surfaces all dust, loose materials, scales etc. are removed by wire brushes. Holes, patches, cracks and surface irregularities should be filled with lime putty or gypsum plaster and allowed to get hard before application of distemper. The surface should be thoroughly rubbed with sand paper, washed clean and allowed to dry before applying the distemper.

   (ii) Applying Prime Coat: After preparation of the surface, a priming coat is applied and left to dry. This coat helps in ensuring good bond between the distemper coat and the surface. The prime coat may consist of materials as recommended by the manufacturer of the distemper or whiting in water or milk.

(iii) Application of Distemper: After applying the prime coat, a coat of good quality distemper should be applied. The prime coat should be allowed to dry completely before distemper coat is applied. While applying the distempers the brush should be first applied horizontally and then vertically. Distempers can be applied with the help of spray pistols. On new lime plastered walls 2-3 coats are required over the priming coat. On old lime plastered walls one coat of distemper with priming coat is sufficient. Distempers which are used on cement concrete on the external surfaces are manufactured with weather resistant ingredients and therefore distempering coat lasts for longer period.

3. Properties of Distemper:

(a) Distempers are available in the form of oil bound washable paints, washable oil free distempers, non-washable distempers etc. They are available in powder form and in the paste form. Powder distempers are called as dry distempers whereas distempers in the form of paste are known as oil bound distempers. Oil bound distempers are superior than dry distempers. Oil bound distempered surface is washable.

(b) Distempers are cheaper than paint and varnishes and also cheaper than cost of white wash in the long run. They are water paints and are easier to apply.

(c) Coating of distempers are comparatively thick and more brittle as compared to other types of water paints.

(d) The film of distemper is porous in nature and allows the water to pass through it. This property helps the new walls to dry out, without damaging the distemper film.

(e) Distempers are generally light in colour and provide a good reflective coating.

(f) They are less durable as compared to oil paints.

(g) Distempers are available in variety of shades, in powder and paste forms. They can be applied on cement plastered surface, lime plastered surface, brick work, insulating boards etc.

(h) On drying, the distemper film may lead to cracking and flaking due to shrinkage.

(i) Distempering gives poor results if the surface is damp.

6.8 VARNISHES

The essential constituent of all varnishes is "resin" or rosin which is dissolved in oils, turpentine or alcohol. The liquid dries or evaporates and leaves a hard transparent, glossy film on the varnished surface. There are various types of varnishes obtainable in the market each suited to a specific work. The preparation of varnishes is a difficult matter, and it is best to purchase readymade. Varnish dries quickly and gives a hard and tough coating. Painted surfaces are also varnished to brighten them.

Water varnishes are used for painting paper surfaces.

Oil varnishes are used for interior or exterior works. Superfine Copal varnish is considered to be the best as it produces a higher gloss and smoother finish. Copal varnish is made from the fossil resins (the copals) which are found in several parts of the world and in many different grades of quality. English copal is considered to be the best. If the varnish is too thick, spirits of turpentine can be added.

Spirit varnishes: Shellac varnish and French polish belong to this class.

Resins used for preparation of varnishes are generally obtained from gums of various trees. The most common being Shellac, Gum, Arabic, Rosin, Amber.

6.9 WALL CLADDING

Wall tiling or cladding is a process of finishing the surface with tiles. They are fixed upto a height of 1.25 m above the floor level or upto ceiling, in passages, bath rooms, swimming pools, kitchens, staircases, boiler rooms, fire places and sometimes on exterior of building for decorative effect or protection from atmospheric agents. They make the wall non-absorbant and easy to clean. The tiles used are either of terra cotta, faience, china clay, natural stones like marble. Faience is similar to terra cotta but it is twice fired. These tiles are available in variety of colours and thicknesses. They are rectangular, square, rounded or corner type.

For cladding, the surface of the wall is first plastered with cement mortar in usual manner and then the tiles, which are immersed in water for atleast one hour are covered with a paste of neat cement on back and laid flat against the wall surface true to line and plumb and pressed with light strokes of a wooden mallet. The joints should be as thin as possible.

Table 6.3: Showing different materials and their uses in the content of wall claddings

Sr. No.	Description of wall finishes	Use
1.	Chettinad/brick tiles	Decorative for both interior and exterior walls.
2.	Clay/ceramic tiles	Doors in kitchen, wash areas and toilets, skirting in rooms with tiled floors.
3.	Mossaic tiles	Doors in kitchen, wash areas and toilets, skirting in rooms with tiled floors.
4.	FRP boards (Fibre Reinforced Plastic)	Maintenance free, pre-painted boards for wall panelling.
5.	Glass tiles/sheets	Decorative finish for walls.
6.	Laminates	Decorative finish for wood and wood-based materials.
7.	Mirror	Reflective, decorative finish used to create an illusion of space and also used at corridor corners.
8.	Gypsum board	Bonded plaster board for interior walls.
9.	PVC sheets	Maintenance free, pre-painted wall panels, skirting and cladding.
10.	Natural stone cuddapah, granite, kotah.	Marble granite is used for interior wall as decorative finish. All natural stones can be used for external cladding.
11.	Reflective acrylic	It is used to create an illusion of space and at corridor corners.
12.	Rigid polyurethane panels	Panels available with several decorative facings for interior walls.
13.	Cork tiles/sheets	Decorative finish for wood/plastered wall. Good acoustic material.
14.	Coir mats, jute mats.	Fixed on wooden frame into interior walls.
15.	Wall fabrics velvet, suede.	Fixed with an adhesive.

6.10 WALL PAPERING

In this process, paper is pasted on the internal surface and ceiling and aesthetics of the room is improved. The papers which are used for wall papering are (a) Satin paper, (b) Common or pulp paper, (c) Flock paper.

While carrying out papering work, first the surface is cleaned and made smooth by rubbing the surface and scrapping it properly to remove dust, white wash and colour wash. Adhesive paste is prepared by mixing flour, glue and water. This paste is applied thoroughly and uniformly on back of the paper and the paper is pasted on the wall. The paper is finished smooth with a roller covered with clean flannel.

6.11 GLAZING WORK

Glazing means fixing glass panels in frames of door and window made up of iron, steel or wood. A frame is an assembly of horizontal and vertical members which are placed at top, sides and bottom of an opening and form an enclosure to act as support for a door or a window. Glass panels which are cut to required dimensions are secured in place means of putty or wooden moulds. The glass panels are fixed in 15 mm rebate of the wooden frame leaving a gap of 1.5 mm all around for expansions. The putty is produced by mixing finely powdered whiting and linseed oil and kneading into a stiff paste. This putty is first applied on back side and glass panel is fixed in position with the help of small steel rails. Putty is then applied on the front side. It is pressed and finished properly to get a smooth surface. When large panels or plate glasses are required to be fixed, they are first placed in rebate by moulded wooden fillets all around with brass or nickel screws, inserting a strip of felt or rubber in the rebate under the glass which act as cushion.

Table 6.4: Difference between Plastering and Painting

Plastering	Painting
1. It consists of application of thin layer of mixture of binding material (such as lime, cement, mud), fine sand and water.	1. It consists of application of coating of fluid material on masonry wooden or metallic material.
2. Thickness of plaster ranges between 3 mm to 25 mm.	2. Thickness of paint is in microns.
3. After plastering curing is essential.	3. No curing is required.

QUESTIONS

1. State step by step procedure for three coat sand faced plaster. Assume thickness of plaster is 25 mm. State specific thickness and care required for each coat.
2. State the types of defects in oil painting work and cause for the type of defect. Enlist types of paints used for metal surfaces.
3. State step by step procedure to provide three coat sand faced plaster to B.B. masonry.
4. State step by step procedure to apply paint on a new wood work.
5. Write down the objectives of plastering. What is ground work for plaster?
6. State different market names of paints. Explain defects in painting.
7. What are the objectives of plastering? Name the various types of plasters and mention the requirements of a good plaster.
8. Explain the various types of paints which are readily available in the market in various colours.
9. Write a note on: Wax polishing,
10. Explain preparation of surface for plastering. Describe defects in painting.
11. State different materials used for wall cladding finishes. Write down the functions of base in a paint.
12. Describe the method of painting in detail. Explain defects in painting.
13. State different building finishes. Explain defects in plastering.
14. What is pointing? Explain defects in plastering.
15. Differentiate between the following:
    (a) Plastering and painting,
    (b) Distempers and paints.
16. Describe the different tools used in plastering with sketches.
17. Explain "Wall cladding" with material used and method of fixing.
18. Enlist the types of plasters and explain cement plaster.
19. Write notes on:
    (a) Varnishing
    (b) Wall papering

■■■

www.ingramcontent.com/pod-product-compliance
Lightning Source LLC
Chambersburg PA
CBHW080422230426
43662CB00015B/2189